The Communion We Share

The Compass Rose

The emblem of the Anglican Communion, the Compass Rose, was originally designed by the late Canon Edward West of New York. The modern design is that of Giles Bloomfield. The symbol, set in the nave of Canterbury Cathedral, was dedicated by the Archbishop of Canterbury at the final Eucharist of the Lambeth Conference in 1988. The Archbishop dedicated a similar symbol in Washington Cathedral in 1990, and one in the original design in New York Cathedral in 1992, demonstrating that its use has become increasingly widespread. The centre of the Compass Rose holds the Cross of St. George, reminding Anglicans of their origins. The Greek inscription "The Truth Shall Make You Free" (John 8:32) surrounds the cross, and the compass recalls the spread of Anglican Christianity throughout the world. The mitre at the top emphasises the role of the episcopacy and apostolic order that is at the core of the churches of the Communion. The Compass Rose is used widely by the family of Anglican-Episcopal churches. It is the logo of the Inter-Anglican Secretariat, and it is used as the Communion's identifying symbol.

The Communion We Share

THE OFFICIAL REPORT
OF THE 11TH MEETING
OF THE ANGLICAN CONSULTATIVE COUNCIL,
SCOTLAND 1999

Edited by James M. Rosenthal

MOREHOUSE PUBLISHING

Published for the Anglican Communion Office
Partnership House
157 Waterloo Road
London SE1 8UT
England

Morehouse Publishing
P.O. Box 1321
Harrisburg, PA 17105

Morehouse Publishing is a division of The Morehouse Group.

© 2000 The Secretary General of the Anglican Consultative Council

All rights reserved. Study questions for The Virginia Report and for The Gift of Authority may be copied for non-profit use. No other part of this book may be reproduced or transmitted in any form or by any means, electronic or mechanical, including photocopying, recording, or by any information storage and retrieval system, without written permission from the copyright owner.

Printed in the United States of America

First Edition   1 3 5 7 9 10 8 6 4 2

ISBN 0-8192-1863-4

Library of Congress Cataloging-in-Publication Data

Anglican Consultative Council. Meeting (11th : 1999 : Dundee, Scotland)
    The communion we share : the official report of the 11th Meeting of the Anglican Consultative Council, Scotland 1999 / edited by James M. Rosenthal.
        p. cm.
    ISBN 0-8192-1863-4 (pbk. : alk. paper)
    1. Anglican Consultative Council. 2. Anglican Communion—Congresses. I. Rosenthal, James. II. Title.
BX5002 .A6326 1999
262'.53—dc21   00-030551

Cover design by Corey Kent

Contents

Mission 21 Hymn vii
The Scottish Episcopal Church viii
Preface x

Acknowledgements xiv
Anglican Consultative Council (ACC) 1
Officers and Members of the ACC and Participants and Staff
    at ACC-11 3
Report of the Standing Committee of ACC-11 10
The Constitution of the Anglican Consultative Council 23
Profiles of Members of the Anglican Consultative Council 36
Photographs 43

Sermons and Addresses 51
Opening Service Sermon: The Burning Mystery 53
Archbishop of Canterbury's Presidential Address 57
Chairman's Address 65
Sermon by the Archbishop of Canterbury at the Solemn Eucharist 69
Launch of the Environmental Project at St. Matthew's
    Church Possilpark 73

Eight Meditations on the Minor Prophets 76

Reports 107
Report by the Secretary General 109
Communications: Summary of Activities 122
Ecumenical Affairs Report 124
Mission and Evangelism: A Brief Report to ACC-11 141
Report of the Coordinator for Liturgy 143

Financial Report 147
Anglican Communion Priorities Working Group 158

Plenary Presentations 165
A Statement by the Chairman: Listening to the Gay and
    Lesbian Community 167
The Anglican Communion and the Four Instruments
    of Unity Briefing 168
The Virginia Report Presentation 179
    Study Questions for *The Virginia Report* 191

Interpretation of Scripture 193
    Presentation on Interpretation on Scripture 203
Hearing on Ethics and Technology 210
Honduras External Debt 221
The MISSIO Executive Summary 226
    MISSIO Presentation 230
ARCIC Presentation 233
    Study Questions for Small-Group Discussion on
    The Gift of Authority 243
    Statement from the Co-Chairmen of the Anglican-Roman
    Catholic International Commission 244
    A Commentary on *The Gift of Authority* 247
A Session on Urbanisation 255
    Some Remarks on Issues of Urbanisation in Japan 259

Networks **263**
Presentation by NIFCON 265
International Family Network 270
The Anglican Indigenous Network (AIN) 273
    A Supplementary Note to the AIN Report 275
Anglican Peace and Justice Network Meeting 278
The Anglican Communion International Refugee and
    Migrant Network 305
International Anglican Women's Network 1999 312
International Anglican Youth Network 314

Anglican Congress **315**
An Anglican Congress in the New Millennium:
    A Background Paper for ACC-11 317
New Heart, New Spirit: Fourth Anglican Congress, 2003 319
Anglican Congress Feasibility Data: Preliminary Financial Appraisal 321
Anglican Congress: Presentation 325

United Nations **327**
Anglican Communion Office at the United Nations:
    Overview Report of the Anglican Observer at the
    United Nations, 1994-1999 329
The Anglican Observer's Office at the United Nations 339

A Millennium Prayer **342**
Prayers for the Anglican Communion **343**

Resolutions of the Eleventh Meeting of the Anglican
    Consultative Council **344**

The Last Word **360**

Directory of Provincial Secretaries of the Anglican Communion **363**

Mission 21 Hymn

—The Scottish Episcopal Church

We have a vision of the Church to share,
One to inspire God's people everywhere;
Open to all, and no one turned away,
All those who enter here will wish to stay.

Here we embrace all people, young and old,
Welcoming those who come into our fold;
Holding the weak, encouraging the strong,
Each person valued, feeling they belong.

Gone is the fear of prejudice and hate,
We seek to cherish, not humiliate;
Here we can own the failures that we know,
Firm in the faith that we can change and grow.

Humbly, we celebrate the good we do,
Working as one towards making all things new;
Using our talents, drawing on our skills,
Grateful for such a vision to fulfil.

Building upon our past that we hold dear,
Knowing tomorrow's task is still unclear;
Each step we take will help us on our way,
One step will be sufficient for today.

Fired with the Spirit, filled with life and light,
Ours is a Church to challenge and excite;
Mission sustained by love and faith and prayer,
Extends God's love to people everywhere.

The Scottish Episcopal Church

The Episcopal Church was formerly the Established Church of Scotland. It was disestablished and disendowed in 1689 by King William III, who, almost entirely on political grounds, set up the Presbyterian Church in its place.

The disestablished Episcopal Church continued strongly until 1746, after the Jacobite rebellion, when, again for political reasons, a severe penal status was imposed upon all Episcopalians. These laws made it illegal for them to possess any churches or chapels; all public services were forbidden, and Episcopalian clergy were not allowed to minister to more than five persons at a time, under penalties of imprisonment or banishment.

The laws continued in force until 1792. Under such conditions it is not remarkable that the persecuted Church dwindled in numbers until it became a "shadow of a shade." Nevertheless, throughout the whole period the bishops maintained their continuity and, in 1784, gave the Episcopate to the American Church by the consecration, in an upper room in Aberdeen, of Bishop Seabury, its first bishop.

Today the Scottish Episcopal Church has seven diocesan bishops, one of whom is elected Primus by the others; about 190 stipendiary clergy; 180 nonstipendiary clergy; and 52,000 members, of whom 32,000 are communicants.

The Scottish Episcopal Church is a self-governing province of the worldwide Anglican Communion.

Its forms of worship, Holy Communion and Morning and Evening Prayers, are recognisably similar to those of other provinces, notably the Church of England, but have their own characteristics. They are to be found in the Scottish Prayer Book of 1929, in a conservative revision of the liturgy in 1970, and in the radically new and original Scottish Liturgy 1982, which is now widely used among us. We also have our own ordination services of 1984, which have been highly acclaimed among international scholars. As with other churches in the Anglican Communion, we are in the process of making experimental revisions to a number of our services, lectionaries, and calendars.

Communicant members of the Anglican Communion and of other Trinitarian churches who are visiting us are warmly invited to receive communion in our churches. Longer-staying residents who are not Anglicans would normally be encouraged to be confirmed after a period of preparation.

We maintain the three orders of bishops, priests, and deacons that have existed since the early centuries of the Church. We celebrate the two Gospel Sacraments of Baptism and Holy Communion, and the Prayer Book makes provision for Confirmation, Marriage, Ordination, Penance, and the Anointing of the Sick.

It is our policy, wherever possible, to work in conjunction with other Christian bodies and, where appropriate, with other faiths in Scotland. To this end, we belong to "Action of Churches Together in Scotland" (ACTS), which has among its membership the Church of Scotland, the Roman Catholic Church, the Congregational Union of Scotland, the Methodist Church, the United Free Church of Scotland, the United Reformed Church, the Society of Friends, the Salvation Army, and several other Christian bodies.

We are also involved with a number of these churches in the common pursuit of Christian unity.

We are seriously engaged in the work of Christian education, involving all age groups; of caring for people in their daily lives, as well as when they are in trouble, need, or sickness; and of reaching out to those who have little or no link with the Church.

Though we are a small Church with about 52,000 members, we are actively involved in the life of the nation at many levels and seem to be able to exercise quite a substantial role in that field.

We have links with the Church in many parts of the world, receiving from them and sharing with them a variety of gifts, both spiritual and material.

In the ordering of our church life, at each level we are represented by clergy and laity, and we try to ensure that the youth have a voice.

Each congregation has an elected vestry, and congregations are grouped in areas in each of the dioceses. Each diocese has its own Synod presided over by the bishop. In the province there are seven dioceses made up of amalgamations of the fifteen ancient dioceses. They are Aberdeen and Orkney, and Moray, Ross, and Caithness in the north; Argyll and The Isles in the west; Brechin, and St. Andrews, Dunkeld, and Dunblane in the centre; and Edinburgh, and Glasgow and Galloway in the south. The General Synod is responsible for ordering the life of the province as a whole. It is presided over by the bishop, who is elected by his fellow bishops to the office of Primus. The General Synod normally meets annually and oversees the life of the Church in all its aspects.

From the booklet *The Scottish Episcopal Church*, published by the General Synod Office, 21 Grosvenor Crescent, Edinburgh, Scotland EH12 5EE.

Preface

The Anglican Consultative Council (ACC) was brought into being by the Lambeth Conference of 1968 "to share information about developments in one or more provinces in other parts of the Communion and to serve as needed as an instrument of common action." In the course of the last thirty years, the Anglican Consultative Council has taken its place—alongside the Archbishop of Canterbury, the Primates' Meeting, and the Lambeth Conference—as one of the instruments of unity. It has retained from the outset the distinctive characteristic of being the only one of the four instruments to bring together bishops, clergy, and laypeople.

The eleventh meeting of the Anglican Consultative Council (ACC-11) was held in Dundee, Scotland, from September 14 to 25, 1999. It brought together eighty representatives from thirty-eight provinces within the Anglican Communion, including those who came from the two newest provinces, the Church of the Central American Region and Hong Kong.

Old hands at these ACC gatherings commented on the efficiency with which business was despatched at Dundee. Certainly there was a brisk pace from the outset as we settled down to a familiar routine of worship, Bible study, presidential address, formal presentations, group discussions, business sessions, civic receptions, and the debating of resolutions.

A robust series of Bible studies on the Minor Prophets by the bishop established the theme of justice as the backcloth to so many discussions. "We are not only supposed to believe in justice and to talk about it, but we are to make justice happen." Meanwhile, the small groups for Bible study shared their discussion insights and experiences, so that fellowship was secured at an early stage.

It was, perhaps, inevitable that the agenda of ACC-11 would mirror to some degree the concerns of the Lambeth Conference of 1998. The most significant formal presentations at Dundee concerned:

- **The Interpretation of Scripture**—tradition and language; translation and interpretation; the centrality of the scriptures; experience, ritual, and belief; interpretation as communication; the ecumenical perspective; and silence and interpretation.

- *The Virginia Report*—the Communion of the Trinity and the Church; belonging together in the Anglican Communion; subsidiary and interdependence; the instruments of communion; and structures and processes.

- **Anglican–Roman Catholic International Commission (ARCIC) Authority in the Church:** *The Gift of Authority*—the understanding of authority within the Anglican Communion; the relation between *The Virginia Report* and *The Gift of Authority;* the concept of a universal primacy; and the consequences for Anglican-Roman Catholic relations at local and provincial levels.

- **Technology and Ethics**—creation, ecology, and our relation to the natural order; the nature of technology; the development of computer technologies; developments in the field of biotechnology; and the characteristics of technological societies.

- **International Debt**—a case study of Honduras and external debt, especially in the aftermath of Hurricane Mitch; the Heavily Indebted Poor Countries Initiative; and debt cancellation and poverty reduction.

- **Mission**—the Report of the Anglican Communion Mission Commission (MISSIO), the Communion's standing commission on mission; case studies from different parts of the Communion; the Decade of Evangelism; structures for mission in the Anglican Communion; and priorities in evangelism.

- **Urbanisation**—urbanisation as the global context for mission and evangelism; the unacceptable social consequences; the experience of Christians in cities at different stages of the urban cycle and in different cultures; the proposals to form an Anglican Urban Network and a "Faith in an Urban World" Commission.

A brief summary of the work of any conference can never communicate the range of personal insights and experiences that any one of the participants is bound to take away. These undoubtedly include for me an appreciation of the many gifts and experiences that are brought together in these international gatherings; an awareness of the isolation that is experienced by some in their ministries as they work in situations that are remote or fragile or violent; and an insight into the gulf that exists between those who find themselves on the cultural boundaries of the Western world—secularism, sexuality, and feminism—and those whose theological background and pastoral context demand of them a more unqualified testimony to the absolutes of the received tradition. And it would be impossible to leave Dundee without acknowledging the warm and generous hospitality of the Scottish Episcopal Church—and, indeed, of the civic authorities of Aberdeen, Dundee, Edinburgh, and Glasgow.

But what happens when a triennial meeting of the Anglican Consultative Council comes to an end? Is it merely a question of old and new friends saying good-bye and expressing the hope that they might meet in Hong Kong in 2002? Are things left to the Secretary General and his staff, to the Standing Committee and the Inter-Anglican Finance Committee, and the Joint Standing Committee of the Primates and ACC, to ensure that issues and resolutions are pursued and that the necessary degree of dialogue is secured both between the various instruments of unity and between the provinces of the Communion?

One part of the answer must be found in the continuing work of the networks, which address particular themes and concerns throughout the Anglican Communion. The reports received at Dundee from the Networks for Peace and Justice, for Inter-Faith Concerns, for Women, for the Family, for Youth, for Indigenous People, and for Refugees and Migrants, indicate something of the range of concerns that are being explored.

But it was also possible to detect at Dundee the signs of some frustration. Is the ACC an effective instrument of communication and of unity? What would be lost if it ceased to exist? What does it mean to refer things to the ACC? Do our structures actually contribute to the developing life of the Communion? Do they ensure that the synodical principle of bishops, clergy, and laypeople taking counsel together is fully acknowledged? Do they make adequate provision for the voices of women and of younger people to be heard?

Some of these concerns were brought to a head in the proposal that there should be in the first decade of the new millennium an Anglican Congress—succeeding the earlier congresses of 1954 and 1963 and possibly meeting alongside the Lambeth Conference. Large questions remain unanswered, however: the size of such a body, the funding that would be required, the authority that it would possess, and the purposes to be served by such a gathering within the life of the Communion. But it is exactly here that we come to the nub of the problem, and it goes far beyond ACC. My brief experience as an observer at the Lambeth Conference in 1998 and as a member of ACC-11 in 1999 has left me with no doubt about two things: first, the importance of the office of the Archbishop of Canterbury as the preeminent instrument of unity; and second, the serious possibility that we may be coming to the end of a chapter where the present instruments of unity are concerned.

The size of the Lambeth Conference and the impossibility of doing business—serious business—in that way must raise questions about its continuing appropriateness in its present form. The ACC is by definition a body for consultation, but if consultation is little more than talk, then it may be judged sooner rather than later that talk is not enough. History may well judge that these are transitional years as the Anglican Communion struggles to work out the meaning of provincial autonomy and interdependence. Are we attempting to reconcile principles of church life that are mutually incompatible, or are we feeling our way slowly—very slowly—toward a degree of executive authority and of discipline?

It was the Anglican Congress of 1963—the Toronto Congress—that led to a widespread acceptance of the document entitled *Mutual Responsibility and*

Interdependence in the Body of Christ. Much that has happened since that time—including the work of the ACC—has attempted to keep faith with that affirmation. It is not yet entirely clear what these things might mean in the life of the Anglican Communion. Questions remain concerning the relation between the Four Instruments of Unity; the structures that are appropriate for an international community; the reconciling of provincial autonomy and executive action at a Communion level; and the nature of the presidential role and, indeed, of the authority of the Archbishop of Canterbury.

But of far greater consequence is whether there is a desire to see the Anglican Communion take its place within the life of the wider Church as an international faith community. An earlier generation had something to say about the incompleteness of Anglicanism. That is not in dispute. But nor is it in dispute that Anglicanism offers to the wider Church an ecclesiology which embraces the model of a reformed Catholicism, a way of doing theology, a rich and diverse pattern of spirituality, and a ministry which is at its best rooted in the needs and aspirations of local communities. If these things matter, if they represent some small part of the contribution that the Anglican Communion might yet make to the coming great Church, then the structures and the processes by which we order the life of the Communion take on a new significance.

It would be manifestly untrue to suggest that these questions loomed large in everybody's day-by-day thinking at Dundee, but they were there in one form or another just below the surface, and they gave for some of us an urgency to the consultation in which we were glad to share.

—John Moses, Dean of St. Paul's Cathedral, London

Acknowledgements

Thanks go to Marjorie Murphy, to the eleventh Anglican Consultative Council Secretariat, Mr. Ian Harvey, and to Mrs. Veronica Elks from the Anglican Communion Office, London, for their help in preparing this report. Thanks also go to Kenneth Quigley, Mark Fretz, Debra Dortch, and Harry Zeiders from Morehouse Publishing for their help in publishing this report.

The grace of our Lord Jesus Christ, the love of God, and the fellowship of the Holy Spirit be with us all evermore.

ANGLICAN CONSULTATIVE COUNCIL (ACC)

Officers and Members of the ACC and Participants and Staff at ACC-11

Officers

President

> Most Reverend and Right Honorable George Leonard Carey
> *Archbishop of Canterbury*

Chairman

> Right Reverend Simon E. Chiwanga
> *Tanzania*

Vice Chairman

> Most Reverend John Campbell Paterson
> *Aotearoa, New Zealand, and Polynesia*

Secretary General

> Reverend Canon John L. Peterson
> *Anglican Consultative Council*

Joint Standing Committee

Primates

> Most Reverend Richard Frederick Holloway
> *The Scottish Episcopal Church*
> Most Reverend William Moses
> *The Church of South India*
> Most Reverend Livingstone Mpalanyi-Nkoyoyo
> *The Church of the Province of Uganda*
> Most Reverend Michael Geoffrey Peers
> *The Anglican Church of Canada*
> Most Reverend Moses Tay (not in attendance)
> *The Province of South East Asia*

Anglican Consultative Council

> Ms. Judith G. Conley
> *The Episcopal Church in the United States*
> Reverend Dr. Jae-Joung Lee (unable to attend)
> *The Anglican Church of Korea*
> Mr. Ghazi Musharbash
> *The Episcopal Church in Jerusalem and the Middle East*

Right Reverend Bernard Ntahoturi
The Episcopal Church of Burundi
Mr. John M. Rea
The Scottish Episcopal Church
Ms. Maureen Sithole
The Church of the Province of Southern Africa
Right Reverend Fernando Soares
The Lusitanian Church of Portugal (extra-provincial to the Archbishop of Canterbury)

Inter-Anglican Finance Committee

Most Reverend Robert Henry Alexander Eames
Chair of Finance Committee—ex officio member of the Joint Standing Committee
Ms. Judith G. Conley
The Episcopal Church in the United States
Most Reverend Alwyn Rice Jones
Primates Representative
Mr. Ghazi Musharbash
The Episcopal Church in Jerusalem and the Middle East
Right Reverend Fernando Soares
The Lusitanian Church of Portugal (extra-provincial to the Archbishop of Canterbury)

Members of the Council

The Anglican Church in Aotearoa, New Zealand, and Polynesia
  Reverend Winston Halapua *(ACC-11, -12, -13)*
  Professor Whatarangi Winiata *(ACC-10, -11, -12)*

The Anglican Church of Australia
  Right Reverend Phillip Keith Newell, AO *(ACC-9, -10, -11)*
  Very Reverend David John Leyburn Richardson *(ACC-9, -10, -11)*
  Mr. Robert Tong *(ACC-10, -11)*

The Church of Bangladesh
  Mr. Samuel Pronoy Sarkar *(ACC-10, -11, -12)* (unable to attend)

Igreja Episcopal Anglicana do Brazil
  Most Reverend Glauco Soares de Lima (substitute for Right Reverend Luiz Osorio Prado) *(ACC-11, -12, -13)* (unable to attend)

The Episcopal Church of Burundi
  Right Reverend Bernard Ntahoturi *(ACC-9, -10, -11)*

The Anglican Church of Canada
  Right Reverend Michael C. Ingham *(ACC-11, -12)*
  Venerable Barbara Anne Clay *(ACC-9, -10, -11)*
  Dr. Stephen John Toope *(ACC-11, -12, -13)*

The Church of the Province of Central Africa
    Right Reverend Bernard Amos Malango *(ACC-9, -10, -11)*
    Mr. Michael Mawaraidzo Kututwa *(ACC-9, -10, -11)*

Iglesia Anglicana de la Region Central de America
    Mr. Luis Roberto Valleé *(ACC-11, -12, -13)*

The Church of Ceylon
    Mr. Yohesan Nicholas Chetty *(ACC-11, -12)*

Province de L'Eglise Anglicane Du Congo
    Right Reverend Sylvestre Tibafa Mugera *(ACC-9, -10, -11)*
    Reverend Basimaki Byabasaija *(ACC-10, -11, -12)*

The Church of England
    Right Reverend Richard Douglas Harries *(ACC-10, -11, -12)*
    Very Reverend Dr. John Moses *(ACC-11, -12, -13)*
    Canon Dr. Christina Ann Baxter *(ACC-9, -10, -11)*

Hong Kong Sheng Kung Hui
    Ms. Fung Yi Wong *(ACC-11, -12, -13)*

The Church of the Province of the Indian Ocean
    Mr. Bernard Georges *(ACC-11, -12, -13)*

The Church of Ireland
    Reverend Canon Michael Burrows *(ACC-11, -12, -13)*
    Lady Brenda Sheil *(ACC-9, -10, -11)*

The Nippon Sei Ko Kai (The Anglican Communion in Japan)
    Reverend Samuel Isamu Koshiishi *(ACC-10, -11, -12)*

The Episcopal Church in Jerusalem and the Middle East
    Right Reverend Riah Hanna Abu El-Assal (substitute for Most Reverend Ghais Abdel Malik) *(ACC-10, -11, -12)* (unable to attend)

The Anglican Church of Kenya
    Mr. Samuel Arap Ng'eny *(ACC-9, -10, -11)*
    Right Reverend Joseph Otieno Wasonga *(ACC-10, -11, -12)*

The Anglican Church of Korea
    Professor Peter Kim Chin Man (substitute for Reverend Dr. Jae-Joung Lee) *(ACC-10, -11, -12)* (unable to attend)

The Church of the Province of Melanesia
    Right Reverend Lazarus S. Munamua *(ACC-11, -12, -13)*

La Iglesia Anglicana de Mexico
    Mr. Antonio Ortega Reybal *(ACC-10, -11, -12)*

The Church of the Province of Myanmar (Burma)
    Most Reverend Andrew Mya Han *(ACC-11, -12, -13)*

The Church of Nigeria (Anglican Communion)
   Most Reverend Peter Akinola *(ACC-11, -12, -13)*
   Very Reverend Dr. David Chidiebele Okeke *(ACC-11, -12, -13)*
   Chief Godwin O. K. Ajayi *(ACC-10, -11, -12)*

The Church of North India
   Reverend Enos Das Pradhan *(ACC-11, -12, -13)*
   Mr. Richard I. Thornton *(ACC-11, -12, -13)*

The Church of Pakistan
   Right Reverend Samuel Azariah *(ACC-11, -12, -13)*
   Mr. Farrukh Marvin Parvez *(ACC-11, -12, -13)*

The Anglican Church of Papua New Guinea
   Reverend Denny Guka (substitute for Sir Kingsford Dibela)
      (ACC-11, -12, -13)

The Episcopal Church in the Philippines
   Mr. Warren E. Luyaben *(ACC-10, -11, -12)*

Province de L'Eglise Episcopal au Rwanda
   Right Reverend Prudence Ngarambe *(ACC-11, -12, -13)*
   Reverend Damien Nteziryayo *(ACC-11, -12, -13)*
   Mrs. Margaret Jolly Bihabanyi *(ACC-10, -11, -12)*

The Scottish Episcopal Church
   Mr. John M. Rea *(ACC-10, -11, -12)* (attended 5 days only)
   Most Reverend Richard Frederick Holloway (substitute for Mr. John M. Rea)

The Church of the Province of South East Asia
   Right Reverend Bolly Anak Lapok *(ACC-10, -11, -12)* (unable to attend)

The Church of South India
   Right Reverend B. Peter Sugandhar *(ACC-10, -11, -12)*
   Reverend Jeedipalli Prabhakar Rao *(ACC-10, -11, -12)*
   Professor George Koshy *(ACC-10, -11, -12)*

The Church of the Province of Southern Africa
   Right Reverend Petrus H. Hilukiluah *(ACC-11, -12, -13)*
   Venerable Margaret Vertue *(ACC-11, -12, -13)*
   Ms. Maureen Sithole *(ACC-10, -11, -12)*

Iglesia Anglicana del Cono Sur de America
   Right Reverend Hector Zavala *(ACC-10, -11, -12)*

The Episcopal Church of the Sudan
   Right Reverend Michael S. Lugör *(ACC-10, -11, -12)*
   Reverend Nelson Koboji Nyumbe *(ACC-9, -10, -11)*
   Mr. Is-hag Kannidi Kodi Kodi *(ACC-10, -11, -12)*

The Anglican Church of Tanzania
    Reverend Canon Mkunga Mtingele *(ACC-9, -10, -11)*
    Mrs. Joyce Luhui Ngoda *(ACC-11, -12, -13)*

The Church of the Province of Uganda
    Most Reverend Livingstone Mpalanyi-Nkoyoyo *(ACC-10, -11, -12)*
    Reverend Canon Job Bariira-Mbukure *(ACC-11, -12, -13)*
    Mr. Edward Seth Mungati *(ACC-9, -10, -11)*

The Episcopal Church in the United States
    Right Reverend J. Mark Dyer *(ACC-9, -10, -11)*
    Reverend Robert Sessum *(ACC-11, -12, -13)*
    Ms. Judith G. Conley *(ACC-10, -11, -12)*

The Church in Wales
    Venerable E. Bryan Williams (substitute for Reverend Canon David Williams) *(ACC-9, -10, -11)* (unable to attend)
    Miss Sylvia Scarf *(ACC-10, -11, -12)*

The Church of the Province of West Africa
    Professor Adrian DeHeer-Amissah *(ACC-10, -11, -12)*

The Church in the Province of the West Indies
    Reverend Robert Thompson *(ACC-11, -12, -13)*
    Mr. Bernard Selkirk Anderson Turner *(ACC-10, -11, -12)*

Co-opted Members

Mr. Ghazi Musharbash *(ACC-10, -11, -12)*
Representing the Laity of the Church in Jerusalem and the Middle East
Right Reverend Fernando Soares *(ACC-9, -10, -11)*
Representing the Lusitanian Church of Portugal
Reverend Canon Lovey Kisembo *(ACC-10, -11, -12)*
Representing Women
Mrs. Lenore Margaret Parker *(ACC-10, -11, -12)*
Representing Women
Miss Andrea Candace Payne *(ACC-11, -12, -13)*
Representing Youth

Churches in Communion

Right Reverend Dr. Joseph Mar Irenaeus
Mar Thoma Syrian Church of Malabar
Right Reverend Joachim Vobbe
The Old Catholic Church of the Union of Utrecht

Observers from Other Churches

Reverend Dr. Alan D. Falconer
World Council of Churches

Reverend Timothy Galligan
Roman Catholic Church
Right Reverend William Boyd Grove
World Methodist Council
Reverend Sven Oppegaard
Lutheran World Federation

Consultants and Presenters

Mr. John Clark
MISSIO (Inter-Anglican Mission Commission)
Reverend Canon Andrew Davey
Urbanisation
Reverend Dean Fostekew
Mission 21
Right Reverend Leopold Frade
Bible studies
Dr. Ida Glaser
NIFCON
Right Reverend Laurence Alexander Green
Urbanisation
Reverend Dr. John Pobee
Interpretation of Scripture
Right Reverend Roger Frederick Sainsbury
Urbanisation
Right Reverend Mark Santer
ARCIC
Reverend Canon John Sargant
NIFCON
Reverend Dr. Israel Selvanayagam
NIFCON
Reverend Clive Wylie
Mission 21

Chaplaincy

Reverend Paul Gibson
Chaplain
Reverend Father James Milne
Assistant to the Chaplain
Mr. Matthew Edwards
Organist

ACO Staff

Mrs. Helen Bates • database coordinator
Reverend Canon Eric Beresford • ethics presenter
Mrs. Veronica Elks • communications
Reverend Canon David Hamid • ecumenical and interfaith

Mr. Ian Harvey • communications and computer network management
Mrs. Deirdre Martin • executive assistant to the Secretary General
Miss Marjorie Murphy • mission and evangelism
Mr. Michael Nunn • finance and administration
Ms. Rosemary Palmer • finance and administration
Ms. Ann Quirke • travel office
Reverend John Rees • legal adviser
Canon James M. Rosenthal • communications and *Anglican World* editor
Mr. Graeme Smith • finance and administration
Mrs. Barbara Stanford-Tuck • Secretary General's office
Mr. Chris Took • communications and web site manager

Archbishop's Staff

Reverend Dr. Herman Browne
Assistant Secretary for Ecumenical Affairs to the Archbishop of Canterbury
Reverend Canon Andrew Deuchar
Secretary to the Archbishop of Canterbury for Anglican Communion Affairs
Miss Fiona Millican
Anglican Communion Affairs
Reverend Lesley Perry
Media Officer

Communications Team

Reverend Ian Douglas (United States)
Deaconess Margaret Rodgers (Australia)
Mr. Manasseh Zindo (Sudan)

Host Province

Right Reverend Neville Chamberlain
Bishop of Brechin
Ms. Pat McBryde
Provincial ACC-11 coordinator

Interpreters

Mrs. Dorothy Evans
Spanish interpreter
Ms. Ruth Lambert
French interpreter
Mrs. Dominique MacNeill
French interpreter
Reverend Paula Mayer
French interpreter
Reverend Rogelio Prieto-Duran
Spanish interpreter

Report of the Standing Committee of ACC-11

March 1998

Membership

> Right Reverend Simon Chiwanga, Tanzania, chairman
> Most Reverend John Paterson, Aotearoa, New Zealand, and Polynesia, vice chairman
> Ms. Judith Conley, United States
> Reverend Dr. John Jae-Joung Lee, Korea
> Mr. Ghazi Musharbash, Jerusalem and the Middle East
> Right Reverend Bernard Ntahoturi, Burundi
> Mr. John Rea, Scotland
> Ms. Maureen Sithole, Southern Africa
> Right Reverend Fernando Soares, Lusitanian Church

The Standing Committee meets with the Standing Committee of the Primates, which in the period of 1997 to 1998 consisted of the following members:

> Most Reverend and Right Honourable Dr. George Carey, England, chairman
> Most Reverend Richard Holloway, Scotland
> Most Reverend Livingstone Mpalanyi-Nkoyoyo, Uganda
> Most Reverend Michael Peers, Canada
> Most Reverend Moses Tay, Southeast Asia

Meetings

The Joint Standing Committees met in Panama on October 19, 1996, at the conclusion of ACC-10; in Jerusalem at St. George's College from March 7 to 10, 1997; and in Canterbury, England, from March 12 to 16, 1998. This report covers those meetings. It is anticipated that a supplementary report will be made available at ACC-11 to include those matters discussed at the meeting due to be held in Dundee immediately prior to the actual ACC meeting.

ACC-10 Evaluation

Less than fifty percent of the membership of ACC-10 had completed evaluation forms before leaving Panama, but consideration was given to the information conveyed in the forms. The material gathered was referred to the group to be set in place to design ACC-11, with particular note being taken of the suggestions relating to:

- Revision of the constitution and simple rules for meeting procedures.

- The taking of full minutes at the meeting.

- The wish to have fewer resolutions tabled.
- The desire for provinces, particularly new provinces, to be able to make some kind of presentation to the whole council.
- The need for an orientation session at the start.
- The suggestion of more cultural variation in worship.
- The need for more free time during the meetings.

A design group for ACC-11 was appointed, to be chaired by the Most Reverend John Paterson, with the Right Reverend Bernard Ntahoturi, the Right Reverend Fernando Soares, Mr. John Rea, and Ms. Maureen Sithole as members. That group subsequently met on three occasions in order to prepare for this meeting of the ACC.

Anglican Congress

The Joint Standing Committees gave consideration to the various expressions of interest in the holding of an Anglican Congress and resolved to ask Ms. Judith Conley and the Secretary General to conduct a feasibility study. The initial study was reported to the March 1998 meeting, at which point the Joint Standing Committees gave approval to the proposal to hold and plan an Anglican Congress early in the twenty-first century. The design group for ACC-11 early in 1999 expressed concern that more work needed to be done in order to give the members of ACC-11 sufficient data on which to make a well-informed decision, and thus further work was done with the staff of the Secretariat, resulting in a report that is to be distributed to members of ACC-11.

Bethlehem 2000

The Joint Standing Committees considered the matter of participation in a project to renovate Manger Square in Bethlehem for the year 2000, as had been outlined at Panama and supported in Resolution 004 of that meeting. The Secretary General was asked to give consideration to the request from the municipality of Bethlehem, with regard to finance and personnel and possible ecumenical participation. Subsequent developments and the awarding to the Swedish government the right to renovate Manger Square led to a proposal for the Anglican Communion to become involved in a nativity museum in Manger Square, which would house a collection of nativity scenes from around the world. The project was described as having three parts:

(a) The gathering of cribs (crèches)

(b) Payment for the interior of the museum and related expenses

(c) Development of an infrastructure and training of staff for the museum

The Secretary General undertook to develop the proposal, and it was made clear that the Joint Standing Committees were not able to agree to the underwriting of any costs.

Anglican Investment Agency

Resolution 033 of ACC-10 had expressed gratitude and support for the initiative that had resulted in the setting up of the Anglican Investment Agency. The Joint Standing Committees received a progress report in 1997 with details of some initial funds invested with the agency. Three persons were nominated to membership of the disbursement trust, viz. Ms. Judith Conley, United States; Mr. Bernard Turner, West Indies; and Professor Whatarangi Winiata, Aotearoa, New Zealand, and Polynesia. An associated effort had also resulted in the setting up of the Archbishop of Canterbury's Anglican Communion fund. The trustees of the latter met in November 1997 and made four grants from the fund. Good progress was reported as having been made with the Anglican Investment Agency.

Anglican Communion Friends

The Joint Standing Committees received information on some initial work that had been undertaken in the United States on the establishment of a friends' group to educate Episcopalians on the life and work of the Anglican Communion and to help finance the work of the Anglican networks. The longer-term plan was to provide a model that other provinces might adopt. We are waiting for further information on this matter.

Compass Rose Society

Good progress has been made with the development of the society. The Right Reverend Frank Cerveny was appointed as a special envoy of the Compass Rose Society. Meetings were held in London in 1997 and Texas in 1998 as the membership of the society grew. The goal was to raise a significant capital sum in order to help with crisis ministry throughout the Communion and with the communications programme of the Communion. Membership was possible on an individual basis, on a parish basis, or on a chapter basis in which people could combine their resources for membership. The initial joining gift was set at $10,000 U.S., but because this was seen as a prohibitive sum in some parts of the Communion, more flexible arrangements were possible.

Personal Emergencies Fund

Grants are made from this fund for medical emergencies or special needs, but the fund has few resources and more donations are required if it is to remain operative. The Joint Standing Committees expressed strong support for the fund and appointed for a further three-year term (from 1997) the following persons as the committee of management: Canon Colin Craston (convenor), the Right Reverend Simon Barrington Ward, and the Most Reverend Robin Eames.

Anglican Observer at the United Nations

The Joint Standing Committees meeting in Panama in 1996 had resolved that an evaluation be made of the purpose and efficacy of the office to be completed early in 1997. At the invitation of the Archbishop of Canterbury, Sir Peter Marshall, former British ambassador to the United Nations, consulted widely on this matter and produced a helpful report, which the Joint Standing Committees considered at length. Mr. Tom Chappell, as chair of the local advisory council, and the Right Reverend James Ottley, the observer, attended the meeting in Jerusalem to contribute to this discussion in person. The Joint Standing Committees resolved to reiterate the importance of the observer's office at the UN, noting that it provides a significant Anglican presence in the United Nations, an important avenue for advocacy, and a vital means of information. The observer and the advisory council were asked to observe budgetary constraints, while gratitude was expressed that the advisory council was raising large sums to finance the expanded work of the office. Noting the need to broaden the advisory council to include other geographic and cultural dimensions, the chair and vice chair of the ACC were appointed to the council. In March 1998, further consideration was given to whether the office should continue and in what form. It was noted that Bishop Ottley's appointment was due to finish at the end of 1998. The Joint Standing Committees again expressed support for a continuation of the office in some form, and subsequently provision for the sum of $40,000 from the inter-Anglican budget for 1998 was made for the observer's office at the UN. A paper was prepared addressing issues of accountability and purpose, which was referred to the advisory council, and is attached to this report as appendix A.

Anglican Centre in Rome

Brief reports were received of the work of the centre, and particular attention was paid to the need to move to new premises in a different part of the Palazzo Doria. Fund-raising was undertaken in order to enable this move, and the hope was expressed that an endowment might be raised to allow the centre a more secure financial base. Information was to be sent to the provinces about the centre.

St. George's College, Jerusalem

Reports were considered from the Anglican Consultative Council representative on the board of the college—Canon James Rosenthal. Budget and income were healthy, and courses were well supported. Three regional committees in North America, the United Kingdom, and Australasia supported the work of the college.

Network Reports

In order to facilitate the work of the various Anglican networks and to improve the communication flow with the Joint Standing Committees, liaison persons were appointed from the Standing Committee to work with each of the networks.

Refugee and Migrant Network

The network last met in Jordan in 1992 and needed to be reestablished. Archbishop Ian George of Adelaide, Australia, was asked to reconvene the network and he has set about this task well.

Family Network

Liaison person: the Most Reverend Richard Holloway. The network has been active and has had good responses to the inclusion of its family newsletter in *Anglican World*. Efforts are now being made for the newsletter to be translated into other languages.

Indigenous Peoples Network

Liaison person: Ms. Judith Conley. The network now attempts to operate through working groups because of budgetary restraints, following the first two meetings in Canada and New Zealand. The particular concerns of the network are as follows:

- Native spirituality in relation to Christianity;
- Theological education and ordination and alternative methodologies for ordination preparation;
- The development and publishing of theological materials; the network is cautious about being linked too closely to the structures of the Communion.

Youth Network

Liaison person: the Right Reverend Fernando Soares. A report was received on Gathering 1997, which was a gathering of young adults from parts of the Communion.

Peace and Justice Network

Liaison person: the Reverend Dr. John Jae-Joung Lee. It was reported that strong support for this network had come from the Episcopal Church in the United States. A meeting was being planned for Korea in April 1999. It was largely an information-sharing network, and it enjoyed useful links with the Anglican observer's office at the UN.

Network for Inter-Faith Concerns (NIFCON)

Liaison person: Mr. Ghazi Musharbash. A support group had been meeting in Birmingham during the time that the Reverend Nigel Pounde had been the convenor, seconded by his diocese for one day per week for this work. The new convenor is the Reverend Canon John Sargant.

Anglican Women's Network

Liaison person: Ms. Maureen Sithole. In November 1997 a consultation of the chairs and presidents of women's organisations around the Communion had been held and representatives of fourteen provinces attended. One result was to establish an Anglican Women's Network. Issues arising from the Beijing World Conference in 1995 were discussed. Mrs. Elizabeth Barnes of Southern Africa was the coordinator of the network. The aim is to have a contact person in each member church of the Communion. An overall goal was to link women from the various church organisations to which they belong, as well as women who are not able to belong to any organisations, so that the network could be an empowering network for all the women of the Communion. Funding needs to be addressed. A report from African women theologians was received.

Inter-Anglican Finance Committee

The Joint Standing Committees have expressed appreciation for the work of the committee, chaired by the Most Reverend Robin Eames. Very full reports and accounts have been received, and these are to be dealt with separately.

Staffing Review

The Joint Standing Committees noted that the appointments of various staff members were due to be completed at a variety of dates, and with pressure mounting in respect of the Lambeth Conference and the need to prioritise the work of the Communion office, resolved that a three-person review group be asked to undertake a review of present staffing structures and the role and duties of the staff members of the Anglican Communion Office. The three persons so appointed were the Right Reverend Simon Chiwanga, Ms. Judy Conley, and the Most Reverend Robin Eames. This was carried out in June 1997, and a confidential report was compiled. The review committee noted that the Communion was served by a godly and committed staff that frequently had to work under stressful and difficult conditions.

Office Location

In March 1997 the Joint Standing Committees resolved to note that the space in the Partnership House is not suitable for the needs of the Anglican Communion Office and the efficient working of the staff and offered encouragement to the Secretary General to make suitable alternative arrangements when possible. In March 1998 a report was received that no progress had been made on this matter, but that discussions were taking place. In 1999 the office is still located in Partnership House.

Anglican Cycle of Prayer

Consideration was given to the respective responsibilities of Forward Movement Publications and the Anglican Communion Office in the production of the *Cycle of Prayer*, as this publication was seen as an important means of communication and a vehicle for prayer and worship. A good deal of consultation has subsequently taken place, and a new two-year format was agreed upon, the first of which was finalised during the

Lambeth Conference and is now in use. Corrections as necessary will appear in *Anglican World* and on the Anglican Communion web site.

Communications

Canon Rosenthal has reported fully on the communications programme in the Communion. Much attention has been paid to the production of *Anglican World* and the need for translation so as to enable greater use and appreciation of the magazine. Valuable funding assistance is acknowledged from the Compass Rose Society for the communications programme. Dr. Joan Ford worked at the Communion office in the telecommunications area and contributed significantly to an enhanced programme. The Anglican Communion News Service had been made available online on a weekly rather than monthly basis, and the web site developed.

Ecumenical

The Reverend Canon David Hamid reports regularly from the Department of Ecumenical Affairs and Relations on the work of the inter-church dialogues and the progress toward forming an Inter-Anglican Standing Commission on Ecumenical Relations. Much of this work was used to inform the ecumenical section of the Lambeth Conference. The various ecumenical dialogues have continued, and good progress has been reported. The Joint Standing Committees resolved to reaffirm Anglican commitment to the World Council of Churches as a vital ecumenical instrument and commented on both the proposed restructuring and the membership of the WCC. It was recommended that the ACC and the old Catholic churches of the Union of Utrecht establish an Anglican-Old Catholic International Coordinating Council. Progress was reported on the matter of a common date for Easter. More detailed material will be presented to the ACC on these and other matters.

Liturgical

The Reverend Dr. Paul Gibson has continued as the coordinator for liturgy and has served the Communion extremely well in this office. In March 1997, the Joint Standing Committees were presented with a draft of a review of the fourteen years of the International Liturgical Consultations. Dr. Gibson retired from his position as liturgical officer for the Anglican Church of Canada, continued until ACC-11 in his post as coordinator for liturgy, and agreed to be the chaplain for this meeting of the council.

Mission and Evangelism

The Reverend Dr. Cyril Okorocha served as secretary for mission and evangelism until 1997 and reported to the March 1997 meeting of the Joint Standing Committees. Much of his time and attention had been taken up with the Second Anglican Encounter in the South. At the expiry of Canon Okorocha's appointment, Miss Murphy picked up this responsibility and reported fully to the March 1998 meeting. MISSIO made a number of recommendations to the Joint Standing Committees, and these were referred as appropriate to the various sections of the Lambeth Conference.

Lambeth Conference

Mr. David Long, manager of the conference, attended the meetings of the Joint Standing Committees and reported fully on preparations for the conference. The regional meetings and the conference itself had required much time and attention from the various members of the Secretariat, and it was hoped that the conference would be a significant event for the Communion. The design group for ACC-11 subsequently worked through the resolutions from the conference with a view to their inclusion as appropriate in the agenda for this meeting of the council.

Legal Advisor

The Joint Standing Committees and the Secretary General have been greatly assisted in recent years by the advice offered by the Reverend John Rees of Winckworth and Pemberton in Oxford. Accordingly, it was resolved to appoint John Rees as the legal advisor to the Anglican Consultative Council. He has produced a revision of guidelines for the conduct of meetings of the council, and the Joint Standing Committees are most grateful for his help in these matters.

Priorities Working Group

At the urging of the Inter-Anglican Finance Committee, the Joint Standing Committees looked at the question of an ordering of priorities for the Anglican Communion and the ACC and asked a small working group to consider these matters in consultation with the Archbishop of Canterbury. The group was comprised of the Archbishop of Canterbury and the Most Reverend John Paterson as co-chairmen, with Mr. John Rea, Ms. Maureen Sithole, the Right Reverend Fernando Soares, and the Secretary General as members. The group met twice and will be reporting to the meeting of the Joint Standing Committees immediately before ACC-11.

New Provinces

The Joint Standing Committees welcomed the progress that was being made toward the formation of the new province of Hong Kong. That process is now complete and Hong Kong is present at this meeting in that capacity. A welcome was also extended at the formation of the new province of La Iglesia Anglicana de la Region Central de America.

ACC Membership

Three resolutions from ACC-10 (resolutions 006, 009, and 026) relating to membership and size of the ACC were referred to a working group for consideration and report. The group was comprised of the Most Reverend Robin Eames, the Reverend Dr. John Jae-Joung Lee, and Mr. Ghazi Musharbash. Subsequently, Ms. Judith Conley joined the working group. Their report was considered in March 1998, and it was resolved to recommend to ACC-11 that membership of the ACC be comprised of the following:

Archbishop of Canterbury	1
9 provinces with 3 members: 1 bishop, 1 priest, and 1 layperson	27
Provinces with 2 members, always 1 bishop and the other alternating between a priest and a layperson	54
7 co-opted members	7
Total	**89**

The rationale behind having seven co-opted members was that ten percent of the current membership of the ACC was seven. It was noted that care should be taken to ensure that the co-opted members would represent a good balance of the recommended qualifications. As the number of provincial representatives increased, so would the number of co-opted members in order to maintain the balance of ten percent of the members being co-opted.

In the light of the increase in numbers of ACC members and the fact that the size of the Standing Committee had remained the same since the ACC was formed, the working group recommended the following proposal: "that the ACC Standing Committee consists of 12 persons: 4 bishops, 4 clergy, and 4 laity. The chair and vice chair shall always be members, and there shall be represented at least two women and one person under 28 years of age at the time of appointment."

Subsequent to the Lambeth Conference, which made some specific recommendations concerning the ACC, the working group met, by conference call, to augment the proposal by offering an alternative based on the Lambeth thinking. Both alternatives, with cost estimates, are included in the report of this working group.

Appendix A: Anglican Observer at the United Nations

I. Ministry Mission Statement

The Anglican Communion is a family of autonomous churches in 165 countries whose ethnic, cultural, and political diversity reflects the complexity and richness of the world.

Recognizing the sacredness of life, the Anglican Communion worldwide works to promote fundamental human rights and freedoms, the empowerment of women and all peoples, the repair and preservation of the environment, and the advancement of justice and peace. We commit ourselves to work with others for a world that is "pro-dignity, pro-nature, pro-people."

In support of the ministry of the Anglican Communion at large, the Anglican Observer seeks to serve:

1. As the eyes, ears, and voice of the Anglican Communion at the United Nations.

2. As a host to deliberations on major world issues, providing an Anglican perspective in responding to injustice in the world.

3. As a resource to inform and support the prophetic ministry of the Archbishop of Canterbury, the Primates, and the wider leadership of the Anglican Communion.

4. As an advocate for human development in its fullest forms, articulating and communicating the views and concerns of the Archbishop of Canterbury, the Primates of the Anglican Communion, and the Anglican Consultative Council.

5. As a convenor, facilitating dialogue and forging creative solutions among decision makers at the UN, its agencies, and other related bodies.

6. As a witness, working to create a network of prayer throughout the Anglican Communion for particular Christian issues.

II. Job Description

Job Title: Anglican Observer at the United Nations

Responsible to: The Anglican Consultative Council and the Archbishop of Canterbury as president, through the Secretary General

Job Purpose: To provide an Anglican presence at the UN

Key Responsibilities: In serving as the eyes, ears, and voice of the Anglican Communion at the United Nations, the observer seeks to:

- Bring to the attention of the Archbishop of Canterbury, the Primates of the Anglican Communion, and the Anglican Consultative Council (through the chairperson and the Secretary General) important global issues, events, and information as they relate to the United Nations and related organisations;

- Share with the United Nations and related organisations information conveyed from the Archbishop of Canterbury, the Primates of the Anglican Communion, and the Anglican Consultative Council;

- Represent the Communion at the UN and related forums as able;

- Serve as an advocate for the Communion on issues of justice, equality, ecology, and development.

Other Specific Responsibilities:

1. Within the programme and budget agreed by the ACC, be responsible for the selection, management, deployment, and development of the staff of the Observer's office.

2. As practical, within the resources available, seek to promote the following:

    (a) Within the Communion:

    - Work closely, where appropriate, with the various Anglican Communion networks;

- Facilitate dialogue and develop forums, which discuss major global issues of concern to the wider church;
- Develop and employ effective means of communicating information on global issues and the work of the office to create awareness within the Communion;
- Work to create a network of prayer throughout the Anglican Communion for particular Christian issues;
- Where helpful, provide theological reflection on selected United Nations issues.

(b) On behalf of the Communion:
- Establish contact with the different programmes of the United Nations and serve as a liaison between the UN, the provinces, and the dioceses of the Anglican Communion;
- Collaborate with other religious and nongovernmental organisations at the United Nations, where appropriate;
- Together with other ecumenical partners, to provide a pastoral ministry to members of the United Nations community.

3. Contribute to the periodic review of the Observer's role and programme.
4. Any other tasks as may be required by the Secretary General, the Archbishop of Canterbury, the Primates, or the Anglican Consultative Council from time to time.

III. Channels of Accountability and Communication

The Observer is accountable to the ACC and line managed by the Secretary General.

It is recognised that the nature of the Observer's role requires occasional direct contact with the Archbishop of Canterbury, the Primates, the Anglican Consultative Council and the advisory council.

In order to facilitate effective and clear communication, the following efforts should be pursued in collaboration with the Archbishop of Canterbury, the Primates, and the Anglican Consultative Council.

- An annual meeting should be scheduled with the Archbishop of Canterbury to share, in person, news and other information about the ministry of the Observer and his office.
- Reports by the Observer should be made at the Primates' Meetings and should be received in writing when they are not in session.
- The Observer will make an annual report to the Joint Standing Committees of the Primates and the Anglican Consultative Council and, on a three-yearly basis, to the Anglican Consultative Council.

- Circumstances permitting, the Observer should be invited to attend special meetings with other church or governmental leaders on global issues of concern to the United Nations and the wider Church.

- The Observer should be kept abreast of the efforts of the wider Church and its leadership in politically sensitive areas such as Rwanda, Burundi, Sudan, and so forth.

- In so far as possible, the Observer should be informed about some of the Archbishop of Canterbury's plans so that current, relevant information about the countries to be visited by the Archbishop may be provided.

- The Observer should have a more clearly defined role in major events throughout the Communion, such as the Lambeth Conference of bishops.

IV. The Role of the Advisory Council

An advisory council was formed from people in the United States to support the work of the Observer. In recent years, this group has been responsible for an impressive amount of fund-raising. The advisory council membership has now been augmented by the appointment of the chair and vice chair of the Anglican Consultative Council and the representative of the Archbishop of Canterbury. Its role and functions are becoming more clearly defined.

In supporting the ministry of the Observer and his office, the advisory council:

- Acts as a local source of counsel and support to the Observer to strengthen the ministry and effectiveness of the office.

- Helps in networking and establishing new contacts with persons who would support the ministry of the wider Church at the United Nations.

- Helps to provide resourcing and funds, as part of the agreed budget through which to achieve the agreed programme.

V. Funding Arrangements—1998 Onward

At the 1998 Joint Standing Committees, a Priorities Working Group was appointed to consider the various ACC activities and make recommendations concerning priorities and funding to the Inter-Anglican Finance Committee.

Given the reaffirmation of support for the role and contribution of the UN Observer's office by the 1998 Joint Standing Committees, the Priorities Working Group is asked to consider the recommendation of a 1998 budgetary allocation that reflects the following principles:

1. The recognition, status, and potential of the UN observer's office, as agreed, by the Joint Standing Committee.

2. The importance of reassuring the advisory committee and UN Observer of the ACC's commitment to this work at a level that encourages the advisory group in their much-appreciated fund-raising role.

From 1999 onward, as part of the ACO budget preparation process, the UN observer will be asked to submit, in consultation with the Secretary General, a rolling three-year business plan reflecting:

- The objectives of the office
- The priorities for action in the coming year
- The working methods, tactics, and targets proposed
- An outline of the resources, both human and non-human, required
- The proposed budget, reflecting both the specific ACC request and the resources to be obtained from other sources
- The arrangements proposed to review the impact and effectiveness of the work of the office

To put this request in context, it is anticipated that the annual provision of a business plan and justified budget request for the IAFC will, in the future, be a requirement for each significant area of ACC activity to enable responsible budgetary decisions to be made, both by the IAFC and the Joint Standing Committees.

VI. *Relationship with the Primates*

We recognise, with appreciation, the work of the Observer and seek to develop further the contribution this role can make toward and on behalf of the work of the Archbishop of Canterbury and the Primates.

As reflected in the job description, through raising awareness and providing briefing information, the observer can contribute to the sensitive and effective exercise of the leadership and prophetic role of the Primates, either acting in a local, individual manner or collectively. The UN observer is potentially well-placed to act as a source of influence at the UN on behalf of the Archbishop of Canterbury and the Primates.

It is recommended that the Archbishop of Canterbury lead a session at the next Primates' meeting to help explore and agree on how the role of UN Observer might best be exploited by the Primates. It is suggested that the Observer and the ACC Secretary General would both be involved in this discussion and commitment.

The Constitution of the Anglican Consultative Council

1. Name

The name of the council is the Anglican Consultative Council.

2. Object

The object of the council shall be to advance the Christian religion and in furtherance of that object, but not further or otherwise, the council shall have the following powers:

(a) To facilitate the cooperative work of the member churches of the Anglican Communion.

(b) To share information about developments in one or more provinces of the Anglican Communion with the other parts of the Communion and to serve as needed as an instrument of common action.

(c) To advise on inter-Anglican, provincial, and diocesan relationships, including the division of provinces, the formation of new provinces and of regional councils, and the problems of extra-provincial dioceses.

(d) To develop as far as possible agreed Anglican policies in the world mission of the Church and to encourage national and regional churches to engage together in developing and implementing such policies by sharing their resources of man power, money, and experience to the best advantage of all.

(e) To keep before national and regional churches the importance of the fullest possible Anglican collaboration with other Christian churches.

(f) To encourage and guide Anglican participation in the ecumenical movement and the ecumenical organisations, to cooperate with the World Council of Churches and the world confessional bodies on behalf of the Anglican Communion, and to make arrangements for the conduct of pan-Anglican conversations with the Roman Catholic Church, the Orthodox churches, and other churches.

(g) To advise on matters arising out of national or regional church union negotiations or conversations and on subsequent relations with united churches.

(h) To advise on problems of inter-Anglican communication and to help in the dissemination of Anglican and ecumenical information.

(i) To keep in review the needs that may arise for further study, and, where necessary, to promote inquiry and research.

(j) To obtain, collect, receive, and hold money, funds, and property, old and new, by way of contributions, donations, subscriptions, legacies, grants, and any other lawful method, and accept and receive gifts of property of any description (whether subject to any special trust or not).

(k) To assist any charitable body or bodies financially or otherwise.

(l) To establish an emergency fund or funds for the support of clergy in special need and for other charitable purposes in any part of the world.

(m) To assist the Inter-Anglican Finance Committee (as hereinafter defined), the Primates' Meeting, and the Lambeth Conference as and when required to do so.

(n) To procure to be written in print, publish, issue, and circulate gratuitously or otherwise any reports or periodicals, books, pamphlets, leaflets, or other documents.

(o) To receive and hold in custody, or cause to be held in custody, any records or legal or historical documents of any member church.

(p) To arrange and provide for or join in arranging and providing for the holding of exhibitions, meetings, lectures, and classes.

(q) To make bylaws, always subject to this constitution, for the better conduct of its business and to repeal or amend the same from time to time.

(r) To do all such other things as shall further the objects of the council.

3. Membership

(a) The council shall be constituted with a membership according to the schedule hereto. With the assent of two-thirds of the Primates of the Anglican Communion, the council may alter or add to the schedule. "Primates," for the purposes of this article, shall mean the principal Archbishop, bishop, or Primate of each of the bodies listed under paragraphs b, c, and d of the schedule of membership.

(b) Members shall be appointed as provincial, national, or regional machinery provides. Alternate members shall be appointed in a similar manner and shall be invited to attend a meeting if the ordinary member is unable to be present for a whole session of the council. Any appointment of a member or alternate member may be revoked by the body that made the appointment.

4. Appointment and Retirement of Members

    (a) Each of the appointing bodies shall have regard to the desirability of ensuring that any member appointed to represent it on the council shall be a member of its own representative structures and that such person shall be given appropriate opportunity to report the proceedings of the council to its own decision-making bodies and to convey the views of such decision-making bodies to the council.

    (b) The term of office for ordinary members shall be either

    (i) six years calculated from a member's first attendance at a meeting of the council, or

    (ii) three successive meetings of the council, whichever period shall terminate the later, or

    (iii) such shorter period as the appointing body shall determine.

    (c) On termination of his or her period of office, no member shall be eligible for reappointment nor shall he or she be appointed an alternate member until a period of six years elapses from the date when such original membership ceased.

    (d) Bishops and other clerical members shall cease to be members on retirement from ecclesiastical office.

    (e) Any appointing body as set out in the Schedule of Membership shall have power at any time and from time to time to appoint any qualified person to be a member to fill a casual vacancy to hold office for the unexpired term specified in clause 4(b).

    (f) Alternate members: an alternate member may be reappointed as an alternate member or appointed an ordinary member unless he or she has already replaced a member at two meetings of the council.

    (g) Any appointing body shall upon making such appointment notify the Secretary General of the name of the person so appointed and all relevant contact information relating to the person.

5. Advisers

The council may invite advisers, Anglicans, or others, to be present at its meetings, but not to vote.

6. Officers

   (a) The Archbishop of Canterbury shall always be a member of the council and its president, and not subject to retirement under the provision of clause 4(b). When present he shall inaugurate each meeting of the council. He shall be an ex officio member of all its committees.

   (b) The council shall elect a chairman and vice chairman from its own number who shall hold office for two meetings of the council.

   (c) The council shall delegate to its Standing Committee the appointment of a secretary for a specified term who shall be known as the Secretary General of the council and whose duties it shall determine. The Secretary General shall not be a member of the council. Remuneration and terms and conditions of service shall be determined by the Standing Committee.[1]

7. Standing Committee

   (a) The council shall appoint a Standing Committee of nine members, which shall include the chairman and the vice chairman of the council. The Secretary General shall be secretary of the Standing Committee.

   (b) The members of the Standing Committee shall be the trustees of the council for the purposes of the Order of the Charity Commissioners for England and Wales sealed on May 6, 1994.

   (c) Ordinary meetings of the Standing Committee shall take place annually.

   (d) At least six months' notice shall be given to every member of the date and place of the annual meeting of the Standing Committee and such notice shall specify the general nature of the business to be transacted thereat.

---

[1] ACC-1, page 59, resolution 42, defined the terms of appointment as follows:

   (a) to be responsible for all secretarial and other duties for the council and for the meetings of the council and of its Standing Committee; and

   (b) to serve the Anglican Communion and its member churches with particular regard to the stated functions of the Anglican Consultative Council and to the recommendations and reports of the Council.

ACC-8, resolution 30:

Meetings of the Primates and the Lambeth Conference

The Secretary General shall be available to serve, as the Archbishop of Canterbury shall require, as staff for meetings of the Primates and Lambeth Conference. The ACC shall not be responsible for the expenses of the Primates' Meetings or the Lambeth Conference. The Primates' Meetings and the Lambeth Conference shall be responsible for expenses incurred on their behalf by the Secretary General and his staff.

8. Powers of the Standing Committee

The Standing Committee shall act for the council between meetings of the council and shall execute such matters as are referred to it by the council. The Standing Committee may exercise all powers of the council as are not by this constitution required to be done specifically by the council, and in particular may borrow money and mortgage or charge the council assets.

9. Meetings of the Council

(a) The council shall meet at intervals of approximately two or three years as appropriate.

(b) As far as possible, the council shall meet in various parts of the world.

10. Amendments to the Constitution

Amendments to this constitution shall be submitted by the council to the constitutional bodies listed under clauses b, c, and d of the Schedule of Membership and must be ratified by two-thirds of such bodies provided that no amendment shall be made which shall cause the council to cease to be a charity at law.

11. Dissolution

If upon the winding-up or dissolution of the council, there remains after the satisfaction of all its debts and liabilities any property whatsoever, the same shall not be paid or distributed among the members of the council, but shall be given or transferred to some other charitable institution or institutions having charitable objects similar to the objects of the council and which shall prohibit the distribution of its or their income and property among its or their members.

The Schedule of Membership

The membership of the council shall be as follows:

(a) The Archbishop of Canterbury

(b) Three persons from each of the following, consisting of one bishop, one priest, and one layperson:

Anglican Church of Australia
Anglican Church of Canada
Church of England
Church of Nigeria (Anglican Communion)
Church of the Province of Rwanda
Church of the Province of Southern Africa
Church of South India
Church of the Province of Uganda
Episcopal Church (United States of America)

(c) Two persons from each of the following, consisting of one bishop or one priest plus one layperson:

Anglican Church of Aotearoa, New Zealand, and Polynesia
Church of the Province of Central Africa
Province of the Anglican Church of Congo
Church of Ireland
Anglican Church of Kenya
Church of North India
Church of Pakistan
Episcopal Church of the Sudan
Anglican Church of Tanzania
Church in Wales
Church in the Province of the West Indies

(d) One person (preferably lay) from each of the following:

Church of Bangladesh
Episcopal Anglican Church of Brasil
Church of the Province of Burundi
Anglican Church of the Central America Region
Church of Ceylon
Hong Kong Sheng Kung Hui
Church of the Province of the Indian Ocean
Nippon Sei Ko Kai (Anglican Communion in Japan)
Episcopal Church in Jerusalem and the Middle East
Anglican Church in Korea
Church of the Province of Melanesia
Anglican Church of Mexico
Church of the Province of Myanmar
Anglican Church of Papua New Guinea
Episcopal Church in the Philippines
Anglican Church of the Southern Cone of America
Scottish Episcopal Church
Church of the Province of Southeast Asia
Church of the Province of West Africa

(e) Co-opted members:

The Council may co-opt up to six additional members of whom two shall be women and two persons not over 28 years of age at the time of appointment.

(f) Additional members:

When the chairman's appointment as chairman extends beyond the date at which his or her membership of the council ordinarily expires, from the time of the expiry of the ordinary membership:

i. the body which made the appointment shall be entitled to appoint a new member of the council;

ii. the chairman shall become an additional member of the council until the completion of the term as chairman;

iii. the same rules shall apply to the vice chairman.

The Bylaws of the Anglican Consultative Council

(adopted pursuant to clause 2q of the constitution)

1. Meetings of the Council

    (a) All meetings of the council shall be called at a minimum of six months' notice in writing. Such notice shall specify the date, the place, and the general nature of the business to be transacted thereat.

    (b) No business shall be transacted at any meeting of the council unless a quorum of members is present at the time when the meeting proceeds to business. A quorum shall consist of members appointed by a majority of the bodies listed in clauses b, c, and d of the Schedule of Membership personally present.

    (c) Conduct of business at any meeting of the council shall be regulated by procedural rules adopted from time to time by the council, and insofar as any procedural matter shall arise that shall not be dealt with in the procedural rules currently in force, the chairman shall have power to determine such matter conclusively after such consultation as he shall think fit.

2. Proceedings of the Standing Committee

    (a) The chairman of the council may and on the request of five members of the Standing Committee shall summon a special meeting of the Standing Committee.

    (b) The Standing Committee may regulate their meetings as they think fit and determine the quorum necessary for the transaction of business. Unless otherwise determined, five shall be a quorum. Questions arising at any meeting shall be decided by a majority of votes. In the case of an equality of votes, the chairman shall have a second or casting vote.

    (c) The Standing Committee may delegate any of its powers to committees as it thinks fit and any committee so formed shall, in the execution of the powers so delegated, conform to any requirements imposed on it by the Standing Committee. Any such committee may call advisers.

(d) In electing members of the Standing Committee the council shall have regard to the desirability of achieving (so far as practicable) appropriate regional diversity and a balance of representation between clergy and laity and between the genders.

(e) Elected members of the Standing Committee shall hold office from the end of the council meeting at which they are appointed until the end of the last ordinary council meeting at which they would be entitled to attend but subject to earlier termination in the event that such elected member shall for any reason cease to be a member of the council.

3. Finance

(a) The Secretary General is responsible to the council for overseeing its financial affairs and the affairs of the Inter-Anglican Finance Committee and shall ensure that proper books of account be kept with respect to:

   i. All sums of money received and expended by the council and the matters in respect of which the receipt and expenditure took place

   ii. The assets and liabilities of the council

   and shall be responsible for presenting the council's audited accounts at each annual meeting of the Standing Committee.

(b) The Standing Committee shall lay before the council properly audited annual income and expenditure accounts, balance sheets, and reports, and such documents to include full financial reports on the Inter-Anglican Finance Committee, the Primates' Meeting, and, where necessary, the Lambeth Conference. Copies of the same shall be circulated to members of the council with the other papers for the meeting at which the accounts are to be considered.

4. Inter-Anglican Finance Committee

(a) The council in conjunction with the Primates' Meeting shall appoint a finance committee of at least five members, to be called the Inter-Anglican Finance Committee, which shall be responsible for coordinating the finances required by the council, the Primates' Meeting, and the Lambeth Conference.

(b) The membership shall consist of at least two members appointed by the Primates' Meeting and at least three members appointed by the council.

(c) Members appointed by the council shall take their place on the committee at the end of the council meeting at which they are elected, and their membership shall continue until the end of the last ordinary council meeting they would be entitled to attend but subject to earlier termination in the event that such elected member shall for any reason cease to be a member of the council. Members appointed by the Primates' Meeting shall serve as long as the Primates shall determine.

(d) The Inter-Anglican Finance Committee shall appoint from its own membership its chairperson and vice chairperson.

5. Inter-Anglican Budget

The Inter-Anglican Finance Committee in collaboration with the Standing Committee shall, in consultation with member churches, be responsible for the annual Inter-Anglican budget, which will include the costs of the Inter-Anglican Finance Committee, the Primates' Meeting and the Lambeth Conference, and shall keep members of the council and member churches informed about each year's budget and about the forecast for each of the succeeding three years. In the light of those draft budgets, the council shall determine the level of expenditure and the income required to meet its purposes. The contributions to the Inter-Anglican budget shall be apportioned among the member bodies as in clauses b to d inclusive of the Schedule of Membership.

6. Casual Vacancies in the Co-Opted Membership of the Council

In the event of any casual vacancy occurring in the co-opted membership of the council, the Standing Committee shall have power to co-opt a member under the provisions of clause e of the Schedule of Membership of the council to hold office until the conclusion of the next meeting of the council. Any member co-opted in this manner by the Standing Committee shall be eligible for election by the council if it so wishes.

7. Casual Vacancies on the Standing Committee

In the event of a casual vacancy occurring in the membership of the Standing Committee between council meetings, the Standing Committee itself shall have power to appoint a member of the council of the same order as the representative who filled the vacant place, and such member shall have full voting rights for the remainder of the term of service of the former member. Such member shall, subject to his or her eligibility for continuing membership of the council, be eligible for re-election to the Standing Committee at the next council meeting.

8. Common Seal

The seal of the council shall at all times be kept in safe custody and shall not be affixed to any instrument except by authority of a resolution of the Standing Committee and in the presence of the secretary or the chairman of the Standing Committee and one other member of the council, each of whom shall sign every instrument to which the seal shall be so affixed in their presence.

Guidelines for Meetings of the Anglican Consultative Council

General

1. All arrangements for the conduct of the business of the council shall be made under the general direction of the president.

Arrangements for Meetings

2.1 The Standing Committee:

   2.1:1 Shall make all detailed arrangements for meetings of the council, and

   2.1:2 Shall settle the agenda and determine the order in which business shall be considered by the council at its meetings, and

   2.1:3 May delegate any of its functions relating to such matters to member(s) or officers(s) as it shall see fit.

2.2 In settling the agenda, the Standing Committee shall pay particular regard to:

   2.2:1 The role of the council as one of the instruments of unity in the Anglican Communion, and

   2.2:2 Specific issues referred by the Archbishop of Canterbury, by the Lambeth Conference, by previous meetings of the council, and by the Primates' Meeting, and

   2.2:3 The need to inform members about the ongoing work of the council, its Standing Committee, and its officers, and

   2.2:4 The finances of the council.

2.3 In its preparation for each meeting of the council, the Standing Committee shall give opportunity to members at the first business session of every meeting (which shall take place within the first three days of assembling) to comment upon the settled agenda and to request the inclusion of additional material.

2.4 The chairman after consultation with the president shall have power to direct the addition to the agenda at any time of such urgent or specially important business as shall seem to them desirable.

Chairing of Meetings

3.1 The Standing Committee shall appoint persons to chair each session of the council who shall be either the president, the chairman, the vice chairman, or such other member of the council as the Standing Committee shall think fit.

3.2 It shall be the duty of the chair of each session to maintain order in debate, to ensure so far as possible that discussion of matters is broadly representative of the full range of views of members of the council as a whole, and to encourage the council to reach general assent on matters under discussion.

3.3 The chair of each session may with or without the request of any member of the council after such consultation as the chair shall think fit suspend debate on any topic under discussion for a specified period or impose any speech limit or direct that any matter under discussion shall be put to the vote or give any other direction as shall seem to the chair to be conducive to the proper despatch of business.

Speakers

4.1 In their contributions to discussion members shall pay proper respect to the chair of the session and in particular shall have regard to the duties of the chair under 3.2 above.

4.2 All members of the council shall qualify to be called upon by the chair of the session to speak in any session of the council, and Primates, ecumenical participants or other persons present at the invitation of the council may address the council at the invitation of the chair of the session.

4.3 The chair of any session may request that members wishing to speak on any particular subject be asked to submit their names in writing to the chair of the session in advance with a general indication of their particular interest or expertise in relation to the matter under discussion.

4.4 Members may not speak unless called upon to do so by the chair of the session and, if called upon to speak, shall address their remarks through the chair.

4.5 Upon being called upon to speak, a member shall first announce his or her name and province or church.

4.6 Subject to any other direction by the chair of the session, a speaker introducing a report or moving a motion may speak for up to ten minutes and all other speakers may speak for up to five minutes.

4.7 The chair of the session shall call a member to order for failure to address remarks through the chair, irrelevance, repetition of previous arguments, unbecoming language, discourtesy, or any other breach of reasonable order of debate, and may order a member to end any speech.

4.8 The person moving a motion (but not an amendment) shall have a right of reply limited to five minutes at the close of the discussion, but no member may otherwise speak more than once in the same discussion except with the express permission of the chair.

Motions and Amendments

5.1 Insofar as daily business shall not have been dealt with in the main agenda, relevant motions shall be made available in writing to members in such form as the Standing Committee shall determine as soon as possible after receipt from the person proposing the motion and in any event not later than the commencement of the session in which it is proposed to be presented or discussed, unless the chair of the session shall permit otherwise.

5.2 Motions for consideration by the council shall be presented:

5.2:1 In the case of motions forming part of the main agenda, by a member of the council nominated by the Standing Committee; and

5.2:2 In the case of motions formulated by a regional or other group set up for a specific purpose as part of the work of group of sessions, by a member of such group; and

5.2:3 In the case of any other motion to be brought to a plenary session designated by the Standing Committee for such business, by any member of the council with a written indication of support signed by ten other members;

and in the case of motions under 5.2:2 and 5.2:3 above, the full text of such a motion shall be submitted in writing not later than the time directed by the Standing Committee in advance of the relevant discussion in order that the full text may be made available for consideration by all members unless the chair of the session shall permit otherwise.

5.3 Members wishing to submit any amendment to an existing motion shall submit the full text of such motion or amendment in writing, signed by the mover and ten other members, not later than the time directed by the Standing Committee in advance of the relevant discussion in order that the full text may be made available for consideration by all members unless the chair of the session shall permit otherwise.

5.4 An amendment shall not be accepted for discussion if in the opinion of the chair of the session it repeats an amendment that has already been withdrawn or disposed or would negate the motion to which it relates.

5.5 Amendments will normally be considered in the order in which they first affect the motion under discussion but may be considered in some other order at the discretion of the chair of the session, and the order in which amendments will be taken shall be announced at the commencement of the session.

5.6 A main motion shall not be put finally to the meeting until all amendments shall have been carried, withdrawn, or otherwise disposed of, and in the event that an amendment shall have been carried, the chair of the session will read to the council the motion as amended before further discussion on the motion or any outstanding further amendment may proceed.

5.7 When all amendments shall have been dealt with, the motion, subject to any agreed amendments, shall be put to the council.

Decisions on Business

6.1 Only members of the council shall be entitled to vote on business before the council.

6.2 The chair of each session shall put the motion under discussion to the council for its general assent, which may be indicated in such manner as the chair shall think fit.

6.3 If the chair of the session shall so direct, or if upon the chair requesting general assent any member shall request that a vote be taken, and such request has the support of not less than one-third of the members present and entitled to vote, then a vote shall be taken by show of hands or on ballot papers as the chair of the session shall decide.

6.4 In the event of a vote being taken, a simple majority shall be required unless the president after consultation with the Standing Committee shall direct that some other majority shall apply.

General

7.1 The chair of a session may after consultation with the Standing Committee suspend the application of these guidelines for part or all of the relevant session if the chair shall think it conducive to the better despatch of the business then before the council.

7.2 The council may at any time with the consent of the Standing Committee revoke, amend, or supplement these guidelines or any part of them for the better conduct of the business of the council.

Profiles of Members of the Anglican Consultative Council

The Very Reverend David L. Richardson,
Clergy representative, Anglican Church of Australia

The Very Reverend David L. Richardson, a liturgical expert who has ministered in three different states in Australia, is the clergy representative from that province. Since his ordination in the Diocese of Brisbane, he has served in University College chaplaincy, theological education, and parish ministry. He is one of a few Australian clergy who has been dean of two metropolitan cathedrals in Australia, in his case, St. Peter's, Adelaide, and presently St. Paul's, Melbourne. He served for seventeen years as a member and thirteen years as executive secretary of the liturgical commission of the Anglican Church of Australia. He is married to Margaret, a psychologist, and they have two adult children.

Speaking of the Anglican Church of Australia, the dean says that it is a culturally and theologically diverse province. Since the end of the Second World War, Australia has moved from being predominantly Anglo-Celtic, with a small population of aboriginal and Torres Strait island peoples, to being one of the world's most multiculturally diverse nations. The major cities are close to the coast, and with one or two exceptions there is a small regional population spread thinly across the vast continent. The Anglican Church is the second largest church in Australia, and currently some twenty-six percent of the population declare they are Anglican adherents. The Church has five provinces, each based on an Australian state, with an Archbishop in the metropolitan city. The Primate is elected from among the diocesan bishops, and the General Synod meets every three years. The 1998 General Synod decided to include among its membership representatives from aboriginal and Torres Strait Islander communities.

His thoughts on the Anglican Communion in the new millennium include, "Challenges for Anglicanism are specific, for present theological trends stretch us in many areas, for example, the Eames and *Virginia* Reports and the ARCIC documents. While they stretch us, they also give us a mechanism to respond to culturally and theologically diverse expressions of contemporary Anglicanism, which in their turn stretch us.

"The Communion we share celebrates the enormous growth we are witnessing in certain parts of the world Church, yet that very growth changes the way the Church responds to certain issues when we gather in our diversity. Certain questions that challenge us can easily be transformed, in our new situation, into questions that may become critical for our unity and self-understanding.

"My hope, encouraged by my experience of our strength of *koinonia* and the strength of our theological thinking, is that we may continue to celebrate both our unity and our diversity, and so contribute to many great Christian centuries to come."

Father Denny B. Guka
Representative from the Anglican Church of Papua New Guinea

Father Denny Guka was trained as a school teacher before he entered theological college to prepare for ordination to the priesthood. He now serves as a parish priest in the Diocese of Port Moresby. He also undertakes many other responsible tasks. He is archdeacon of Port Moresby, diocesan youth chaplain, and ecumenical officer for the province. He is a member of the executive committee of the Papua New Guinea (PNG) Council of Churches and is their representative on the PNG Government's Committee for Early Release of Prisoners. Father Denny is married to Marinda, and they have four children.

Father Guka tells us that the first missionaries landed in Papua New Guinea 108 years ago. Originally an extra-provincial diocese of the Anglican Church of Australia, the province of PNG came into being in 1997, with five dioceses and altogether about 120 parishes throughout the entire country, though new areas are now being opened up. The Church provides education and health services that are vital to the nation. It has two training centres for lay evangelists and one theological college for ordination training. Most clergy are PNG born. Significant ministry arms of the Church are three religious orders, the Mothers' Union, and youth and Sunday school ministries.

Speaking of the Anglican Communion in the new millennium, Father Denny says, "Most Anglican Christians have grown up to understand church ministry as just priest's ministry. But this is not so, now lay ministry is essential to the life and witness of the Church, but a major emphasis on lay training programmes is vital.

"Beyond 2000, the Church should look to make church ministry become people's ministry. The Mothers' Union and youth are well established in their networking, but they still need training and resources. The clergy must be trainers and teachers. Having been part of the youth ministry most of my life, I see youth as an important channel of the Church's ministry. As a Communion, we need, through the ACC, to establish networks and an exchange of reliable personnel and resources to assist bringing renewal and growth in the Church as a Communion."

Mr. Warren Luyaben
Lay representative from the Episcopal Church in the Philippines

Warren Luyaben is a second-generation Anglican; he belongs to the cultural minorities of the northern Philippines. He is a trial lawyer and also manages a small construction firm. He holds many responsible positions in his church. He is the chancellor to the prime bishop of the Episcopal Church in the

Philippines, and he is a parliamentarian in the Annual Diocesan Convention of Northern Luzon and of the provincial Synod that meets every three years.

Mr. Luyaben told us that the Episcopal Church in the Philippines originated as a missionary district of the Episcopal Church of the United States at the turn of the century. Though they are full of gratitude for their founding church, the five dioceses were pleased to achieve their autonomy on May 1, 1990. The church has a membership of about 120,000, mostly located in the highlands of northern Philippines. The Episcopal Church of the Philippines is in communion with the Eglesia Filipina Independiente (the Philippine Independent Church) and is a member church of the National Council of Churches in the Philippines, where it makes a lively contribution to the ecumenical dialogue of the churches of the Philippines. The prime bishop is located in Quezon City, Manila.

On the matter of the Anglican Communion in the new millennium he said, "Both the relevance and the growth of the Anglican Communion in the new millennium will depend in a great degree on how we translate our love of God and that of our neighbours into reality. To those in the so-called Developed World, the least of our brethren are all around you, but most of all the migrant workers. Make a commitment to mission a reality to them."

Mrs. Margaret Bihabanyi
Lay representative from the Church of the Province of Rwanda

Margaret Bihamanyi was born in Rwanda but has lived for half of her life as a refugee in Uganda. She was educated by her church and graduated as an economist. After the genocide in 1994 she returned to Rwanda and is currently director of handicrafts in the ministry of trade. Margaret is the mother of Sandra and Samson and is the fond grandmother of one-year-old Ryan.

She told us that the Church of the Province of Rwanda has nine dioceses and nine diocesan bishops. Anglican Christians are trying to rebuild the Church once more after the devastating genocide. They sing praises of the ACC for facilitating them to elect bishops through resolution 15 of ACC-10 in Panama. There is a spirit of rebirth as the programme of reconciliation develops within the government.

Speaking about her views of the Anglican Communion in the new millennium Margaret said, "I hope that the ACC will continue to be the voice of the voiceless without fear or favour. I hope the sharing and unfolding in the discussions between the different faiths will be put into action and translated into visible results that minister to the Christians in the name of the Lord Jesus Christ."

Miss Sylvia Scarf
Lay representative, Church in Wales

Sylvia Scarf is a single laywoman and retired senior probation officer. She worked across the spectrum of the probation service, including training and family court welfare (mediation), and served for the last two years in a forensic psychiatric unit. She is a member of the governing body of the Church in Wales (one of the panel of chairpersons) and is also deputy chair of the board of mission and chair of a panel of bishops' representatives on child protection. She is involved in the Girl Guide Movement with a drug prevention project and is a member of a number of charitable organisations.

Sylvia tells us that the Church in Wales is a small province of six dioceses that, in the eighty years since Welsh disestablishment, has gained in confidence and has made a significant contribution to the Anglican Communion. The Archbishop and Primate is elected from among the six diocesans, and the diocesan bishops are chosen by an electoral college of bishops, clergy, and laity. It is a bilingual Church, with the governing body meeting twice a year.

Speaking of the mission of the Anglican Communion in the new millennium Sylvia says, "My hopes are for a Communion that is open to the Holy Spirit and is where no one province or Church leadership is able to veto any discussion on important issues, but that we may move forward in a spirit of graciousness—able to listen to and value each other, even the smaller provinces.

"I would also hope for a real wave of justice for the underdeveloped countries and their peoples. I feel that Anglicans in the developed and affluent countries are not aware enough of the suffering of others.

"I also hope to see a greater movement of ecumenism—could it be to the extent that we no longer have an Anglican Communion?"

The Right Reverend Lazarus S. Munamua
Episcopal representative from the Church of the Province of Melanesia

Bishop Lazarus Munamua is one of six brothers from a family who lives on the Island of Tikopia in the Temotu province, eastern Solomons. He is the only son to have received an education in both church and a government secondary school. He studied for three years in Fiji and then entered the civil service in the Solomons. After independence he worked as a personnel officer in an agroindustrial company, but soon felt a call to ministry. In this he was doing as his father, a village catechist, advised "when he sent me to the mission school." He studied at St. John's College, Auckland, and, after ordination served in parish ministry, as secretary to the Archbishop of Melanesia. In 1987 he was consecrated bishop of Temotu, a diocese formed in 1981.

Bishop Lazarus informed us that the province of Melanesia, with originally only five dioceses, now has nine, for a commitment to mission and evangelism has seen an ongoing process of growth in the Anglican Church in the South Seas of the South Pacific. The vision for the Church is "striving to achieve unity among diverse cultural groups through the proclamation of the gospel of Jesus Christ and the development and enrichment of the community."

The bishop said, "My hopes for the Anglican Communion in 2000 and beyond are simply these—that our Communion stands firm in the life we offer the broken world and fearlessly witness in the bearings of the Anglican faith in and within which we discover God's love and mercy again and again."

The Reverend Robert Thompson
Clergy representative from the Church of the Province of the West Indies

The Reverend Robert Thompson is the Jamaican-born rector of a three thousand member parish in the Church of the Province of West Indies. A major focus of the ministry is work among youth, but the Church also serves three inner-city communities. These are major commitments for the congregation, which allocates about one-third of its annual budget to these projects. Robert is married to Charmaine, and they have two teenage sons.

He tells is that the Church of the Province of the West Indies became self-governing in 1883. It comprises eight dioceses: Barbados, Belize, Guyana, Jamaica, Nassau and the Bahamas, Trinidad and Tobago, Windward Islands, and northeastern Caribbean and Aruba. The Primate, Most Reverend Drexel Gomez, is bishop of Nassau and the Bahamas.

Speaking of the Anglican Communion in the new millennium, Father Thompson said, "I believe that the Anglican Communion, its liturgical tradition, its dialectic in thought and the ties of fellowship in spite of diversity, is well positioned to respond to the challenges of our world. My hope and prayer is that individually and collectively we will claim these gifts."

The Reverend Enos Das Pradhan
Clergy representative from the Church of North India

The Reverend Enos Das Pradhan was born and brought up in Darjeeling. Coming from a Presbyterian background he is an ordained minister of the Church of North India and commenced service as its full-time treasurer in May 1995.

The Church of North India's clergy representative explained that the Church of North India is regarded as one of the provinces of the Anglican Communion. It is a united church that came into being with the union of six large denominations in North India in November 1970. There are twenty-six dioceses in the province, with a total membership of 1.5 million.

His views on the Anglican Communion in the new millennium are many. He said, "Unity is not uniformity, yet unity is the key issue in the next millennium. The role and the status of the united Church in the Anglican Communion must be defined clearly.

"There are several networks established in the Anglican Communion. One, which is very important for the new millennium and which must be established in the Communion, is a network for ministry to children. The new millennium belongs to the children and it would be a wise investment of ministry and resources."

Ms. Maureen Sithole
Lay representative from the Church of the Province of Southern Africa

Maureen is the mother of two children and also the guardian of her brother's children. But this energetic Anglican from Southern Africa still has time to work for her government as a health worker. She is very involved in the activities of her church both locally and at the provincial level. She represents her diocese of Highveld at Synod, and she is also a member of the Mission and Transformation Commission of the Church of the Province of Southern Africa (CPSA).

She told us that the Church of the Province of Southern Africa is now emerging into the post-Apartheid era. The Church played a substantial and important role in bringing about positive change. They continue to be a church that speaks out against injustice, a theme that was the thread throughout ACC-11. The CPSA comprises people of many different cultures, languages, and backgrounds who hold on to one another as they face the many issues challenging them in their society. They continue to be a province where much laughter and dancing is found, knowing that God reigns.

Speaking of the Anglican Communion in the new millennium, Maureen said, "I hope and pray for more openness in all the issues before the Church, and I look for more involvement of women in decision-making. There is real growth in church membership where this is the case. I look to the building up of a strong Communion that addresses issues that affect the poor with more action rather than talk."

Mr. Nicholas Yohesan Casie Chetty
Lay representative from Sri Lanka

Mr. Nicholas Chetty was educated at St. Thomas' College, Mt. Lavinia, which is one of the oldest and best known public schools in Sri Lanka. He gained an LLB from the University of Colombo and then worked with the government Attorney General's Department for five years. He then read for his postgraduate degree at the University of Kent at Canterbury and gained an LLM in law and development. Returning to Sri Lanka, he practised law for some years and then was appointed headmaster of St. Thomas' Preparatory School. He is actively involved in the life of the Church, being a member of the Standing Committee of the Diocese of Colombo since 1989, and a member of the constituent assembly. He was chairman of the House of Laity from 1991 to 1992 when Bishop Kenneth Fernando was elected the thirteenth bishop of the Diocese of Colombo. He is active on other church committees and also on government bodies. He is presently a member of the Fair Trading Commission of Sri Lanka.

He told us that the Church of Sri Lanka became an extra-provincial entity comprising the two dioceses of Colombo and Kurunagala in 1970, when the General Assembly met for the last time and the province of India, Burma, Pakistan, and Ceylon was disbanded.

He has many hopes for the Anglican Communion in the new millennium. Nicholas said, "The Sudanese proverb rings clearly in my ears: 'Empty stomachs have no ears.' In the vast majority of the provinces represented in our Anglican Communion, social justice, poverty, marginalisation, oppression, hunger, war, and disenfranchisement loom ominously large on our agenda. The Anglican Communion will either stand or fall on how sensitively and meaningfully, and how realistically, we face up to these manifold issues.

"Failure to do so, or even to attempt to confront these challenges half-heartedly, will surely be to our peril. We will continue to be recognised and identified as a relict of a bygone colonial era and as a quintessential construct of Western imperialism meant to salve the consciences of the fortunate few in the First World.

"That is precisely the challenge we face in the new millennium—our best efforts to spread the word of our Lord and Saviour will surely fall on deaf ears if we do not confront these challenges with due seriousness."

Antonio Ortega Reybal
Lay representative from the Anglican Church of Mexico

Antonio Reybal is a mechanical and electrical engineer, and he also has an MBA. He has his own business that supplies electrical parts for industry. He is married to Dora, and they have two sons. He is a member of the Standing Committee of his diocese and is president of the local Chamber of Commerce.

He told us that the Anglican Church of Mexico has five dioceses: Cuernavaca, Mexico, northern Mexico, southeastern Mexico, and western Mexico. The Primate is Archbishop Samuel Espinoza-Venegas, who is also bishop of western Mexico. The province works together especially in maintaining its own identity alongside the dominant Roman Catholic Church.

Antonio said, "I hope that in the new millennium we will have a strong Anglican Communion. To achieve this aim we must work hard to take the ideas we share together at ACC-11 home with us to our provinces so that they may become part of our local mission and ministry."

A business session at ACC-11

The Scottish Episcopal Church delegation

The Primus of Scotland

46   The Communion We Share

Sightseeing in Dundee

Photographs   47

The traditional group photo

48   *The Communion We Share*

The Global Children's colourings of St. Nicholas display

Scottish flare—piper leads the procession at the civic centre

The Archbishop of Canterbury and Mrs. Carey with the Sudan delegation

SERMONS AND ADDRESSES

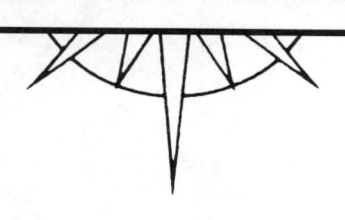

Opening Service Sermon: The Burning Mystery

—THE MOST REVEREND RICHARD HOLLOWAY, BISHOP OF EDINBURGH, PRIMUS

St. Andrew's Cathedral, Aberdeen
September 14, 1999

At a midnight service on Christmas Eve, I began my sermon in a cathedral in Edinburgh by pointing out that an ancient manuscript had recently been discovered, dated by scholars to about 70 A.D. I explained that, while they disagreed about its authenticity, all agreed that it was a remarkable and interesting document. It appeared to be an autobiographical meditation, written as an old man, by Jonathan the son of Simon, innkeeper at Bethlehem at the beginning of the first century. An American scholar, Professor Capote, I went on, had made a translation of the document, and instead of a sermon, I was planning to read his version of the document. It started like this: "I, Jonathan son of Simon, of Bethlehem in Judea, wish to set down my memory of events that are now being spoken of and written about, most recently in a strange text called *The Good News* according to Luke, a physician, which has recently come to my attention."

The sermon I preached that night was published in a newspaper a few days later, and I was soon getting letters from people, asking how they could acquire copies of this ancient document. There was, of course, no ancient document. I was following an ancient tradition, by making up a story in order to convey a message. I had even planted a clue about what I was doing in the text of my sermon. I gave the name Capote to the scholar who had translated the document because Truman Capote, author of *Breakfast at Tiffany's*, had pioneered modern versions of this ancient technique in his book *In Cold Blood*, which is about a multiple murder in a Kansas farmhouse. That book was neither fiction nor pure documentary, so the commentators dubbed it *faction*. He used the form of fictional narrative, including imaginative reconstructions of lengthy, unrecorded conversations, to get inside the complexity of a hideous event. In a modest way, my Christmas sermon in 1993 was a similar exercise.

The Hebrew word for this technique is *midrash*, from a verb meaning to search out, to seek, to enquire. All religious traditions develop a literature of imaginative responses to their sacred canon. C. S. Lewis's *Screwtape Letters* is a good example. This book, one of the most famous Lewis wrote, purports to be letters from a junior demon to his supervisor about his work of tempting a hapless human. A person, unaware of such literary conventions, might believe that the letters were authentic; and maybe C. S. Lewis got letters from some of his readers, asking for copies of the originals. There is a lot of *midrash,* or imaginative construction of this sort, in the New Testament. If we want to understand the Bible properly, we have to read it within its own literary conventions. For example, most scholars believe today that the whole of John's Gospel is *midrash,* an imaginative theological construction that is the fruit of years of meditating on the meaning of Jesus.

One way of interpreting the story of the birth of the Church in the second chapter of the Acts of the Apostles is to see it as belonging to this same kind of literature. It is an extended exercise in theological code, and you get the message only if you know the background, just as my Christmas sermon made sense only to people who already knew the Gospel of Luke. One of the favourite *midrash* techniques used by the New Testament writers is to take great events from the Old Testament and to repeat or echo them in a different context, in order to show that Jesus had assumed the role that was previously filled by one of the great heroes of the Hebrew scriptures, such as Moses. The reading from the second chapter of the Acts of the Apostles echoes and develops several themes from the Old Testament. The great, foundational event in the life of Israel was the exodus from bondage in Egypt. The early Christians described the resurrection of Jesus as his exodus from the bondage of death. Fifty days after the exodus from Egypt, the children of Israel arrived at Mount Sinai, where, in the midst of thunder and lightning, God made a contract with Israel, establishing them as his own people. According to one Jewish writer, quoted by Father Raymond Brown in his exposition of this passage, angels took the news of the bargain struck between Moses and God on Mount Sinai and carried it on tongues to the people of Israel camped out on the plain below. So, fifty days after Easter, our exodus, something like the same process, is repeated at the feast of Pentecost, our Mount Sinai, when the followers of Jesus are established as the nucleus of a new people of God, commissioned to take the good news of Jesus to the whole world.

So the important thing to understand about this complex story is that it is making a simple claim: since that first Pentecost, it has been through the Church that the meaning and message of Jesus has been shared with the world. Unfortunately, that claim is easier said than demonstrated, because there is something about Jesus and organised institutions that do not mix well. Let me explain.

Whenever any new vision or idea is born, it requires a process to carry it through history. The process is invented to mediate the vision, to carry it through time. The great sociologist Max Weber called this process, "the routinisation of charisma." The great, gifted, given thing, the charism, has to be embodied in a routine—whether it is a political party or a church. Two related and unavoidable things happen in this process. By definition, charisms cannot be perfectly routinised or institutionalised, so the very process that gives them continuing life also begins to kill them. That is bad enough; what amplifies this process of corruption is that the people who are brought in to supervise the routine are usually more interested in the process than in the purpose or vision it is meant to serve. The process itself becomes fascinating, takes over, and you get church for church's sake; so the protection and maintenance of the institution becomes the institution's primary purpose.

This happens to all institutions, but it is deeper and more tragic in the case of the Church than of other institutional compromises. The Church has the impossible task of being an organisation, with an unavoidable power structure, that exists to preserve the memory of one whose mission was to oppose the processes and sacrifices of power, because they are almost always exercised at the cost of the individual—and it was individuals he was interested in, especially those who had been beaten up by the world's power systems. He expressed God's absolute love for those outside the great institutional enclosures, with their ethic of survival and power. It was the victims of institutional power he went after. He lived among them and died as one of them, because, as Caiaphas pointed out with impeccable institutional logic, it was expedient that one man die rather than the whole people perish. That is always the way systems work. Jesus did the precise opposite. He always went after the lost, the ones outside all the systems, the broken ones. Yet, and this is one of the most heartbreakingly beautiful things about him—he understood the corrupting compromises institutions and their leaders have to make; he had compassion on their need to follow the ethic of expediency and even forgave them the necessity of his own crucifixion. "Father, forgive them, for they know not what they do." It is this uncompromising unconditionality of Jesus that is so breathtaking.

The pain of being a Church comes from recognising that we are supposed to express that same unconditionality and acceptance of all, while knowing that the system we have invented to do the job is not up to it, because it is run by us and not by Jesus. So, in trying to embody the absoluteness of God's love, we cannot help but contradict it. No wonder Paul said that the Church was an impostor through whom the truth was spoken. But the really extraordinary thing about this institution we call Church, whose ambiguous reality we express here today, is that without it we would know nothing about the Jesus whose message it so consistently compromises. I would not be beating my breast about the failings of the Church today and my part in those failures if the Church had not introduced me to that mysterious, unavoidable man from Nazareth. So the truth of God's unconditional love does get through the Church, in spite of its own compromising timidity. That is why, week after week in the Church's liturgy, I am still able to stand and say, "I believe in one holy, Catholic, and apostolic Church." In spite of all our compromises and confusions, in spite of the uncertainty of our love and the way we disfigure his image, the memory of the man of Nazareth is kept alive in history.

Mysteriously, but certainly, he will be encountered in our meetings of the Anglican Consultative Council this week, as we struggle to be faithful to the mind of Christ, knowing full well that we all encounter it in different ways. He will be mysteriously present as we struggle in our weakness and fallibility to respond to the challenge of his burning love. No one can say why or how it happens, only that it does. He will meet us, as he met by the lakeside those of old. No one has expressed the mystery of this encounter better than Albert Schweitzer in his classic study, *The Quest of the Historical Jesus*, which ends with these mysterious but captivating words:

> He comes to us as One unknown, without a name, as of old, by the lakeside, He came to those men who knew him not. He speaks to us the same word: "Follow thou me!" and sets us to the tasks which He has to fulfil for our time. He commands. And to those who obey him, whether they be wise or simple, He will reveal Himself in the toils, the conflicts, the sufferings which they shall pass through in His fellowship, and, as an ineffable mystery, they shall learn in their own experience Who He Is.

Archbishop of Canterbury's Presidential Address

September 15, 1999

As President, I welcome you all to this eleventh meeting of the Anglican Consultative Council. On your behalf, I would like to thank the Primus of the Scottish Episcopal Church, Bishop Richard Holloway; Bishop Neville Chamberlain; all those in the local Church and the national Church who have been involved in the preparations; and the staff of the University of Dundee for the warmth of their welcome.

Our last meeting took place in Panama in 1996—a memorable conference, in which we dealt with a number of important issues on behalf of our Communion, many of which are featured on the agenda this time, as are some of the vital matters on which we focused our attention at the Lambeth Conference last year. So I hope you will all feel a sense of continuity about our discussions.

It is very good to be here in Scotland as guests of the Scottish Episcopal Church. If there are occasions when some Scots feel overshadowed by their southern neighbours, few will deny that this year Edinburgh has had a pretty good share of the headlines, both in the political and the ecclesiastical spheres! I am sure I can speak for us all in offering our best wishes to the new Scottish Parliament in these early days of its life, as it seeks to promote a renewed sense of identity for the Scottish people and to make a very significant contribution to the political life of these islands. It was good last night to be reminded in Aberdeen of the important part which the Scottish Episcopal Church played in the formation of the Anglican Communion. It was a church ready to take risks in the eighteenth century, and clearly the tradition continues! The lively debate on morality to which your Primus has contributed in a substantial way, though not uncontroversially, is a very important one, and a little later in this address I will offer one or two reflections of my own, as well as offer some thoughts concerning how we should handle matters where there is substantial disagreement among us.

Just recently, I saw again a film I first saw a number of years ago. It moved me then, and it moved me again this time. It is called *Mr. Holland's Opus*. It tells the story of a young composer whose dream is to produce one great piece of music. In order to survive financially, he takes a temporary job teaching music in a school whose pupils have little interest in the subject. After a difficult start, he warms to his task, and over the years he manages to enthuse successive generations of pupils with a love for music; but his great opus remains a distant dream. He tinkers with it, jotting down a few notes and phrases from time to time. Suddenly, retirement is in view, and all his frustration and bitterness boils over. At a retirement party given by his past pupils, it transpires that they have gotten a hold of the manuscript, and Mr. Holland is persuaded to conduct the orchestra in a performance of the work; but the punch line is spoken by one of the pupils. "Mr. Holland," she says, "we are your great opus; we are your work of art."

In the letter to the Ephesians, there is a similar reflection, which has always caught my imagination. In chapter 2, verse 10, the writer says: "For we are his workmanship, created in Christ Jesus for good works, which God prepared beforehand, that we should walk in them." Or, as the New English Bible has it, "we are his handiwork." The Greek word is *poema*, from which our word *poem* comes. It means that the body of Christ is God's "work of art," created to set forth God's love and God's good news.

Isn't that a beautiful image? We, God's people, created and called by him, are crafted by him to be what he wants us to be, to do what he wants us to do. We are not required to be good and to do good in order to gain God's favour, or to placate him. Quite the opposite. It is God's intention in moulding us in the first place that we should walk in his way. God's grace takes us as we are and forms us in the image of the Creator. We are the "clay in the potter's hand" (Jeremiah 18:6), the handiwork of God. In other words, the impulse for mission, the living and preaching of the word of God, is not something that we decide to do. It is what we do, it is what we are created to do; and if we do not do it—either as individuals or as the Christian community—we are being rebellious, we are breaking the mould in which we have been made.

Of course, that is easy to say. We know, and scripture constantly reminds us, that we *are* a rebellious people. God has given us the freedom to choose our path, and how readily we accept that freedom. The world in which we live offers us a myriad of temptations—to selfishness, to greed, to immorality of so many kinds. But God has also given us everything we need to "choose life" in Christ Jesus, the word made flesh, the way, the truth, and the life. And even when we turn away from God and choose ways other than the one he has given us, we are freely offered a way back. God always restores those who are penitent and turn to him. So the extraordinary truth of our faith is that God gives us everything we need to be faithful disciples.

We know only too well, however, that it is not as simple as that. The struggle to discern what is right and what is wrong, what is of God and what is not, is the story of the human race from the beginning of history, as the stories in Genesis so dramatically remind us. But the fact that we are constantly facing an apparently insurmountable challenge does not excuse us from it. The search for a "godly morality" is of the essence of what it is to be part of God's handiwork, not because it is imposed on us by some dictatorial and judgmental divinity, but because we have been given the gift of creation in the image of God and the grace to explore the call to full humanity.

Last time many of us met was in Canterbury for the Lambeth Conference. The more I reflect on the conference, the more I am sure that it achieved a very great deal. On many things there was considerable agreement. Central to all, of course, was prayer, worship, and Bible study. We paid attention to one another; we were drawn into new experience and new understanding of the struggles of our brothers and sisters in different parts of the world, and so much of what was framed in the resolutions demonstrated clearly that longing to be faithful instruments of God's love in the world. I felt that from that meeting of bishops there was a longing for the Church to be more effective as "God's workmanship."

For example, there was energy and determination in the resolution on international debt, not just to preach to others about their responsibilities but also to challenge ourselves. I know of one church at least—the Church of Ireland—that has taken that seriously and resolved to increase its giving; and the campaign has continued and developed throughout the world. The Archbishop of Cape Town has continued to give a lead—and so has the Presiding Bishop of the United States—and I know that many provinces have taken action with their governments. The huge demonstrations in London—which I was able to share in—and in Cologne around the time of the group of seven (G7) summit in June have again made a profound impression on political leaders.

And then our concern, so powerfully expressed during the conference, about our relations with Islam has been further explored in a very important consultation hosted by the Church of Nigeria, under the auspices of the Evangelical Fellowship of the Anglican Communion. I believe this was a very positive experience for all involved, and it underlines the importance of working together and supporting one another as we explore our developing relations with other faiths, which can vary so much around the world. It is vital work, not just for our own comfort as a Communion, but also for the well-being of the world, for which all faith communities bear such a responsibility. So I want to underline my support for work in this area. I will be making a return visit to the University of Al Azhar in Cairo later this year, at the invitation of His Grace, the Sheikh, to further our common search for the right way to relate to one another as faithful Christians and Muslims.

Another important ministry flagged up by the Lambeth Conference was that of how we relate to young people and minister to them. In all provinces this is a huge challenge. But Lambeth gave fresh inspiration to us and has led to several initiatives. For example, I was delighted that, at my invitation, four thousand young English Christians came to London, with their bishops—fifty-seven of them!—for a weekend of celebration and encounter, the main priority being to signal to the rest of the Church the importance of young people and the enormous contribution they can make to God's kingdom. We all learned a lot! And we enjoyed ourselves as well, though whether St. Paul's Cathedral has recovered from the experience, you must ask the dean! I know that other gatherings are being planned—for instance, in the United States in 2000 and in Latin America in 2001.

And then mission and evangelism. Section 2 of Lambeth 1998 offered very significant challenges to us all and warned against putting mission and evangelism on the back burner. In a real way the "decade of evangelism" never ends. We are constantly called to be a missionary church proclaiming Christ until he comes again. Thus it behoves ACC to ask: How may we take forward the mission of the Church? How may we deepen learning and teaching in this area? So I am glad that in the course of ACC-11 we shall have the opportunity to hear more—from the Anglican Communion Mission Commission (MISSIO) about their work and the whole question of how we develop our mission and evangelism in the future (and in this context, I am especially looking forward to our visit to Glasgow and to hearing from the Scottish Episcopal Church about their Mission 21 project). We shall hear about urbanisation and the challenge to learn from one another as we seek to meet the challenges of the dramatic process of urbanisation in every part of the world; about the continuing developments in technology and their implications for matters of life and death, into which the Christian tradition must make a contribution. All these are examples of how the Lambeth Conference can initiate, share, and encourage the common task of fulfilling our role as the "handiwork of God," and there are many more.

You don't need me, however, to tell you that there is so much more to do. The world has recently faced so many crises and disasters. Natural disasters, as in Central America and Turkey, and the renewed threat of famine in Ethiopia and Somalia stretch global compassion to its limits. It is a stark and urgent task for our Communion, together with all people of goodwill, to keep that compassion alive and to feed it. The violent eruption in the long-running political sore of East Timor is a potent reminder to us today of the knife-edge on which humanity treads, between just and peaceful development and chaos. The people of Kosovo, the people of Sierra Leone, the people of Kashmir and of Ireland need no reminder of the precipice on which they stand or have stood. And still the wars in Sudan, the Great Lakes region, and so many other places continue. If these are some of the crises, which have horrified us all, each one of us will know many other stories of struggle within our own countries and communities. All of them call for Christians to enter the struggle and to wrestle, in all humility, with the challenges they present, not in order to cast the stones of judgement, but so that the vision of God and his kingdom, which he has created us to pursue, may be realised.

But we do not always agree. In some of these problems which tax us, right and wrong appear easy to identify. In others, as a body, we are unable to discern an agreed course of action. There are many reasons for that—sometimes cultural, sometimes theological, and sometimes contextual. Whatever the reason, the fact of division and disagreement is very uncomfortable to live with.

Some months ago, I had the opportunity to give a lecture to a gathering in Charleston, South Carolina. In that address, which sought to address this matter of how we cope with disagreement, I referred to that classic book of Michael Ramsey's, *The Gospel and the Catholic Church*. He was addressing the wider problem of Christian unity, and he said this: "The movement towards the problem of the reunion of Christendom is also compelled to see its problems in close connection with the Passion." He goes on to say that the unity question will not be solved through easy humanistic ideas of fellowship and brotherhood but by the hard road of the cross. He concludes his passage with these words:

> The Cross is the place where the theology of the Church has its meaning, where the unity of the Church is a deep and present reality, and where the Church is already showing the peace of God and the bread from heaven to mankind.

He might have gone on to say that where Christians are able to meet with the cross at the centre of conflict they will find sufficient resources to meet in understanding—even if, for some time, they will not find agreement.

You see, the process of opening ourselves to the creative will of God, of being the clay in the potter's hand, must inevitably lead us into difficult areas, which may indeed bring us into conflict with others; and the more strongly we hold our faith, and the clearer our minds are about lines between belief and unbelief and between heresy and orthodoxy, the sharper will be the challenge. Now, some have said that the diversity and comprehensiveness that have been our bywords can be held up as the defining characteristic of Anglicanism. I do not accept that. Of course we rejoice in our diversity, our openness, our blurred edges. That denotes a generosity of spirit, which can sometimes be lacking in other parts of the Christian family. It is also a recognition that we cannot claim the whole truth for any one part of the church. We need each part to enrich the whole. We are all searching for that wholeness and fulfilment. We readily recognise the common but diverse search for truth, and we welcome honest seekers.

However, we do not live by the principle "Anything goes." I, and I guess most of us, do not accept that there are no cardinal doctrines, beliefs, or limits to orthodoxy. *The Virginia Report,* which will be the focus of much debate later on, emphatically contradicts this mischievous notion and makes it clear that the limits of diversity are precisely conformity to the "constant interplay of Scripture, tradition and reason." So we must be very wary of any understanding of comprehensiveness that masks doctrinal indifference. Instead, we need to view it as the breadth of a Communion exploring the fullness of a faith rooted in Scripture, anchored in the creeds, expressed in faithfulness to the dominical sacraments, and embodied in a faithful episcopally led Church.

This means that we are a Communion constantly being moulded into God's handiwork, immersed in Scripture and the Church's teachings and exemplified in the life of the Master we seek to follow.

And such a Communion will always be asked to be charitable and generous in our treatment of one another, as well as to be under God's word and teaching.

Two things have crossed my desk recently that relate very closely to the tension that we are experiencing at the moment. I made a light-hearted reference to Bishop Richard Holloway's recent exposure to the media in my introduction. His book, *Godless Morality*, is generous in intention. He is concerned to understand our world and make the gospel relevant. I find myself in agreement with some parts of it, but have to say that I disagree with his central thesis that God must be left out of the moral debate. In his introduction, he comments that "By claiming divine authority for the commandments and prohibitions, with eternal punishment for those who disobey them, religious moral systems operate on the basis of fear." It is certainly true that in history some parts of the Church have behaved in this way, and some sects, even today, continue to operate on the basis of fear. But surely, to conclude that we must turn our back on scriptural insights and teachings, the body of doctrine in the Church formed over the years, and theological learning is an unacceptable option for us. If there is a godless morality, it cannot be a fully formed Christian morality. But all of us will have ample opportunity to talk this over with Bishop Richard informally during our conference.

The other thing that has crossed my desk is the decision of Archbishop Moses Tay, a member of the Primates' Standing Committee, to absent himself from ACC-11. In his letter to me, he expressed profound disappointment with the way some parts of the Communion appear to be ignoring or rejecting key resolutions of the Lambeth Conference. The heart of his concern, which I know is shared by others, is that the Communion is deviating from its traditional roots of faith.

Now I sincerely hope that no one is in any doubt as to where I stand in these matters. For the nine years that I have been Archbishop of Canterbury, I have made the encouragement of the Church, confident in expressing its faith, outward looking and missionary in its vision, a central theme of my ministry. But I am under no illusion that the process of arriving at such a position of confidence in the fundamentals and openness to the world in all its pain and all its glory has been or ever will be easy. Nor were we ever promised an easy ride. Even less were we assured that we would always get it right, or that the church would be protected from error, and we hardly need to explore our history very far to see the truth of that. I said earlier that we need to approach one another and the world in humility. There is no place for triumphalism of any sort. The great philosopher Søren Kierkegaard once wrote:

> A Church triumphant is nothing but a sham. In this world we can truthfully speak only of a militant church. The Church Militant is related to and feels itself drawn to Christ in humble obedience. The Church triumphant, however, has taken the Church of Christ in vain. . . . The triumphant Church assumes that the time of struggle is over; that the

> Church, because it has expanded itself, has nothing more about or for which to struggle . . . . This is not the way of Christ. . . . Christ's Church can only endure by struggling—that is by every moment battling the world and battling for the truth.

Now, we might want to take issue with that style of language, but in essence what he says rings true. Once any church or any part of a church steps away from the struggle, divorces itself from our continuing search, it loses part of what it is to be Christian. If we start to build fences around our particular perception of the truth and to cut ourselves off from others who are different, we are in danger of saying to God, "We are your perfect creation. There is no more need of your craftsmanship." But none of us would say that; and it is, at least partly, in that encounter with one another, with the crucified Christ at our heart, that God continues his process of moulding us into what he wants us to be.

Does this then mean that truth no longer matters? By no means. Some have said to me, following my address in the United States, that truth must take precedence over unity, and therefore the status quo of the Communion or of a province must be challenged. To that I say, Challenge by all means. Vigorous debate and healthy intellectual engagement on the basis of the faith we share are important ingredients of informed Christians struggling to share their faith with the world around. I have made it clear that we must engage in the reality of the life of the church and of the world.

But unilateral action is different. Let me remind you of what I said in that SEAD address. No one has the right to make decisions that affect the whole. The moment the "local" wrests decisions from the whole, it is engaging in division. No diocese should take unilateral action, impairing the life of the whole province. Every House of Bishops must seek unity of vision for the sake of the province it leads—and deviation from agreed constitutions will only weaken the Church bishops claim to serve. No province should take unilateral action, affecting and impairing the whole Communion—that only denies the nature of communion and declares that we are in reality no more than a federation of independent churches. That clearly is not our ecclesiology, and we have to say so again and again and again.

And let me take that one step further: to engage in division is itself to undermine truth. The call to unity is at least as strong in Scripture as is the call to purity and holiness. "I believe in one holy Catholic and apostolic church." It is there as a fundamental tenet of our faith. So I hope that those who are tempted to go their own way, wherever they are and for whatever reason they feel frustrated with the Communion, will hold back and have faith in the loving purposes of God. The unity of the Church is, after all, God's gift to us. It is not of our making. It is we in our disobedience that have fragmented and fragmented again and again.

My brothers and sisters, we require a much bigger doctrine of the Church than we currently possess. The unity of the body is so precious that those who risk undermining it are hurting the One whose body it is. I have often been struck by St. Paul's doctrine of the church in Ephesians. He says later in the epistle, "Christ loved the Church and gave himself up for her." How can we despise what he loves? How can we turn our back on a "handiwork" that he has created—the opus that he is composing? We are God's handiwork, and he has crafted us for a purpose. He has assured us over and over again that in his Son Jesus Christ he will be with us always, even to the end of time, so the process of moulding continues in order that his mission will grow and develop. We are like clay in the potter's hand, and if we are to do the work of the gospel and further the vision of the kingdom of God, we have to engage with all the challenges that present themselves to us, whether internally or externally. Each one of us here has been called and has responded freely to that call. We are not slaves of some perverse dictator in the sky who likes nothing better than punishing us when we do wrong. Our faith in God is a liberating faith. "God is rich in mercy, and because of his great love for us, he brought us to life in Christ when we were dead because of our sins" (Ephesians 2:4-5). The message we are called to proclaim is life giving; it is a message of freedom from that which enslaves us. We need to recognise and own our history, which, again, should prompt us to the greatest humility as we approach our missionary task. But to recognise and repent of our failings and to seek with God's help to be more effective and true in our task is our constant quest. I cannot see how Christians can with integrity take God out of the equation. Our faith is in God the Creator who seeks the fulfilment of everything that is. As we seek to collaborate in the building of that kingdom, we have been given a glorious and life-giving message. The challenge is not to leave God out of the search for good and truth, but to redouble our prayer, our waiting on God, and our readiness to be crafted for the task to which God calls us. Why? Because our God is about, to paraphrase that most beautiful of passages in Philippians, "whatever is true, whatever is honourable, whatever is just, whatever is pure, whatever is lovely, whatever is gracious" (4:8). And that is a vision for the world, which is worth battling and struggling for.

I am reminded of a beautiful story, which I came across some months ago. A woman in a dream imagined a shop where God the Holy Spirit gave the fruits of the Spirit free of charge. In her dream she went along and said to the shopkeeper, "I want peace, and love, and joy—and while you are at it, perhaps some holiness as well."

God the Holy Spirit beamed at her and said, "I think you have been misinformed, we don't offer fruits here—just seeds."

So, as we get this eleventh ACC meeting under way, perhaps we may be sowing a few seeds of the Spirit, which in many different ways will grow into fruits of the Spirit in our Communion. There is no need for fear, because God has not given us the Spirit of fear but of power and a sound mind. Let us use that collective mind together for the sake of God's body, his handiwork, his opus, and for his glory.

Chairman's Address

—The Right Reverend Dr. Simon Eliya Chiwanga

In keeping with the best tradition of the chair's statement at the beginning of the ACC meeting, my address is going to be short, at least compared to the length of a normal sermon in Tanzania. I had intended to include a section on the role of the ACC and its relationship to the other instruments of communion. Bishop Mark Dyer's excellent introduction of the Four Instruments of Communion has helped me, so I will not have to include that section in my address.

To begin with, I would like to join our president in thanking the Scottish Episcopal Church and Primus Richard Holloway for welcoming us to this warm and gracious country. I thank the design group, under the leadership of our vice-chairman, the Most Reverend John Paterson, for the organizing they have done. I also want to thank the staff of the Anglican Communion, under the devoted and able leadership of the Secretary General, Canon John Peterson, for their tireless work over the last three years and for giving themselves so generously to the mission of God. There is no group of people on earth that I know of who accomplish so much with so meager resources and remuneration. One sister of mine among the staff sometimes responds to my "Hello, how are you my dear sister?" by saying humorously, "Overworked and underpaid!" I know very well that she does not mean it, but still the truth is that they deserve more than what we are able to give them, and yet they never complain. From the bottom of my heart and on behalf of the ACC, I thank each one of them.

When I was elected chairman of ACC in 1996, our president, Archbishop George Carey, told me of his intentions to involve me as much as possible in the activities of the Communion. I have indeed witnessed that and have constantly enjoyed his support and encouragement. I shall always cherish that unique and rare honor he gave, not only to me but also to the ACC as a whole, by inviting me to preach at the opening Eucharist of the 1998 Lambeth Conference.

And finally, I want to thank members of the Standing Committee for their dedication and exemplary leadership. I would like them to please stand up so that you may recognize them and their devoted service. I am proud to be their servant. You will see the wonderful work they have done in the three years since the last council when the vice-chairman presents the report of the Standing Committee after my address.

To the delegates of the ACC, ecumenical participants, spouses, and all our invited guest speakers, I want to extend a warm welcome, karibu sana! I am most delighted that you were able to come, and this shows how much you value the role of the ACC. I am most encouraged to note that provinces have been careful to select committed and capable delegates who can effectively express the mind of their churches to the council and the mind of the council to their churches. I appeal to you, therefore, to speak freely and openly at this meeting. Since we are all baptized into the one body of Christ, we all have the authority to speak the truth in love, and to love and speak the truth. Our registrar, the Reverend John Rees, has worked hard, together with our Constitutional Review Committee, to simplify the rules of procedure with respect to debate at our council meetings. Please read and familiarize yourself with these rules. They are intended to facilitate more open and free exchange. Let us not miss the opportunity to do so. When we go home from Dundee, we all have the responsibility to report back to our churches. This is a very crucial responsibility, for consultation is more than what we do here these ten days.

The theme of this meeting is "The Communion We Share." What is that communion? What is it that we share?

First, What is that communion? The Anglican Communion today is at a very important time of change and transition. Old ways of knowing and old ways of relating have begun to evolve into a yet unknown world filled with hope and possibilities in the Risen Christ.

A half century ago the majority of Christians lived in the industrialized West. When most of us in this room were born, the Anglican Communion was identified with Anglo-American culture and socio-political realities. Those Christians in the Southern Hemisphere who called themselves Anglicans usually lived under colonial rule and worshiped in churches that were still missionary districts of the mother churches. But all this began to change radically in the 1960s with the emergence of independent nation-states in previous colonies and the advent of self-supporting, self-governing, and self-extending Anglican churches in the former missions.

The turning point of the Communion from that of givers and receivers to a family of equals was the 1963 Anglican Congress in Toronto and its far-reaching imperative known as "Mutual Responsibility and Interdependence in the Body of Christ," or MRI for short. MRI proposed a radical reorientation of mission priorities stressing equality among all Anglican churches. MRI and the 1963 congress were hailed as breakthroughs that would transcend the paternalism and dominance of Western patterns of mission. For the first time, the younger churches in the Anglican Communion saw themselves as equal to the older, "richer" churches of the West. MRI challenged the historic sending churches of the Anglican Communion to change their attitudes and theologies of mission to be in line with the emerging realities of a new Anglican Communion.

It has taken three and a half decades, but today, as we stand on the eve of a new millennium, we can say without question that the vision heralded by MRI is beginning to become a reality. There is no turning back.

The real question for Anglicans today is "How does this mutual responsibility and interdependence play itself out in a community of thirty-eight equal and autonomous churches? With the loss of old ways of relationship, how do we come together as the body of Christ, the Church catholic? What are the limits of our identity, now that we do not share a common language or culture? Where does authority lie in a global community of many different churches?" These are some of the questions we will address at this meeting of the Anglican Consultative Council.

In these times of profound change, many who are fearful of the future may seek security and solace in what they perceive as safe and sound. For some, such safety is thought to be found easily in a clearer articulation of and uncritical appeal to doctrinal positions and/or theological truths. Suddenly the Chicago Lambeth Quadrilateral, the 39 Articles, or even *The Virginia Report* becomes the defining document of what it means to be an Anglican today. Others may be tempted to seek security in ecclesial structures or offices that have developed over time. The Lambeth Conference, the Primates' Meeting, The Archbishop of Canterbury, and yes, even the ACC can suddenly be seen as holding ultimate authority on one issue or another. Whether confession or curia, catechism or conference, constitution or council, the fearful are looking for easy answers.

Listening to conversations at the meetings of some of our Instruments of Communion, my mind is led to paraphrase Luke 22:24–27 in the following way. "A dispute arose among the Instruments of Communion as to which one was regarded the greatest. But he said to them, 'The kings of the Gentiles lord it over them; and those in authority over them are called benefactors. But not so with you; rather the greatest among you must become like the youngest, and the leader like one who serves. For who is greater, the one who is at the table or the one who serves? Is it not the one at the table? But I am among you as one who serves.'" "But I am among you as one who serves" are words I have ever kept before me in my ministry, particularly since I was consecrated bishop. Bishop Mark Dyer was again most helpful here when he emphasized the interdependence and mutual responsibility of the Four Instruments of Communion. The scramble for greatness is a sign of fear and leads to the weakening of the mission of the church.

In the meantime, the world is dying to hear, to know, and to experience the good news that we have found in Jesus Christ. The divisions that we wrestle with in the Church are minuscule in relation to the evils and pains of the world. Capitalism and international debt, militarism, religious persecution, civil wars, the drug trade, the environmental crisis and devastation of this fragile earth, nuclear arms proliferation, the continuing marginalization of women and youth in some of our cultures—all seek to undermine the commonality of creation we have with and in God.

The mission of God, *the missio Dei,* however, stands in stark contrast to these demons of division. We are all called to participate in the restoration of all people and all creation to unity with God and each other in Christ. This is the truth at the center of our baptismal call. This is the truth that we find in Jesus. In the mission of God is the answer to the question, What is it we share? We share the truth of our common call to a redeemed and restored life in Jesus.

But the truth that we find in Jesus, the truth that we know when we meet our Lord and one another in the poor and the suffering and around the table, is not an easy answer. No, God in Jesus came into the world so that all might come to him and be saved. *It is in following Christ, in all our differences and particularities, and very often in the very messiness of our life,* that we can begin to see and appreciate what God is doing for each and every one of us through his saving love.

The great Church Mission Society (CMS) missionary strategist Max Warren once said: "It takes the whole world to know the whole gospel." No one person, no one group, no one episcopate, no one church possesses the whole truth. We all have a piece of the truth and only by being together in all of our Pentecost diversity can the fullness of God's love be revealed in all the world.

And so St. Paul in his letter to the Romans speaks of the Christian duty to love one another. In following Jesus, Paul says: "Let love be genuine; hate what is evil, hold fast to what is good; love one another in mutual affection" (Romans 12:9–10). "Live in harmony with one another; do not be haughty, but associate with the lowly. Do not claim to be wiser than you are. Do not repay anyone evil for evil, but take thought for what is noble in the sight of all. . . . Live peaceably with all" (Romans 12:16–18).

As Christians we are called to follow Jesus' example. We are called to live in love and in the promise of forgiveness and new life in Christ. Following Jesus means that we are called to seek communion and be in right relationship with God and with each other in all of our difference and all of our diversity. As we sang in that wonderful Communion hymn in our opening Eucharist in Aberdeen:

> I come with Christians far and near
> to find, as all are fed,
> our true community of love
> in Christ's communion bread.
> As Christ breaks bread for us to share,
> each proud division ends.
> The love that made us, makes us one,
> and strangers now are friends.

My prayer for the Anglican Consultative Council, especially in this time of transition, is that we will continue to seek to live together in communion, speaking the truth in love, acknowledging our faults, and loving our enemies. To separate ourselves from one another and from God is contrary to all that Jesus came to do. In his life, death, and resurrection is the true and genuine promise that every individual, the whole Church, and all of creation can be restored to unity with God and each other. In Jesus *is* our commonality: one Lord, one faith, one baptism. This is the communion we share.

"For in Christ Jesus you are all children of God through faith. As many of you as were baptized into Christ have clothed yourselves with Christ. There is no longer Jew or Greek, there is no longer slave or free, there is no longer male and female; for all of you are one in Christ Jesus" (Galatians 3:26–28).

Sermon by the Archbishop of Canterbury at the Solemn Eucharist

St. Mary's Episcopal Cathedral, Edinburgh
September 19, 1999

May I on behalf of the Anglican Consultative Council thank the provost of St. Mary's for his welcome to this lovely cathedral. We are glad to be here in this fair city and diocese of Edinburgh to share in this act of worship with you. Thank you again to Bishop Richard Holloway for his welcome and hospitality.

The cabin boy was mystified by the daily routine. Every day he brought the great captain of the ocean liner his cup of tea. He would bring it to the bridge; the captain would smile at him, take a sip, pick up his binoculars, and survey the empty ocean. Then, with a dramatic gesture, he would take a piece of paper from his pocket, consider it carefully, then replace it in his pocket with the same care. The cabin boy was overawed. What a privilege to bring the captain his daily cup of tea—but what was written on that piece of paper? What instructions were they that required such thought? He longed to know.

One day he found out.

As usual he brought the captain his cup of tea. He received the customary smile. The captain picked up his binoculars and surveyed the empty ocean, and then with a flourish he took the piece of paper from his pocket and read it with close attention. The cabin boy craned his neck and was able to read what was written there on. It read: "Port is left. Starboard is right."

There are times too in our Christian pilgrimage, whether as individuals or as churches, when it is right to pay particular attention to what lies at the root of our faith. Times when we need to be reminded afresh of what is basic to our existence and of the faith once delivered to the saints.

Now, in one sense, today's reading from the epistle of Philippians, chapter 1, is doing just that. Indeed, with a little thought we can see several similarities between Paul's day and his situation and the world Church today, some twenty centuries on. He was in prison; for him persecution was a daily, personal reality. He was experiencing opposition within the church as well as from without. He was uncertain about the future and perhaps worried now and again about what lay ahead. Above all, he felt the pain of being cut off from his congregations and lacking the fellowship and support that meant so much to him.

Clearly for some of us here many of those experiences are far removed from our daily lives. The terrible events currently taking place in East Timor remind us all too tragically of the bitter reality of some of these things—persecution is all too well-known to a number of members of ACC; some here have been imprisoned for their faith, and others along with them can speak with sadness of the death of loved ones for the sake of Christ. But all of us, I suspect, know something of Paul's deep concern for his churches and the value of having others with whom we can share the challenges of leadership.

Paul's letter to the Philippians, then, speaks into our experience as Christians. Paul speaks first of the hope at the heart of the gospel we preach: "For me to live is Christ and to die is gain." That quiet conviction, which is the heartbeat of faith.

But Christianity is not "pie in the sky when I die," and it never has been. St. Paul goes on to hammer home the fact that faith has to be lived out in the uncertainties of life. It is interesting that in the translation I used for my preparation two different verbs had been translated by the word "stand." Both of them are vivid, and no doubt military images lie behind them. Images that would have strongly resonated with Paul's readers. The city of Philippi itself was a Roman colony with a large number of former soldiers as its citizens. Paul himself was writing from prison in Rome, the capital of the empire, with his military guards around him. The calls to "stand by" and to "stand firm" convey the outlook of soldiers fighting for their homeland: facing the foe, unafraid, but not underestimating the nature of the conflict either.

The first occurrence of "stand" is in verse 25. It conveys the meaning of helping others and serving them—I shall stand by you to help you forward in your faith *(parameno)*. This is the bread and butter of leadership: to help others in their journey, to be there for them and to be with them through thick and thin. And this has a meaning for all of us. For the politicians present—that the ideals that have formed your lives should constantly have as their reference point the good of others. Likewise for teachers, social workers, and parents—indeed, all people in their varying professions—need to ask: The work I currently do—who is it for? Am I standing by those whose concerns I am supposed to meet?

And no group has greater reason to ponder this than Christian leaders. That is why St. Paul's own practice continues to be such an inspiration. No doubt, at times, he exhausted the patience of his tiny congregations and his band of friends; no doubt his single-mindedness, his obsession with certain things, must have driven them to exasperation. But he never lost his love for his Lord nor his passionate concern for those he had been given to care for. In other words, he remained in love.

And isn't that a challenge to us all? To remain in love with our ideals and to cherish that vision of our Lord which led us to offer ourselves to him?

The most effective leaders are not necessarily those with the most finely honed public skills or who are great administrators, but those who remain in love with their Lord and with their people: people who will be able to say in the twilight of their lives with St. Paul: "I was not disobedient to the heavenly vision."

That is my prayer for us all and for the Communion we represent. As the later chapters of Philippians remind us, it is tempting to be self-seeking in any position of leadership, whether religious or secular. Such leadership can be outwardly successful, but will ultimately never be a real benefit to a church or society. Truly beneficial leadership comes from those who stand alongside others in love, who desire the very best for them, and who have the courage and persistence to stay the course. Some years ago one of our leading London stores had an advertising slogan: "We grow by caring." It is not a bad one for a Christian Church either. Ministers like that, churches like that, will always produce the fruit that Christ longs to see in our lives.

However, there is another reason why Paul wished to stand alongside them. It was, he says, "to add joy to your faith." Joy takes the slog out of what we do: it lightens our step, it refreshes our way, and it gives enthusiasm to our work. I am reminded that if you go to a certain church near Cambridge you will find a plaque on the wall, dating back two hundred years, commemorating the vicar. It says devastatingly: "This plaque is erected to commemorate the Rev. _____ who worked among us for thirty years without the slightest trace of enthusiasm." Today we read that as a backhanded compliment. Not so in his day. Rather, it was a tribute to his ability in keeping the enthusiasts—the Methodists—out of his parish! But this is not a model to emulate for ourselves! Rather, we should always seek to stand firm in the joy of our faith and express it enthusiastically.

The second reference to "standing" occurs just two verses later, when Paul speaks of "standing firm" for the faith of the gospel. Here his argument moves from the personal to the corporate. And again Paul draws upon the image of Roman life. As I have said, Philippi was a Roman colony. The people there were proud of being counted Roman citizens. They were a homeland in miniature. And Paul makes the parallel with being citizens of a heavenly country. The literal translation of verse 27 is "exercise your citizenship worthily of the gospel of Christ." The verb is *politeuomai*, from which our word *politics* comes. Here is the charter of our commitment to the world in which we live—because to exercise our citizenship takes us irrevocably into the whole of life. We are sometimes told that churches and church leaders should keep their noses out of politics. Well, if we are to be faithful to our calling as Christians, we simply cannot do that. Our political calling comes from a citizenship that embraces all those made in God's image. That has usually been true of Anglicanism, and it is a heritage we should seek to foster.

Nevertheless, honesty compels us to acknowledge that we have not always lived up to this high calling. Sometimes in our history we have ignored the needs of those in distress; sometimes we have stressed evangelism and left undone the claims of mission. Sometimes we have ignored the urging of Amos: "Let justice roll on like a river and righteousness like an ever-flowing stream."

Happily, I have witnessed time and again that there is a passion for the application of the gospel in all its forms throughout the Communion. I think, for example of the small Anglican church established in Recife, Brazil. It stands close to the site of a rubbish dump where, six years ago, a young woman priest was horrified to see people living. Their despair led her to act and galvanise the city authorities and bully the church until the place began to be transformed. Such "standing firm" will never be easy, will always be costly. and at its best will always be holistic—never separating mission and evangelism. Here in Scotland, I think of a project that has employed a community worker in one of the more difficult areas of Glasgow to provide support for families under pressure. This is an excellent example of working together with the diocese, the Mothers' Union, and more recently the Church of Scotland to provide resources for the work. Such projects, and there are many others that I could cite, go to the heart of what we believe, our passion for justice and our desire for God's mission.

But it not always easy to keep our ideals uppermost in our thoughts and prayers. I was struck by Bishop Richard Holloway's address at Aberdeen Cathedral on Tuesday. He spoke of the way we Church people may confuse the Church structures with the good news we share. The result may be that we end up loving the Church more than the gospel and seek our own survival rather than obeying the Lord of the Church.

Yes, that is a subtle danger. As Paul reminds us, there is a gospel to contend for and we can do it effectively only when we do it together and are open to the leading of God.

To say that we live in exciting times is a truism. This century has seen the encouraging growth of our Communion. What is more, we have grown most spectacularly where our Church has suffered and where it has had to live out its faith by exercising a daily trust in God. God beckons us into his future: a future that will daunt the strongest among us and call forth from us, possibly, depths of faith, love, and hope that we have never previously fathomed. And when the chips are down, it is the love we have for our Lord, the concern we have for the hungry, needy, and poor, and our passion for God's kingdom that will sustain us. For that we need to be reminded of those lessons of faith, which have sustained us on previous journeys. We need, like that captain, to take out our piece of paper day by day and to be reminded afresh of the roots of our Christian faith. That hope which sustains us, that gospel which guides us, and those foundations of faith on which we rest. So the apostolic call comes down the centuries: Stand firm with God and with each other—allow him to direct our lives. "Port is left and starboard is right"—even the best of captains must ponder that daily.

Launch of the Environmental Project at St. Matthew's Church Possilpark

—THE MOST REVEREND RICHARD HOLLOWAY, PRIMUS OF THE SCOTTISH EPISCOPAL CHURCH

September 22, 1999

In his book *The Good Society*, Kenneth Galbraith, the Harvard economist, writes these words: "There is the inescapable fact that the modern market economy accords wealth and distributes income in a highly unequal, socially adverse and also functionally damaging fashion." Galbraith knows better than most how good the market economy is at generating wealth, but he is concerned at the way those who benefit from the system refuse to address the damaging effects it has on the most vulnerable members of society. Most unprejudiced thinkers today would acknowledge the failures as well as the successes of the global market economy. At the meeting of the Anglican Consultative Council in Dundee this week, we have listened to harrowing descriptions of the effect of the global economy on the poor of the Third World, but we also have to acknowledge that the Third World is with us in the midst of the Developed World. Few people today argue for the complete abolition of the capitalist system. Increasingly, however, they are calling for a candid acknowledgement of its failures. "We created the thing," they say, "so why can't we learn to modify or correct it?" And we have started to do this in certain areas. We have learned about the cost to the planet of unregulated industrial activity, so we no longer tolerate businesses that pollute our rivers and destroy the quality of the air we breathe. So far, however, we are uncertain about how to respond to the effects of the global market economy on the human environment. We could make a start by acknowledging that the system that has made most people in this country more prosperous has plunged a significant proportion of our fellow citizens into poverty and despair.

One of the undisputed facts of the history of human industry is that change in the methods of production always has a disproportionate impact upon the most vulnerable in society. History, like nature, seems to be indifferent to the pain it causes the weak. Think of the way the Industrial Revolution chewed up and spat out generations of the poor, before we learned how to protect them from its worst depredations. The paradox of our time is that it is the death of heavy industry that is now devastating the poor. In a recent essay, Professor David Donnison claimed that in Scotland we are in the midst of a massive social disaster, and Glasgow is its epicentre. He writes: "Nearly three fifths—58%—of the most deprived postcode districts of Scotland are in this city. 37% of Glasgow's households with children in them have no-one in a paid job, and 27% have only one adult." Poverty is heavily concentrated in and around Glasgow, but other cities have their share, including prosperous Edinburgh. Much of this is the consequence of global economic changes, coupled with the closure of pits and defence industries. Heavy industry has been replaced by the knowledge economy, and we are only now trying to catch up with its consequential impact upon the poor and ill-educated. And, as if that were not enough, social change has combined with the economic revolution to destroy the cultural cohesion of the most vulnerable sections of our society. When the culture revolution of the 1960s met and married the economic revolution of the 1980s, there was a potent instrument of social change created that has transformed the social landscape of Britain, and its most devastating impact has been upon young, ill-educated workless males. The institutions that once gave them a motive for responsible living, such as holding down a tough, demanding job with its own culture and honour, and presiding, however clumsily, within a marriage and family that was the primary context for the nurture and socialising of children, have largely disappeared, and with them the main ways the human community traditionally disciplined and integrated what the Prayer Book calls "the unruly wills and affections of sinful men." This shattering of the structures that once gave the poor significance and purpose has created a breeding ground for despair and alienation. Whenever I refer to these facts in certain circles, someone inevitably points out that no one in Britain is starving today, because absolute poverty has been eradicated. That may be true, but minority poverty has a cruelty that is all its own. When most people were poor, as they were when I was born here in 1933, there was a camaraderie and cultural cohesion in belonging to the working class that gave them a strength and pride that transcended the structures that excluded them. But in a society where most people are prosperous and the poor are a minority whose culture has disintegrated, the pain and anger they feel is heightened.

It is the mark of a humane society to acknowledge this pain and try to tackle the factors that produce it. Because the British government has acknowledged that the endurance of poverty in a prosperous society is a scandal, we are currently embarked upon an ambitious programme to tackle the human tragedy created by the revolutions of our time. We have acknowledged that the system that benefits most of us has had the unintended effect of excluding many of our fellow citizens. So we are working to correct that tragic imbalance by policies and projects designed to counteract the effects upon the poor of the revolutions of our time. We know that they lead shorter and less satisfying lives than the rest of us; that their health is worse (yet they are less well served by the health service); and that many of them go through the education system with little benefit, so they are heavily handicapped in their attempts to find work. And we know that they are more prone to those devastating addictions that are such a feature of our complex society. All of these characteristics are found here in Possilpark, which has been rated by the government as the most deprived community in Scotland. The project we have opened today is a good example of the way we are beginning to tackle poverty in our society. St. Matthew's has secured money from the Glasgow City of Architecture and Design initiative, which has been supported by the European Regional Development Fund. The Scottish Arts Council has also sponsored the project. All of these initiatives are helping the regeneration of this Priority Partnership Area. The way back to justice, the way back to the good life for all our people, has to begin by giving them hope. That is why I am delighted that we have created this place of beauty in the heart of Possilpark. The tree I planted is a sign of hope, but it must be more than that: it must be a sign of our determination to work for a more just and equal society. When the Irish poet W. B. Yeats was an old man, he feared that the gift of poverty had left him. He had once thought that his poems came to him from outside himself. Then he realised that they had come from his own heart, so he must go back there and start climbing out of despair. The poem he wrote to express this insight ends like this: "Now that my ladder's gone I must lie down where all the ladders start / In the foul rag and bone shop of the heart." We are doing something like that today; we are building something from the human heart, "where all the ladders start."

Eight Meditations on the Minor Prophets

—The Right Reverend Leo Frade, bishop of Honduras

As I begin this meditation, I must confess that I do it with a lot of fear and trepidation. Actually, it is not so much because I face this august body of Anglicans and other assorted Christians, but rather it is because I am really concerned about my accent. Since I came to England, I realised that I speak something very different from English. I must apologise to the British that invented this very hard language, because I have learned my English from the Americans. Now I realise that they taught me something else that sounds somewhat similar to English.

Maybe I should try to get my money back because they taught me faulty English. Of course, Americans can be excused because they are far away from England, so the English could not do a good job. But alas, I have now spent a couple of days in Scotland, and I have not been able to understand a word of what they are saying to me. There is no excuse here because Scots are very close to England. But anyway, nevertheless I will do my best with this American English with a Cuban-Honduran accent.

I am proposing to share with you eight meditations taken from the twelve minor prophets. here is a common thread in their thinking that has to do with justice, that has to do with the poor and our responsibility to them, and that has to do with the religious institution and its role in a suffering world. Please be aware that because I have only eight days, you will not be hearing much from Obadiah, Nahum, Haggai, and Malachi. I am reserving them for future meditations.

I come to you also as a Latin American person who was born in Cuba, educated and ordained in the United States, and now has been the bishop of Honduras (the poorest Spanish-speaking country in the world) for sixteen years—the bishop of a diocese that was fulminated by nature less than a year ago under the effects of Hurricane Mitch. I would like to point out that our church is a rapidly growing church, like many of the churches in the Anglican Communion. We are not shy about being Anglicans and proclaiming the gospel of Jesus Christ at all times and in all places, but our church is also one that is surrounded by the poor and is made up mainly by the poor.

We are constantly struggling with this tension, of what is the role of the church as we go around with our prayer book, Bible, and hymnal, facing children that are hungry, seeing the desperation of parents that have nowhere to go and nobody to help them—all situations created by an unequal system of distribution, coupled with classism, racism, and imperialism.

So let us begin.

First Meditation: Hosea 6:1-6

Today's meditation is taken from Hosea 6:1–6, where we can find this familiar quotation: "For I desire steadfast love and not sacrifice, the knowledge of God rather than burnt offerings" (verse 6). Our Lord Jesus Christ used this quote twice: "Go and learn what this means, 'I desire mercy, not sacrifice. For I have come to call not the righteous but sinners'" (Matthew 9:13) and "But if you had known what this means, 'I desire mercy and not sacrifice,' you would not have condemned the guiltless" (Matthew 12:7).

Let's read Hosea 6:1–6.

> "Come, let us return to the LORD; for it is he who has torn, and he will heal us; he has struck down, and he will bind us up. After two days he will revive us; on the third day he will raise us up, that we may live before him. Let us know, let us press on to know the LORD; His appearing is as sure as the dawn; he will come to us like the showers, like the spring rains that water the earth. "What shall I do with you, O Ephraim? What shall I do with you, O Judah? Your love is like a morning cloud, like the dew that goes away early. Therefore I have hewn them by the prophets, I have killed them by the words of my mouth, and my judgment goes forth as the light. For I desire steadfast love and not sacrifice, the knowledge of God rather than burnt offerings.

"For I desire steadfast love and not sacrifice, the knowledge of God rather than burnt offerings." Our Lord Jesus Christ uses this quotation. The first time he uses it is when he is accused by Pharisees for hanging around with publicans and sinners. He tells them: "Go and learn what is the meaning of 'I desire mercy and not sacrifice.'"

Later on, he is challenged again because his disciples were plucking grain on the Sabbath. The Pharisees counter Jesus, and he uses this Bible verse one more time and tells them: "If you had known what this means, 'I desire mercy and not sacrifice,' you would not have condemned the guiltless."

Our Lord knew that when religion begins to give preferences to issues of liturgy, dogma, nuances of languages, architecture, etc., but forgets the humans that are suffering, those who are exploited and in pain, then what we have is cultic correctness completely void of the presence of God. We may end up having all the faith and may be able to understand all the mysteries and knowledge, the most pure dogma, but then we still have nothing because it is void of love.

Our Lord is reminding us not to understand religion in terms of church growth, biblical decency, and doing what our cultic and cultural requirements demand from us. We must be sure that we haven't reduced religion to a common denominator where our goal is just to conform to doctrine, correct liturgy, and the growing of churches—forgetting the issue of love.

I must say that the key word here is the Hebrew word *ḥesed*. It appears in Hosea 6:4 when Yahweh says: "Your love is like a morning cloud, like the dew that goes away early"—your *ḥesed* is like a morning cloud.

It appears again in verse 6: "For I desire steadfast love and not sacrifice." I desire *ḥesed*. Both love and steadfast love are translations of *ḥesed*. It is used in 1 Samuel 18:1–3, where David and Jonathan made a covenant with each other, and 1 Samuel 20:14–15, where Jonathan asks David to never abandon his family and he says: "Show me the faithful love *(ḥesed)* of the LORD, but if I die, never cut off your faithful love *(ḥesed)* from my house."

We could explain *ḥesed* as a form of covenant love. In marriage it is used also as the loyal love between two persons that marry. In the book of Hosea, he uses *ḥesed* to talk about the love that God has for his people and also for the love that people have toward their neighbours.

Our Lord understood the words of the prophet, and he reminds us that there are two fundamentally different notions of religions. The Pharisees described one that sought to satisfy their religious duties by a series of rules and sacrifices that they had confused with God's will. Jesus reminded them that they were required to offer *ḥesed* in order to fulfil their duties to God and their fellow human beings.

The question for us is to make sure that we understand the fundamental differences of the notion of our religion. For me in Latin America, I must respond to what I must do when I am faced with the claim of the Garífuna people to the oceanfront land that they have been occupying for over 150 years and that the government is now claiming in order to develop tourism and development in an area that has paradise beaches. What can I do to help the native people of Honduras that are spitting on the cross of Jesus because it was the symbol under which the conquerors received their strength to take over their land and their women?

What can we do when faced by sexual tourism that feeds on the hunger of our children and is paid with the money of those that come to our shores in search of thrills of both heterosexual and same-sex encounters?

How can we respond in a loving way to nations that have sucked our blood, invaded our lands, exploited our resources, forced us to emigrate because of the civil wars they financed to fight their enemies from afar and, now when we are not needed, send our people back in shame and chains as undocumented aliens to a devastated land where there are no jobs?

Should we tell our people who insist on violence to put their weapons and guns away? Should we tell them that they should have patience and ignore one of the highest rates of infant mortality of the world and laws that protect the powerful?

Should we as Anglicans do like some of our evangelical brothers and sisters who concentrate on issues of religion and church growth and give a blind eye to the poor around us, ignoring also the injustice of those who govern?

Should we then, if we decide to respond to help the poor, concentrate on just giving minor Band-Aid solutions that just cover a major sore, ignoring the root causes of poverty and exploitation?

We struggle with questions like this daily, as many of you do in your churches. We hear our Lord demanding from us that we must be faithful in the knowledge of God, but always and above all desire steadfast love and not sacrifice.

I don't pretend to have an answer. Most of those questions continue to be unanswered. We don't want to encounter the wrath of those in power. We know that it is safer to feed the hungry but not to get in the way of those who take away the food from the poor. We are careful and we also have very little time left because we must make sure that our church continues to grow rapidly.

I don't want you to provide me with the answers that are for me to find out through my dialogue with God and with my sisters and brothers as we search the Lord's will. But I would like you this morning to search your ministry, your experience, and your involvement in your world where the Lord has planted you.

Do you practice *hesed* and not sacrifice? Is your ministry one that is able to reach to those in need, those who are discriminated, and those who are pushed aside because of our cultic regulations? And then ask yourself if there is something that we can do to respond to their plea. My prayer is that our commitment as Anglicans is not like a morning cloud, like the dew that goes away early.

I pray that we can offer our God the steadfast love that he desires, because without it we will be totally empty—just satisfying religious duties, ignoring both God our Creator and our fellow brothers and sisters that are his creation. Amen.

Second Meditation: Joel 3:1–21

There is what is probably a mythical story that I grew up listening to in my history classes in Cuba. The story has to do with an Indian Chief named Hatuey. After 1492, after the discovery of the Americas by the Europeans, the conquest of the New World began to take place. At the beginning it seemed that it was going to be a peaceful settlement by the Europeans, but greed took over and the systematic enslavement of the Native Americans began to take place.

In Cuba an Indian chief named Hatuey rallied the tribes to resist the Spanish conquest. He fought for many months until he was captured. He was condemned to die, but before he was killed, a priest offered to baptise him in order for him to go to heaven. The story says that Chief Hatuey asked the Spanish priest if those who were baptised went to heaven and those who were not baptised went to hell. The priest said, "Yes, that was the way it works." Hatuey then asked if the Spaniards were baptised and if they were going to go to heaven. The priest said: "Of course, they are baptised Christians and they will be with God in heaven." Hatuey then told the priest that he didn't wanted to be baptised, just to make sure that he would end up in hell where there were no Spaniards.

We in Latin America are revisiting our sad past, struggling to live our cruel present, and hoping to improve the future of our children. The book of Joel begins with the statement that says to let the children know and for the children to tell the children in another generation that horrible things have happened in the past. We have experienced the disaster of such a magnitude that must not be forgotten.

While reading the book of Joel and his description of such a destruction, I could not but be reminded of what we went through in Honduras when Hurricane Mitch brought to us destruction greater than arrows and greater than spears and swords.

In Joel's times, natural disasters were as frightening and unpredictable as in our times. A plague of locusts could wipe out an entire food supply in a few hours, just as Hurricane Mitch did to the whole nation of Honduras in a couple of days.

In Joel's times nobody was spared. In my diocese, which is the country of Honduras, just a few months ago I was trying to explain to many parents that lost their children that God was merciful and loving. I did get in touch with the words from Joel that say: "Truly the day of the Lord is great; terrible indeed—who can endure it?"

It is when we face disasters of the magnitude of Hurricane Mitch that we have to try to explain why God allows disasters to happen. Joel had no doubts that God was behind the plague. He also believed that God, after a nationwide day of prayer and fasting, would roll back the damage done by the locust. He was sure that the people would emerge from the experience with a new and durable confidence in God's love.

I have gone back to many of the people that cursed God's name when they lost everything, including their loved ones. After many months they have reconciled with their God and accepted their destiny. They came to the realisation that it was the cycle of nature that was responsible and not God. Many of those that died lived in areas where the poor dwell in huts along the river. Should they blame God or perhaps an unjust neo-liberal system that puts profits ahead of people and won't allow them to escape the cycle of poverty. Many have also finally realised in Honduras that ecology must be taken seriously if we are to survive another major disaster.

There are many of us in Latin America who call ourselves Christians that are ˙ing to our past and are saying today that we must take strong corrective measures to guarantee that our children and the children of our children won't have to suffer what we have suffered in our past and are suffering in our present.

I must confess to you that in this concern for a better tomorrow in Latin America and the world, I am indeed worried that our historical enemy has disappeared. From the time I was born, more than half a century ago, I feared and even fought them, but now that they are gone, I miss them. They were always there, demanding rights for the poor, organising struggles for social justice, willing to give of their time, their money, their support, and many times even their lives in order to change the evils of a materialistic and capitalistic society that has no concern for the poor and the workers.

I am referring to the communists and the nations that were ruled by a Marxist-Leninist system. I will agree with you if you tell me that they did not practice what they preached. I will concede that today those countries that are ruled by communists are not perfect and a lot of social injustice takes place there. But allow me to tell you that capitalism and neo-liberalism, as we experienced it, can be as oppressive and unjust as those societies that we all like to criticise and condemn.

Allow me, before you discard me in your thinking, to share my pain and my frustration. But also allow me to try to explain why I said that I missed my enemy. Yes, communists were my enemy when they existed, and I fought them and will fight them again if they ever come back. But I will repeat myself, I miss them.

Today in Latin America, and I am sure that the same goes for Asia and Africa and all the nations of the South, we have been left defenceless to face injustice, to organise our struggle for equality, to have the resources to change the inequalities of our social system, to have a place to escape to and hide when being persecuted, tortured, and killed by the oppressors.

It is not surprising for me that the Northern Hemisphere nations like to quote Isaiah 2:4, "They shall beat their swords into ploughshares and their spears into pruning hooks." Many cannot understand how those who propose liberation for the poor and the oppressed using the name of God in Latin America can have turned to violence at times. It seems that we in the South are so desperate with our oppression that we would rather read Joel 3:10, where it says: "Beat your ploughshares into swords, and your pruning hooks into spears; let the weakling say, 'I am a warrior.'"

It has been over 500 years and the native people of the Americas are still living in oppression. In Honduras the authorities were indignant when, during an October 12 celebration remembering the discovery of Christopher Columbus of the new world, one of the Indians tribes vandalised a statue of Columbus, knocking it down, cutting themselves, and covering the statue with their blood.

We have also seen how multinational companies have been able to have laws approved that benefit them but exploit the workers. We have seen how powerful nations can hold hostage a small nation to guarantee that things are done in that small nation to benefit the powerful ones. We have seen how economic embargoes are forced on the people of countries that just disagree with the mighty powerful countries.

Before, I could count on the communists to cry out and demand justice. They were professionals and knew how to do it well. The fact that they were my enemies and blamed the church for our alliance with the powerful classes did not take from their struggle for justice.

Today the poor have nobody but the voice of the church to defend them, to demand justice, to protect them from their persecutors and oppressors. That puts us in a very hard situation that accounts for a lot of risk and anger because the oppressor is not going to take it sitting down. They didn't take it from the communists, and they will not take anything from us either. That is why I miss my enemy, because now we are stuck with the job to defend the poor. The poor of this world have only the voice of the church to defend them. We are it!

"They have divided my land, and cast lots for my people and traded boys for prostitutes, and sold girls for wine, and drunk it down" (verses 2 and 3). The words that Joel wrote are a reality in our lands. They have divided our lands, they have cast lots for the people in Latin America, our boys have been used for prostitution, and our girls are sold for less than wine. What a sad commentary for me and my church when I dare to say that I miss my enemy because I fear to face the consequences to defend the poor and struggle for justice and equality.

How can I find the courage to tell the invader that has taken over our lands, raped our sisters, our mothers, and our daughters, killed our children, and now comes to us with a cross in the name of God proposing for us to turn the other cheek. If Chief Hatuey is presently burning in hell and some of those cruel European conquerors are enjoying the joy of heaven, then there is indeed something wrong with our religion.

But the promise of Joel is also that there will be retribution for our suffering because of the violence done to our people, in whose land they have shed innocent blood. We, in the meanwhile, need to become the voice of those who are suffering and to remember that our struggle is against rulers, authorities, and the devil himself. We are reminded by our Lord Jesus Christ that what really counts for him, at least what the Bible tells us counts for him, is that we feed the hungry, give drinks to the thirsty, welcome the stranger—and I will add, not to shackle them like criminals into deportation—to also clothe the naked, take care of the sick, visit the prisoners, and be sure that we make the least of God's creation a member of our own families.

My question for you is, Are we as the Anglican Communion willing to take on this task? Are we willing to confront the oppressors of our societies and demand justice and mercy for the poor? Are we willing to defend those who are exploited, those who are marginalised because of their sexual preference, those who have different skin colour or language or different nationality or ethnic origin? Are we willing to confront those who deny medical knowledge that could save millions of poor people dying from AIDS in Africa, Asia, and Latin America? Are we willing to be radical about it and make sure we find a solution, or are we going to do just enough to look good and keep our conscience clear?

Archbishop Temple, who preceded all the liberation theologians of Latin America, reminded us that "unless the Church has something to stand for, it has no place of its own in the ordering of life, and becomes merely a group of people who like or value their association with one another."

Third Meditation: Jonah 4

Jonah is the only Old Testament prophet with whom Jesus directly compared himself. There is no question that Christ considered Jonah's experience and mission of great significance. Both Jonah and Jesus were Galileans. Jesus was from Nazareth, and only a few miles north is where you will find the town of Qath-hepher. Any student from St. George's College, Jerusalem, will know that it was only less than an hour away if you walked. We can imagine Jesus visiting that town and meditating on the significance of Jonah's mission as well as his own.

Jesus referred to Jonah in Matthew 12:38–41 and Luke 11:29–32 and talks about Jonah's mission and the repentance of the people of Nineveh. The people of Nineveh had responded to the preaching of Jonah and repented, but the Jews had failed to repent while hearing the preaching of Jesus that was "the sign of Jonah."

While reading the book of Jonah, one gets the idea that he was a reluctant evangelist and definitely not very ecumenical. The book of Jonah tells a story of a man who had received implicit orders from God to love his enemies. We are astonished at his reluctance and his daring disobedience to God's command. If we look on a map, Jonah is asked to go east but instead he manages to find a boat that is going west. Jonah is asked to love his enemies and save them from destruction, but he chooses to turn his back on them and "escape" the presence of the Lord.

I wonder how many Jonahs I know. Maybe I am one of them myself. There have been many opportunities in life to reach out that I have turned down because it was not convenient, or too dangerous. There have been many times when I could have been compassionate and forgiving, but instead I chose to be judgmental and strict. The poet Robert Frost said, "After Jonah, you could never trust God to be merciful again." Jonah's major problem was that he was completely aware that God is loving and forgiving. The book of Jonah ends with a poignant statement that asks: Can anyone put limits on how much love, mercy, and forgiveness God is willing to give?

How do we deal with people that we strongly disagree with? Not only with those that are far away and of different cultures but also with those who get in our way because they live very close and for some reason keep crossing our path, challenging our beliefs, and demanding space that is ours—or at least we think that it is ours.

I can only tell you of my shortcomings and my inability to hear others when they disagree with me: to be able to put them down, to prove that they are wrong, and to guarantee that their cause and their beliefs will never rise up again to challenge mine.

Nineveh was indeed a sinful city, and I am sure that they deserved punishment, but God had compassion on them and was willing instead to offer love, pardon, and mercy. Jonah was not even willing to hear about it, and he was not willing to be part of any understanding or acceptance. He did not want to look like a fool by announcing a judgement that was not going to materialise. He felt that God was too kind, and we see by the story in chapter 4 that Jonah has more concern for a vine that shaded him than for the people of Nineveh.

Are we willing to listen to others when they make a statement that is different from ours? Are we going to appeal to our Holy Writ and quote chapter and verse to guarantee that we are right and to assure that others are wrong?

A little over a year ago the bishops met in Southern England for the Lambeth Conference. In that meeting we spent days trying to achieve consensus on the issue of sexuality, and more specifically on the issue of gays and lesbians. I remember seeing a bishop going around with a big sign full of Bible verses that condemned homosexuality as a grievous sin. It reminded me of Jonah when God asked him to go east and he decided to go west. Somehow, a prevalent attitude of total rejection and a lack of wanting to listen to one another began to take over. We began to embark the church toward Tarshish and away from Nineveh. We were not willing to hear that there were more than a hundred twenty thousand persons that wanted to be heard by our church and that claimed to speak for a God that, according to the Holy Bible, tends to relent from punishing, that turns always from his fierce anger, that is gracious and merciful, and is slow to anger and abounding in steadfast love.

Why do I say this? Is it because I have a liberal position on this issue? I don't think so. I can be described as many things, but not as one that is liberal on this issue. I adhere to a biblical position on this matter that can be supported by tradition. Still, it is that same Holy Bible that compels me to reach out and be willing to hear those that I disagree with and are challenging me. It is God's Holy Word and teaching that call me to reach out in love to my sisters and brothers. I cannot be indifferent to their suffering. It is also reason that makes me realise that I must pay attention to new findings and a different way to look at the same thing.

Why do I say this? It is not because I like to make anyone feel bad or angry. It is because the issues of the minor prophets have to do with justice, they have to do with the religious institutions and their role in a suffering world. Why do I say this? Probably because I also want to challenge myself. You see, I also got in the boat that was going west, even if my heart and compassion were calling me to hear those who were suffering and wanted to be heard. Like Jonah, I have been in the belly of the fish, because steadfast love put me there, and now I want to be spit out and be willing to say that if I believe in justice and mercy, then I must not be selective in who receives it. I want to be willing to listen to God and to all the men and women he created, regardless of their sexual preference.

I do not know about Africa and Asia. Maybe there are no gays or lesbians there, but in Latin America there are gays and lesbians. And do you know what? They are our mothers and fathers, our sisters and brothers, our wives and husbands, our sons and daughters. They are people like you and me and they suffer, they are discriminated and beaten and many times tortured and killed. Are we suppose to look the other way and let their blood be on us?

I know that in industrialised countries this is not as acute as in Latin America, but discrimination also happens there. What must we do to alleviate their pain and their suffering? Some may say to convert them, to heal them, to expel the demons from them. Others claim that we must listen to them and reach to their pain and be willing to accept them as they are. After all, there are more than a hundred and twenty thousand persons, and we know that our "God is gracious and merciful, slow to anger and abounding in steadfast (*ḥesed*) love and ready to relent from punishing."

I may be wrong, but during the sessions of sexuality in Lambeth, bishops seemed to stop listening to each other and decided, very conveniently, to put aside *ḥesed*. I am sure that steadfast love is at the centre of the gospel of Jesus Christ. Christ's message is all about love and forgiveness and acceptance. I am not saying that the other side of the issue of sexuality should have won the vote. But what I am trying to express is my perception that God's *ḥesed* seemed to evaporate under the bishops' tent that afternoon.

When I walked out of the tent where we were meeting in Lambeth, I could not but think of the words of St. Paul when he wrote to the Corinthians: "If I have prophetic powers, and understand all mysteries and all knowledge, and if I have all faith, so as to remove mountains, but do not have love, I am nothing" (1 Corinthians 13:2). Truth may be intolerant of error, but God's truth is also intolerant of intolerance. Truth, as St. Paul conceives it in 1 Corinthians 13, is intolerant of any self-righteous belief that is void of love and compassion.

If gays and lesbians of this world are sinners, then we should be sitting down with them to eat and drink as our Lord did during his time with those that were called sinners. I want to make sure that they are able to see the Lord among them—the compassionate Christ that keeps appearing in the gospels in the company of sinners.

How many of our provinces and our dioceses have begun to listen to what gays and lesbians have to say? That was also included in the resolution that was passed. When you do that, if you do that, then you will begin to hear stories of pain, suffering, and persecution. You will also realise that much of that pain, suffering, and persecution has been done by the church.

I can recall many sermons I heard in the late 80s and early 90s that insisted that AIDS was God's punishment for homosexuals. Those sermons were preached in Honduras and all of Latin America by Protestant churches of many denominations and by Roman Catholic churches also. Sadly, more than one Anglican preacher managed to agree with that horrendous belief.

I have watched with horror on the television of San Pedro Sula when a known and respected Pentecostal preacher suggested that the demons that possess the gays can be expelled by beating the homosexuals. He encouraged parents to challenge their sons and daughters and beat them up if necessary.

The book of Jonah, dating sometime in the post-exilic period, most likely in the fifth century B.C., is still a forceful and dynamic story to challenge our thinking on how we deal with those that we disagree with.

I am aware that the realities of Africa and many areas of Asia where Islam imposes its criteria on the pain of death makes a difference on how you respond to this. I'm sure that those areas have a different reality than ours in Latin America. But please do not discard me yet or close your eyes and ears to my reality and the reality of other parts of the planet. We must try to listen to each other in love and respect. Yes, we should be free to disagree with each other, but even in disagreement we must show God's love and try to imitate a God who is willing to love and forgive in any continent of this planet. Until we learn to do that, we are going to be in the darkness of the belly of that big fish of intolerance, knowing that we are completely right, but unable to move anywhere because God is demanding from us to reach out and listen to those with whom we completely disagree.

If doctrinal purity has no room for mercy and steadfast love and is not willing to embrace sinners and publicans, then the so-called orthodoxy is going to be well received in the eastern city of Tarshish if they can make it all the way there without storms. But most probably there will be a gathering of the select and doctrinally pure inside the belly of a big fish.

I know that it is very hard to imitate God when it comes to *ḥesed*, to steadfast love. But we must try it if we are willing to do God's will. Can we talk to each other, hear each other, and try to understand each other?

Are we willing to challenge some of our strongly held beliefs, as Peter did when faced with the Gentile question? Are we willing to establish a serious conversation with those who differ from us or those who have questionable morality, like the Samaritan woman that Jesus met at the well?

Are we willing to let diversity take place and recognise that *my* biblical interpretation is different from the interpretation of others?

Are we willing to welcome one another as Christ welcomed us?

These are just some of the questions that I propose for us to discuss this morning. May we do it in love, willing to hear one another. I am not pretending to change anyone's mind—just some of our attitudes toward each other.

I gave up trying to save the Church when I realised that Jesus Christ had done just that on the cross. May we be willing to share that cross in order to love one another.

Fourth Meditation: Micah 6:6–15

What does God want? What does the Lord really require of you and me? In the gospels we see that our Lord Jesus challenged the scribes and Pharisees, calling them hypocrites. "You tithe mint, dill, and cumin, and have neglected the weightier matters of the law: justice and mercy and faith. It is these you ought to have practised without neglecting the others. You blind guides! You strain out a gnat but swallow a camel!"

The Pharisees, who literally strained water through a cloth in order to filter unclean gnats, surely felt Jesus' sarcasm. I am sure that Jesus was not that angry with them for being ritually strict, but for ignoring what was important: justice, mercy, and faithfulness to God.

Micah lived during very hard times for Israel. It was a time of struggles, both from within and without. Micah was concerned about all the idolatry that was creeping south into Judah. The same judgement that Yahweh had imposed on the kingdoms of the north was going to be imposed on Judah unless they repented.

Micah could see further ahead from all their sins and spoke of a God who punished in order to purify his people. Micah also foresaw peace and talks about peace and security through obedience. He, as Isaiah, prophesied of a time when "they shall beat their swords into ploughshares, and their spears into pruning hooks" (4:3).

Reading Micah could be very confusing because this book of only seven chapters is full of prophetic statements. In a short space you have fragments that talk about the Messiah, and then all of a sudden he begins to talk about the battle against Assyria. It is a collection of speeches, all put together. The speeches are a combination of God speaking, Micah speaking, and the rebellious people also giving their opinion.

Actually, I could have done the eight meditations just on Micah. There is a lot here. I always have loved that quotation from Micah 6:8. I was still in seminary when President Jimmy Carter took his oath of office on a Bible that was opened to Micah 6:8: "He has told you, O mortal, what is good . . . but to do justice, and to love kindness, and to walk humbly with your God?"

Phillips Brooks wrote the hymn "O Little Town of Bethlehem" that picks Micah 5:2: "But you, O Bethlehem Ephrata, who are little among the clans of Judah . . ."

The writings of this prophet, who lived in the time of King Jotham, probably after Ahaz had become co-regent and possible all the way after the Assyrian invasion of 701 B.C. gives us a testimony of what God wants for his people: to do, to love, and to walk.

Not only are we supposed to believe in justice and to talk about it, but also we are to make justice happen. Micah tells us what we must do to please Yahweh and that is to do justice. The notion is a dynamic one because it is something a person does. To carry out *mishpat* or justice; to do it not just to believe in it or talk about it. How many resolutions can we accumulate if all of our Anglican churches around the world add their beautiful and positive statements about justice. I am sure that there are many, and luckily for us there are also many of our clergy and laity that not only talk about it but also do justice and practice justice. But we live in a world of injustice, with people who are suffering as a product of that injustice. Micah's writings of two thousand seven hundred years ago could have been written by any Latin American reformer or revolutionary just last week. "Alas for those who devise wickedness and evil deeds on their beds! When the morning dawns, they perform it, because it is in their power. They covet fields, and seize them; houses, and take them away; they oppress householder and house, people and their inheritance" (2:1–2). This sounds like an editorial from one of our leftist newspapers!

> But you rise up against my people as an enemy; you strip the robe from the peaceful, from those who pass by trustingly with no thought of war. The women of my people you drive out from their pleasant houses; from their young children you take away my glory forever. (2:8–9)
>
> Its rulers give judgement for a bribe, its priests teach for a price, its prophets give oracles for money. (3:11)
>
> Can I tolerate wicked scales and a bag of dishonest weights? Your wealthy are full of violence; your inhabitants speak lies, with tongues of deceit in their mouths. (6:11–12)
>
> The faithful have disappeared from the land, and there is no one left who is upright; they all lie in wait for blood, and they hunt each other with nets. Their hands are skilled to do evil; the official and the judge ask for a bribe, and the powerful dictate what they desire; thus they per-

vert justice. The best of them is like a brier, the most upright of them a thorn hedge. (7:2–4)

Micah sounds quite similar to a report from our human rights commissioner. These statements describe with full details what is going on in most of our countries, if not all of them. The Christians in Latin America, as well as Christians everywhere, know that to do justice means to work for the establishment of equity for all, especially for the powerless.

But who are the powerless? In my country and in my diocese I am talking about eighty percent of the people. I meet them every day as I open the gates of my beautiful house, surrounded by the traditional walls that we use in our area. They are there in the street corners, with their hands uplifted asking for alms. To quench my conscience I give them one or two pesos, about seven to twelve American cents. They smile with joy, thankful that I had mercy on them. Then I drive to see the *campesinos,* the peasants that are landless, and I rejoice in the social projects of our church. We do it with money that our brethren from the north sent down.

I do many things that make my conscience feel good, but what is very hard to do, and what I tend to avoid, is to work to change the injustice that comes out of unjust laws and an unjust economic system. I do nothing or very little to change that unjust system that continues oppressing the poor and powerless of our lands.

Who should we blame for all of this suffering? Not me, not you. Let's blame the International Monetary Fund (IMF), or the Americans that everybody loves to blame for all the ills of the world, or the Paris Club, or the World Bank. Maybe we need to blame the Liberal Party that is in power in Honduras or the National Party that will probably get elected in our next elections. Yes, let's blame the politicians. Let's blame everybody, but not you and me, and of course not our church.

Let's not forget that who is to be blamed is the least of the worries of those who are suffering. The poor and powerless know that it is almost impossible to escape the cycle of poverty. They also know that the church is their only connection to hope. That is, of course, if the church is willing to do justice and not just to talk about it. If the church is willing not to avoid confronting the root causes of poverty and oppression—even if that confrontation has a price to pay.

Secondly, Micah says that the Lord also wants us to love kindness. He uses Hosea's same theme and says that we must love *ḥesed*. Remember *ḥesed* from the first meditation? When used in a relationship between humans, it means love with the strong element of loyalty, such as that between a husband and wife who love each other and are faithful to each other. We saw that it was also the love between two friends, a loyal love. When we use it to speak of the human relationship with Yahweh, it again means love and loyalty.

To please our God, we must above all seek ḥesed. The prophets, even though they questioned the mechanics of some of the cultic rites, never advocated doing away with sacrifices and offerings, and they also never called for the abolishment of the cult. What we see in their message is a call for reformation or, even better, a rediscovery of a religion that is able to recall what God has done and how he has blessed and delivered his people from oppression. But this message also strikes to the heart of the community of the faithful and articulates what our answer should be, as a people that have known God's grace, to the less fortunate around us. You cannot read the Minor Prophets without wanting to go out and confront the exploitation, the abuses, the corruption, the existing oppression of the poor, the lack of morality, and the materialism of today's society.

If your heart is not touched by the pain of the powerless of today's world, the pain of those who are unable to go to bed with food in their stomach or a roof over their heads, without an opportunity to have a decent job, or without the same rights that other citizens have, or even to have access to medicine and medical care—if your heart is not touched, then you have no ḥesed.

If the churches of the Anglican Communion are unable to make this our first priority, then do not be surprised if prophets from God will rise up again to tell us:

> Therefore I have begun to strike you down, making you desolate because of your sins. You shall eat, but not be satisfied, and there shall be a gnawing hunger within you; you shall put away, but not save, and what you save, I will hand over to the sword. You shall sow, but not reap; you shall tread olives, but not anoint yourselves with oil; you shall tread grapes, but not drink wine. (6:13–15)

We must not be silent and we must not ignore the reality of what is going on in this planet of ours, where two percent of the people partake of ninety-eight percent of the goods and the other ninety-eight percent of the people have access to only two percent of the goods available in the planet. If I sound upset, it is mainly because I am one of the bishops of the ninety-eight percent that have access to only two percent. This issue is real for me.

Thirdly, Micah claims that what Yahweh requires from us is to walk humbly with our God. He wants us to walk carefully with a sense of circumspection. The New English Bible quotes the word "wisely" instead of "humbly." But the important word is not the adjective, but the verb, the word "walk." Micah is using "walk" to describe the whole orientation of what our life should be. "For all the peoples walk, each in the name of its god, but we will walk in the name of the LORD our God forever and ever" (4:5).

In Judaism, we are told by Limburg in his commentary that the word for ethics is *halacha*, which means "walking." In the book of Deuteronomy, the Lord makes the same requirement when he explains the essence of the law:

"So now, O Israel, what does the LORD your God require of you? Only to fear the LORD your God, to walk in all his ways, to love him, to serve the LORD your God with all your heart and with all your soul, and to keep the commandments of the LORD your God" (10:12–13).

This call to "walk" is very similar to what Jesus said, which was really not an invitation to believe but rather to walk or to follow him. It is step-by-step living with God and living for others, acting as advocates for the powerless and showing care for those who are hurting and are in need of help.

How could we move from talking justice to doing justice? From passing a resolution to be able to resolve the pain and suffering of the poor?

Is ḥesed or steadfast love for the poor our first resolve? Not just to give alms but to do something to transform their predicament into hope?

Are we willing to "walk" the walk wherever God calls us? To take our cross and follow Christ even to confront our societies if they are oppressive? Is the Anglican Communion an advocate of the powerless of this world? Are we willing to say and do like Jesus did when he said: "The Spirit of the Lord is upon me, because he has anointed me to bring good news to the poor. He has sent me to proclaim release to the captives and recovery of sight to the blind, to let the oppressed go free."

May Yahweh give us the strength to do it, but to do it with conviction and vigour. Amen.

Fifth Meditation: Habakkuk 2:6–20

I am sure that sometime in your lives you had an opportunity to surprise someone with your wit. I got to do it during my last flight. As you know, flying is a time when people are very nervous. Just before coming here, the weather was stormy back home and people were apprehensive of getting into a plane. One of the local businessmen of my city mentioned how good he felt knowing that a clergyperson was going to be on the plane. His thinking was that because I was a man of the cloth, nothing bad was going to happen. He was convinced that in case of trouble, I could always send a special prayer that was surely going to be immediately answered. He said to me, "You, being a bishop, surely have influence up in heaven." I answered him by saying, "Unfortunately, I only work for the sales department. Administration tends to run things their own way."

Habakkuk surely felt that way. He began his book with a complaint. Habakkuk is kind of unique because he doesn't confront Israel. Instead, he confronts God. This book is a conversation of the prophet with Yahweh. He wants to know why the people of God were being punished by a nation that was so unworthy and sinful. Why can't God do something to help his people? Why is God deaf to their cries for help? God answers Habakkuk, but with an answer that he doesn't like. How could God allow the Babylonians to punish Judah in such a ruthless way that will completely destroy his people?

In this book we see God's answers. First, God points out that those who destroy his people are going to be destroyed in the end. Second, as he says in 2:14: "But the earth will be filled with the knowledge of the glory of the LORD, as the waters cover the sea." Even if God is silent for a while, in the end Yahweh's mighty voice will be heard and his people will rejoice in the Lord, the God of our salvation.

Habakkuk is dated around the year 600 B.C., or a little earlier. That makes him probably a contemporary of the prophet Jeremiah. Of course, instead of carrying the message of God to the people like Jeremiah did, Habakkuk was involved exclusively in a conversation with the Almighty.

How many times have I felt like Habakkuk? Here I am working very hard telling the people of God's mercy and care for them, and the answer seems to be more pain and suffering. Maybe this time the little nations of the world, especially those countries in the Southern Hemisphere, are not being threatened by an invasion from the Babylonians and their powerful armies. Instead, the threat is more insidious and silent, but as effective in creating death and pain to a suffering people.

"Alas for you who heap up what is not your own! How long will you load yourselves with goods taken in pledge? You have plundered many nations, you get evil gain for your houses, setting your nest on high to be safe from the reach of harm!" You have devised shame for your houses by cutting off many peoples."

Today, we are going to be dealing with the burden of the world debt. We did it in Lambeth too. I hope that we could be a little more enthusiastic on this issue than the bishops in Lambeth. You may say that I am wrong for making such a statement, because the bishops gave an unanimous approval to the resolution dealing with the world debt. Well, you are right. The bishops did approve the resolutions by unanimity and quickly passed to the next issue at hand. The world debt issue was rapidly buried. I wish that they would have become emotional about the resolution and even rebelled at the content of it—that they would have screamed loudly and gone into caucuses to defeat or to improve the resolution. If that would have happened, maybe our provinces and dioceses today would have the world debt issue as number one on their agenda. Our Primates now would be dealing with committees and subcommittees of interested people trying to care for the pain and desperation that is taking place around the world and that is directly related to the world debt. Instead, other issues are occupying that place of honor in our agenda and discussions. The issue of preponderance for the nations of the Developing World, or Third World as others prefer to call us, is the issue of world debt because it creates affliction and hunger, and is instrumental in our oppression and underdevelopment.

We must continue to deal with the aggression and exploitation of the developed countries of the Northern Hemisphere, hoping to alleviate and remove this shameful economic violence that is inflicted on the developing nations of the south.

Yes, we passed resolutions, but we must be reminded of what the New Zealand Prayer Book says in one of its Daily Devotions prayers: "Lord God, when you give to us your servants any great matter to do, grant us also to know that it is not the beginning, but the continuing of it, until it is thoroughly finished which yields the true glory" (Monday, page 111).

We do have a great matter on hand and we had a good beginning. But now we must concentrate our efforts to make sure that we do not forget the distress of a great number of people in this planet. They came to us for refuge, and we must not turn our backs to them. We have to make sure that we finish what we have started.

It is important that we raise our voices when it is appropriate and also when it is not appropriate or welcomed. The world must hear the cry of the forsaken, and that voice can come only from us, because the weak of the world cannot speak loud enough to be heard over the deafness created by greed and complacency.

Politicians also must be reminded that there is a task at hand and that the Christian churches of the world will not cease to demand justice. We must reach the final solution to this oppression that the developed nations of the North have imposed upon the developing nations of the South.

At the beginning of this year I had the privilege to be invited to meet American President Bill Clinton during his visit to Tegucigalpa, the capital of Honduras. He was there to see for himself the vast and horrible destruction that Hurricane Mitch had caused in my country. For this meeting they selected forty persons from different backgrounds to be with the American president and the Honduran president. For a while, I thought that I was among the forty that were going to meet Moses. They were wise enough to choose me and, of course, the Roman Catholic Archbishop of Honduras, Monsignor Oscar Rodriguez. We were the only two persons selected from the religious sector. It was the Roman Archbishop that made the presentation about our needs and about our suffering. Of course, the issue of the world debt was first among his description of horrible things that had happened to us and that were hurting us. He asked for help and quoted also the various statements from the Vatican that speak clearly to the issue of the international debt.

What I found very enlightening was Clinton's statement in answer to the Archbishop. He thanked him and reminded him of the importance of constantly challenging the politicians on this issue. He was candid enough to share with us that many times even if politicians agree with you and want to do something to solve the matter, it is much easier for them to do it (and with less political danger), if the Pope or the Archbishop of Canterbury or a religious leader from a particular district that can affect votes be the one to encourage senators, representatives, deputies, or ministers of parliament to do the right thing.

With Jubilee 2000, the Christians of the world have begun a battle that will be remembered by future generations. My prayer is that we will be able to say, like Habakkuk in triumph, "Oh Lord, you came forth to save your people, to save your anointed" (3:13).

To those who oppose us I will also say, "I wait quietly for the day of calamity to come upon the people who attack us" (3:16).

We don't know the details of how everything will work out in the end. It is a mystery for me as it was a mystery for Habakkuk. But I am called to live by my faith, because "the righteous live by their faith" (2:4).

Maybe we cannot see God's power very clearly at all times, but it is our faith that will keep us going until our task is thoroughly finished, and then we will yield the true glory.

I am sure that there is much more than what we have done that could have been done. We in the debtor nations of the South spend all of our time trying to influence the creditor nations of the North. Have your deacons, priests, bishops, Archbishops, and Primates, and more important, have your laity done what they can do to influence their politicians and economists from the creditor nations to work to forgive or at least seriously alleviate the debt?

What can we do as individuals and also as representatives of our churches and provinces to assure that the issue of world debt takes a place of priority?

Is there an interrelation of justice issues between the priorities of the Developed World and the priorities of the Developing World? Can we reconcile these issues and work together for justice?

Are we able to face the world in faith, regardless of circumstances, and assure the people of the world that no matter how hard things get, God still cares for his people? Are we convinced that even if evil seems to reign, it will eventually be defeated by the righteous?

Sixth Mediation: Zephaniah 1:7–12

"Before him there was no king like him, who turned to the LORD with all his heart, with all his soul, and with all his might, according to all the Law of Moses; nor did any like him arise after him" (2 Kings 23:25).

These words from 2 Kings are in reference to King Josiah, the eight-year-old boy who assumed the throne after his father, the evil king Amon, was killed.

The changes that he was able to make led to a radical reformation that cleansed Judah from idolatry. Zephaniah was also a young man when he began to prophesy. He can be dated as a contemporary of Jeremiah and Habakkuk. He lived under good King Josiah and begun to prophesy under the evil kings Manasseh and Amon.

Before Zephaniah, seventy years had passed since Isaiah and Micah had been heard. The voice of the prophets was not being proclaimed in the land. Instead of that, under King Manasseh, both idol worship and child sacrifice had become a common practice in the land. The Bible tells us that he had built altars for star worshipers in the temples and even male prostitution had become common as part of their religious rituals (2 Kings 21).

It is in the twenty-first chapter of 2 Kings that we are told that "Manasseh had misled the people to do more evil than before. . . . He shed very much innocent blood until he had filled Jerusalem from one end to another, besides the sin that he caused Judah to sin so that they did what was evil in the sight of the LORD" (21:9, 16).

After Manasseh was killed, his son Amon continued to do evil in the sight of the Lord, as his father had done. Eventually we are told that the servants of Amon conspired against him and killed the king in his house.

Then came King Josiah, after his father was killed. The Bible tells us that he did what was right in the sight of the Lord; he did not turn aside to the right or to the left. He led a reform that changed the land and organised the first Passover that had been celebrated in many years.

Zephaniah spoke just before King Josiah's transforming changes that brought the people back to Yahweh. He spoke during the time of the long reign of the evil Manasseh, who ruled for more than fifty years, from 696 until 642 B.C. And he also lived under King Amon and all of his two years of evil doings.

Regardless of the evil governments of his day and the hopelessness of the situation at the time, the message that we hear from Zephaniah is for his people to change and to take action. He began with a tale of tremendous gloom, not being afraid to condemn the sins of his nation and assure the sinful nation that God was going to punish them. The coming judgement on Judah was inevitable unless a change of heart took place. Zephaniah also spoke of the "great day of the Lord" that was going to bring such distress to the people as never before and that was going to cleanse the planet from sin. Perhaps only a few could be safe, he suggested. Only people humble and lowly, the remnant of Israel, could be sheltered from disaster and pain if they turned to God.

The book of the prophet Zephaniah starts with dark clouds of gloom but ends with a rainbow of hope. God will indeed bless all the nations that are willing to call upon his name and serve him with one accord. How wonderful it is to know the end of the story and to look into the history of the world after things have happened. But how difficult it was for Zephaniah to challenge his people and his king. It took a lot of courage to remind them of their sins, to challenge his compatriots that were living by force, fraud, and wickedness. Something had to be done, he claimed, and must be done quickly; if not, death would come inside the gates, inside the quarters, and destruction would be within the wall.

There is one verse from Zephaniah that especially caught my attention. It was written around 600 B.C. about two thousand six hundred years ago. It is still true today, and sadly so prevalent in the minds of our churches and the behaviour of our societies that it could be scary. Says Yahweh: "At that time I will search Jerusalem with lamps, and I will punish the people who rest complacently on their dregs, those who say in their hearts, 'The LORD will not do good, nor will he do harm.'" (1:12).

I am sure that Zephaniah was convinced that God was going to take care of Kings Manasseh and Amon. No king was going to be stronger than Yahweh. But the words of verse 12 show the frustration that the prophet had with people that didn't give a damn. Those complacent people had given up on God and, after fifty evil years of King Manasseh and the reign of Amon, had already become used to things as they were. God for them was powerless.

It seems to me that after two thousand six hundred years, humans have not changed much. Complacency is still prevalent. How many times have I heard that things have been like this for a long time and no one is going to be able to change them?

How many people do we know that have given up on God acting and making a real difference in the problems of their lives and world?

Zephaniah reminds us that there is no room for complacency and apathy in our churches and in our lives. God will search all over for any one of us who rests in complacency—those who today are saying in their hearts, "The Lord will not do good, nor will he do harm."

I don't know if I should talk about my wife, who is definitely not a very complacent person. But I will talk about her anyhow. It was about eleven years ago that after seeing the plea of the abandoned, orphaned, and abused girls of Honduras she decided to do something about it. She started the home for girls "Our Little Roses" in the city of San Pedro Sula, Honduras. At the time, any girl with problems was sent to the women's penitentiary for care, where she ended up worse than she had begun. There were many homes for boys, but none exclusively for girls. After all, street boys could end up as juvenile delinquents and criminals. Girls, on the other hand, can be used for cheap labour or even worst, as sex workers. No one was interested in cutting the supply. But my wife Diana was convinced that God was calling her to do something about the female children. She had a vision that was going to make it possible for those girls to be what they wanted to be, according to their capacity and effort. Today, after a decade, several girls are now in the university, preparing themselves as professionals with an honest future and an opportunity for success. Some of these girls were begging or were being sexually abused less than a decade ago. Now their lives are radically changed because one woman decided that God's intention was to bless the girls that he had created and she was indeed willing to do good to them. She was also willing to challenge a society that had become complacent and had given up on them.

If today you are of the opinion that the Anglican Communion, with all of our provinces and churches and, more important, with all the millions that we claim as members, is unable to radically transform this planet and to be agents of change to improve our world, then you are wasting God's time by being here. Please leave, because I also believe that, if necessary, God will search Dundee with lamps and will punish the people who rest complacently, those who say in their hearts, "The Lord will not do good, nor will he do harm."

Can we make a difference for the Christians in Sudan? Yes, we can. The Archbishop of Canterbury was willing to take a chance to make it happen. There was no guarantee for success. If you look at the predicaments of prophet Jeremiah, you begin to realise that not everyone who speaks in God's name is rewarded. But what we must be really sure about is that God will not tolerate us sitting on our behinds and saying: "Why should we care? What can we do? The Lord will not do good, nor will he do harm."

Archbishop Oscar Romero of El Salvador was willing to speak to a people that had decided to destroy themselves in a bloody civil war. He spoke of peace while others cried for war. He spoke of forgiveness when others were demanding revenge. He asked for justice when injustice was the norm. He challenged the Christians of El Salvador and Central America—notice that I said Christians and not just the Catholics. He challenged us to make a difference in our midst, to speak up, to confront injustice, to be willing to take chances, to dream dreams of redemption. He saw hope where others were unable to see shame turned into praise among all the peoples of the earth. He assured us that we could do all of these things in the name of our common Lord Jesus Christ. Today, Christ can still make a difference in the lives of those who are suffering in this world—something that many of us seem to have forgotten.

We could see the same commitment in the lives of the African Archbishop Janani Luwum of Uganda and in the American Dr. Martin Luther King, Jr., who confronted the evil of racism. Both were murdered by the hand of injustice, hatred, and intolerance. The same evil force that throughout the ages is not willing to tolerate the message of God's prophets.

As Anglicans, we also have the example of the Church of Southern Africa and in particular of the people of South Africa, with their past and present

Archbishops Tutu and Ndungane. They were and are willing to make a difference. One of them against the burden of apartheid and the other one against the burden of the world debt.

Rigoberta Menchu in Guatemala, Archbishop Helder Camara in Brazil, our Episcopalian Rosa Cisneros of El Salvador, and many others were willing to face evil and injustice. Some were killed and others survived, but like Zephaniah they were not going to be idle or silent when facing injustice, regardless of the consequences.

Do you really think that it is possible for our Church to find the stronger unity it needs? Could there be a forgiveness of the international debt? Can we achieve peace in the world or an end to ethnic conflicts? Can we bring justice to the suffering people of this world? Can we do something that can make a difference for our sisters and brothers around the world who are discriminated and abused due to their sex, skin colour, religious belief, language, national origins, or sexual preferences?

If you think that nothing can be done, then you better think again. Because what we are doing here in Dundee at the eleventh Anglican Consultative Council is not only important and necessary for our Communion, but is also something that could make a difference in this world, because you can be assured that God really cares about his people. He empowers his Church to effect changes that can make a difference in order to achieve a more just and perfect world. Be assured that the Lord will indeed do good if we are willing to make it happen!

Seventh Meditation: Zechariah 7:8-14

The book of the prophet Zechariah talks about a new start. The people of God had come back from exile after the Persian Emperor Cyrus the Great took power. A decree was promulgated that allowed the Jews to return from exile in Babylon to the land where they had been uprooted. They also were given a license to rebuild the temple of the Lord at Jerusalem.

Zechariah probably returned from Babylon with his grandparents around 537 B.C. His father had died while he was still young, and the head of his clan had raised him. He probably grew up in the city with a family of faith. He witnessed when the foundation of the temple was laid and when its construction began. He probably felt the disenchantment of the people when the rebuilding of the temple went so slow and heard the locals that opposed the reconstruction. When he returned from exile with his family, they found a sad scene. The city that his parents left was now in ruins and deserted. There was nothing worthwhile or of value left. The fields that were once fertile and lush were now full of worthless desert brush. To make things worse, he found a region that was almost deserted. Almost no one lived there. Everything wonderful that his family had said about the land that they had left behind when they were forced into exile was now nothing more than a wishful dream that looked more like a nightmare

And so it went for twenty years; the temple stayed unfinished until Zechariah and Haggai were called by Yahweh to get his house completed. Their message warned the returning Jews that as long as the temple was unfinished, their God was not going to act in their time. If they wanted to continue to be called the people of God, they had to complete God's dwelling; that would restore their special relationship with the Almighty.

It took four years to finish the temple, and its completion was partly due to Zechariah's message. But there is something in Zechariah's message that makes him distinctive. He was not only interested in the construction of the building, even if that building was going to be the house of Yahweh. What was more important for him was the type of relationship that the people had with their God and their fellow humans. He reminded the people to not make the same mistakes from the past, to make sure that they were not repeated. After all, it was the disobedience of the people and their lack of morality and justice in the past that had brought their predicaments. They had a temple before, but the temple was worthless for protecting them, because they didn't have a true relationship with their God.

If they were going to begin anew, it was important that the people truly returned in obedience to Yahweh. "Return to me, says the LORD of hosts, and I will return to you, says the LORD of hosts" (1:3).

The verses from the minor prophet that we heard today referred to the type of life that God wants for the people that worship at the temple. Zechariah was convinced that all cultic rites were useless unless the people that practised them, regardless of how proper they performed the ceremonies, had lives that were transformed and were willing to live in justice and steadfast love with God and their fellow humans.

"Thus says the LORD of hosts: Render true judgements, show kindness and mercy to one another; do not oppress the widow, the orphan, the alien, or the poor; and do not devise evil in your hearts against one another" (7:9–10).

Zechariah recorded God's words as both advice and a warning. He condemns the hypocrisy of religious ceremonies like fasting. For him, those ceremonies were inconsequential compared to what God really demands from his people. True religion, for the prophet, requires from the people not only certain cultic obligations but also a change of heart that enables them to fulfil their moral obligations to society. The people, on the other hand, were failing to manifest their social responsibility with those in need among them.

That's why I like Zechariah, even if his writings are sometimes difficult to understand. Nevertheless, he has a clear message for his people, to this effect, that combines their cultic obligations with a complete commitment to social justice. And better still, he is not afraid to say it loud and clear.

The Book of James, in the New Testament, supports this idea even further when it demands from us to be doers of the word and not merely hearers. James insists that faith can only be active along with works, and faith is brought to completion by works.

Today in Latin America we see how there is a great appeal for a new type of preaching that only calls the people to repentance and to a close personal relationship with Jesus Christ as Saviour. You may ask, "Isn't that great?" Well, not necessarily. Because that same preaching is totally devoid of a commitment for justice and a steadfast love for human beings that are different from them. If you have a personal belief in Jesus Christ, that is enough. Nothing else is needed. That is why this type of religion is so attractive to dictators and oppressors and is so popular among the powerful classes that don't care to be challenged because of their social carelessness over the needy, who are so abundant in our societies.

Many are afraid when their religious beliefs do something more than just casually inform them that there are poor in the world and that there are many that are suffering. When you share with them what God is saying about the poor and suffering people, they begin to accuse you of being involved in politics. Well, we will continue reminding them, like Zechariah did, that the poor, the hungry, the disenfranchised, and those who are suffering are our sisters and brothers, those who Christ calls his own. They must be reminded that our Lord will not tolerate that we abandon them to their fate. If we want to be saved, if we want to make it to heaven, then we better start feeding them, clothing them, giving them water, healing and welcoming them, and also, when needed, visiting them in jail. But remember that to give the poor and hungry bread, you must start by giving them of your own bread. Then you can really find Jesus. Just raising your hand in an evangelistic crusade or coming forward to the altar, ignoring the poor that you pass along the way, is not enough to satisfy the Lord. If you say that, you probably skipped a few chapters of the Bible. Cultic requirements may be necessary, but they are not the fullness of what God wants for his people. I have a good friend that is a Roman Catholic priest with whom we have worked closely in social and political issues, trying to bring change to the existing social order of our area. He keeps blaming me of somehow being associated, as a Protestant bishop, with those fundamentalist churches that are growing so fast in Latin America. I found a way to make him stop. I told him that if he continued charging me of being allied with those fundamentalists, I was going to start charging him, because he is a Roman Catholic priest, of being part of the *Opus Dei*.

The other day he said something that I found so true. He was frustrated upon hearing the type of confession where an upper middle-class businessman repents of his lust for his pretty secretary, but at the same time feels no remorse for the mistreatment and abuse of the workers at his clothing factory and also to those who work at his own home. Somehow the type of sins that deals with sex are the ones that the church has impregnated in people's conscience, but the ones dealing with social injustice and the lack of practice of steadfast love in society have somehow failed to penetrate our innermost beings.

I have to say that I do agree with him. Anglicans have managed to do likewise. Now, do not get me wrong. I do not condone sexual sins, but I find them less destructive at times than the ones that exploit and dehumanise our societies. I find it very hard to recognise as a true Christian a judge that is willing to put the poor in jail for even minor infractions and at the same time look the other way in order to exonerate the rich and powerful, as well as the murderers and exploiters of our people. That is why a person like General Pinochet could not be brought to justice in Latin America. There are too many of our judges that are unable or unwilling to render true judgements.

We live in a society that looks down on those who show kindness and mercy to one another. Our economic laws strangle and oppress the widows and anyone that gets in the way of progress. In too many countries the orphans and abandoned boys and girls are hunted and killed like wild animals. In Latin America we are encouraged by all the foreign powers to take the necessary economic measures to have our economies take off. If we do so, it will surely mean prosperity for all. But the reality has been different. Prosperity was only for a few select that became richer, but the poor became poorer and more abundant. The neo-liberal system proposed by Milton Friedman has captivated many of our governments. But the cost of implementation is now fuelled by the suffering and pain of the poor classes. Every time that new demands come from the IMF, the World Bank, the Paris Club, or the U.S. Agency for International Development, what I call the Four Horsemen of the Apocalypse, our people end up with deprivation and a diminishing of the quality of life.

Be assured that God doesn't care if you were converted by Billy Graham himself; if through your words and actions you reject the alien in your land, then you have no right to call yourself a Christian.

When you practice racism and classism, you also exclude yourself from the people of God. Our God demands from us to not be like our ancestors. "Thus says the LORD of hosts: Return to me . . . and I will return to you."

I think that it is very important for us to be loyal, to keep that relationship with God that we can make true, through our relationship with everyone that God has placed along our way. The lesson from Colossians reminds us that if we are God's chosen, at once we must clothe ourselves with compassion, kindness, humility, meekness, and patience. We must bear with one another and forgive each other. Above all, we must clothe ourselves with love, which binds everything together in perfect harmony.

Florence Nightingale said that the "kingdom of heaven is within, indeed. But we must also create one without." God has chosen you and me to make a difference in this world. We must minister to each other, rescue each other, and heal each other. If we claim to be Christians, let's make sure that we don't get fined by God's police for impersonating one.

What are the challenges in our area that the churches of our provinces must face? Are we responding to the cries of the poor in our lands? Can there be church growth where our churches also proclaim a demand for social justice? How much involvement should the church have in the economic issues of our day that affect society?

Eighth Meditation: Amos

Recently I heard the story about a wealthy businessman who died suddenly. At the Pearly Gates he had to face St. Peter and ask to enter heaven. St. Peter looked through the list and couldn't find the man's name, so he told him that he couldn't let him in. The man asked him if there was any way that he could get into heaven. St. Peter felt sorry for this rich young man and said that maybe if he could think of something really good that he had done on earth, at least one true act of mercy, maybe God give him the OK and he could pass through the Pearly Gates.

The man desperately thought very hard, trying to remember at least one good thing that he had done. Finally, his face lit up and he said to St. Peter: "I just remembered that about this same time last year, I was coming back from one of my trips, and as I was leaving the first-class section of the Heathrow Express at Paddington Station, I was encountered at the outside door by a woman with a child that needed money for medicine. Beside her, there was this young student that had been mugged and needed money for the train, and at the same time there was this old lady that was asking money for food. I normally don't like to give money to beggars because as you know they would probably use it for drinking. But in this case, I dug inside my pocket, and even though I had bills of twenty and fifty pounds, I was at least moved by compassion and gave them a one-pound coin and told them to divide it among themselves. The man added, I know it is not much, but you cannot deny that it was a bona fide act of mercy and I should be allowed to get into heaven.

St. Peter said that he had to check with God and went into the Lord's palace to present his case. He went over the details with God of how the man had aided the woman with the child that needed the medicine, the distraught young man, and the hungry old woman that was asking for his help. He told God how he was at least moved to take a one-pound coin from his pocket and gave it to them and told them to share it among themselves.

God thought about it for a while and then he began to dig into his long robes searching into his multiple pockets. (As you know, God handles many currencies and has just added one more to his pocket for the Euros.) But nevertheless, he finally found his pound sterling pocket and took out a one-pound coin and told St. Peter: "Here is the coin that he gave. Give it back to him and tell him to go to hell."

Micah appeared in Israel coming from Judah in the south, all the way from Tekoa, where he was a shepherd. He appeared to let the people of Israel know that they were going to hell. Life was good in Israel at that time. There were no wars, the economy was flourishing, businesses were doing quite well, profits were up, and luxury was the name of the game. It was the right time to live in Israel.

Besides that, one thing that you could tell about the Israel of that time was that they were very religious and devoted people. They indeed had plenty of religion and also many places that they frequently visited for worship.

Then, in the midst of that splendid way of living, Amos, a prophet from Judah, appeared to tell the people that they were in a heap of trouble. He was the carrier of bad news. A kind of a party-pooper, challenging their materialistic way of life. To make things worse, he was even challenging their religious practices that they were so proud of. How could he dare tell them that Yahweh despised their festivals and took no delight in their solemn assemblies? Who was Amos to say that the Lord was not going to accept their offerings and even refused to listen to the wonderful hymns of praise from their new and revised hymnal?

It seems that Amos, though he came from a small town, was interested in the world around him and was also a powerful speaker. We can see that even though he was a shepherd, he was familiar with things besides sheep. The name Amos means "to load" or "to carry a load." And surely he carried a load that included many natural disasters, famine, drought, various plagues, and wars. He began to challenge their assurance of being the people of God by telling them that God was extremely upset with them. All throughout the book of Amos there is a cry for justice that can surely move your soul.

Amos challenged their exploitation and accused them of trampling the heads of the poor into the dust of the earth. He accused them of violating God's law, as for example, when he accused bill collectors that took not only money from the poor but also their garments. These were used as collateral even if the law didn't allowed the collectors to leave a person without clothes. The creditors used those same clothes as bedding to rest when they went to their holy shrines for worship, while the poor were left literally naked. Religion had become just social gatherings, and participation in their cultic rites had become an end in itself. It was a way to improve your social standing or your self-esteem. And now Amos was saying that God was not happy with their solemn gatherings and their elaborate feasts because the soul of it was gone. There was no longer any communion with Yahweh, and the only thing left was communion among those who had prospered in business.

Amos is very clear that it was not only what they did at worship in the holy places but also what they did the other six days of the week that was upsetting the Lord. There were many abuses taking place that he describes in detail. The farmers were being charged an exorbitant percentage for the rental of the land, and the wealthy were taking more than their fair share. To make things worse, if the poor went to court to complain of injustice, because of bribes from the rich and powerful, they were pushed aside at the gate. There was even fear of retribution if you dared to complain because it was an evil time, the Bible tells us. It sounds so familiar, so real. It seems that injustice in the world is like a videocassette that keeps rewinding itself and playing over and over again!

The poor and the powerless were as oppressed as they are today by an unfair economic system. Amos was not afraid to tell it like it is. His message also rings true for us today in a society that has not changed much. A few days ago I was telling you that Micah's writings could be the same writing, almost to the word, that a reformer or revolutionary could write in a liberal newspaper of Latin America. I can also tell you that today in Latin America any person that would dare to boldly speak the words of Amos would surely have a great chance of being arrested or tortured or would just "disappear," as in most of the "democratic" countries of Latin America.

I would like to quote for you not a revolutionary, but a person that represents the almighty empire of today's world. Madeleine Albright is the Secretary of State of the United States of America. During the Council of the Americas, celebrated last April in Washington, D.C., she described the dark clouds that hang over Latin American these days. Surprisingly, she was very naive in her description of the region and was willing to admit of the grave and unnecessary risk for the peace of the area if the process of globalisation continues going forward without taking a human face. She warned the delegates of instability and turmoil that were leading to the return of authoritarian rule, as in years past. We have seen this already at work in Venezuela, where citizens became so disgusted with the corruption and abuses of their "democratic" leaders that they have welcomed a strong ruler to take over.

She continued by saying, and I quote, "None of this needs to happen. But much of it may, unless we address the gaping inequality in our hemisphere between those who have and those who have not, between those with the access and skills to make it in the new world economy, or those denied that access. She further continued:

> Latin America and the Caribbean continue to have the world's most unequal distribution of income. The top twenty percent of Latin America's population currently accounts for a fourth of the region's income—more than in Africa or Asia—while the poorest thirty percent receive only eight percent of the income, a lower proportion than anywhere else, according to Inter-American Development Bank figures. One in every three people in Latin America must live on less than two dollars a day—a potential threat to economic stability and political free-

> dom. One-fourth of Latin American adults have had no education at all, and the majority have less than five years of schooling. Meanwhile, children from wealthy families are going to the best schools, and are the most likely to graduate from universities. The policies of free markets and open investment . . . are vulnerable to challenge if too many people feel shut out or left behind.

How could anyone in this world dare to tell the Christians in Latin America, and other places of the world where there is injustice, to be idle and resign ourselves to accept the existing order? If we really believe the Word of God and the message that it contains, then we must seek justice. We have no choice but to proclaim justice if we pretend to be faithful to Christ and the message that the prophets proclaimed before him and the apostles after him.

But let's not forget what the Bible means by justice. The Bible's idea of doing justice is a dynamic notion. Remember Micah 6:8? "What does the Lord require of you but to do justice, to love kindness and to walk humbly with your God."

The Western image of justice is a frigid blindfolded white woman holding a set of balances. She is just standing there, static and not moving a finger, to insure that the balance brings forth justice. But Amos presented a totally different idea to us: "Let justice roll down like waters, and righteousness like an ever-flowing stream" (5:24).

For Amos, justice is like the mighty waters that are willing to push everything aside like the waters that we saw in Honduras during Hurricane Mitch—so mighty and powerful that no one could stop them. Waters rushing and crushing, always in motion and creating lots of commotion. This torrent of waters always flowing is what should be the image of our Church when it confronts injustice. We must be willing to be ever-flowing, cleansing, surging, never giving up, and pushing with force to bring forth what God wants for his people. Doing justice is doing God's will in response to what God has done for us. We were rescued by God and now we are called to rescue others.

Amos is not giving us a suggestion. He really means for us to seek good and not evil, if we want to live. We must not be neutral when facing evil. It clearly says: "Hate evil and love good and establish justice in the gate. Maybe if you do that the Lord, God of hosts, will be gracious to you."

The church—I am referring to you and me—must continue proclaiming our prophetic voice, allowing the world to see into the eyes of mothers who have to watch their children die because of a lack of medicine and resources to obtain it. We must erase the existing apathy that has overtaken our materialistic neo-liberal societies that seem to believe that they have no responsibility with those less fortunate.

Yes, business has never been better in many developed countries of the North; there are no major military threats that can confront the mighty power of the northern nations. Trade routes are open for those who comply, and embargoes are imposed on those who dare to rebel. It is indeed the days of big profits. Luxury is definitely in, and the promises of the new millennium forecast even more riches—except that two percent of the people that share this planet have access to ninety-eight percent of the existing goods and ninety-eight percent of the people can manage to access only two percent of the existing goods. As the Americans taught me to say, "Hey, there is something wrong with this picture!"

If the Anglican Communion is willing to give bread to the hungry, we must start by giving of our own bread. To make justice a priority, we must be intentional about it. If not, even if we would be liturgically and theological correct, and have the most beautiful cathedrals of the world, and our choirs sing the most pleasant and delightful hymns and chants, a prophet will rise again from Tekoa, Judah, to repeat the words of the Lord: "I hate and despise your festivals and take no delight in your solemn assemblies. Take away the noise of your songs, I will not listen to the melody of your harps." During these past days I have shared with you the pain of the part of the world that usually takes a back seat in the Anglican Communion. We are also prophets from the South appearing in the North as party-poopers, saying that there is something wrong with the way society and the church behaves in the North. We saw our native people being forcefully baptised by Europeans, and in exchange for getting wet and receiving a cross, they had their land taken away from them. Thank you very much!

We abhor the industry of sex tourism that uses our children as instruments of pleasure and is advertised and promoted in the mighty civilised cities of the North through the most advanced technology.

Also in the past days, I challenged you to be compassionate with those who think different from you on the issue of sexuality. I want to challenge you again. The Jewish *midrash* suggests to us that the voice of God mutated into seven different voices. Jewish thought always endeavours to find a common ground with Jews who happen to hear the voice of God differently than another person heard it. I think that Anglicans have a rich history to do likewise without any group surrendering what they hold as truth.

To bring justice also means to respond to the plea of the southern nations on the issue of world debt. We must not rest until the shackles of bondage are removed from our starving people.

We must not say that things cannot change. Let's make sure that God doesn't have to get his lamp and come after us who are resting and complacent, saying that the Lord will not do good, nor will he do harm. As Joan of Arc said, "Act, and God will act."

Let's pray that we have not been wasting God's time in this beautiful part of the world. We have a job to do and that is to let justice roll down like waters and righteousness like an ever-flowing stream.

Dios los bendiga. May God bless you. Amen.

REPORTS

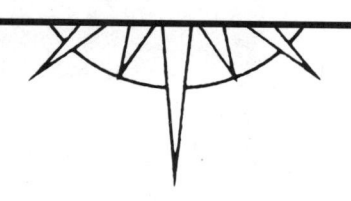

Report by the Secretary General

—THE REVEREND CANON JOHN L. PETERSON

September 16, 1999

Grace be unto you and peace from God our Creator and the Lord Jesus Christ.

It is again with a sense of great privilege and rejoicing that I stand before you as the Secretary General of the Anglican Communion to share with you, the members of the Anglican Consultative Council, where we are at this moment as a worldwide Communion of churches as scenes of our global family pass in front of your eyes. As we approach the next millennium, I hope to be able to share with you some of the hopes, dreams, and expectations that I have been privileged to experience in our Anglican family since our last council meeting in Panama. But with the joy there are some painful and hurtful moments that individuals and churches have experienced. Our days here in historic Scotland will be revealing and a blessing if we are open to the Holy Spirit's call to each of us.

As we are virtually on the eve of the millennium, I have learned one thing over the past few years, and that is that we are in God's time. God has a plan for us, both as individuals and as a Church. Life is not magic, but it is a mystery.

I want to begin my remarks today by remembering some of the faithful servants of Christ who now rest from their labours. I want to remember before God the extraordinary work and episcopate of Bishop Daniel Zindo of the Sudan, who died tragically in a car accident just after the Lambeth Conference last year. He will be remembered forever as a great servant and soldier of Jesus Christ in the midst of such hostility, pain, and difficulty. We are privileged to have at this ACC meeting Daniel's son, Manassah, who is a part of the communication team.

I want to remember the ministry of Bishop Alastair Haggart, one-time Primus of this church. Alastair was one of the early leaders in the Anglican Consultative Council, and he served the ACC with distinction as its vice chair. He firmly believed in the synodical form of government in the ACC. Through his vision and leadership he helped to mould the ACC into what it is today. In the early 1980s, Alastair participated in the Eloff Commission, and he went to South Africa in support of Desmond Tutu's struggle against the horrors of apartheid. Today his widow, Mary, has joined us and I would like all of us to recognize her.

When we met in Panama for ACC-10, Archbishop Brian Davis of New Zealand co-chaired the design group along with Diane Maybee. Little did we know at that time that soon Brian's body would be wracked with cancer. Brian loved the ACC. He truly believed in lay and clergy participation in the Church, and he always wanted the ACC to be a strong voice for the whole Church. I had the great privilege to represent you at a special celebration for Brian in Wellington Cathedral just before he, Maria, and Fiona moved to Napier. At that celebration there was a great outpouring of love by the whole church, giving thanks for Brian's visionary ministry.

And although there are many others that are now at rest from their labours, I particularly want you to remember one of the great lay leaders of this Church who has died, Berta Sengulane. Berta, age forty-three, was a sign of joy, peace, and faithfulness, a loving wife, a true proclaimer of God's goodness and love to her people and those beyond. Her life on this earth was tragically ended in a car accident while she was touring parts of Mozambique with guests from their companion diocese of London. The party had no way to call for emergency help. A sad reality in Mozambique is that there are no emergency services. She left behind her husband, one of the shining lights in the episcopal office of this Communion, and wonderful children, two of whom have serious medical problems, but who persevere knowing as Christians that life changes, but it does not end at death. How my heart aches for Bishop Dinis and his children, knowing the difficulty they must face without the love, care, and support of Berta. She helped establish congregations, and she was a leader of women's work. Now Bishop Dinis wants to open a health post near the scene of the tragic accident. If you have not done so already, might I urge you to read Berta's own story in Eileen Carey's book, *The Bishop and I*, which was written for the Spouses' Conference last year.

As your Secretary General, it has been my privilege to visit several provinces since we last met. I have seen firsthand the challenges faced by Anglicans in Nigeria. I have witnessed the incredible ministry of Bishop Josiah Idowu-Fearon and his wife, Comfort. The church in Kaduna is in desperate need of resources to make Christ's love known to the people in northern Nigeria. The bishop has pleaded with me to help him find the means to provide medical care in the scores of villages in the bush where the Kaduna Diocese is planting churches. Can you imagine a place where sixty percent of the children born will die before they reach three years of age? Can you imagine that one out of every eight mothers will die in childbirth? I travelled with members of the Compass Rose Society, the Society that so generously supports the ongoing ministry of the Anglican Communion Office. This visit has left an incredible impression upon me. It gets me on my knees in prayer, and it also inspires me to want to inspire others to help. Perhaps the greatest gift I have received since becoming your Secretary General is when Bishop Josiah wrote to me after the Compass Rose Society visit and said,

> A major thing has taken place as a result of your visit; the small congregation at Rafin Rimi where we intend setting up a health clinic has suddenly grown. The non-believers there were encouraged by your visit

to them that they have decided to become Christians. We had a congregation of 16 at the time of the visit, but we now have to cope with between 36–40 members! Would you please get the team back please? The visit has also affected this year's Mission positively, we were able to plant two more congregations in the same Kwassam area and the cry now is for education.

I look at the challenges I have seen in our Church in Japan. How over the years since World War II they have become a church of love and reconciliation. A church that demands of itself reconciliation and penitence. A church that has been able to say, "We're sorry." And at the same time having to face a certain amount of economic instability in a country that most people think is one of the most stable in the world.

Bishop Michael Mayes recently wrote a fascinating article in the Church of Ireland's *Gazette* on the Peace and Justice Network meeting in Seoul, Korea. I knew about the outstanding work that the Church in Korea is doing trying to build bridges between North and South, but I did not know about the serious problems of unemployment and homelessness faced by the people. Korea does not have a social security net, so if someone loses his job, that someone also loses his income, house, and as often as not, wife and children as well. The Anglican Church in Korea has twenty-five to thirty social mission centres in the poverty-stricken parts of Seoul. I am so glad that the Seoul Cathedral features so prominently in the current Anglican World.

When the Compass Rose Society had its meeting last year in the Diocese of Texas, where Claude Payne is bishop, we were introduced to a creative new evangelism programme that promotes a vision of the diocese as a missionary church. The programme is called the Community of Miraculous Expectation, and it confronts the different cultures in Texas today. Its purpose is the active transfiguration of lives instead of a static emphasis on culture and membership. As a result of transforming lives, the diocese is expecting to double its membership in six years. Already in two years they are well on their way.

To change cultures, there must be a miracle. One attribute of the Diocese of Texas is that it is an enormously diverse diocese. Think of the vast expanse of Texas—its big cities, its country settings, and all the people of Spanish-speaking origin in its cities. What this Community of Miraculous Expectation programme has already done is reduce racism, and it has enabled the Church to direct divisive issues in a most positive way. No longer is the diocese afraid to look at divisive issues; instead, when the parishes do, Bishop Payne says they become "miracle parishes." It is always exciting to be in the Diocese of Texas, because miracles are taking place there.

The Episcopal Church in the United States has taken new strides in support of the Inter-Anglican budget under Presiding Bishop Frank Griswold. Today the Episcopal Church is giving one hundred percent of its asking, along with all of the other Communion programmes which it supports. This is something for which all of us can rejoice and give thanks. As the Anglican Communion Office, we live within the province of the Church of England. The generosity of that province is so evident, and I would like to mention the important lead they took in the Lambeth Conference bursary fund.

Our Church is growing in leaps and bounds throughout the world. If you read church papers stating that is not the case, maybe you are reading the wrong papers. If you want to know what is happening, I encourage you, and I encourage others, to read *Anglican World,* to visit our web site, and to regularly check the Anglican Communion News Service.

The bishops of the Church gathered last year at the Lambeth Conference along with six hundred spouses. Lives have been changed, challenges have been set before us. The Lambeth Conference has asked the Anglican Consultative Council to consider many resolutions and requests. In your preparatory mailings you have received much of this material, and in the next few days many important presentations will be made to you and important decisions will have to be made by you.

At the Lambeth Conference *The Virginia Report* was welcomed and given to the Communion for reception. At this ACC meeting, Bishop Mark Dyer will help us to understand how we can shape our structures and Communion life in light of *The Virginia Report.* Certainly critical issues like the relationship of the Four Instruments of Unity, as well as ecumenical concerns, will be put into focus because of this important document.

The work of our small but dedicated Anglican Communion staff continues to be a blessing to the Church around the Communion. I speak for the staff in our thanksgiving to our president, the Archbishop of Canterbury; our chairman, Bishop Simon Chiwanga; and our vice chairman, Presiding Bishop John Paterson, all of whom have given much time and effort so that we can exercise our ministry on your behalf. The members of the staff are, of course, here at this ACC meeting and they are eager to hear from you about the work happening in your own province. We look to you, the ACC members, to be our primary source for information gathering and sharing in the Communion. The Anglican Communion is only a phone call, a fax, an e-mail, or a letter away. We want to hear from you on a regular basis. You are our major link with the provinces.

Canon David Hamid has led the Anglican Communion Ecumenical work for the last three years in the Anglican Communion Office. He has been tireless in his ecumenical efforts as the Communion participates in twelve different conversations, dialogues, and informal talks.

The Anglican Communion maintains dialogues with as broad a spectrum of Christian churches as any other denomination. Our official dialogues are with the Lutherans, Methodists, Oriental Orthodox, Orthodox, Reformed, and Roman Catholics. These dialogues have been running for several years.

The Lambeth Conference reaffirmed the importance of these and mandated new dialogues with Baptists, Pentecostals, new churches, and independent church groups. In the report of the director of Ecumenical Affairs you can read in more detail what has been happening in these relationships over the past three years.

The dialogues with Lutherans, internationally and regionally in North America, Europe, and Africa, are moving from theological agreement to changed relationships called full communion or visible unity. The dialogue with the Orthodox continues to make steady advance on some important matters of Trinitarian theology, which provides a solid base for future work on topics of ecclesiology and ministry. On the remarkable progress in the dialogue with the Roman Catholics, we shall be hearing more in the Anglican-Roman Catholic International Commission (ARCIC) presentation on Tuesday, September 21.

The new work, which will begin shortly, with the Baptists and potentially with the Pentecostals and new churches and independent Christian groups will break new ground for Anglicans and open some yet unexplored horizons in the search to reveal the unity of Christ's body. Work will resume in the near future with Methodists, Oriental Orthodox, and the Reformed churches. For the first time in the history of the Anglican Communion we will have a mechanism to begin to relate these dialogues one to another, and to give guidance in the context of the ever more complex ecumenical map. The mechanism to which I refer is the Inter-Anglican Standing Commission on Ecumenical Relations (IASCER).

The process is now under way to appoint members and plan for the first meeting of the IASCER. I am delighted that the Archbishop of Canterbury has invited Archbishop Drexel Gomez of the West Indies to chair this important commission. It is a sign that our ecumenical work is advancing and making progress when we come to the stage that such a commission is needed. It is important that we strive to be consistent in our conversations with different partners and that there be some mechanism at the level of the Communion to monitor the fruitful work happening at regional and provincial levels. It is important to encourage such progress to benefit the whole Communion. The commission will hopefully give leadership in identifying issues to be addressed by the Communion as a whole in its ecumenical work. It will help with the complex task of reception, beginning with facilitating the circulation of documents and ecumenical resources throughout the Communion.

If there is one challenge that is facing the whole ecumenical movement today, including the Anglican churches, I would highlight the challenge related to the question of reception. How do we receive the fruits of all these bilateral dialogues, not to mention the important multilateral dialogue of the Faith and Order movement, with which Anglicans have been associated since its inception? How do we effect change in our lives as churches, based upon the agreements we have reached? *The Virginia Report* is one clear example of how our ecumenical conversations are beginning to shape how we structure and order our life as a Communion of churches.

Those of us who are gathered here as leaders of the Communion from every part of the world have a key role to play in the ongoing process of reception of ecumenical agreements. Anglicanism, by its very nature, perhaps has some particular challenges in this regard. Our "dispersed authority" makes any decision-making process a little untidy. The various contexts in which we live means that receiving the fruits of a particular dialogue might seem odd. For instance, in the Pacific Islands, how does the Anglican-Orthodox dialogue achieve reception? Sometimes, sadly, there are nontheological factors that impede reception. Historical and cultural prejudices do get in the way! And of course, our people are facing other issues each day. Some are life-threatening: famine or war, for example. But nevertheless, Anglicans hear God's call to unity, and we must strive to be obedient to it, and I am grateful for your commitment to this call.

In March of this year, the Right Reverend James Ottley completed his contract as the Anglican Observer at the United Nations. His dedication to the mission of the observer's office was greatly appreciated by the staff, Advisory Council, and many supporters of this ministry throughout the Anglican Communion. The Advisory Council recommended that the Right Reverend Paul Moore, Jr., supervise the operation of the office until an interim observer was appointed. The day-to-day business of the office is handled by Yasmeen Granville, the office manager, and Richard Sabune from Rwanda, who also attends nongovernmental organization (NGO) briefings at the UN on a regular basis. The Reverend Canon Jeff Golliher continues in his environmental work for the observer's office.

This last week the office of the Anglican observer hosted a significant panel discussion entitled *Principalities, Powers and Peace.* You will be receiving recommendations from the Inter-Anglican Finance Committee and from the Joint Standing Committee on the future of the Anglican observer's office at the United Nations.

For some years the Anglican liturgists who meet as the International Anglican Liturgical Consultation (IALC) have been working their way through the great themes of baptism, Eucharist, and ministry, to which particular focus was given in the Lima document of the Faith and Order Commission of the World Council of Churches (WCC). Members of the IALC have tried to identify the cutting edge of an Anglican understanding of these themes and to suggest ways in which that understanding must shape and influence the liturgical texts and practice of the future as the process of liturgical renewal goes on.

A conference of Anglican liturgists met in Finland in 1997 under the auspices of the IALC and began work on the theology and practice of ministry and its implications for our rites of ordination, installation, appointment, and so forth. The purpose of the Finland conference was to set the agenda for a larger and fuller consultation in 1999 in Kottayam, India. A great deal of effort was expended by some members of the IALC to raise money which would enable Anglican liturgists in underfunded countries to attend the consultation and guarantee the fullest possible representation.

The Steering Committee of the IALC met in 1998 to put finishing touches on the agenda of the 1999 consultation. They distinguished between topics on which some consensus had been achieved, topics on which further work was needed, and topics that had not yet been addressed in-depth. Papers were solicited on these latter subjects, especially on episcopacy and authority, on the use of the terms *priest* and *presbyter,* on the role of bishops with nondiocesan constituencies, and on indelibility.

Unfortunately, the intentions of the Steering Committee to implement a challenging and productive program were in some measure frustrated by unforeseen events. About twelve of the sixty-three intending participants who had registered for the consultation (approximately one-fifth of the whole) were unable to attend because they did not receive or were denied visas to enter India. Almost of all these were members of provinces in underfunded countries. Their absence seriously affected the balance of participation, and the Steering Committee, in a preconsultation meeting, asked if the intention of the body to be as representative as possible had been seriously frustrated.

These problems were sharpened when the chair of the consultation received written notice that foreigners were forbidden to attend the consultation as planned. The Steering Committee recommended to those present that the consultation as such be abandoned and that those present meet informally in a hotel near the intended site of the event. They agreed.

In spite of these problems, the members present attacked their subject with vigour. Meeting in three groups, they addressed the theology of ordination as it relates to liturgical acts, the structure of ordination and related rites, and the relationship of the processes of discernment of vocation and ministerial formation for ordination rites. The groups reported regularly to plenary sessions, and the whole body agreed on a process by which their preliminary reports would be edited, circulated for comment and amended, and presented in documentary form to a full consultation, which was deferred until August 2001, when it will meet in California in the United States.

It would be premature to anticipate the completion of work that is still very much in progress, but it is possible to report that the meeting approached the subject of ordination in the Church from the point of view of a baptismal ecclesiology in which the people of God are engaged in ministry and in which specific orders of ministry find their place. Areas of consensus and areas of disagreement will be addressed within this framework.

In accordance with IALC guidelines, the chair of the Steering Committee, Ronald Dowling, whose term of office would have been completed if a full consultation had been held, will remain in office until the deferred consultation in 2001. Paul Gibson assists the Steering Committee as coordinator for liturgy for the Anglican Consultative Council. Recently, the Joint Standing Committee of the Primates and the ACC renewed Paul Gibson's contract until 2001, when the liturgical consultation will meet in San Francisco.

When I visited Brazil two years ago, I saw firsthand the impact that the Decade of Evangelism has had on the Brazilian Church under the leadership of its primate, Dom Glauco Soares de Lima. In Brazil I found the dioceses engaged in forming a cohesive and integrated ministry, where all are encouraged to participate and where the bishop, clergy, and people walk together in proclamation and service. So many of the great global challenges to human life and dignity are found in Brazil today: globalisation of the marketplace, migration of peoples to the cities, increased marginalisation of the poor, and threats to the delicate ecosystem.

The Church in Brazil continues to take bold and creative steps to address these challenges. Each parish of the Church is encouraged to explore new ways of engaging in ministry and mission that address the realities of the sociocultural context, be it supporting landless farmers or working with street children. Archbishop Glauco has continually stressed that the strength of his church is the diversity of gifts and insights: evangelicals, Anglo-Catholics, charismatics, and supporters of liberation theology. All have a place and all share in a fundamental unity, because the Church is clear about its role: the calling of the people of God to worship, nurturing community, and engaging in outreach, mission, and evangelism.

A mainstay in the life of the Anglican Communion Office in London is the work done by Marjorie Murphy. I believe I would not be too inaccurate if I were to say that Marjorie is one of the most "Anglicanized non-Anglicans" within the geographical boundaries of the Anglican Communion. I know all of us appreciate the wonderful job Marjorie is doing as the director of the Secretariat here at ACC-11.

Since January 1998 the portfolio of mission and evangelism has been carried by the Secretary General with the capable support of Marjorie, who has been coordinating mission and evangelism affairs for the Communion. The work of the department has included responding to everyday inquiries, maintaining data of companion relationships throughout the Communion (including resource material for the Decade of Evangelism and a list of provincial evangelism and mission coordinators), extensive preparation for the Lambeth Conference, the coordination of the Anglican Communion Mission Commission (MISSIO), and the gathering of information on the progress of the Decade of Evangelism throughout the provinces of the Communion. An effort has been made to be kept informed of developments in mission throughout the Communion.

MISSIO has met twice since ACC-10, in Recife, Brazil, in September 1997, and in Harare, Zimbabwe, in April 1999, with arrangements made by the Anglican Communion Office. Two reports have been made, first the interim report, entitled "Sing a New Song," for the Lambeth Conference, and second MISSIO's final report, "Anglicans in Mission: A Transforming Journey," with an executive report for ACC-11. Plans are being made for the reports to be published and distributed in book form.

Because the MISSIO meeting in Harare was the last meeting of this term of MISSIO, a chairs' advisory group has been formed to operate until new members of the Inter-Anglican Standing Commission on Mission are appointed.

A questionnaire survey on the Decade of Evangelism was sent to the provinces and to some dioceses around the Communion. This survey explored the strengths and weaknesses of the Decade of Evangelism, the lessons learned, and the future direction as we look forward to the new millennium. The signs of "shifting the Church from a maintenance mode to a mission orientation" are evident. The data gathered has been compiled and summarised in the MISSIO report. The MISSIO report and recommendations will be presented to ACC-11 on Monday, September 20.

One often incredibly difficult task—and one that receives not much glory—is that of the work of the treasurer. Besides his professional skill, Mike Nunn also brings to his office his own personal Christian testimony as well as a sense of humour. I am grateful for his exactitude and the attention which he and his staff give to detail. Mike makes sure that every single pence that is received is properly used for the mission of the Anglican Communion.

During the last three years, the major challenge has been to manage the financial administration of the Lambeth Conference. We were very grateful to have the assistance of Canon John Rye, of the Anglican Church of Canada, who joined the Secretariat for three months during 1998 to administer the distribution of the Lambeth Conference fund. The generous response to the Lambeth Conference Fund Appeal, which made it possible to provide help with conference attendance costs to all those who needed it, was a source of great satisfaction. Because of this fund, the costs of the conference were completely covered by the income provided.

Of utmost importance to our life as a Communion is our communication programme. Jim Rosenthal brings to communication his personal devotion and love for the Anglican tradition, as well as his excitement and care when he can share our good news with our fellow Anglicans and others. The opportunities abound, but the limitations that the communication programme faces are great. So much is accomplished in this realm with so few resources.

This work is very humbling at times. Jim recently received the following extraordinary letter.

I always gladly and gratefully receive your magazine. The spirit is willing, but the pockets are weak (confer. Mat. 26:41). Our Diocese is located in the Western region of Uganda which is ravaged by the civil war, which destabilise our Christians. So we fail to get money of even buying essential commodities of our families, but the Lord has mercifully sustained us.

Let me hope that you will continue to send the magazine to me, and I promise that by God's Grace, we shall stabilise and contribute towards the continual publication of our precious, impressive, informative and educative magazine.

May Our Good Lord richly bless your efforts.

When it comes to communication, the last couple of years have been milestones in many ways. *Anglican World,* through the generosity of the Compass Rose Society, has taken a new lease on life. Thanks to the good advice of Mandy Murphy, formerly a magazine coordinator from New York, fresh ideas have been shared with the editor and now *Anglican World* offers feature sections in each issue. So far we have had successful pieces on icons and stained glass that featured works from parishes around the Communion. Local people are very proud that they are in *Anglican World.* The current issue has a refreshing look at the new Christianisation of the St. Nicholas custom, and the last issue of 1999 will focus on Jesus Christ 2000. The comments we continuously receive are very supportive, and yet so few of the 70,000,000 Anglicans actually see the magazine. *Anglican World* now increasingly puts us in touch with the real folk at the parish level. It also addresses timely and critical issues through the family network section, a foundational part of the magazine.

Another wonderful experience over the last few months has been a children's page to celebrate St. Nicholas. Hundreds of drawings have come in, and they are on display for you to see how beautiful they are. Yes, through this competition we have reached another level of communication with the local congregations, which must be our goal. The people whom we have never really reached before are now being reached. This is something I want to hold up as a sign of the good work that has been done. Maybe we can maintain these links and expand our relationships to reach not only the children, but also young adults and especially the neglected elderly.

The accomplishments in telecommunications at the Lambeth Conference, under the direction of the Reverend Dr. Joan Butler Ford and volunteer staff, were phenomenal. The cooperation of these two units meant that people at home, those who were able to retrieve information by e-mail and the World Wide Web, were informed instantaneously of what was happening at Lambeth. The communication department's role was to serve our constituency, and they did that with great vigour, enthusiasm, and expertise. For this we are grateful. Dr. Ford has now retired, and due to financial limitations, she has not been replaced. However, the important programme that she put in place is being continued by the communication staff and in particular Chris Took from Ireland, who is helping to maintain our web site. Chris's part-time work is being sponsored by Trinity Church, Wall Street. We hope to have an intern from Africa in early 2000.

We were very fortunate to welcome the Reverend Canon Raphael Hess, the newly appointed communication officer to the Archbishop of Cape Town, to the communication department for a short internship programme. The experience proved to be helpful as Canon Hess assumed his new ministry. This is an example of how our work in the communication department can be shared with the different provinces in the Communion that need the expertise and training.

I am continually grateful for the ministry of Deirdre Martin, who has now been at the Anglican Communion Office for more than twenty-three years. Her role is ever changing, but one to which she adjusts with a great sense of alacrity and goodwill. There were additional staff members brought onboard for the Lambeth Conference, but the core staff remains small and dedicated. I want to extend my special thanks to Frances, Graeme, Rosemary, Barbara, Veronica, Helen, Christine, and Ian, and also to Canon Geoffrey Cates, who, although retired from active parochial ministry years ago, still takes the train from Ipswich once a week and volunteers and helps us with the Communion archive work. Canterbury Cathedral chorister Jon Williams works on a commission basis as the advertising person for Anglican World.

One of the comments I heard most in Jerusalem following the 1988 Lambeth Conference had to do with travel for the 1988 conference. Little did I know then that I would have something to do with the Lambeth Conference ten years later. But when that became a reality I knew I wanted to do something about travel. If people can travel to meetings without hassles, if there is always someone at the end of the telephone line who understands your problem and who cares about you, travel will go much better. As a result, a travel office was set up in the Anglican Communion Office (ACO) in 1997 and staffed by Ann Quirke. It has been a marvellous success story. However, we could not do it on our own.

The office was set up with the help of Menno Travel Service (MTS) in New Jersey. With their help, Galileo Focalpoint, a globally recognised system of airline booking, was installed. Because of United Kingdom laws, ticketing facilities are not available to the ACO, so we rely on MTS to print most of our international tickets for us. For our local tickets, we also work closely with Voyageur Travel, Covent Garden. But regardless if MTS or Voyageur prints the tickets, the bookings are done by Ann in the ACO office.

In view of the ever-changing face of technology and to make the ACO travel office more cost-efficient, MTS is planning to install a programme that will allow access to airline bookings via the Internet. It is expected that this will be up and running soon after ACC-11. Shortly it is hoped that some information regarding the travel office will be available on the Anglican Communion web page.

Ann Quirke is here in Dundee; if you have any travel problems, see her. She has been known to perform miracles.

I come to this ACC meeting with mixed emotions. I come with a wish list—not my own wishes, but the wishes of those who write, telephone, fax, and e-mail me day by day, week by week, month by month, year after year. Some of that communication has come from people in this room. I am grateful for it, but I often wish that we as a Communion could respond in a more fulfilling way, and most of all, in a more practical way. The challenge is before us. The challenge is to you as the ACC, not just to me as the Secretary General. As we seek to implement the programme that the ACC puts before the Communion, I am increasingly aware of the importance that the ACC brings to the Anglican forum of discussion. Here in the ACC you are the representative voice of the whole Church. We represent all orders of ministry, bishops, priests, deacons, and laity. Many of you are leaders by your own right in your own provinces. I know the challenges and demands on you are enormous, but please know how much we count on your participation in the worldwide Church concerning the work of the Communion. You are the ambassadors, the apostles of our communal message. Your apostolate is to share the good news we have as a family, as a Christian family dispersed in 38 provinces in more than 160 countries.

It is with a special sense of thanksgiving and joy that we welcomed into this ACC meeting members from our two newest provinces, the Church of the Central America Region and Hong Kong. I had the privilege of attending both of their inauguration services when they became provinces. It is undoubtedly one of the greatest gifts that we now have a strong voice from the people of Hong Kong and the people of Latin America in the work of the Communion. We specially welcome Ms. Fung Yi Wong from Hong Kong and Mr. Luis R. Vallé from the Central American Region.

The issue of *Anglican World* you have today shows some exciting pictures of visitors to the Bethlehem Peace Museum as part of the Bethlehem 2000 celebrations in preparation for the millennium. Because of resolutions passed at ACC-10 and at the Joint Standing Committee meetings, Anglicans are a part of the Bethlehem 2000 project. This project is in the capable hands of Compass Rose Society members, the Reverend Hamilton Fuller from the Diocese of Southwest Virginia and Mrs. Barbara Payne of Houston, Texas. Our participation in the Bethlehem 2000 project gives us an opportunity for rejoicing and a sense of pride in what we are doing. The basic task assigned through the ACC and the Anglican Communion has been to secure a crib museum that is becoming a reality. Already over eighty donations have been received from all over the world. We have received everything from a beautiful Chaucer crib set to peasant crib figures from Taiwan and Japan. Might our gift to Bethlehem always remind us of the gift that Bethlehem gave to the world. Our participation is not only a celebration of the millennium, but also an affirmation of the faithful ministry and witness of our brothers and sisters in the Diocese of Jerusalem.

This morning I want to make it perfectly clear, as I hope you can see from the reports which I have shared with you, that the purpose of our office is to be a servant, a servant to the ongoing work of all Four Instruments of Unity. All of us in the Secretariat prayerfully see our role in this way. When one thinks of servants in the Anglican Communion Office, there is one person whom I have not yet named, namely Joan Christey. For twenty years Joan served the office as a servant of the servants. When anyone from around the Communion would call the office, Joan would make him or her feel welcome. Earlier this year Joan experienced a neurological disorder and she had to resign. When Joan resigned, her concern was not about herself, but about "letting the Anglican Communion down." We give thanks for Joan's faithfulness.

Let us think of a verse we all know well—John 8:32: "And you shall know the truth, and the truth shall make you free."

We all know that the Truth is Christ, none other. We all are warned in Scripture not to make idols of anything whatsoever, and yet we bring so much baggage with us. In one of the baptismal rites it asks, "Do you turn to Christ?" And the answer is, "I do." But do we? Do we allow Christ to permeate every aspect of our work? Do we listen to his words? Do we believe in his abiding presence with us to this day? Do we truly celebrate his gift to us of himself in the Eucharist? Do we really come face to face with him in a living, lively way in this day and age? Do we ask in our hearts and our minds "What would Jesus do?" in those areas that confront us and challenge us as we become a Community of Miraculous Expectation.

The millennium celebrations allow us to rethink this relationship with the Prince of Peace. It allows us time and space to come to grips with whom we are and whose name we bear. May Christ give us the strength to be his hands, his feet, his eyes, and his ears in a world that is aching so much, in a world that also deserves to share in his good news. Why does the world deserve it? Because the world is God's and God created it and loved it. God loved the world enough to love, transform, and redeem it by sending Jesus Christ. I ask you to loose the bonds of those who are often hindered in their work by lack of facility or resources. Let us go into the new millennium with a new start, a new hope, a new beginning, and a new challenge. Let us be faithful to Christ who is the same yesterday, today, and forever.

Communications: Summary of Activities—Post Panama ACC-10 through Pre-Scotland ACC-11

—The Reverend Canon James M. Rosenthal, director

Main Accomplishments

- Publication of ACC-10 report. Huge savings through generosity of Morehouse Publishing, Harrisburg, Pennsylvania, United States, with low-cost editing by staff
- *Anglican World*
- Anglican Communion News Service
- Publication of *The Essential Guide to the Anglican Communion*
- Photo library
- Other publication: *A New Spirit*
- Drafting and research writing
- Information services

Visits

with Archbishop Carey
- Uganda, Southern Cone, Rome (papal visit)

with Canon Peterson
- Brazil, Costa Rica (new province), Hong Kong (new province)
- Scotland (Pre-ACC)

with Compass Rose Society
- Nigeria and Northern Ireland

with General
- New York (Pre-Lambeth Conference) and Dublin
- Jerusalem (St. George's College Board)
- Jacksonville, Florida, United States (St. George's College Board)
- Washington, D.C., United States (Enthronement of Bishop Griswold)
- Harare (World Council of Churches)
- Canterbury (1,400th Augustine Feast)

Lambeth Conference

- Two-year preparation
- Director of communications during event
- Managed over sixty volunteers (self-paying)
- Negotiated report, again at great savings through Morehouse Publishing, Harrisburg, Pennsylvania, United States
- Managed all publications: *Lambeth Praise,* and so forth

Thanks

- Nicola Currie (left post after ten years)
- Veronica Elks, secretary
- Dominic Brant (Lambeth Conference staff)
- Trinity Church Grants Programme, United States, Father James Callaway, director
- The Reverend W. Clement Lee, Episcopal Church Center, United States

Awards

- *Anglican World,* Anglican Communion News Service, Family Network Newsletter
- Posters and pamphlets-all won Polly Bond awards for excellence in religious publications (USA Episcopal Communicators).

Soli Deo Gloria

Ecumenical Affairs Report

—The Reverend Canon David Hamid, director
—Mrs. Christine Codner, programme assistant

Introduction

Ecumenical engagement and work occurs at every level of the Church's life. However, the constitution of the Anglican Consultative Council mentions three specific ecumenical tasks that pertain to this central international instrument of the Communion:

- To keep before national and regional Churches the importance of the fullest possible Anglican collaboration with other Christian Churches.

- To encourage and guide Anglican participation in the Ecumenical Movement and the ecumenical organisations; to co-operate with the World Council of Churches and the world confessional bodies on behalf of the Anglican Communion; and to make arrangements for the conduct of pan-Anglican conversations with the Roman Catholic Church, the Orthodox Churches and other Churches.

- To advise on matters arising out of national or regional church union negotiations or conversations and on subsequent relations with united Churches.

It is clear, then, that the official international dialogues fall under the responsibilities of the ACC. Consequently, the Ecumenical Affairs staff at the Anglican Communion Office is responsible for the care, nurture, support, logistical details, and follow-up related to these conversations. A close working relationship is maintained with the Archbishop of Canterbury's advisor for Ecumenical Affairs, Canon Richard Marsh, recognising the particular ecumenical role inherent in the office and ministry of the Archbishop.

In so many ways, what Anglicans learn from our ecumenical dialogues with other Christians touches upon our very life as a Communion. Ecumenical dialogue and commitment are not optional extras. As *The Virginia Report* states in its final paragraph,

> By virtue of our baptism we have in a communion in the Holy Trinity and therefore with the universal Church. The long history of ecumenical involvement, both locally and internationally, has shown us that Anglican discernment and decision-making must take account of the insights into truth and the Spirit-led wisdom of our ecumenical partners.

The Lambeth Conference 1998

The preparatory document for Section IV (Called to be One) was completed at the St. Augustine's Seminar in April 1997. This paper first of all invited the bishops to explore major themes facing Anglicans in their ecumenical work, such as the nature of visible unity and the challenge of consistency and coherency in dialogues. Then, systematically, the existing dialogues and relationships in which Anglicans find themselves, internationally, locally, and around the world, were examined one by one. A third section of the paper broke new ground for Anglicans, encouraging the exploration of relationships with new churches and independent Christian groups, including the Pentecostal churches. The style of the paper was open-ended, like a work sheet, pointing to issues raised in the existing documentation (such as bilateral and multilateral dialogue reports), as well as the reflections distilled in *The Agros Report*, which was prepared by the Ecumenical Advisory Group of the Communion as a resource for the Lambeth Conference.

The Archbishop of Canterbury invited thirty-six ecumenical participants to the conference. They were introduced at a service of Vespers, which celebrated ecumenical life and achievement. The homily at this service was delivered by Cardinal Edward Cassidy, the president of the Pontifical Council for Promoting Christian Unity. It challenged Anglicans to examine our own internal unity within the Communion, as well as to take seriously the communion, *koinonia*, we share with other Christians. The Niceno-Constantinopolitan Creed was led by Metropolitan John of Pergamon, who represented the ecumenical patriarch at the conference.

A substantial report of the work in the section, as well as twenty-five resolutions, provides a useful snapshot of the state of ecumenical relations involving Anglicans around the world, as well as lays down some useful markers for work in coming years.

Inter-Anglican Standing Committee on Ecumenical Relations

One of the most significant resolutions at the Lambeth Conference was IV.3 on Inter-Anglican Standing Commission on Ecumenical Relations (IASCER). The Ecumenical Advisory Group (EAG), which met in Cyprus in 1996, first suggested such a body, and the suggestion was subsequently affirmed by the ACC-10 meeting in Panama in 1997. The Lambeth Conference resolution includes some clear purposes for the Standing Committee and some helpful suggestions as to membership.

A planning group met in New York in January 1999 to work on a detailed proposal that took into account the thinking from the EAG and the Lambeth Conference discussion. The members of the IASCER are now in the process of being named. Because one of the major tasks will be reviewing and ensuring consistency in ecumenical conversations, the majority of members will come from the official ecumenical dialogues. Other focus areas of work for the commission include enabling reception and response processes throughout the Communion and addressing theological issues that arise in the dialogues, such as "bearable anomalies" and the understanding of "visible unity/full communion." Therefore, membership will include those with regional experience, theological expertise and adult education, and communication skills, along with a link to the Inter-Anglican Doctrinal Commission. The Archbishop of Canterbury has appointed Archbishop Drexel Gomez (CPWI) to be the chairman of the IASCER. The first meeting of the commission will be in 2000.

Relations with Other Communions and Churches

Anglican-Baptist Relations

The Lambeth Conference of 1988 called for dialogue between the Anglican Communion and the Baptist World Alliance (BWA). This was never implemented, principally due to a lack of resources. However, on September 30, 1997, an informal meeting was held, sponsored by the Church of England, to review the Church of England-Baptist relationship. At that time, some thought was given to the possibilities for an international dialogue. The Anglicans present for this discussion were Dr. Mary Tanner, The Reverend Dr. Flora Winfield (local unity secretary, CCU, Church of England), and Canon David Hamid. Baptists present were The Reverend Tony Cupitt (director of evangelism and education, BWA), The Reverend Keith Jones (deputy general secretary, Baptist Union of Great Britain), and The Reverend Dr. Chris Ellis (moderator of the Doctrine and Worship Committee, Baptist Union of Great Britain). In looking toward an international dialogue, an interesting model was proposed which would creatively use a minimum of resources. The 1998 Lambeth Conference in resolution IV.15 gave added impetus to move forward. Discussions with the BWA were held in May 1999, and a firm proposal for an Anglican-Baptist International Forum was drafted (appendix 1).

The BWA is a fellowship of 192 Baptist unions and conventions comprising a membership of more than 42 million baptised believers and a community of more than 100 million Baptists worldwide.

Anglican-Lutheran Relations

Lutheran World Federation (LWF)

Close working relationships exist between the LWF and the Anglican Communion. Frequent staff consultations and exchange of observers at major meetings of each Communion are now commonplace. The Anglican Communion was represented at the ninth assembly of the LWF in Hong Kong, July 8 to 16, 1997, by Bishop David Tustin (Grimsby), The Reverend Dr. Eric Chong (Hong Kong), and Canon David Hamid. This meeting marked fifty years of the LWF. Bishop Christian Krause of the Evangelical

Lutheran Church of Brunswick was elected president, replacing Dr. Gottfried Brakemeier of Brazil. Bishop Krause spoke of his priorities during his period of office to include the promotion of the role of women in the Church, to work toward a eucharistic communion with Catholics, and to forge stronger links with the Reformed.

The ecclesiological identity of the LWF has evolved over the past fifty years. In 1947 there was no widespread "altar fellowship" among the member churches. Today, increasingly, bishops, pastors, and members are not seen as just members, pastors, and bishops of local churches, but of the entire Communion. The ordination of women is still in a process of reception, despite LWF reaffirmation of its commitment to women's ordination (seventy percent of member churches ordain women). There have been some instances of trying to influence member churches through manipulation of financial and personnel resources. At Hong Kong, one of the liveliest debates was on the question of human rights in China.

At its assembly the LWF reaffirmed its commitment to full communion with churches of the Anglican Communion and welcomed the work of the Anglican-Lutheran International Commission. Significant for the wider ecumenical movement is the Joint (Roman Catholic-Lutheran) Declaration on the Doctrine of Justification. The LWF urged member churches to study the agreement and submit responses to the LWF Council by the middle of 1998. Positive responses were received from a large majority of member churches. Following some negotiation with the Roman Catholic Church regarding its response, these two Communions are set to sign the Joint Declaration on October 31, 1999, in Augsburg, thus achieving a significant breakthrough on an issue which has divided these churches for centuries.

Anglican-Lutheran International Working Group

The Lambeth Conference in resolution IV.16 recommended consultation with the LWF about the continuation of the work of Anglican-Lutheran dialogue. The consultation has taken place, and an Anglican-Lutheran International Working Group has been formed. It consists of four members plus one staff member and one consultant from each Communion. This group will continue to work at outstanding issues, including differences in terminology and issues connected with the threefold ministry.

Pan-African Anglican Lutheran Dialogue

Since 1992 several consultations have been held in Africa (in Harare in 1992 and 1994, and in Johannesburg in 1993 and 1997). The 1997 meeting in Johannesburg completed a report that spelled out the goal of the continental dialogue, elements toward a declaration of mutual recognition, commitments to further steps toward full communion, and proposals for immediate joint actions (appendix 2).

> ### Anglican-Lutheran International Working Group
>
> *Anglicans*
>
> Right Reverend David Tustin (England) (co-chairman)
> Right Reverend Sebastian Bakare (Zimbabwe)
> Reverend Canon Alyson Barnett-Cowan (Canada)
> Right Reverend Orlando de Oliveira (Brazil)
> Reverend Dr. Bill Peterson (United States) (consultant)
> Reverend Canon David Hamid (co-secretary)
>
> *Lutherans*
>
> Bishop Ambrose Moyo (Zimbabwe) (co-chairman)
> Professor Kirsten Busch-Nielsen (Denmark)
> Reverend Dr. Hartmann Hˆvelmann (Germany)
> Professor Michael Root (United States)
> Professor Ola Tjørhom (France/Norway) (consultant)
> Reverend Sven Oppegaard (co-secretary)

An interim committee was named to carry forward the preparatory work toward the formation of a pan-African committee. This interim committee met in Harare in March 1999 and prepared a report (appendix 3).

Specific to the Anglican-Lutheran dialogue in Africa is its emphasis on the pastoral and diaconal dimensions to the Church's life. *The Hanover Report* (The Diaconate as Ecumenical Opportunity) is seen to be particularly important in this context. This regional dialogue faces some challenges. In some areas of the continent, further education is required in the churches about the desirability of relations with Anglicans or Lutherans, as the case may be. In some parts, the presence of either the Anglican Church (e.g., in Ethiopia) or the Lutheran Church (e.g., in Kenya) is minimal. Also, it will be important to link this initiative to the international agreements in *The Niagara Report* and to other developments in Anglican-Lutheran relations around the world.

Anglican-Lutheran Developments in Other Regions

Although not directly involved in the proposals in Canada, the United States, and Europe, the Anglican Communion Office has been communicating regularly with the ecumenical officers of the relevant provinces and providing support when requested.

The United States of America

After the Episcopal Church in the United States (ECUSA) General Convention of 1997 gave overwhelming approval to the *Concordat of*

> ### African Anglican-Lutheran Interim Committee
>
> *Anglicans*
>
> Right Reverend Sebastian Bakare (Zimbabwe) (co-chairman)
> Professor Denise Ackerman (South Africa)
> Most Reverend Donald Mtetemela (Tanzania)
>
> *Lutherans*
>
> Bishop Ambrose Moyo (Zimbabwe) (co-chairman)
> Reverend Edward Ishaya (Nigeria)
> Mrs. Faith Lugazia (Tanzania)
>
> Reverend Sven Oppegaard and Canon David Hamid provide liaison with the LWF and the Anglican Communion Office, respectively.

Agreement, the Church Wide Assembly of the Evangelical Lutheran Church in America (ELCA) failed to approve it by only six votes (short of the required two-thirds majority). A new drafting team has presented a revision of the *Concordat, Called to Common Mission,* which will be considered by the ELCA in August 1999. Concern in the ELCA seems to centre around a changed role for Lutheran bishops and their incorporation into the historic episcopate. Also, some members of the ELCA, itself a recent product of a Lutheran merger, are concerned about the effect of another unity scheme that may affect the ecclesial life of the denomination.

Canada

A Joint Working Group of the Anglican Church of Canada and the Evangelical Lutheran Church in Canada (ELCIC) have prepared a text, *The Waterloo Declaration,* which will be considered by the National Convention of the ELCIC and the General Synod of the Anglican Church in 2001. If approved, these two churches will be in full communion. The Canadian Anglican House of Bishops and the Council of General Synod agree that they are prepared to view the historic episcopate in the context of the understandings of apostolicity articulated in *BEM, The Niagara Report,* and *The Porvoo Common Statement.* The National Convention of the ELCIC agrees that it is prepared to take the constitutional steps necessary to understand the installation of synodical bishops as ordination. A study resource, entitled *Called to Full Communion,* containing the draft joint declaration and other useful background material has been published. A more academic theological commentary is also available. At the Lambeth Conference the bishops reviewed (in section IV) the Canadian initiative and commended the progress as set forth in *The Waterloo Declaration* for consideration by both churches in 2001. The proposal has also been circulated to Anglican provinces for comment.

Europe: Porvoo

The Porvoo Contact Group continues to oversee the implementation of the Porvoo agreement signed by the four Anglican provinces in Great Britain and Ireland and six Lutheran churches in the Scandinavian and Baltic region. The relationships are deepening through diocesan twinnings, a common prayer cycle, a hymn collection, mutual participation in episcopal consecrations, and consultations. The Archbishop of Canterbury invited the Primate of each Porvoo Lutheran Church to send one bishop to take part in the Lambeth Conference, by virtue of being bishops in communion with the See of Canterbury. Three bishops, from Finland, Norway, and Sweden, attended.

Europe: Meissen

The Meissen Common Statement is an agreement between the Church of England and the Evangelical Church in Germany (which includes Lutheran, Reformed, and United churches). The Meissen Commission is continuing with further work on the specific issue of episcopacy and the mutual recognition of ministries and on the meaning of "full visible unity."

Europe: Reuilly

Conversations between the British and Irish Anglican churches and the French Lutheran and Reformed churches have led to an agreed text: *The Reuilly Common Statement*. This agreement is more of a Meissen type than a Porvoo type, since it does not entail full interchangeability of ordained ministers. The Lutheran and Reformed churches involved are not episcopal churches.

Anglican-Methodist Relations

In 1996 the Anglican-Methodist International Commission completed its report, which was submitted to the 1998 Lambeth Conference. This report includes two resolutions that were adopted unanimously by the World Methodist Council (WMC) at its meeting in Rio de Janeiro in 1996. The Lambeth Conference adapted the wording of the resolutions in *Sharing in the Apostolic Communion* for the sake of consistency with other dialogues and to recognise the variety of relationships between Anglicans and Methodists in different regions. The Lambeth Conference recommended the establishment of a Joint Working Group with the WMC to monitor and promote regional developments and to move where appropriate from mutual acknowledgement to the reconciliation of churches and ministries. Consultation with the WMC will now be held to establish such a working group.

Regional dialogues with Methodists can be found in England (with the Methodist Church of Great Britain), Scotland (a multilateral dialogue), Wales (multilateral), South Africa (multilateral), and New Zealand. Talks are being considered in Canada with the United Church of Canada and in the United States with the United Methodist Church. (ECUSA has a multilateral conversation, which includes Methodists, through the Consultation on Church Union, [COCU]).

Anglican-Oriental Orthodox and Assyrian Relations

The Coptic Orthodox Church, the Syrian Orthodox Church, the Armenian Apostolic Church, the Ethiopian Orthodox Church, and the Malankara Orthodox Syrian Church. Churches of the Anglican Communion have a lengthy relationship with these five ancient, non-Chalcedonian oriental churches. In many countries Anglicans and members of these churches experience a close pastoral and ecumenical relationship, and several national bilateral dialogues are flourishing.

Various complicating factors have impeded activity related to the Anglican-Oriental Orthodox International Forum over the past couple of years. Nevertheless, all of these churches were invited to send representatives to the 1998 Lambeth Conference, and all but the Ethiopian church were able to attend. This provided opportunity to explore how the official conversations could continue and be deepened. Indeed, the Lambeth Conference recommended that the forum be upgraded to an International Theological Commission, to seek an agreement on Christology and to consider other theological and ecclesial issues.

In February 1999, the Archbishop of Canterbury completed official visits to all the Oriental Orthodox jurisdictions. A small planning group of Anglicans and Oriental Orthodox will now meet to plan for the joint formation of an International Theological Commission. The Eritrean Orthodox Church has recently claimed autonomy from the Ethiopian. It remains to be seen if and how this Church will participate in the dialogue, although a protocol exists to permit that Eritrean relations be handled by the Copts.

The Assyrian Church of the East

This ancient church, whose official name is the Holy Apostolic Catholic Assyrian Church of the East, is not a member of the Oriental Orthodox family (it recognises only the first two ecumenical councils) and thus will not participate in the Anglican-Oriental Orthodox International Theological Commission. Nevertheless, the Assyrians have an equally long history of contact with Anglicans, and significant bilateral relations flourish where there is a large Assyrian diaspora community in Great Britain, North America, and Australia. Such regional conversations are to be encouraged, noting that previous Lambeth Conferences (1908 and 1920) have determined that there are no longer major Christological obstacles to closer relations.

Anglican-Orthodox Relations

International Commission of the Anglican-Orthodox Theological Dialogue (ICAOTD)

Progress continues to be made in this dialogue, following a work plan drafted by the Commission at New Valamo in 1989. The first phase of the New Valamo work plan was completed in June 1998 in Bucharest, and three interim statements *(The Trinity and the Church; Christ, the Spirit and the Church; and Christ, Humanity and the Church [Parts 1 and 2])* were com-

---

ICAOTD

Anglicans

Right Reverend Mark Dyer (United States) (co-chairman)
Right Reverend Riah Abu El-Assal (Palestine)
Reverend Dr. Timothy Bradshaw (England)
Right Reverend Sigqibo Dwane (South Africa)
Reverend Dr. Donald Edwards (Australia)
Reverend Professor William Green (United States)
Reverend Canon John McNab (Canada)
Reverend Professor John Riches (Scotland)
Reverend Canon Dr. Joy Tetley (England)
Right Reverend Maxwell Thomas (Australia)
Right Reverend Rowam Williams (Wales)
Reverend Canon Hugh Wybrew (England)
Reverend Canon David Hamid (co-secretary)
Reverend Canon Dr. Richard Marsh (England) (co-secretary)

Orthodox

Metropolitan John of Pergamon (Constantinople) (co-chairman)
Metropolitan Peter of Aksum (Alexandria)
Bishop Gabriel of Palmyra (Antioch)
Bishop Nifon of Slobozia and Calarasi (Romania)
Metropolitan Chrysostomos of Kition (Cyprus)
Professor Constantine Scouteris (Greece)
Father Andrezej Minko (Poland)
Dr. Peter Gilbert (Albania)
Metropolitan Ambrosius of Oulu (Finland)
Reverend Dr. Christos Christakis (United States) (co-secretary)

mended by the Lambeth Conference to the bishops of the Communion for study. Their responses are due to the Anglican co-chairman of the dialogue, Bishop Mark Dyer, by December 31, 1999. The second phase of the New Valamo plan will begin in October 1999, with work on episcopacy and conciliarity.

Annual informal talks continue to be held with representatives of the ecumenical patriarch and the Anglican Communion, which share concerns of a pastoral and practical nature and which monitor the progress of the theological dialogue.

Relations with Pentecostals, New Churches, and Independent Church Groups

This is a new area of ecumenical relations for Anglicans. The Lambeth Conference of 1998 called for the Anglican Communion to pay some attention to these two groups of Christians. Resolution IV.21 refers to Pentecostal churches and invites the Inter-Anglican Standing Commission on Ecumenical Relations (IASCER) to explore the possibility of conversations between the Anglican Communion and Pentecostal churches. This matter is on the agenda of the IASCER. Resolution IV.25 on new churches and independent church groups encourages the development of relations, bilaterally, multilaterally, locally, and informally, where this is appropriate and possible.

The Ely Group

To begin to analyse the implications of these resolutions, a small reflection group has met twice, under the chairmanship of Bishop Stephen Sykes (Ely). This group has done some useful preparatory work, which will be a resource to future conversations and for relations with Pentecostals, new churches, and independent church groups. The Ely Group recognises its role as preecumenical and predialogue, inasmuch as its function is distinct from formal conversations with ecumenical partners. It is a service unit for

---

The Ely Group

Right Reverend Stephen Sykes (convenor)
Reverend Dr. Christ Cocksworth
Reverend Canon David Hamid
Dr. Harriet Harris
Reverend Canon Graham Kings
Dr. Bernice Martin
Reverend Professor David Martin
Reverend Mark Savage
Reverend Dr. Chris Sugden
Dr. Bridget Nichols (secretary)

Anglicans who are interested or concerned about relations with new churches and independent church groups.

This group sees itself as having three functions: the provision of support to bishops and others in local situations, the provision of information and resources, and the dissemination of accounts of good practice in relations with these groups around the world. Some specific tasks that may be addressed include the preparation of a "who's who" of new churches and the preparation of study guides which help to theologically "unpack" the Lambeth resolutions. Some preliminary correspondence has gone out to the Primates of the Communion regarding the work of this group.

Anglican-Reformed Relations

The World Alliance of Reformed Churches (WARC)

The Anglican Communion was represented by the director of Ecumenical Affairs at the twenty-third General Council of the WARC in Debrecen, Hungary, from August 8 to 19, 1997. The outgoing president, Dr. Jane Dempsey Douglass (Presbyterian Church, United States), presented the theme "Break the Chains of Injustice." Choan Seng Song (Taiwan) was elected president of WARC. The General Council spent considerable time reflecting on issues of gospel and culture, economic justice, the question of Korean reunification, the ecological crisis, and human rights.

There are 197 member churches in the WARC. More than twice as many Reformed churches are outside the alliance than within it. The General Secretary Milan Opocensky drew attention to the disunity that is, sadly, characteristic of the Reformed family and, reflecting on the theology of *koinonia,* urged the taking of steps to transform the WARC into "a more committed communion of churches."

Ecumenical relations and dialogues were not a major feature of the agenda of the General Council. Nevertheless, a resolution with ecumenical implications called for future meetings of the WARC General Council to be organised jointly and concurrently with the World Council of Churches (WCC) and LWF. Another resolution supported an initiative of Dr. Konrad Raiser of the World Council of Churches to begin preparations for a universal Christian council engaging the main Christian families of churches.

Anglicans should note that the churches of South India, North India, and Pakistan are members of WARC, as well as of the ACC. The full significance of this for our ecumenical relations has yet to be explored.

Anglican-Reformed Joint Working Group (ARJWG)

It was hoped that *God's Reign and Our Unity,* the 1984 report of the Anglican-Reformed International Commission, would be studied by Anglican and

> ### ARJWG
>
> *Anglicans*
>
> Right Reverend Robert T. Halliday (Scotland) (co-chairman)
> Reverend Dr. Alfred Moss (United States)
> Reverend Courtney Sampson (United States)
> Reverend Canon David Hamid (co-secretary)
>
> *Reformed*
>
> Professor Stephen Farris (Canada) (co-chairman)
> Reverend Douglas H. Rollwage (Canada)
> Reverend Margrethe B. J. Brown (United States)
> (No WARC co-secretary at present)

Reformed churches around the world, with the response to be collected by the WARC and the ACC. The response to this rich report has, unfortunately, not been overwhelming. As a result, the WARC and ACC agreed that a joint working group would be the best way to carry forward this relationship at present. ARJWG has had one meeting, in 1996. It recommended a regional dialogue in South Africa to locally explore some of the issues in *God's Reign and Our Unity*. Both the ACO and WARC have written to member churches in South Africa, but there appears to be little energy for a local dialogue at present.

It should be noted that Anglicans are in formal dialogue with Reformed Christians through the Meissen, Reuilly, COCU, and Scottish churches' initiative.

Anglican-Roman Catholic Relations

Archbishop Carey paid an official visit to Pope John Paul II from December 3–6, 1996. During a full programme, the Archbishop met with the Pope on four occasions. A joint service of vespers was celebrated at the Church of San Gregorio al Celio, and a joint declaration was signed (appendix 4). Archbishop Carey also had a brief private conversation with the Pope on February 13, 1999, at the time of the official opening of the new Anglican Centre in Rome.

Annual informal talks continue to be held between the Vatican and the Anglican Communion to share concerns of a pastoral and practical nature.

Anglican-Roman Catholic International Commission (ARCIC)

In is plenary session in Italy in 1998, ARCIC completed a report called *The Gift of Authority: Authority in the Church III*, which was published on the Eve of the Ascension in 1999. As the second half of the title indicates, this is the third study on authority undertaken by the commission. The text roots Church authority in the scriptures, deals with the question of Scripture and tradition, explores the concept of synodality in the Church's exercise of authority, and finds some significant areas of convergence in regard to the primacy of the bishop of Rome. Two commentaries, one Roman Catholic and one Anglican, are available to help interpret the text. *The Gift of Authority* has been translated into French, Italian, Portuguese, and Spanish. The statement and the commentaries have been circulated to members of the ACC and sent to all Primates of the Communion, along with some questions to stimulate discussion.

With the completion of *The Gift of Authority,* the Anglican co-chairman, the Right Reverend Mark Santer, the bishop of Birmingham, retired from the commission. Archbishop George Carey has appointed the Most Reverend Frank Griswold, the Primate of ECUSA, as the new Anglican co-chairman.

Anglican-Roman Catholic Bishops' Consultation

The proposed consultation between Anglican and Roman Catholic leaders, which came about as a result of the Archbishop of Canterbury's visit to the

---

ARCIC

Anglicans

Most Reverend Frank Griswold (United States) (co-chairman)
Right Reverend John Baycroft (Canada, Italy)
Dr. E. Rozanne Elder (United States)
Reverend Professor Jaci Maraschin (Brazil)
Reverend Canon Richard Marsh (England)
Reverend Dr. John Muddiman (England)
Right Reverend Michael Nazir-Ali (England)
Reverend Dr. Nicholas Sagovsky (England)
Reverend Dr. Charles Sherlock (Australia)
Reverend Canon David Hamid (co-secretary)

Roman Catholics

Right Reverend Cormac Murphy-O'Connor (England) (co-chairman)
Sister Sara Butler MSBT (United States)
Reverend Peter Cross (Australia)
Reverend Dr. Adelbert Denaux (Belgium)
Right Reverend Walter Kasper (Vatican) (appointment expected)
Most Reverend Patrick A. Kelly (England)
Reverend Jean M. R. Tillard OP (Canada)
Reverend Liam Walsh OP (Switzerland)
Reverend Timothy Galligan (co-secretary)

Pope in 1996, is now scheduled for May 14 to 20, 2000, just outside Toronto, Ontario, Canada. The Pope and the Archbishop felt that the time was opportune "to consult further about how the relationship between the Anglican Communion and the Catholic Church is to progress." The initial response to this idea has been encouraging. The Primate (or his episcopal representative) of the churches in Aotearoa, New Zealand, Australia, Brazil, Canada, England, Ireland, South India, Nigeria, Papua New Guinea, Southern Africa, Uganda, the United States, and the West Indies have been invited by the Archbishop of Canterbury. The counterparts from the Roman Catholic Church in these countries have been invited by Cardinal Cassidy. The staff of the Pontifical Council for Promoting Christian Unity and the ACO will be overseeing the detailed planning for this high-level meeting.

World Council of Churches (WCC)

Eighth Assembly, Harare

The eighth assembly of the WCC was held in Harare, Zimbabwe, from December 3 to 14, 1998. All Anglican churches, which are members of the WCC, sent delegates, and many Anglicans attended in other capacities as stewards, staff, journalists, consultants, and observers, including the director of Ecumenical Affairs of the Anglican Communion, who attended as a delegated observer. The theme of the assembly, which was also the fiftieth anniversary of the founding of the WCC, was *Turn to God: Rejoice in Hope*.

Highlights included the agreement on a statement of *Common Understanding and Vision (CUV)*, which went through several drafts in the years leading up to the assembly, a process with which Anglicans were significantly involved-through their member churches and through comment from the Communion itself. Major celebrations marked the council's jubilee and the end of the decade of the churches in solidarity with women. The host continent, Africa, made a powerful impact in worship, drama, and presentation. Halfway through the assembly, a marketplace (*Padare* in Shona) of workshops, seminars, and cultural presentations were staged. The *Padare* provided the opportunity for attendees to sample and explore various issues and movements, some central to the agenda of the assembly itself, and others more peripheral. Substantial reports from the moderator of the Central Committee Catholicos Aram I of Cilicia (who was reelected for another term) and from the General Secretary, Dr. Konrad Raiser addressed several concerns facing the council, including dwindling finances and the unhappiness of Orthodox churches with the style and agenda of the WCC. Resolutions were passed concerning the relationship of the WCC to the Christian World Communions and encouraging the exploration of a Forum of Christian Churches and Ecumenical Organisations that may be a way of drawing into conversation (without any agreed, clear commitment) a wider range of ecumenical partners, including, it is hoped, the Roman Catholic Church and Pentecostal and evangelical churches.

Two gatherings of Anglicans were organised by the Anglican Communion during the assembly. One provided a forum to hear views and concerns from around the Communion concerning items on the WCC agenda. The other was a social event at the time of the Archbishop of Canterbury's visit, to which members of the local province and diocese, as well as members of churches in the Communion were invited.

At Harare, Dr. Mary Tanner (England) completed her term as moderator of the Faith and Order Commission, a work with which she has been closely involved since 1974. The Anglican Communion is justifiably proud of Mary's immense contribution and key leadership in this multilateral dialogue.

Toward a Common Date for Easter

The World Council of Churches and the Middle East Council of Churches jointly sponsored a consultation in Aleppo, Syria, from March 5 to 10, 1997. The Anglican Communion was represented by the Reverend Canon John Halliburton of St. Paul's Cathedral, London. The report was welcomed by the Lambeth Conference, and the provinces of the Communion are currently engaged in endorsing the recommendations.

Churches in Communion: Anglican-Old Catholic Relations

A relationship of communion has existed for a number of years between the churches of the Anglican Communion and the Old Catholic churches of the Union of Utrecht, by means of the 1931 Bonn Agreement. The challenge before both families of churches is how to deepen the communion between them, including ways of taking counsel and making decisions together and addressing the anomaly of overlapping jurisdictions. Regular participation in each other's councils is one way of making visible the communion we share.

In recent years, the Union of Utrecht has been under some strain as some member churches move to ordain women. At present there is no consensus among the churches of the Union of Utrecht regarding the ordination of women. The Germans, Austrians, and Dutch now ordain women priests, but the Polish National Catholic Church (PNCC) has made it clear that it is not in communion with Old Catholics who do so; nevertheless, it remains in the Union of Utrecht. Several years ago, the PNCC broke communion with the Anglican Church of Canada and ECUSA on similar grounds, but it has not declared any alteration in relationships with the Church of England or with any other Anglican province. The Swiss ordain women deacons but not priests.

Anglican/Old Catholic International Coordinating Council (AOCICC)

ACC-9 mandated the formation of an Anglican-Old Catholic Coordinating Council specifically to deepen the relationship formed through the Bonn

Anglicans Elected to Positions in the WCC

Presidents

Dr. Agnes Aboum (Kenya)
Bishop Jabez Bryce (Aotearoa, New Zealand, and Polynesia)

Vice Moderator

Ms. Justice Sophia O. A. Adinyira (Ghana, West Africa)

Central Committee (*Executive Committee)

Ms. Keshini I. Arulendran (Sri Lanka)
Mr. Victor Avasi (Uganda)
Right Reverend Samuel Azariah (Pakistan)
Ms. Susan Janelle Bazzana (Australia)
Dr. Pamela P. Chinnis (United States)
Ms. Inamar Correa de Souza (Brazil)*
Reverend G. Dyvasirvadam (Church of South India)
Ms. Donnalie E. C. Edwards (Antigua, West Indies)*
Ms. Alice-Jean Finlay (Canada)
Right Reverend Godfrey M. Mhogolo (Tanzania)
Ms. Pragyan Mohanty (Church of North India)
Right Reverend Dr. Barry Morgan (Wales)
Right Reverend John R. W. Neill (Ireland)
Right Reverend Bernard Ntahoturi (Burundi)
Ms. Jenny Siama Paul (Sudan)
Most Reverend Rémi J. Rabenirina (Madagascar, Indian Ocean)
Right Reverend Barry Rogerson (England)
Mr. Albert A. K. Samadder (Bangladesh)

Faith and Order Standing Commission

Right Reverend John Hind (England)
Reverend Jane Namugenyi (Uganda)

Joint Working Group between the WCC and the Roman Catholic Church

Ms. Susan Janelle Bazzana (Australia)
Reverend Canon David Hamid (consultant)

Agreement. For a few years this council was never constituted. In December 1997, a meeting was held between Anglican and Old Catholic representatives in Amersfoort, Holland, to take action on the ACC resolution. The recommendations from ACC-9 were somewhat streamlined, making the council more affordable to both Communions. The Joint Standing Committees of the Primates and the ACC in 1998 and the International Bishops' Conference of the Union of Utrecht approved the modifications. The first meeting of the Council was held in Frankfurt from November 23 to 25, 1998 (appendix 5).

AOCICC

Anglicans

Right Reverend Jonathan Gledhill (England) (co-chairman)
Reverend Gabriel Amat (Switzerland)
Reverend Sarah Rowland Jones (Wales)
Mrs. Gillian Ratcliff (Sweden)
Reverend Canon Dr. Robert Wright (United States)
Reverend Canon David Hamid (co-secretary)

Old Catholics

Bishop Joachim Vobbe (Germany) (co-chairman)
Reverend Professor Dr. David Holeton (Czech Republic)
Mrs. Teresa Kropielnicka (Poland)
Reverend Wietse van der Velde (The Netherlands)
Reverend Professor Dr. Urs von Arx (Switzerland)
Reverend Dr. Thaddeus A. Schnitker (co-secretary)

Mission and Evangelism: A Brief Report to ACC-11

—Mission and Evangelism Department

Since ACC-10 a transition has taken place in the Mission and Evangelism Department. Since January 1998 the portfolio of this department has been carried by the Secretary General with the capable support of Ms. Marjorie Murphy, who has been coordinating mission and evangelism affairs for the Communion. The work of the department has included responding to everyday inquiries, maintaining data of companion relationships throughout the Communion and other such lists, the extensive preparation for the Lambeth Conference, the coordination of the Anglican Communion Mission Commission (MISSIO), and gathering information of the progress of the Decade of Evangelism throughout the provinces of the Communion. An effort has been made to keep informed of developments in mission, including attending various events in England.

MISSIO

MISSIO has met twice since ACC-10, in Recife, Brazil, in September 1997, and in Harare, Zimbabwe, in April 1999. Two reports have been made: an interim report, "Sing a New Song," for the Lambeth Conference, and their final report, "Anglicans in Mission: A Transforming Journey," with an executive report for ACC-11. All the coordination of travel, accommodation, mailings, preparatory materials, and agenda-setting was arranged from this office, working together with a small planing group of MISSIO members. Plans are being made for the report to be published in book form and distributed to the Primates, bishops, and mission agencies of the Anglican Communion, along with an in-house publication of the MISSIO interim report "Sing a New Song."

As the meeting in Harare was the last meeting of this term of MISSIO, a chairs' advisory group has been formed to operate until new members of the Inter-Anglican Standing Commission on Mission are appointed.

In their report, MISSIO members set out guidelines of agenda and appointments of the next term of the Mission Commission, as well as for the future director of the ACO mission desk.

Decade of Evangelism

A questionnaire on the Decade of Evangelism was taken in the provinces and some dioceses around the Communion; it included strengths, weaknesses, lessons learned, and future direction. Through the questionnaire we learned of the impact that the Decade of Evangelism has made in the Communion and signs of "shifting the Church from a maintenance mode to a mission orientation" are evident. The data gathered has been compiled together and summarised in the MISSIO report.

Resource Materials

The survey also included the gathering of resource materials used during the Decade of Evangelism and resource people with various abilities in mission and evangelism training, which would be available to the provinces on invitation.

The resource materials where compiled into categories and are available upon request to the provinces through *Anglican World* and the ACO web site. A separate catalogue of resources for mission and evangelism leadership training for both clergy and laity will also be made available as the research revealed a growing need and demand in this area throughout the Communion. A list of resource people available to the provinces, on invitation, will also be made available through the same means.

Prayers from around the Communion

The survey included the gathering of prayers for mission and evangelism, and plans are being made to publish a book of prayers for mission, gathered from around the Anglican Communion.

Provincial-Diocesan Mission Coordinators

The list of the provincial-diocesan mission coordinators is being updated with the intention of increasing communication and sharing stories and resources of the mission around the Communion.

Companion Diocesan Links List

The list of all the companion diocesan links throughout the Communion is constantly being updated. Many new links were initiated during the Lambeth Conference and are in the process of being formed. The guidelines for various links and partnerships related to mission have been put together in a booklet for easy reference and will be distributed along with the updated list of companion diocesan links.

Booklet of Anglican Communion Guidelines for Mission

- Five marks of mission
- Principles of partnerships
- Priorities in evangelism
- Networks
- Companion diocesan links
- Development programmes
- Partnership visits

Report of the Coordinator for Liturgy

—THE REVEREND CANON PAUL GIBSON

International Anglican Liturgical Consultation (IALC)

For more than ten years the agenda of consultations and conferences of the International Anglican Liturgical Consultation have been shaped around baptism, Eucharist, and ministry—the subjects addressed in the celebrated Lima statement of the Faith and Order Commission of the WCC. These discussions have issued in a number of statements and collections of papers, including *Growing in Newness of Life: Christian Initiation in Anglicanism Today*[1] and *Renewing the Anglican Eucharist: Findings of the Fifth IALC, Dublin, Eire, 1995*.[2] Since the last meeting of this council, an interim conference organized by members of the IALC met at Järvenpää, Finland, to prepare the groundwork for a full consultation on the subject of ordination. The essays considered at the Järvenpää conference and the reports of the working groups have been published as *Anglican Orders and Ordinations*.[3]

At the time of writing, the consultation for which the conference at Järvenpää was preparatory had not yet been held, although it was imminent. The steering committee of the IALC designed the agenda of the consultation (held in August 1999 at Kottayam, India) with the following goal.

> To continue reflection from the point of view of liturgy on baptism, Eucharist, and ministry, by development of statements on ministry and order in the framework of a Church which is defined by the gospel and its effective expression in baptism and Eucharist, and which exists to minister in and to the world.

The steering committee first identified areas on which consensus had been reached at Järvenpää:

- Baptismal ecclesiology, although in a divided Church
- Affirmation of the orders of bishop, presbyter, and deacon
- Recognition of the diaconate as a distinctive order
- That ordination is by the whole church (not by the bishop alone)

---

[1] David R. Holeton, ed., The Anglican Book Centre, Toronto, 1993. Includes the Toronto statement, *Walk in Newness of Life*.
[2] David R. Holeton, ed., Grove Worship Series 135, Grove Books Limited, Cambridge, 1996.
[3] David R. Holeton, ed., Alcuin/Grow Joint Liturgical Studies 39, Grove Books Limited, Cambridge, 1997.

- call, formation, ordination by prayer, laying on of hands, and sending out
- the inextricable link between ordained ministry and pastoral ministry

Areas on which consensus had not yet been reached (papers were invited on most of them) are as follows:

- Direct ordination to the presbyterate or episcopate
- Interchange of ministry with non-episcopal churches
- The understanding of *episcope*
- The relationship and tension between ordination and office
- The question of authority and government in the church
- The place of the diaconate as a full and equal order in the threefold ministry
- The full implications of the ordination of women and the universality of ordination
- Issues concerning qualification and disqualification for ordination, e.g., age, educational attainments, ethnicity, sexuality, and gender
- The tension between small and large diocesan structures whose roots are respectively in ancient settled "southern European" models and "northern European" missionary models
- The nature of the jurisdiction and the experience of *episcope* of nonterritorial bishops, such as ethnic, suffragan, assistant, episcopal visitors, and some Primates of the Anglican Communion
- Priest or presbyter terminology and implications for ordination prayers

Areas that had not yet been addressed in-depth are as follows:

- The nature and meaning of validity
- The ontology of ordination
- The indelibility of ordination
- The direct, prophetic role of Christian leaders in certain social situations

Practical implications of the steering committee's findings are as follows:

- Making a baptismal ecclesiology visible in ordination rites
- The value or demerits of the *porrectio* of various objects in ordination rites
- The appearance of new rituals, like anointing at ordinations
- concelebration, for selection and for models of training

It is my intention to make a report on the Kottayam Consultation available to ACC-11 in Dundee.

The 1998 Lambeth Conference welcomed the emergence of the IALCs, endorsed the recognition given to them by the Standing Committee of the ACC and the joint meeting of Primates and the ACC, asked them to report regularly to the Primates' Meeting, commended the study of their documents, asked provinces to send representatives to the consultations, and commended the principle of bursaries for representatives of provinces that cannot afford to meet the cost of participation. All of this will be important as some provinces settle down to the next round of liturgical revision.

Inculturation

A second consultation on African culture and Anglican liturgy was held at the Kempton Park Conference Centre near Johannesburg in November 1996. The consultation received papers by Jo Seoka, who discussed African practice against the background of an interpretation of African religion and spirituality as simply "human being," and John Pobee, who emphasized the social and contextual implications of religious experience and the importance of the ecumenical dimension. The consultation addressed a number of subjects energetically, including an African sense of the unity of identity and belonging and the attendant risks of tribalism, the need for inculturated attention to initiatory and puberty rites, and the need for a more contextual eucharistic theology. Provinces reported to one another on their own activity in the area of liturgy. Members expressed interest in the names of Africans appearing in the calendars of the various African provinces. The Kempton Park Consultation did not reach firm conclusions or a strong consensus, but the conversations were important and the pattern should be encouraged and supported, not only in Africa but also throughout the Communion, and especially where there are people whose culture cannot be described as Western or North Atlantic.

Documentation

The collection of liturgical documents (housed in the Partnership House library in London) reflecting revision and reform since the 1960s continues to grow, although there are still some notable gaps. A list of holdings was sent to the provinces a few months ago and should be examined against the titles of the actual publications, which have been approved and produced. This collection is, to the best of my knowledge, unique and will provide an important base for study and reflection in the future.

In response to expressions of interest in commemorations and memorials, I have begun to create a database that will document the various calendars of the provinces. This will, when completed, not only provide a fund of information to provinces engaged in calendar revision (see Resolution 21 of the Joint Meeting of Primates and the ACC, Cape Town 1993), but will also encourage better coordination of the calendars of the Communion, which sometimes appear to be unnecessarily out of touch with one another. This is a time-consuming task, much of which can be done only in the Partnership House library, where the necessary documentation is available.

Filioque

In November 1998 I reported that eight provinces have a version of the Nicene Creed in one or more of their approved liturgies in which the words "and the Son" (Filioque) are not printed in the final paragraph. In two provinces this is their only version of the Nicene Creed. One province reported significant resistance to the use of the Nicene Creed without the Filioque clause. Two provinces not using the clause indicated that the matter is under consideration.

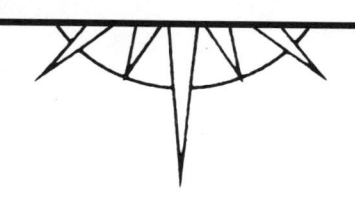

FINANCIAL REPORT

Financial Report

—The Most Reverend R. H. A. Eames, chairman, Inter-Anglican Finance Committee
—Michael Nunn, treasurer

Annual Audited Accounts of the Council

Every year, following approval of the ACC Standing Committee, council members are sent copies of the audited accounts. These include information about the income and expenditures related to the core budget, as well as about the various designated and special funds held. The report for 1998 was circulated with the papers for this council meeting.

The audited accounts for 1996, 1997, and 1998 are laid before this meeting. Extra copies can be made available if individual delegates need them.

Report to the Council

This report summarises the core budget related figures for the years 1996 to 1998 and the budgets for the years 1999 to 2002.

Financial Resources

The primary source of finance for the core budget is the membership. In principle, the ability to enter into increased financial commitments depends on the ability of member churches to increase budget contributions.

The reality, however, is that while some member churches have been able to increase their contributions, others have found it difficult. Overall, in the period from 1996 to 1998 the annual totals contributed have fallen significantly short of the total requests and have not, in fact, reached the level of contribution achieved in 1993. The result of this has been constant difficulty in balancing budgets.

As will be seen from the figures in this report, financial viability has been achieved only through special fund-raising efforts. Special thanks are due to the membership of the Compass Rose Society for their generous core budget support, mainly of the communications activities of the council.

In the final analysis, however, it is important to recognise that the ownership of the budget is with the council membership and that the capacity of the budget is directly related to the ability of the membership to provide the finance. Increased financial commitment needs to be matched by increased contributions to ensure the viability of the council.

Summary of Core Budget Figures: 1996 to 1998

Core budget figures for the years 1996 to 1998 are summarised on Table 1 with highlighted comments on Table 2.

Details of member church contributions, requests, and receipts are given on Table 3. Each year shows contributions actually credited in the year. *In some cases the figures include arrears paid for prior years.*

Core Budget Figures: 1999 to 2002

The bylaws of the council stipulate that the Inter-Anglican Finance Committee, in collaboration with the Standing Committee, shall keep members of the council and member churches informed about each year's budget and about the forecast for each of the succeeding three years. The bylaws further stipulate that the council, in consultation with the Primates, shall determine the level of expenditure and the income required to meet its purposes.

The budget for 1999 and the forecast for the years 2000 to 2002 are summarised on Table 4. A commentary on the figures is included on Table 5.

A detailed projection of member church contribution requests is given on page Table 6. The amounts for 1999 and 2000 have been advised to churches. Figures for 2001 and 2002 are recommendations.

These figures have been approved for presentation to the council by the Inter-Anglican Finance Committee and the Standing Committee of the council. The expenditure figures are based on the existing commitments. Any changes to those commitments mandated by the council will affect the figures and, if, overall, commitments are increased, increased income will be required.

Compass Rose Society support has been pledged only up to the year 2000. Thereafter, no clear undertaking has been given, so a considerable underfunding is, at present, reflected in the figures for 2001 and 2002.

On the basis of the existing commitments and expected contributions, additional funding needs to be secured as follows:

Year 2000: £21,000
Year 2001: £250,000
Year 2002: £236,000

The council holds insufficient reserves to sustain deficit budgets, so, during the period, the Standing Committee and Inter-Anglican Finance Committee will need to carefully monitor the progress in securing funds to cover these shortfalls.

Acknowledgements

The council is invited:

- To recognise with gratitude the strong commitment of many of the member churches to the support of the Inter-Anglican budget and the generous support that has been given by the Compass Rose Society membership.

- To resolve to encourage the member churches to adequately support the Inter-Anglican budget in the coming years.

- To acknowledge the generous support given by the Episcopal Church of the United States of America, the Church of England, the Anglican Church of Canada, Trinity Church Wall Street, and others in assisting in areas not reflected in the core budget of the council.

Table 1

Anglican Consultative Council
Financial Report for ACC-11

Inter-Anglican Budget Outturn 1996 to 1998

INCOME	1996 Budget £	1996 Actual £	1996 Variation £	1997 Budget £	1997 Actual £	1997 Variation £	1998 Budget £	1998 Actual £	1998 Variation £
Interest on deposits	14,000	28,317	(14,317)	15,000	18,464	(3,464)	15,000	19,822	(4,822)
Publications income	5,000	3,394	1,606	5,000	17,292	(12,292)	5,000	5,941	(941)
Services to other bodies	550	500	50	500	500	-	500	500	-
Rent receivable	11,300	7,078	4,222	5,850	5,780	70	6,500	5,723	777
Grants for equipment		1,742	(1,742)		1,437	(1,437)	900	924	(24)
Donations & miscellaneous income	650	3,306	(2,656)	500	2,697	(2,197)	500	2,612	(2,112)
Lambeth Conference towards staff costs							37,000	37,000	-
	31,500	44,337	(12,837)	26,850	46,170	(19,320)	65,400	72,522	(7,122)
Contributions from member churches	1,009,500	839,251	170,249	909,330	853,850	55,480	1,011,863	858,216	153,647
Total normal income	1,041,000	883,588	157,412	936,180	900,020	36,160	1,077,263	930,738	146,525
Special Fund Raising		53,846	(53,846)	243,555	238,578	4,977	320,300	281,188	39,112
	1,041,000	937,434	103,566	1,179,735	1,138,598	41,137	1,397,563	1,211,926	185,637

EXPENDITURE									
Secretary General's office	174,350	164,209	10,141	167,669	158,261	9,408	188,500	174,463	14,037
Communications department	98,775	120,766	(21,991)	169,944	156,472	13,472	132,900	114,897	18,003
Telecommunications/database department							89,000	88,757	243
Anglican World magazine	25,500	46,602	(21,102)	136,750	99,711	37,039	123,000	81,047	41,953
Mission and Evangelism department	83,250	83,301	(51)	80,383	100,805	(20,422)			
Liturgical co-ordinator	7,300	4,790	2,510	6,000	3,761	2,239	6,500	6,250	250
Ecumenical Relations department	57,750	63,170	(5,420)	74,365	88,506	(14,141)	88,500	87,747	753
Finance and Administration department	111,750	133,642	(21,892)	126,294	121,290	5,004	130,900	127,116	3,784
Overheads (rents, office expenses, etc)	137,100	146,244	(9,144)	156,830	141,370	15,460	160,400	157,282	3,118
	695,775	762,724	(66,949)	918,235	870,176	48,059	919,700	837,559	82,141
Provision for meetings etc:									
Inter-Church conversations	40,000	40,000	-	29,000	29,000	-	48,000	48,000	-
Missio	12,000	21,000	(9,000)	15,000	15,000	-	15,000	15,000	-
Council and Standing Committee	60,000	60,000	-	60,000	60,000	-	90,500	90,500	-
Primates	50,000	50,000	-	20,000	20,000	-	25,500	25,500	-
Lambeth Conference	120,000	120,000	-	130,000	130,000	-	140,000	140,000	-
UN Observer's Office				5,000	5,000	-	24,000	24,117	(117)
Research	2,500	2,500	-	2,500	2,500	-	2,500		2,500
Youth Network		4,000	(4,000)						
Inter-Anglican Information Network		2,000	(2,000)						
Provincial Emergencies Provision		10,282	(10,282)		946	(946)	25,000	25,000	-
	980,275	1,072,506	(92,231)	1,179,735	1,132,622	47,113	1,290,200	1,205,676	84,524
Contingencies	40,000		40,000				107,363		107,363
	1,020,275	1,072,506	(52,231)	1,179,735	1,132,622	47,113	1,397,563	1,205,676	191,887
Surplus/(Deficit)	20,725	(135,072)	155,797		5,976	(5,976)		6,250	(6,250)

Table 2 Inter-Anglican Budget Outturn 1996 to 1998
Notes on Annual Figures:

	1996		1997		1998
Presentation:	**Income:**		**Income:**		**Income:**
The audited accounts for the years 1996 and 1998 are set out in the format required by legislation.	Member church contributions were £170,249 under budget.		Overall, the contribution requests to member churches were scaled down. Nevertheless contributions were £55,480 under budget.		Member church contributions were £153,647 under the requests. A significant underpayment had been expected and the contingency provision of £107,363 budgeted under expenditure partially offset this.
This paper presents the core budget figures in an abbreviated and simplified form.	Special fund raising of £53,846 covered the expense line 'Provincial Emergencies Provision, £10,282' and helped mitigate the contributions underpayment.		In setting the budget, it was realised that substantial support would be needed in addition to the member church contributions. Compass Rose Society giving provided £238,578, mainly in support of Communications expenditure.		It was necessary to supplement the contributions with support from Compass Rose Society giving. This provided £281,188, in support of Communications and the 'Provincial Emergencies Provision' expense lines.
For the purpose of budget comparison, this presentation gives a different view from that shown in the annual accounts. The annual accounts break down the budget figures into expense categories, e.g., employment costs, travel, etc, while this presentation gives the figures in departmental totals.	**Expenditure:**		**Expenditure:**		**Expenditure:**
	The comparison between budget and actual item by item is distorted, because some staff costs were switched between departments.		While relocation and termination provisions produced expenditure in excess of budget in the Mission and Evangelism and Ecumenical lines, overall, expenditure was within budget.		Due to changed arrangements, the cost of a Mission and Evangelism assistant is included under the Secretary General's office.
	Excluding the 'Provincial Emergencies Provision' line, expenditure in excess of budget was £41,949.		The Inter-church Conversations line is a net figure. The vote for the year was £40,000, but the budget also allowed for a one-off plough back of £11,000 unspent in the previous year.		Overall, expenditure was under budget, with savings in employment costs and travel and Anglican World. The Anglican World figure is net of earnings and a contribution of £15,000 from the Lambeth Conference budget towards the cost of the post-Lambeth issue.
General Reserve:	Significant variations were in: employment costs, where, inter alia, termination and recruitment costs were incurred; staff travel; office expenses; and Anglican World magazine.		The bottom line shows an excess of income over expenditure for the year of £5,976.		The bottom line shows an excess of income over expenditure for the year of £6,250.
Resolution 49 of ACC-6 provided that the General Reserve should be maintained at a level equivalent to four months' expenditure of the Secretariat.	It should be noted that the Anglican World figure is net of the income generated and some £50,550 of special donations raised through an appeal.		The General Reserve stood at £98,897 at the year end, £148,430 less than required.		The General Reserve stood at £105,146 at the year end, £140,826 less than required.
	The bottom line shows an excess of expenditure over income for the year of £135,072. This was covered by the General Reserve brought forward of £227,923.				
	The General Reserve stood at £92,921 at the year end, £143,499 less than required.				

Table 3

Anglican Consultative Council
Financial Report for ACC-11

Member Church Contributions 1996 to 1998

INCOME	1996 Budget £	1996 Actual £	1996 Variation £	1997 Budget £	1997 Actual £	1997 Variation £	1998 Budget £	1998 Actual £	1998 Variation £
Aotearoa, New Zealand and Polynesia	30,284	33,645	(3,361)	33,645	31,147	2,498	33,645	23,317	10,328
Australia	105,997	84,135	21,862	94,000	78,933	15,067	97,760	67,861	29,899
Brazil	5,048	-	5,048	4,500	3,785	715	4,680	-	4,680
Burundi	150	-	150	200	350	(150)	208	-	208
Canada	111,044	64,009	47,035	64,000	59,613	4,387	66,560	66,877	(317)
Central Africa	12,619	-	12,619	6,500	13,000	(6,500)	6,760	2,000	4,760
Ceylon	1,010	1,010	-	1,100	-	1,100	1,144	1,100	44
Congo Democratic Republic (formerly Zaire)	323	323	-	500	500	-	520	-	520
East Asia [CCEA]	6,764	1,092	5,672	-	5,192	(5,192)	-	-	-
England [inc. Diocese in Europe]	284,173	288,000	(3,827)	295,600	295,600	-	307,424	307,500	(76)
Hong Kong Sheng Kung Hui	-	-	-	-	-	-	-	10,000	(10,000)
Indian Ocean	2,524	2,524	-	2,700	2,700	-	2,808	2,808	-
Ireland	22,714	22,714	-	23,740	22,714	1,026	24,690	24,690	-
Japan	12,619	12,619	-	13,120	13,120	-	13,645	13,645	-
Jerusalem & the Middle East	3,533	3,177	356	3,680	3,068	612	3,827	4,797	(970)
Kenya	15,143	-	15,143	8,000	2,000	6,000	8,320	8,320	-
Korea	3,331	5,291	(1,960)	3,500	-	3,500	3,640	7,140	(3,500)
Melanesia	1,010	1,010	-	1,100	1,100	-	1,144	1,144	-
Mexico	-	999	(999)	1,200	1,130	70	1,248	1,137	111
Myanmar	1,010	1,972	(962)	1,100	1,100	-	1,144	-	1,144
Nigeria	15,143	15,343	(200)	15,250	10,000	5,250	15,860	11,110	4,750
Papua New Guinea	1,010	1,063	(53)	1,100	1,100	-	1,144	1,144	-
Philippines	5,048	4,946	102	5,250	-	5,250	5,460	880	4,580
Rwanda	1,343	1,343	-	1,000	-	1,000	1,040	-	1,040
Scotland	15,143	15,143	-	16,000	16,000	-	16,640	16,120	520
South East Asia [see note ***]	-	-	-	20,000	2,352	17,648	20,800	-	20,800
Southern Cone of South America	2,524	896	1,628	2,630	5,279	(2,649)	2,735	2,742	(7)
Southern Africa	17,666	11,100	6,566	12,480	13,197	(717)	12,979	12,979	-
Sudan	2,524	2,000	524	2,630	-	2,630	2,735	-	2,735
Taiwan	-	-	-	-	1,020	(1,020)	-	1,013	(1,013)
Tanzania	5,048	5,048	-	5,250	5,250	-	5,460	5,460	-
Uganda	7,570	400	7,170	1,000	-	1,000	5,460	6,372	(912)
United States of America (including Province	275,088	221,055	54,033	225,490	220,287	5,203	297,595	216,741	80,854
Wales	22,714	22,714	-	23,740	23,740	-	24,690	24,690	-
West Africa	3,533	1,000	2,533	2,000	3,000	(1,000)	2,080	2,080	-
West Indies	10,095	10,095	-	10,500	10,500	-	10,920	10,095	825
United Churches:									
United Church of Bangladesh	505	24	481	525	1,006	(481)	546	546	-
United Church of North India	1,010	653	357	1,100	1,457	(357)	1,144	1,144	-
United Church of Pakistan	1,010	505	505	1,100	1,010	90	1,144	-	1,144
United Church of South India	1,514	1,514	-	1,600	1,600	-	1,664	1,664	-
Extra-Provincial Dioceses:									
Bermuda Diocese	1,010	1,010	-	1,500	1,500	-	1,560	-	1,560
The Lusitanian Church	353	526	(173)	500	500	-	520	500	20
The Spanish Refrmd Episcopal Church	353	353	-	500	-	500	520	600	(80)
	1,009,500	839,251	170,249	909,330	853,850	55,480	1,011,863	858,216	153,647

Note ***

The request to South East Asia was set by Inter Anglican Finance Committee on the formation of the new province. Following correspondence, it has been agreed to significantly scale down the request and this is reflected in the budget figures from the year 2001 onwards

Table 4

Anglican Consultative Council
Financial Report for ACC-11

Inter-Anglican Budgets 1999 to 2002	1999 £	2000 £	2001 £	2002 £
Interest on deposits	15,000	15,000	15,000	15,000
Publications income	5,000	5,000	5,000	5,000
Services to other bodies	500	500	500	500
Donations & miscellaneous income	500	500	500	500
	21,000	21,000	21,000	21,000
Contributions from member churches	1,073,636	1,116,586	1,128,400	1,174,800
Total normal income	1,094,636	1,137,586	1,149,400	1,195,800
Special Fund Raising	235,000	235,000	-	-
	1,329,636	1,372,586	1,149,400	1,195,800
EXPENDITURE				
Secretary General's office	196,750	206,450	215,100	224,000
Communications department	110,850	114,950	117,400	121,500
Telecommunications/database department	48,100	51,400	53,300	55,300
Anglican World magazine	110,000	110,000	110,000	110,000
Liturgical co-ordinator	6,500	6,500	7,000	7,500
Ecumenical Relations department	86,180	93,780	95,300	99,500
Finance and Administration department	143,400	154,400	162,050	166,300
Overheads (rents, office expenses, etc)	161,500	154,930	162,180	167,580
	863,280	892,410	920,330	951,680
Provision for meetings etc:				
Inter-Church conversations	48,000	48,000	48,000	48,000
Missio	15,000	15,000	15,000	15,000
Council and Standing Committee	90,500	125,000	125,000	125,000
Primates	25,500	25,500	25,500	25,500
Lambeth Conference	140,000	140,000	140,000	140,000
UN Observer's Office	24,000	24,000	24,000	24,000
Provincial Emergencies Provision	25,000	25,000	25,000	25,000
	1,231,280	1,294,910	1,322,830	1,354,180
Contingencies	96,000	99,000	76,400	77,600
	1,327,280	1,393,910	1,399,230	1,431,780
Surplus/(Deficit)	2,356	(21,324)	(249,830)	(235,980)

Table 5 Anglican Consultative Council
Financial Report for ACC-11

Inter-Anglican Budgets 1999 to 2002

Commentary on Budget Figures

Income

A small amount of income is expected from interest on deposits, publications sales, etc. The primary income source is **Member Church Contributions** (81% in 1999). At present these contributions do not provide sufficient income to cover the expenditure commitments. It has therefore been necessary to seek additional help through **Special Fund Raising** efforts (18% in 1999). The **Compass Rose Society** provides most of these funds and the United States Chapter of the Society has committed itself to continue support to the end of the year 2000. For the years 2001 and 2002 the situation is still unclear.

Expenditure

The projections for the years 2000 to 2002 are based on the programmes and commitments in place in 1999.

The figures are grouped by activities. The **Secretary General**'s portfolio includes Mission and Evangelism, with one staff member dedicated to that aspect of the work. The **Communications and Telecommunications** sections deal with internal (through the computer network) and external communications issues including the maintenance of the Anglican Communion Office database. Communications department also produces *Anglican World* magazine which is widely distributed through the Communion, partly on a complimentary basis and partly to subscribers. The **Liturgical Co-ordinator** is a part-time post. **Ecumenical Relations** department services the Inter-Church Conversations and deals with other ecumenical matters. **Finance and Administration** department deals with the finance and accounting, office administration and much of the logistical work for meetings. The **Overheads** include the rent and other office premises costs as well as the general office expenses, audit fees, etc.

The section **Provision for Meetings, etc** includes the annual provisions for the various meetings which have to be held. Also included is a contribution to the **Office of the Anglican Observer at the United Nations**, the overall budget for which (in 1999) is about £140,000. The item '**Provincial Emergencies Provision**' is related to the Compass Rose Society contribution and provides a fund from which assistance can be given to churches where crisis situations have severely affected the provincial infrastructure.

The main cost increases, after 1999, are in two areas:

Staff costs. These costs are included in the departmental figures. From the year 2000, following an actuarial valuation of the staff pension scheme, employer's pension contributions have to rise. Otherwise, the figures include scheduled increments for newer members of staff and an estimate of required cost of living increases for all staff.

Meetings of the Council and Standing Committee. The procedure is to provide an annual amount from the budget which is kept in a fund. The costs of the three-yearly Council meeting, the meetings of Standing Committee, Inter-Anglican Finance Committee and other sub-committees set up by the Standing Committee are charged to the fund. Following the meeting of ACC-11, the fund will be in deficit. It is therefore necessary to increase the annual provision. The revised provision is based on an estimate of costs of the meetings as presently constituted.

Surplus/Deficit on the Budget

Subject to successful fund raising and satisfactory payment of member church contributions, 1999 should be slightly in surplus. For 2000 an overspend of £21,324 is in prospect. This is mainly due to the increase in the Council meetings provision. For 2001 and 2002, when Special Fund raising income has not been assumed, additional funds of £249,830 (2001) and £235,980 (2002) need to be found to meet the expenditure.

Table 6

Anglican Consultative Council
Financial Report for ACC-11

Member Church Contributions 1999 to 2002

	1999 Budget £	1999 Paid by 10/09/99 £	1999 Unpaid Balance £	2000 Budget £	2001 Budget £	2002 Budget £
Aotearoa, New Zealand and Polynesia	34,991	18,615	16,376	36,391	27,800	28,900
Australia	101,670	25,795	75,875	105,737	110,000	114,400
Brazil	4,867	2,450	2,417	5,062	5,300	5,500
Burundi	216	424	(208)	225	300	300
Canada	69,222	27,963	41,259	71,991	74,900	77,900
Central Africa	7,030	-	7,030	7,311	7,600	7,900
Central America	1,298	-	1,298	1,350	1,400	1,500
Ceylon	1,190	1,190	-	1,238	1,300	1,400
Congo Democratic Republic	541	-	541	563	600	700
England [Inc Dio in Europe]	319,721	239,775	79,946	332,510	345,800	359,700
Hong Kong Sheng Kung Hui	20,000	20,000	-	20,800	21,700	22,500
Indian Ocean	2,920	2,920	-	3,037	3,200	3,300
Ireland	25,678	25,678	-	26,705	27,800	28,900
Japan	14,191	14,191	-	14,759	15,400	16,000
Jerusalem & the Middle East	3,980	3,980	-	4,139	4,300	4,500
Kenya	8,653	8,653	-	8,999	9,400	9,800
Korea	3,786	-	3,786	3,937	4,100	4,300
Melanesia	1,190	1,190	-	1,238	1,300	1,400
Mexico	1,298	1,199	99	1,350	1,400	1,500
Myanmar	1,190	-	1,190	1,238	1,300	1,400
Nigeria	16,494	-	16,494	17,154	17,900	18,600
Papua New Guinea	1,190	1,190	-	1,238	1,300	1,400
Philippines	5,678	2,709	2,969	5,905	1,900	2,000
Rwanda	1,082	-	1,082	1,125	1,200	1,300
Scotland	17,306	12,574	4,732	17,998	18,200	19,500
South East Asia	21,632	5,852	15,780	22,497	4,400	4,600
Southern Africa	13,498	-	13,498	14,038	14,600	15,200
Southern Cone of South America	2,844	2,988	(144)	2,958	3,100	3,200
Sudan	2,844	-	2,844	2,958	3,100	3,200
Taiwan						-
Tanzania	5,678	5,678	-	5,905	6,200	6,400
Uganda	5,678	-	5,678	5,905	6,200	6,400
United States of America (including Province IX)	309,499	182,001	127,498	321,879	334,800	348,200
Wales	25,678	25,678	-	26,705	27,600	28,900
West Africa	2,163	2,163	-	2,250	2,400	2,500
West Indies	11,357	-	11,357	11,811	12,300	12,800
United Churches:						
United Church of Bangladesh	568	568	-	591	600	700
United Church of North India	1,190	1,190	-	1,238	1,300	1,400
United Church of Pakistan	1,190	-	1,190	1,238	1,300	1,400
United Church of South India	1,731	-	1,731	1,800	1,900	2,000
Extra-Provincial Dioceses:						
Bermuda	1,622	3,182	(1,560)	1,687	1,800	1,900
Lusitanian Church	541	500	41	563	600	700
Spanish Rfmd Episcopal Church	541	-	541	563	600	700
	1,073,636	640,296	433,340	1,116,586	1,128,400	1,174,800

Anglican Communion Priorities Working Group

Arising from a concern expressed by the Inter-Anglican Finance Committee and the need to prioritise a variety of requests for funding, a small working group was asked by the Joint Standing Committee to consider and recommend priorities for funding purposes in close consultation with the Archbishop of Canterbury. The membership included Archbishop George Carey and Bishop John Paterson as co-chairs, Mr. John Rea, Ms. Maureen Sithole, and Bishop Fernando Soares.

The Group identified five main areas:

- The promotion of mission
- Ecumenical relations
- Communications
- Enabling the Communion to meet at various levels
- A strong and effective Secretariat

The group responded to the immediate financial situation by recommending a freeze on expenditures, alternative funding for the cost of communications such as *Anglican World,* and a ten percent cut in expenditures where possible and appropriate. These measures were immediately put in place voluntarily by the Secretariat. Attention was also given to the fact that the inability of some member churches to meet their full contribution was the main cause of the current financial difficulty.

Consideration was then given to more specific details of the five priority areas identified earlier.

The working group acknowledged that two items were prime objectives: the promotion of mission and ecumenical relations. The other three were means to achieving goals in relation to these prime objectives.

The working group also pointed out that these five primary areas had been identified from the objectives of the Anglican Consultative Council as expressed in the constitution.

A. Priority One: The Promotion of Mission

> The object of the Council (the ACC) shall be to advance the Christian religion. (Constitution of the ACC)

With this in mind the working group returned to the reports of ACC-6 and ACC-8 for a definition of mission that had already been accepted by the Anglican Communion.

Page 101 of the printed report of ACC-8, entitled "Mission in a Broken World," contains the following statement:

> There has been a consistent view of mission repeated by ACC, the Lambeth Conference, the Primates' Meeting, and others in recent years, which defines mission in a fourfold way:

The mission of the Church is:

(a) to proclaim the good news of the kingdom;

(b) to teach, baptize, and nurture new believers;

(c) to respond to human need by loving service;

(d) to seek to transform the unjust structures of society.

We now feel that our understanding of the ecological crisis, and indeed of the threats to the unity of all creation, mean that we have to add a fifth affirmation:

(e) to strive to safeguard the integrity of creation and sustain and renew the life of the earth.

The working group notes that this definition of mission for the ACC sharpens the focus on the requirement "to advance the Christian religion." Each department in the Anglican Communion Office contributes to this overall priority. It gives purpose, meaning, and direction to the work of the Secretary General; the finance, communication, and ecumenical departments; and the Anglican Observer's Office at the United Nations. It also implies support for the staff of the Anglican Communion Office to be involved directly with enabling the efficient operation of various networks, commissions, and consultations in the Communion.

B. Priority Two: Ecumenical Relations

The working group noted that amongst the constitutional powers of the ACC, items e, f, g, and h detail the following:

(e) To keep before national and regional churches the importance of the fullest possible Anglican collaboration with other Christian churches.

(f) To encourage and guide Anglican participation in the ecumenical movement and the ecumenical organisations; to cooperate with the World Council of Churches and the world confessional bodies on behalf of the Anglican Communion; and to make arrangements for the conduct of pan-Anglican conversations with the Roman Catholic Church, the Orthodox churches, and other churches.

(g) To advise on matters arising out of national or regional church union negotiations or conversations and on subsequent relations with united churches.

(h) To advise on problems of inter-Anglican communication and to help in the dissemination of Anglican and ecumenical information.

The working group believes that it is important for the Anglican Communion to maintain an ecumenical department as a point of contact and reference for ecumenical matters in full support of, but quite distinct from, the important work of the Archbishop of Canterbury in these matters.

In order to carry out these two primary functions, the following support structures are seen as essential.

I. *Communications*

An effective communication operation in the various areas of:

- telecommunications
- web sites
- broadcasting
- print

are essential in order to:

- share
- support
- inform
- influence.

Objectives a, b, d, e, and h have particular reference here.

(a) To facilitate the cooperative work of the member churches of the Anglican Communion.

(b) To share information about developments in one or more provinces of the Anglican Communion with the other parts of the Communion and to serve as needed as an instrument of common action.

(d) To develop as far as possible agreed Anglican policies in the world mission of the Church and to encourage national and regional churches to engage together in developing and implementing such policies by sharing their resources of manpower, money, and experience to the best advantage of all.

(e) To keep before national and regional churches the importance of the fullest possible Anglican collaboration with other Christian churches.

(h) To advise on problems of inter-Anglican communication and to help in the dissemination of Anglican and ecumenical information.

II. Enabling the Communion to Meet at Various Levels

The Anglican Communion faces a number of issues and tensions as it seeks to promote Christ's gospel in mission to the world. In order to maintain a sense of unity in diversity on such matters as faith, worship, order, values, and understanding of Scripture, the Communion needs to be able to meet at various levels. We identify the following meetings as important:

- The Anglican Consultative Council
- The Primates
- The Joint Standing Committees
- Inter-Anglican Finance Committee
- Lambeth Conference
- Anglican Congress
- ACC and Lambeth commissions
- MISSIO
- Inter-Anglican Theological and Doctrinal Commission

III. A Strong and Effective Secretariat

The Communion is well served by a dedicated and hardworking staff. In order to assist in the shaping of policies in relation to the two main priority areas in association with the appropriate elected bodies in the Communion and then to implement policy, the members of the Secretariat should be adequately supported and resourced. In this respect the working group draws attention to the need for adequate office accommodation for the Secretariat.

The working group further believes that some clarity on the matter of process would assist the Secretariat in functioning effectively.

IV. Proposal of Priorities

i. Anglican Communion priorities may be proposed by:
- Archbishop of Canterbury
- Primates
- Anglican Consultative Council
- Lambeth Conference
- ACC or Joint Standing Committees
- Commissions
- Anglican Communion Secretariat

Anglican Communion priorities are decided by the Joint Standing Committees.

ii. Strategic Plans

Strategic plans are taken by the Joint Standing Committees.

Proposals about strategy, tactics, and targets in relation to agreed priorities might be proposed by the same groups as IV(i) above. Decisions on strategic plans are taken by the Joint Standing Committees.

iii. Budgets

(a) Budget proposals, relating to agreed activities, are prepared by the Secretariat.

(b) Budget recommendation results from Inter-Anglican Finance Committee consideration.

(c) Budget decision taken by the Joint Standing Committees.

IV. Budget Cycle

The council's bylaws state:

The Inter-Anglican Finance Committee in collaboration with the Standing Committee shall, in consultation with member churches, be responsible for the annual Inter-Anglican budget, which will include the costs of the Inter-Anglican Finance Committee, the Primates Meeting and the Lambeth Conference, and shall keep members of the council and member churches informed about each year's budget and about the forecast for each of the succeeding three years.

The effect of this is that we are always dealing with four years, the current year and the three following years. Thus, year one of a triennium will always be the year following the current year.

The Inter-Anglican Finance Committee normally meets annually and needs to have its meeting early in the calendar year in order to deal with the annual report and accounts for the previous financial year.

Taking this factor into account, the cycle needs to be as follows:

- **Early January:** After consultation with the chairman of the Inter-Anglican Finance Committee and Secretary General, the director of finances issues the year's planning timetable and budget guidelines.

- **January and February:** Preparation of separate departmental plans and budgets to agreed format:

    – Brief review of previous year's and current year's activities to date and planned activities for current year.

    – Identification of any significant change factors.

    – Three-year strategy for activity area starting with the year following the current year.

    – Detailed tactics, targets, and resource implications for year one of the three-year strategy.

    – Budget request for year one and indicative budgets for years two and three.

- **Early March:** Agreement of departmental plans and associated budget requests by the Secretary General.

- **March or April:**

    1. The Secretary General submits ACO budget (including the UN office) to the Inter-Anglican Finance Committee.

    2. The director of finances and the Secretary General provide up-to-date income information and any other relevant contributions, ideas, or proposals to the Inter-Anglican Finance Committee.

    3. The Inter-Anglican Finance Committee reviews current year budget expenditures and so forth.

    4. The Inter-Anglican Finance Committee considers proposed strategic plans and associated budget requests and agrees on the budget to recommend to the Joint Standing Committees for decision.

    5. The Joint Standing Committees consider and agree on strategic plans and budgets.

PLENARY PRESENTATIONS

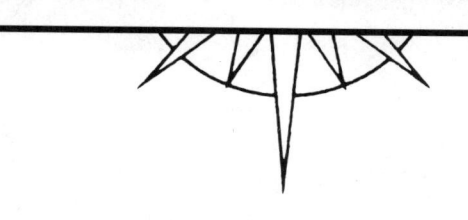

A Statement by the Chairman: Listening to the Gay and Lesbian Community

—THE RIGHT REVEREND SIMON CHIWANGA, BISHOP OF MPWAPWA, CHAIR OF THE ACC

September 19, 1999

Members of the Anglican Consultative Council (ACC) meeting this week in Scotland have today shared in a unique experience of testimony and witness. A group of gay and lesbian Christians have shared with us their own story and pilgrimage. As the ACC is a representative gathering of the worldwide Anglican Communion, the reaction to such testimonies is broad and diverse. The whole area of human sexuality is complex and personal and comes wrapped in cultural understandings. Speaking for myself, I come from Tanzania in Africa, from a church that holds the traditional teaching on human sexuality and marriage.

I am thus grateful for this hearing today, as it is consistent with the communion we share and the nature of a consultative body such as the ACC. Listening to everyone and to each other is a cardinal principle of consultation and communion. Hence, the call from the 1998 Lambeth Conference that there should be a listening process with church members who are homosexuals has begun today. Today's sharing has provoked in me and in many of us the desire to pray for one another, remembering that we are all children of God in need of redemption and the freedom found in our relationship with the Risen Christ and in our fellowship with each other.

As part of the response to the Lambeth Conference resolution, the Archbishop of Canterbury, in consultation with the Presiding Bishop of the Episcopal Church of the United States, has initiated a consultation between bishops representing all shades of opinion within the Communion. The first gathering of the group will take place in November 1999 in New York.

The Anglican Communion and the Four Instruments of Unity Briefing

—THE RT REVEREND MARK DYER, VIRGINIA THEOLOGICAL SEMINARY, UNITED STATES

I would like, if I might, to begin with a prayer. It's one of my favourite prayers. It comes from Alcuin of Tours in the seventh and eighth centuries. Let us pray:

> Eternal light, shine into our hearts; eternal goodness, deliver us from evil; eternal power, be our support; eternal wisdom, scatter the darkness of our ignorance; eternal pity, have mercy upon us, that with all our heart and mind and soul and strength, we may seek your face and be brought to your infinite mercy, to your holy presence through Jesus Christ our Lord. Amen.

My task, at the invitation of the Standing Committee, is to speak about the instruments of unity, those Four Instruments of Unity that have come to us historically as members of the Anglican Communion: the Archbishop of Canterbury, the Lambeth Conference, the ACC, and the primates—their ministry in the Church, their history, and their inter-relatedness. Tomorrow when I speak about *The Virginia Report,* as John has just said so well, I will place these in their theological context. That is not my task this afternoon. My task this afternoon is simply to explain them, and their relationship with one another, and their relationship with the Church. I'll do that then by review of the Four Instruments of Unity. And after the review, give a recent historical example of how the Four Instruments of Unity really work, and how they have worked on what I would suggest is the most contentious issue that the Anglican Communion faced in its recent history.

The Virginia Report, when it begins its presentation of the instruments of unity—and as we know, *The Virginia Report* has been received by the Lambeth Conference—reminds us clearly that there is no legislative authority in the Anglican Communion above the provincial level; that we are a Communion that is episcopally ordered, but provincially governed. *The Virginia Report* also reminds us that why we face and have these instruments of unity is because of culture and context; that within various cultures and contexts from the various provinces from which we come, and dioceses within those provinces, we will read, interpret, and try to make present again the living Gospel in the ways that come out of context. Therefore, the provinces have tremendous gifts to offer to one another, precisely because of the different cultures and contexts through which the Gospel is interpreted and lives within those contexts. We are richer because of the diversity within the provinces; because the very diversity itself opens to us new ways of looking at the mystery of God—Father, Son, and Holy Spirit—that comes to us from the various provinces, and we have them throughout our history.

So, in the development of the Anglican Communion historically, we know there is no legislative authority above the provincial level. But—and we have a very profound and helpful *but* here in *The Virginia Report*—autonomy intends a legal juridical right of each province to govern its own way of life. But in practice, autonomy has never been the sole criterion for understanding the relation of the provinces to one another. They share an implicit understanding, a kind of holy intimacy among us as Anglicans—as I like to call it. I would suggest a holy intimacy that is much stronger and much deeper and much more sound than any legislation that has ever been offered in the Church. That holy intimacy, that we have with one another as provinces as we gather as a world Communion, calls us always to allegiance to inter-dependence. So, autonomy has never stood alone. It has always gone face to face with mutual inter-dependence as a world Communion. This inter-dependence of the province, then, is now served by Four Instruments of Unity. And obviously, historically the first instrument of unity is the Archbishop of Canterbury.

Let me tell you a story of how the Archbishop of Canterbury in the personhood of the present Archbishop of Canterbury stood as a symbol of unity, continuity, and coherence in a very significant way a few years ago. It was December of 1995; it was the official patriarchal visit to Canterbury of the Patriarch of Constantinople. Unbeknownst to me at that time, twelve Lutheran bishops were doing a retreat at Canterbury Cathedral. In another month I would be debating a Lutheran bishop on "Towards Full Communion," the concordat for unity in the United States with Lutherans and Episcopalians. One of them there was directly opposed to our unity, and would be facing me off in a month's time in America after that wonderful liturgy with our Archbishop and the Patriarch of Constantinople. And that next month as I appeared at that debate, that bishop got up and said this: "On retreat in Canterbury with the Patriarch of Constantinople and the Archbishop of Canterbury, as the doors of the Cathedral opened, as the procession started down the aisle and the choir started to sing, I looked and I said to my Lutheran brothers, 'My God, look at the history that these two men embody. Look at the See of St. Andrew represented— embodiment, a personal embodiment—in Bartholomew, Archbishop of Canterbury. Look at the Benedictine heritage from Gregory I, Bishop of Rome, and Augustine and his forty monks—that's nearly 1400 years old." Two years hence we would celebrate the 1400th anniversary. He said moving down that aisle is the embodiment of continuity, of unity, and of history. And he turned to me in the debate, and said, "You know, Mark, I was converted that day. And I said to my brother Lutherans, 'We need to be part of that, that personal embodiment of continuity and unity.'"

That's essential—isn't it—that personal embodiment of historic succession. And for us, the Archbishop of Canterbury and only the Archbishop of Canterbury can represent that. No other bishop in the Communion can have that representative and personal function and ministry, because it is only at the See of Canterbury from which all of us have grown our roots. Therefore, it was the 1930 Lambeth Conference that gave focus to that very fundamental reality. And I quote—talking about Anglicanism it said we must speak about Anglicanism in this way: "It is part of the whole catholic and apostolic church. Its centre of unity is the See of Canterbury. To be an Anglican is necessarily to be in communion with that See." Why? Because of the history in the story of that Lutheran bishop—that's why.

Lambeth 1968 developed that a little bit further when it said, "Within the college of bishops, it is evident that there must be a president. In the Anglican Communion, this position is at present held by the occupant of the historic See of Canterbury, who enjoys a primacy of honour, not of jurisdiction. The primacy is found to involve in a particular way that care of all the churches which is shared by all the bishops." And then Lambeth 1978: "The unity of our Communion is personally grounded in the loyal relationship of each of the Churches with the Archbishop of Canterbury, who is freely recognised as the focus of unity."

Therefore—well let me put it this way: the incarnation is not virtual reality. The incarnation is a communal event with Jesus Christ at the centre. This historic embodiment of that communal event, that is the incarnation with Jesus Christ at the centre, must be personified in face-to-face people. It must be embodied in that literal sense of embodiment, as the Church carries out throughout its history. Therefore, the Archbishop of Canterbury as an instrument of unity is a personal embodiment of that particular ministry for us. Therefore, the Archbishop's task has been described in a particular way: that care of all the churches, which is shared by all the bishops. So, it is a sharing life. Also it is, as we say at Lambeth, the Archbishop's task not to command, but to gather, to gather the Communion in service and caring and never coercive power. So, our first instrument of unity is the historic See of Canterbury and the resident of that historic See, because we are an incarnational community. And therefore that kind of history is terribly important, as a people without history has lost its identity.

The Archbishop of Canterbury, as we have developed the Anglican instruments of unity, also serves as we know as the President of the ACC, as the one who presides and calls and gathers together the Lambeth Conference, as the first among equals who presides and calls together the meeting of the primates. So, there is a historicity and an interconnectedness in that awesome and really fearsome task before Almighty God to sit in the historic See of Canterbury.

The second instrument of unity that comes to us is the Lambeth Conference, historically. The Lambeth Conference, as we all know, met for the first time in 1867 at the request of the bishops of Canada with—I am told with a neighbour who joined that request from the State of Vermont—the Bishop of Vermont requested the calling together. Why? Because the missionary expansion of the Church of England had reached such a stage where provinces were developing, not knowing how to develop; the development of archbishops and primates were beginning to emerge; and the mission of the Gospel had to be spread indigenously. What do you do about that? So they asked the Archbishop for a conference in 1867. Striking for its identity, the Lambeth Conference would say of itself in 1867 a very cautious statement. But I need to say personally the caution expressed in this statement runs to the heart of what I understand being an Anglican is all about. So, in 1867, in its cautiousness, it said, "It has never been contemplated that we should assume the functions of a general synod of all the churches in full communion with the Church of England." We need to keep that before us these days when we look at what happened at Lambeth 1998, when some of us may want to express a charism of infallibility about resolutions that have yet even to be thought about, discussed, or received into the provinces of the Communion. Lambeth in 1867 said,

> It has never been contemplated that we should assume the functions of a general synod of all the churches in full communion with the Church of England, and take upon ourselves to enact canons that should be binding upon those represented. We merely propose to discuss matters of practical interest and pronounce what may seem expedient in resolutions.

1920 gathered that further in its own self-understanding. Lambeth 1920: "The Lambeth Conference does not claim to exercise any powers of control. It stands for the far more spiritual and Christian principle of loyalty to the fellowship."

The Archbishop quoted Ephesians very powerfully this morning. Father Raymond Brown—whom we all know as one of the greatest New Testament scholars that has been given to the Church over the years—Father Brown in writing about the ecclesiology of the Church in Ephesus says it was precisely the loyalty of that community expressed in the Epistle that was the authority residing within the community. So the community itself was defined by what? Loyalty to Christ, not in the authority above that loyalty. He argues that it was basically an unstructured community that lived on loyalty. I think it's fantastic when we say to one another what keeps us together therefore, is not the kind of issue of control, but loyalty to one another. I'll talk tomorrow about the theology of that loyalty if I might; I'll reserve that for tomorrow.

They go on to say the Churches represented are indeed intra-dependent; but independent with the Christian freedom which recognises the restraints of truth and love. The Churches we represent are not free to ignore the fellowship. The Conference is a fellowship in the Holy Spirit. So what we have is the Lambeth Conference understanding itself as an instrument of unity— of what? Loyalty to the fellowship; restraint when one another belongs to us but denying any power of compulsion over anybody.

But what has happened is that the Lambeth Conference then went to proceed to establish the next two instruments of unity. That's part of the paradoxical nature of the Anglican Communion. Over and over again it said it had no authority to compel, but nevertheless it began in 1958 the development of what was to become the Anglican Consultative Council. So, we are a creature of the Lambeth Conference—although the Lambeth Conference says it has no authority to make us the creature we are. It's a wonderful paradox. But I think those paradoxes are important to what it means to be an Anglican, because it forces us to go within rather than out, when we talk and share with one another. It forces us to be attentive to one another, to be loyal to one another, to have that holy intimacy that I'm speaking about. I'm not going to spend too much time on the ACC, because John did a marvellous job expressing to us this morning the constitutions and the development of the ACC and the responsibility of the ACC.

As one who has worked on a number of commissions over the years, I just want to say and add to that, that we could not function, nor perhaps could the Communion function without the loyalty and the very hard work of the Anglican Communion Office. An awful lot of what we say the ACC does, we don't do. The ACO does—the Anglican Communion Office and that devoted very small staff of people who carry out what we say and how we say it without us having to need to carry it out.

What we need to develop and understand, and the question before us, is, "How do we as a representative body of the Anglican Communion function as an instrument of unity for the Communion?" And I suggest that what we need to do is look at the nature of our agenda when we meet, and say our task—after the things that John said, the work that we have to do, the overriding task we need to do—is to function as a community of people, that communal event that is the incarnation with Jesus Christ at its centre. How do we nurture and sustain the inter-dependence and the unity of this Communion for the sake of the Gospel of Jesus Christ and his mission? I wonder if we have developed that over-riding logical rubric that says this is who we are? And it's critically important—because of theology and of baptism—that there be lay persons, presbyters, I would say deacons, and bishops, as representatives at this meeting. Because, as I'll say tomorrow, no one of us has the charism of teaching and authority that comes because of our baptism. And we, therefore, must listen to one another. I—for one, if I might put my cards on the table—I, for one, would like to see this as widely representative as possible. And allow the primates to have their meeting; but allow us to have our meeting. And with bishops coming from provinces represented here who are not primates, we'd have a richer understanding of Anglican identity. But that's where I'm laying it out, if I might—and that's not in *The Virginia Report*. So, we meet every three years. The Standing Committee meets annually. We're the only legally incorporated body within the Anglican Communion, as John said this morning. But our task is a mutual attentiveness to our dioceses, our province, and this whole Communion to be instruments—of what? Of unity and inter-dependence for the sake of the Gospel. That's what I would say our main purpose is.

In 1978, I believe Archbishop Coggan in his address to the Lambeth Conference stressed the necessity of this inter-relatedness. We know now how the Archbishop is intimately and personally inter-related with the Four

Instruments of Unity, as the one who calls, who gathers, and presides over all the Four Instruments of Unity. So, there is that inter-connectedness. So, the personal experience and life of the Archbishop of Canterbury there is a spokesperson within the four. The call to gather; never to compel or make us comply, but to be attentive and to listen to one another.

But how are the ACC and the primates related? And how is the ACC related to Lambeth? We're a long way off, I would suggest, to seeing how the ACC is related to the Lambeth Conference. Had I not another job that took a significant amount of time at Lambeth 1998—if I were just there as a member of the ACC—I am afraid I would have felt lost and not incorporated, as I don't know that I would have had an agenda. I'm not asking to vote, I'm not asking for a voice. But, I'm asking for some kind of voice in small groups or something where the ACC can make its impact. So, I'd say *The Virginia Report* at the end suggests that the ACC does need some kind of identity—if it's invited to a Lambeth Conference—but also a level of authority and responsibility for its life at Lambeth. And we have ten years to work that out; to see how it works out. But *The Virginia Report* does pose the question, "If ACC members are invited to Lambeth, what do they do? How are they incorporated? And, what would their task be?" That gives people the feeling that they are wanted; they're needed and incorporated into the whole life of a wider meeting.

Archbishop Coggan spoke significantly, then, of the relationship of the ACC to the primates. For, it was Lambeth 1978 that formally established the primates' meeting as an instrument of unity for the Communion. He said this—it's a bit of a long quote from his speech, but it's very significant, I think:

> I, Donald Coggan, am coming to believe that the way forward in the coming years may be a slow process. It will be along two lines. First, to have a meeting of the primates of the Communion reasonably often for leisurely thought, prayer, and deep consultation. There have been such meetings, but on a very informal and rare basis. I believe they should be held perhaps as frequently as once in every two years. But if that meeting now were on some fairly regular basis, if it is to be fruitful, those primates would have to come to the meeting well-informed with a knowledge of the mind and will of their provinces and their dioceses they represent. They are to be channels of thought through which the voice of the member Churches would be heard, then a real interchange of mind and will and heart could take place. That's the first thing. The second line I think on which we might make progress would be to see that the body of primates as they meet should be in the very closest and most intimate contact with the ACC.

The question *The Virginia Report* asked the Lambeth Conference members to reflect on this particular time was what? "Is that happening? And, if it isn't—or how is it happening?" How can we deepen, in Donald Coggan's words, that close and intimate contact between the meeting of the primates and the meeting of the ACC? Questions that I am not able to answer, as I have not served in either position, but: Is the Standing Committee meeting of the primates and ACC enough? Is the dissemination to the whole ACC of what happens at a primates and ACC Standing Committee meeting sufficient? A lot of questions we need to ask, I suggest, as members of the ACC is "How do we do that?" Because I think Archbishop Coggan was right on the task when he said it needs to be personal, it needs to be intimate, and it needs to be close.

The primates' meeting, then, a creature of 1978; their first meeting is 1979. They said of themselves, "The role of the primates' meeting should not be, and was not desired as, a higher synod." Can you hear that refrain in everything everybody is saying? Every instrument of unity in defining itself has said that—including that of the Archbishop of Canterbury. The role of the primates "should not be, and was not desired as, a higher synod." Rather, it's a clearinghouse for ideas experienced through free expression, the fruits of which the primates might convey to their Churches. Each meeting of the primates gathers in the context of Eucharist, prayer, and Bible study—as we do. And in 1991, at the meeting in Newcastle in Ireland, they had three very important points that they wanted to make about themselves, and how they saw their ministry in the Church. Their primary importance of meeting is the building and maintenance of their personal relationships—what first is a sign of unity of the catholicity of the Churches. Therefore, they wanted to be a public embodiment and visible sign of the unity and communion of all the Churches as primates meeting; to give high profile to important issues that may be coming up; and for mutual support and counsel of one another.

Standing before the primates is a resolution of Lambeth 1988 and Lambeth 1998. Lambeth 1998 repeated the theme that was expressed in the words in 1988. The resolution passed significantly at both Conferences.

It's a holy struggle I believe that primates do have to deal with, because the question we ask in *The Virginia Report* is, "Is the internal unity, coherence, and inter-dependence of the Communion strong enough to make the necessary witness, that one must make to the Gospel, as a world Communion?" Is our inter-dependence, our unity, our life in the Gospel as a world Communion—not as individual provinces or dioceses—is that strong enough, is it coherent enough, is it visible enough to make the necessary witness that is needed in terms of the Gospel with a Church that is disintegrating and a history that is thoroughly dehumanising, and where the call of the Gospel is radically needed? Is the Communion strong enough when contentious issues arise out of a particular context and culture, and a province goes ahead in its own specific way out of that context and culture, because it is the last legislative authority in the Communion? Is the Communion strong enough to stay in the deepest level of Communion possible in Christ and with one another? And are the instruments of unity strong enough to allow this to happen and make this happen?

Unity is an essential characteristic of the life in Christ. It's also an essential characteristic for evangelism and mission. ". . . that they may all be one. As you, Father, are in me and I am in you. . . . so that the world may believe." So the world may believe, goes John 17. Evangelism and mission. Unity is essential to mission. I remember a South African bishop at Lambeth 1998 saying, "For too long a divided Church was too weak for the strength of apartheid." Mission of the Gospel in the oppression of people. "For too long," too long, "a divided Church was too weak for the power of apartheid." So, we must see how essential these instruments of unity are—both for the inner life of the Church and the Gospel, and for the outer life of evangelism and mission, because a world that does not believe will not believe with Christians who are divided with one another. So, will they not believe from a Communion with the same identity who does not love one another and care for one another?

Finally then, let me wrap this up with this example that I wanted to give of what Dr. Mary Tanner has called the credible model of decision making and implementation in Church—and the fantastic paper she has written has been published in a number of languages through the World Council of Churches. She wrote it as moderator of the Faith and Order section of the World Council of Churches. For those of you who don't know who Mary is—this is my prejudice, and I have worked with Mary for a good many years now—I would say, Mary is the most significant ecumenical person that the Anglican Communion has given birth to. She is one of the principal authors of DEM, the Lima document; moderator of the World Council of Churches; a member of ARCIC, the Anglican-Roman Catholic International Commission; and drafter of most of our Communion documents on unity with a team of people. Here's the story I want to tell you. And I tell this story because it will incarnate for two reasons: number one, I'm Irish and I can't step down without telling a story; and number two, because it offers a cohesion to show how the instruments of unity, one with another, really work when we face a very contentious issue:

The contentious issue happened with us, the United States Church, when our bishops a few years before Lambeth 1988 voted in its interpretation of our canons to ordain women to the presbyterate, the priesthood, that there was sufficient clarity within that canon that in no way did it also inhibit—to the contrary in every way it fostered—the possibility of a woman bishop, and therefore if due canonical process was followed by a particular diocese of the Episcopal Church and a woman was elected a bishop, the bishops had no right not to assent to that election if all the canonical processes had been followed fully and the person was an appropriate candidate to be a bishop. The gender would have nothing to do with it. Here we are. Here's a province that has its own authority to do that. It made up its mind it's going to do that. But then it said, "Wait a minute. That is an issue that touches on the whole Communion. It is not simply an issue that's alone to the American Church, although it may have been engendered by our context and culture."

So, our primate, Ed Browning, was asked by the bishops who said, "Ed, you've got to take that to the primates' meeting, because unity is important and consultation is important. Yes, we have the sole authority to do that as a province of the Anglican Communion, but our loyalty to one another, our sacred intimacy, and face-to-face reality of the Communion as a world Communion means take that to the next primates' meeting." Ed said—and he's confessed to us that he was dreadfully frightened to do it. This was his first meeting of the primates. He'd never met with the primates before. They met in Canada. Ed brought it to the primates. Archbishop Runcie was in the chair. Ed presented what we had intended to do. And I must say, the intention was there to carry it out, what we intended to do. But inter-dependence was important to us; the intimacy of the Communion was important to us. "I need to tell you this. What are we going to do about it?" The primates discussed it. So, one province touches one instrument of unity, namely the primates. The primates discuss all of this and say, "Well, then we now have to do something about this because it does touch the whole Communion. It's an issue that will divide the Church. It's a reality that will divide the Church. It's literally an incarnational embodiment that will divide the Church. It's the only thing that does divide it anyway."

So, the primates together with the Archbishop of Canterbury turned to John Grinrod, the Archbishop of Australia, and said, "John, we want you to work with a team of primates and others who will help you to speak to all the provinces of the Communion about this issue between now and the Lambeth Conference." Now, some of you have read and seen—those of you who like myself are old-timers in this business—the "Grinrod Report," an absolute masterpiece of a report. Many provinces responded, and some were unable to respond. Again, you have the primates touching all the provinces as primates; the reports coming in.

John arrived at Lambeth—and now we touch the next base of the instruments for unity and how they are inter-related. He arrives at the Lambeth Conference. He has three suggestions for the Conference. The first was don't do anything, knowing that America would anyway. That was one thing he heard from the Communion, "Don't do it." The second thing he heard from the Communion was, "Well, do it," from those who thought it was appropriate to do. And the third was what ended up in our resolution of the Lambeth Conference of 1988. This resolution would then come to the ACC and back to the primates, if it were passed.

Note Anglican polity here. We struck the heart in writing this resolution, the heart of Anglican polity. We didn't ask any bishop whether they agreed or disagreed to the ordination of women to the episcopate. We did not think that was appropriate. What we did ask the bishops was, "Are we committed to provincial authority?" So, the first resolve was that each province respects the decision and attitudes of other provinces in the ordination and consecration of women to the episcopate; without such respect necessarily indicating an acceptance of the principles involved; maintaining, however, the highest possible degree of communion with provinces that disagree with one another.

Note that resolution, then. Each province must respect the decision and attitudes of the other provinces in the ordination and consecration of women to the episcopate without necessarily indicating acceptance of that or its principles, but always committed to maintaining the highest degree of Communion possible. The second resolve was that bishops now exercise courtesy and maintain communication with bishops who may differ and with any woman, ensuring open dialogue in the Church, to whatever extent Communion should now become impaired. Third, that the Archbishop of Canterbury, in consultation with the primates, appoint a committee that (a) would provide for an examination of the relationship between provinces of the Anglican Communion, and ensure that the process of reception includes continuing consultation with other Churches as well. Finally, (b) to monitor and encourage the process of consultation within the Communion, and to offer full pastoral guidelines for any province where reconciliation on these issues is necessary. Any diocesan bishop facing this problem would be encouraged to seek continuing dialogue with, and make pastoral provision for, those clergy and congregations whose opinions differ from those of the bishop in order to maintain the unity of the diocese. And finally, recognise the serious hurt which would result from the questioning of some of the validity of the episcopal act of a woman bishop. Likewise, the hurt experienced by those whose conscience would be offended by the ordination of a woman to the episcopate. The Church needs to exercise its sensitivity, patience, and pastoral care towards all concerned.

That's how we've formed the resolution. John Grinrod says this is probably the best one to go with. We went with that at the Lambeth Conference. Let me give you the vote. You can remember, I'm sure, in 1988 how many provinces opposed the ordination of women, even to the priesthood. A vast majority did. What was the vote? 423 bishops for, 28 against, and 19 abstentions. Why? Because the resolution went to the heart of what Anglicanism is: province, a provincial authority, consultation, inter-dependence, and respect, and how we kept together.

As you know, coming out of that—let me continue—the story continues. Coming out of that was the formation of the Eames Commission—which I was privileged to serve on—The Archbishop's Commission on Women in the Episcopate. Our task was to form the theological framework of *koinonia*, communion, to see how that theological framework of communion would reach all the provinces; and then understand what it means to stay on the deepest level of communion with one another and at the level of the most profound disagreements, and how we could nurture that; and see how the process of reception of women in the ordained ministry was going on in the Anglican Communion. We offered our final report to Lambeth 1998, when we polled all the provinces—I don't have all the statistics with me. The key is we did not divide over that issue—that's what I want to lift up to you—because we put into play all the instruments of unity. During that ten-year period, two instruments of unity became critical as the Eames Commission kept reporting back. First was the ACC meetings during that period. And secondly was the primates' Meeting during that period. The Eames Commission kept reporting and reporting.

So what we had in history is the inter-relationship of the Four Elements of Unity. And, my sisters and brothers of Christ, it really works. And it works with as contentious an issue as I think the Church faced for an awfully long time: namely, women as bishops and then for those who disagreed that women could be bishops, even those men that those women ordained would not be valid within the Communion—an incredible break in the historic succession of the order of presbyterian bishop if you did not agree, that a woman could not be a bishop. And yet we have lived through that.

The final monitoring report has shown how wonderfully we have lived through that as a people of respect, attentiveness, and holy listening, and holy care for one another. We wonder in *The Virginia Report*, Does that not present a model also for ecumenical unity, where people who disagree over issues can still be one in communion and in Christ together? And then, we wonder even more boldly in *The Virginia Report*, Wouldn't it be a model for nations and people? When we disagree, how do we find the deepest level of communion possible so that we can live and love together, even though we disagree? And may disagree not forever, because when we go to heaven, we're not going to have that burden of disagreement. It will be different, but it will be more fun, and then we'll live together.

So, what I need to say before I close, then, is that the instruments of unity have developed historically within the Communion. They are our way of inter-dependence, of mutuality, and unity. And history has taught us that it really works, and can work if we work at it. Therefore, as we face contentious issues today, I would suggest some of the major contentious issues around which we are talking have not been submitted to that discipline. And that's why we are in trouble now. They have not been submitted to that discipline of the Four Instruments of Unity. In some of the contentious issues today, we have sort of run around them, and we do that as Anglicans to our peril. I would say the spirit of God in the laity, the spirit of God in deacon and presbyter and bishop and archbishop will speak, because the heart of Anglicanism is not virtual reality. It's face to face. And each one of these instruments of unity, as I've tried to explain it, is one. It's face to face. So, when we're on one side and on the other side, together we bring one another back to the centre, for the incarnation is a communal event, with Jesus Christ at the centre and he who brings us together.

The Virginia Report Presentation

—THE RT. REVEREND J. MARK DYER, VIRGINIA THEOLOGICAL SEMINARY, UNITED STATES

Introduction

Whenever I lecture before such a prestigious and learned group such as the membership of the Anglican Consultative Council, my anxiety level is quickly rested by the words of a very saintly Benedictine monk who once said to me, "Don't worry, brother Mark. Silence is the language of God; everything else is a bad translation." And now I must talk about God and God's Church, so I will be offering a bad translation of the most holy mystery of God and God's Church. Hence we ought to begin with prayer. It is a prayer from the ancient Celtic tradition.

> Come O Father, Son, and Holy Spirit and weave a silence upon my life; weave a silence upon my mind; weave a silence within my heart. Close my ears to distractions; close my eyes to attentions; close my heart to temptations. Calm me, O Lord as you stilled the storm. Still me O Lord, keep me from harm. Let all the tumult within me cease. Enfold me O Lord in your peace.

We are here to share and discuss *The Virginia Report*, that is, "The Report of the Inter-Anglican Theological and Doctrinal Commission" to the Lambeth Conference 1998. The 1988 Lambeth Conference recognized that there was a need to describe how the Anglican Communion makes authoritative decisions while maintaining unity and interdependence in the light of the many theological issues that arise from its diversity. To address this need the Conference resolved that there should be:

> As a matter of urgency further exploration of the meaning and nature of communion with particular reference to the doctrine of the Trinity, the unity and order of the Church, and the unity and community of humanity. (Lambeth Conference 1988, Resolution 18)

In response to this Resolution the Archbishop of Canterbury appointed a doctrinal and theological commission under the chairmanship of the Most Reverend Robin Eames, Archbishop of Armagh and All Ireland. *The Virginia Report* represents the Commission's work. We are here in Dundee, Scotland to study and discuss this report in response to Resolution III.8 of the 1998 Lambeth Conference which "requests the Primates to initiate and monitor a decade of study in each Province of *The Virginia Report*." As representatives of the Provinces of the Anglican

Communion we are being asked to bring the *Report* back home for further study and reception. Hence *The Virginia Report* is a document waiting for response and reception by the separate but interdependent Provinces of the Communion.

I. The Context

The task we face is how do we as a world Communion of Churches maintain unity and order and strive to be faithful to the Gospel within our own particular contexts and cultures. Fidelity to the Gospel requires all of us in our own local way to respond to issues of justice and human rights, human sexuality, the family, the status of women, racial equality, religious freedom, the use and distribution of resources.

The question to be answered is, "How do we avoid alienation from those who by baptism are our brothers and sisters in Christ, who are embraced in the communion of God the Holy Trinity and yet disagree? How do we stay in Communion with God and each other, how do we behave towards each other in the face of disagreement and conflict? What are the limits of diversity if the Gospel imperative of unity and communion are to be maintained?"

II. Theology of God's Gracious Gift: The Communion of the Trinity and the Church

I'd like to go, if I may, immediately to Chapter 3. This is the controlling chapter of *The Virginia Report*. It is the most serious and the most important chapter of *The Virginia Report* because in it we relate the doctrine of the Holy Trinity to the doctrine of the Church and who we are as God's people. God's love and God's faithfulness, as we know, is understood first and foremost biblically as being an act of creation. God's promise is an everlasting covenant between God and every living creature on earth because of the act of creation. The promise is renewed over and over and over again, and God's promise finds a deeper and more fundamental fulfillment in the creation of Israel as God's people. Let's think about that for a few moments as it appears in *The Virginia Report*. You remember with me the story in Exodus 3:14, where the tradition places Moses in Midian caring for the flock of his father-in-law, and there he sees a bush that appears to be burning. He approaches that bush, and as he approaches he hears a voice saying, "Moses, Moses, this is holy ground. You, take off your shoes." And he approaches again, and he hears God speak to him about God's identity, about the character of God: "I am the God of your father, I am the God of Abraham, Isaac, and Jacob." And the Scriptures tell us that Moses was afraid to look at the face of God, and turned his head down. And then God went on, "I have observed the misery of my people . . . I have heard their cry . . . . Indeed, I know their sufferings, and

I have come down to deliver them." The pivotal element in the history of God's people. God is reaching into the vitals of who God is and what God is like, and entering history and saying,

> Moses, let me define what my I am is. My I am is personal, it is relational because the fact that I am the God of people, the God of Abraham, Isaac, and Jacob. But I am also a God of liberation. Why? Because I hear; I hear their cries; I observe their misery; I know their suffering. I have come to deliver.

And out of that moment, a people began to be gathered together in the most wonderful ways of personal, relational intimacy with God. Later, as they passed through the desert, they would ask Moses, "What does this mean for us? What's our identity now? If God had reached into the vitals of who God is and what God is like, and said this is who I am for you, who are we now that there's been a radical change in identity? Who are we now?" Remember the words attributed to Moses:

> You are a people holy to the Lord your God. The Lord your God has chosen you out of all the peoples of the earth to be his people, his treasured possession. It was not because you are more numerous than any other people that the Lord set his heart upon you and chose you, for you are fewer than all the peoples of the earth. It is simply because the Lord loved you and kept the oath he made to your ancestors. (Deuteronomy. 7:6–8)

I want you to think with me now of our identity, our biblical identity. And let me rehearse these words again, because they are central to *The Virginia Report* and the whole theology of *The Virginia Report*: You are a holy people. You are chosen. You are God's people. You are God's treasured possession. You are the ones God has set his heart upon. You are the ones loved by God.

We have inherited that identity and that tradition. This truth is obviously further deepened as it comes to us in the Prophets, particularly the Prophets of the Return. Isaiah speaks so intimately of the relationship with God:

> You shall be called My Delight Is in Her, and your land Married; for the Lord delights in you, and your land shall be Married. For as a young man marries a young woman, so shall your builder marry you, and as the bridegroom rejoices over the bride, so shall your God rejoice over you. (Isaiah 62: 4–5)

What powerfully intimate language: As the bride and the bridegroom rejoice on their wedding night, so is God's relationship with God's people. So you will never, ever again be termed forsaken or abandoned or lost.

From the later Jeremiah and the return again:

> But this is the covenant that I will make with the house of Israel after those days, says the Lord: I will put my Law within them, and I will write it on their hearts; and I will be their God and they shall be my people. (Jeremiah 31:33)

Torah will be heart-written. *Torah* will be written in their heart.

The amazing thing for us as God's people is that Jesus spoke of this God of steadfast loving kindness and faithfulness as his Father. He prayed:

> I thank you, Father, Lord of heaven and earth, because you have hidden these things from the wise and the intelligent and have revealed them to infants; yes, Father, for such was your gracious will. All things have been handed over to me by my Father; and no one knows the Son except the Father, and no one knows the Father except the Son and anyone to whom the Son chooses to reveal him. (Matthew 11:25)

What we did in *The Virginia Report* is to start to build a theological foundation that makes it virtually impossible for us to unbind our relationships with one another. That's our purpose. To so bind us into the theology of God such that we have no right, after that, to unbind ourselves—however severe the disagreements that come our way. We must be bounded together until the disagreements are no longer with us, because the Good News of the Gospel is that Jesus' life is God's life among us—God breaking down the barriers of our bondage, and our sinfulness, and our divisions. In Jesus, God is faithful even to the cross. And on the cross we encounter a God who is willing to suffer with us, at our side, for us, and even at our hands—but always on our behalf. That is the God of the cross—isn't it? A God who is willing to suffer with us, for us, at our side, and even at our hands—but in every instance for us, on our behalf. Jesus is God with us. To know Jesus is to be with God. We know God as we live with Jesus. So we must say that Jesus' life is the expression of God with us.

Now the climax of the revelation of the Son of God occurs in the last discourse in John's Gospel just before he dies, on the night before he died. Remember these words from the fifteenth chapter of John's Gospel: "As the Father has loved me, so I have loved you; abide in my love." This is a very clear theological statement: As the Father loves me, so I love you; abide in my love. What then is the love within which we abide? It is the love that is between the Father and the Son. Jesus goes on to say, "No one has greater love than this, to lay down one's life for one's friends. I have called you friends, because I have made known to you everything I have heard from my Father." So, we are identified as a friend of Jesus who has received both everything from him about God the Father, and the bonding of love that is the love of the Holy Trinity. Jesus goes on to say, "You did not choose me but I chose you. And I appointed you to go and bear fruit, fruit that will last so that the Father will give you whatever you ask in my name. I am giving you this gift so that you may love one another as I have loved you." The *torah* of Jesus is to love one another as he has loved us, and we can only understand that from the cross.

What does the cross say about staying together in the midst of disagreements? Would it be a violation to walk away from the foot of the cross and say that someone is not my sister and someone is not my brother? But do we stay together long enough into one another's pain and one another's sorrow and one another's anguish and into one another's cross until we can look at one another and say *yes* to one another? Do we take that time? Thus our unity with one another in the Church is grounded in the life of love, unity, and communion of the Godhead. The eternal, mutual self-giving and receiving of love of the three persons of the Trinity is the source of identity and unity of the Anglican Communion and of all Christian Communions. It is a source of our fellowship with God and one another. And through the power of the Holy Spirit we are drawn into a divine fellowship of love and unity.

I want to expand that thought because it is very important that we look at the doctrine of the Trinity with some intimacy: The God of the Gospel is Father, Son, and Holy Spirit, and it should be clear that the Holy Trinity is not primarily a creed, nor is it primarily a doctrine. We don't believe in a creed; we don't believe in a doctrine. We believe in God whom creeds and the doctrines express. The Holy Trinity is a Communion of persons, the living God whose name is Love and who seeks to share divine love with all creatures, and to draw all creatures into a sharing of that same divine love. God remains God, a mystery beyond our understanding, and we remain creatures. Yet the God who is a Communion of Persons invites us to share the divine life, and become more complete persons ourselves as we learn to live in Communion in Christ with other human persons. God the Holy Trinity is a model for all human community: different persons united in a bond of mutual love. The Holy Trinity is, therefore, the model of life of the Church, whose life is meant to reflect that of the Trinity and anticipate the unity God intends for the whole human race. The Holy Trinity, therefore, is neither a creed nor a doctrine. It's a life: a life into which we are invited to enter, a love we are called to accept and pass on, a unity in which we as Church must grow, so that we may foster the Communion of all human persons within that communion of Persons who creates us, redeems us, dwells in our midst, and seeks fulfillment only in the life of divine love.

The Holy Trinity is not simply a model of life of the Church it is the very life, identity, and unity of the Church. The Church happens when in baptism we are gathered into the life of God the Holy Trinity.

> You have received a sprit of adoption. When we cry 'Abba! Father!' it is that very Spirit bearing witness with our spirit that we are children of God, and if children, then heirs, heirs of God and joint heirs with

Christ if, in fact we suffer with him so that we may be glorified with him. (Romans 8: 15-17, Galatians 4:6)

The Church is the place of mutual indwelling with God. Our unity is God-given. The Holy Spirit takes us into community with Jesus, the Son of God, and we thereby become, in Jesus Christ, sons and daughters of God, the Father. So we pray, "Abba, Father."

So, the Church's identity is not of human making. Everything in the Church is gift and derivative. Authority is derivative; life is derivative; everything we have is derived from a gift: the gift of the life, death, and resurrection of Jesus; the coming of the Holy Spirit; and our life in the Holy Trinity.

For this reason, the Church is the Body of Christ (1 Corinthians 12:27), the temple of God (1 Corinthians 3:16), a chosen race, a royal priesthood, a holy nation, God's own people (1 Peter 2:9). These images, therefore, speak of a community of people, a Church, which is in communion with God, the Father, the Son, and the Holy Spirit.

Now this communion should determine our relationship with one another. That is the argument of *The Virginia Report*. This is the relationship that needs to determine how we relate to one another. As 1 John would say, "We declare to you what we have seen and heard so that you may also have *koinonia* with us; and truly our fellowship is with the Father and with the Son Jesus Christ." Communion with God and one another is both gift and divine expectation for the Church.

This Church—that is the Body of Christ, the Temple of God, the chosen race, a royal priesthood, a holy nation, God's people—is an eschatological community. A word theologians like to use today is that we are a *proleptic* community. What *proleptic* simply means is that we are meant to be the community of "coming attractions." The Church as a proleptic community, or as an eschatological community, is gifted by the Holy Spirit with a grace to live out the end time in the meantime. If we don't live the end time in the meantime, then who is going to recognize Christ when he comes back at the end time? Who is going to recognize Jesus when he comes back again unless there is a community of people living at the end times in the meantime? We are living at the end of history in the midst of history—this is what eschatology means. When we live as Jesus lived, we manifest the character of his coming again.

What *The Virginia Report* does is theologically to draw a line between the life of the Holy Trinity and the life and mission of the Church, the Body of Christ. Hence, our unity with one another is grounded in the life of love, unity, and communion of the Godhead—the eternal and mutual self-giving and receiving-love of the three Persons of the Trinity that is the source and ground of our Communion, our fellowship with God and one another. Now, the question: How does the life of God, Father, Son, and Holy Spirit that is revealed in the life, teaching, death, and resurrection of Jesus determine how we live together when we disagree over critical issues on the practice of Gospel-life? I'll do it again in one full statement: How does the life of God, Father, Son, and Holy Spirit—revealed in the life, teaching, death, and resurrection of Jesus Christ that is gracefully given to us—determine how we live together when we disagree over critical issues on the practice of the Gospel? That is the question that runs to the very heart of the theology of *The Virginia Report*.

III. Belonging Together in the Anglican Communion

We have spoken about life in communion, the church as the Body of Christ, the Temple of God, the chosen race, a royal priesthood, the holy nation of God's people. This Church must have some historical visibility. We've got to see it. We are seen as Church-visible by certain, defining elements that express our identity and mission in the Gospel. First, we share a common confession of faith expressed in the historic creeds of the church.

Secondly, we share a life of common prayer. And we know that Scripture comes to us as the word of God in the liturgical cycle of the Common Prayer: morning prayer, evening prayer, Eucharist. That liturgical cycle brings the scripture to us in prayer and praise, and identifies us in a specific way. During the Reformation we defined ourselves with a Prayer Book, and said, "This is what we look like." We are a people who identified as a people who offer Common Prayer. We make the grace of God the Holy Trinity, and who we are as Church, visible through creed and through prayer.

Thirdly, we are a community that believes in the authority and primacy of the Holy Scriptures. That is the basis of our life. The biblical narrative couldn't come to us otherwise. The Scriptures come to us as God's living word in the lived experience of Word and Sacrament: Baptism and Holy Eucharist. We do it all in memory of him, and his memory deepens and sustains us. We do it also with the servanthood and service of the ordained ministry in the historic succession of bishop, priest, and deacon. We do it in a Church that is synodically governed and episcopally ordered. And we do it, finally, in a shared common life of serving and mission for the sake of the Gospel.

These are elements in *The Virginia Report* that are elements of defining. They take the vision of God, the vision of the Church, and they bring it into concrete historical reality.

So, as we look at the life of the Trinity, the life of the Church, and the essential ways *The Virginia Report* says how we live this reality, can you recognize yourself in that portrait? That's what *The Virginia Report* wants to say. Do we recognize ourselves in that portrait? That is, a portrait of the people of God receiving God's gracious gift of life of communion in the Holy Trinity lived out in the confession of a common faith, the celebration of Baptism and Holy Eucharist, a life of common prayer, the service of an ordered ministry, conciliar structures, shared service and mission. These elements are lived out in a distinctly Anglican way.

We are held together in a visible communion of life. Baptism is God's gift of unity. It is a means by which persons participate in the life of God, Father, Son, and Holy Spirit. It is the way we are brought into a living faith within the community of faith. The change that occurs at baptism is even more radical than the change that occurs at our natural birth. At natural birth you will be born and die, with baptism you're born and we live forever. We have opened the gates of heaven, and we are on our way to eternity, and we have been given all the gifts of the Holy Spirit that are necessary for the salvation and life of the Church.

Now let us look at the Anglican way of Scripture, tradition, and reason, as presented in *The Virginia Report*. Anglicans affirm the sovereign authority of Holy Scripture. It is the medium, or the way, or the word, through which God by the Spirit communicates God's word in the Church. It enables people to respond with faith and understanding. The scriptures are, indeed, uniquely inspired witness to divine revelation. They are the primary norm for Christian faith and love. The Scriptures are inspired because they are the word that allows us to encounter the living God. The Scriptures are a series of narratives of the people of God. And if we enter with faith into the narrative of the people of God and Jesus of Nazareth, we then enter into the very life of God through that word. And that's why it is primary; that's why it is word that rules and orders our life.

But we also say that Scripture is understood and read in the light afforded by tradition and reason. In a very real sense, biblical scholars will tell you that the Scripture itself is tradition, because before the Scripture ever became the written word it was the received word and the lived word and the interpreted word. So, tradition is itself a creature of the scripture, and scripture itself is a creature of tradition. Tradition is the faith that once delivered to the saints. *The Virginia Report* says, therefore, tradition is the living mind and nerve centre of the Church. Anglican appeal to tradition is appeal to the mind of the Church that is carried by prayer, worship, teaching, and spirit-filled life of the people of God. So how is the tradition carried? First by prayer, then by worship, teaching, and the spirit-filled life of a Christian who is a person in community and lives that spirit-filled life. Tradition, therefore, denotes the ongoing spirit-guided life of the Church which receives and interprets God's message again and again through history. Tradition is the *regula fidei*, the "rule of faith." A very important contribution to an understanding of tradition is found in

The Gift of Authority. This latest agreed statement of the Anglican-Roman Catholic International Consultation defines tradition this way: Tradition is the revealed word to which the Apostolic community originally bore witness as it is received and communicated through the life of the whole Christian community. Tradition refers to this process. The Gospel of Christ crucified and risen is continually handed on and received in the Christian Churches. This tradition of handing on of the Gospel is the work of the Holy Spirit, especially through the ministry of word and sacrament, and in common with the life of the people of God. So, we have Scripture as the primary authority of our life. But we also have the spirit-filled interpretation of Scripture generation after generation which keeps the apostolic message alive and stays alive.

But the third step really needs to be considered, namely, reason. But when we speak about reason we are not talking about naked, rational reason. What we are talking about is what one of the greatest theologians that ever sat in the chair of St. Augstine at Canterbury, St. Anselm, said: that the work of reason is always a subject to faith, *fides quaerens intellectum.* "Faith seeking an understanding." We talk about reason in the faith-light of Scripture and tradition. It is a spirit-filled reason, the reason of faith.

So, we are people of Scripture, tradition, and reason; we are people of sacrament and worship. The Scriptures come to us and they are interpreted in our communities in a round of daily prayer and celebration of the sacraments. The revelation of God comes to us in word and sacrament. The place of primary theology where all of the baptized, laity, bishop, priest, deacon, live, interpret, and minister in the Gospel.

I want to spend some time with the structures of ecclesial interdependence because this runs to the heart of Anglicanism in a very special way. The structures of interdependence and unity, namely the interdependence of charisms in the life of the church, are how Anglicans express the charisms in the life of the church. In speaking of the laity in *The Virginia Report* we put it this way: "the calling of lay persons," that is, "all who are baptized" into the life of God "live out their calling as members of the Anglican Communion" and "are given the charism of the Holy Spirit for the life of the Communion." All of the baptized live out the life of God and their calling as members of the Communion by the gifts of the Holy Spirit for the life of the Communion and for the service of others. So, every baptized Christian has the charism for ministry in the Church and for the mission of the Gospel. So, what are those charisms? We outline them in the report. We say, for example,

> The calling of lay persons is to represent Christ and his Church; to bear witness to him wherever they may be; and according to the gifts given to them, to carry out Christ's work of reconciliation in the world, and to take their place in the life, worship, and governance of the Church.

Because we believe that the baptized have the charism of the Spirit we therefore in our synodical structure—whether it be parish, diocese, province, or communion—take our place in the life, worship, and governance of the church. So, no one may be excluded because all have been called and gifted.

The Virginia Report also speaks of the charisms of the ordained ministry.

> To enable the community of faith to respond to Christ's call, God has given to the Church the charism of ordered ministry: the episcopate, the presbyterate, and the diaconate. The ordained ministry is exercised with, in, and among the whole people of God.

The ordered ministry has its special charisms.

> The calling of a bishop is to represent Christ and his Church, particularly as apostle, chief priest, teacher, and pastor of the diocese; to guard the faith, unity, and discipline of the whole Church; to proclaim the word of God; to act in Christ's name for the reconciliation of the world and the building up of the Church; and to ordain others to continue Christ's ministry.

The ministry of the priest is:

> To represent Christ and his Church, particularly as pastor to the people; to share with the bishops in the overseeing of the Church; to proclaim the Gospel; to administer the sacraments; and to bless and declare pardon in the name of God.

The deacon is called also according to the gifts of Holy Spirit.

> The calling of a deacon is to represent Christ and his Church, particularly as a servant to those in need; and to assist bishops and priests in the proclamation of the Gospel, and the administration of the sacraments.

Therefore, *The Virginia Report* says, "The complementary gifts bestowed by the Holy Spirit on the community are for the common good and for the building up of the Church for service to the world, and mission and evangelism."

Did you notice that in every step along the way, the layperson, the bishop, the priest, and the deacon there is a common phrase? "To represent Christ." The baptized are called to represent Christ. The bishop is called to represent Christ. We are all called to represent Christ. But what we are saying is that there is one ministry in the Church, and that ministry is the ministry of Jesus Christ. And we all—in one-way or another—are gifted and responsible for the ministry of interdependence and unity. We are all called into the one ministry. And that one ministry is the ministry of Jesus

Christ, in the ordered way that comes with the gifts of the Holy Spirit. There is one ministry. All in one way or another have the ministry of oversight, *episcope*. The Report goes on to describe the critically important ministry of *episcope*. Namely, the ones who oversee the well-ordered life in Christ that is the life of the community.

The Virginia Report presents a vision of *episcope* as a ministry at the service of the unity of the Church, the unity that Christ wants. This is related to the important principle in *The Virginia Report*, the levels of communion and principle of subsidiarity. What is meant by the principle of subsidiarity? Here the report is talking about the local church and the authority of the local church. Subsidiarity is defined this way: "Central authority should have a subsidiary function, performing only those tasks which cannot be performed effectively at a more immediate or local level." That is the heart of Anglicanism.

But it is true that where the church is—is local (that is, the face-to-face meeting of the people of God, baptized, presbyter, and bishop)—is where, in local context and local culture, we develop our indigenous ministry and live out our full church-life. But never in the history of the Church has the local church ever conceived itself as the only church. *Koinonia* is established when local churches are fully in the communion of a common faith, a shared life, and service, and mission of the gospel. Churches must be in communion with one another to be the catholic Church. Catholicity means the communion of local churches in faith, life of prayer, primacy of Scripture, celebration of baptism and Eucharist, service of the ordained, and mission. These realities enable the local church in union with all the other churches to effect change in the world. This is where, I believe, as Anglicans we need a lot of work to do, that is, how can we do this most effectively?

IV. Anglican Structures of Unity and Interdependence

So, we consider in *The Virginia Report* the local church, the universal Church, and interdependence. How does the church maintain its unity in the face of issues that indeed divide locally, provincially, and internationally? Over the years, Anglicans have developed instruments of unity and interdependence that are at the service of the churches. While no one of these, nor all of them together, have any juridical authority, they have served the churches well and helped deepen our communion together for the sake of the Gospel. The final juridical authority within Anglicanism is the Provincial Synod or in a few instances the local Diocese. However, the four instruments of communion, unity, and interdependence serve the Anglican Communion when called upon by the Church. Over the years, the four instruments of unity and interdependence have emerged in the life of the Anglican Communion. They are the ministry of the Archbishop of Canterbury, the ministry of the Lambeth Conference, the ministry of the Anglican Consultative Council, and the ministry of the Primates Meeting.

The ministries of interdependence, accountability, and discernment are essential at all levels of the Church's mission and ministry. Fr the sake of the Church's well being, they must be exercised at every level in a way that is personal, collegial, and communal. Oversight can never be isolated from the community. The purpose of all instruments and structures of the Church is to serve the *Koinonia*, the Trinitarian life of God in the Church, and help all baptized embrace and live out Christ's mission and ministry in the world.

Study Questions for *The Virginia Report*

Chapter One: The Context

1. When Christians find themselves passionately engaged in the midst of complex and explosive situations, how do they avoid alienation from those who, by baptism are their brothers and sisters in Christ and who are embraced in the communion of God, the Holy Trinity, but with whom they disagree?

2. How do they stay in communion with God and each other?

3. How do they behave toward each other in the face of disagreement and conflict?

4. What are the limits of diversity if the gospel imperative of unity and communion are to be maintained?

Chapter Two: Theology of God's Gracious Gift: The Communion of the Trinity and the Church

1. What does it mean to say that the identity and life of the Church is a gift of God's gracious love?

2. What does this mean for living together in unity and diversity as member churches of the Anglican Communion?

3. A living faith in the God of Jesus Christ draws us into the life of the Holy Trinity. What does this mean for the mission and ministry of the Church?

Chapter Three: Belonging Together in the Anglican Communion

1. What holds Anglicans together in a life of visible unity?

2. The Anglican Way is presented as a way of life—embracing Scripture, tradition and reason, sacrament, and worship—and the interdependence of charisms in the life of the Church. Discuss these elements of the Anglican Way.

3. How do bishops exercise the ministry of oversight *(episcopé)*?

4. What are the structures of Anglican interdependence? Describe each of them.

Chapter Four: Levels of Communion—Subsidiarity and Interdependence

1. What is the principle of subsidiarity? How is it meant to function in a diocese?

2. Does our experience of handling the issues regarding the ordained ministry of women in the churches of the Anglican Communion present a credible model of decision making in the midst of deep disagreement?

3. How can one say that the local church is fully the catholic Church? What theological elements need to be present to make this claim?

4. Can a local embodiment of the church ever simply be autonomous?

Chapter Five: Koinonia: Purpose and Principle for Developing Structures

1. What does it mean to say that the ministry of the bishop is personal, collegial, and communal?

2. What is the meaning of Christian attentiveness? Why is it necessary, given the consultative character of the Anglican Way?

3. What part does discernment and reception play in discovering the mind of Christ for the Church?

Chapter Six: The Worldwide Instruments of Communion: Structure and Processes

1. How does the Archbishop of Canterbury exercise his ministry as Primate of the Anglican Communion?

2. How does the Lambeth Conference strengthen the spiritual, theological, pastoral, and missionary life of the Anglican Communion?

3. How does the Anglican Consultative Council serve the Anglican Communion? What is its mission?

4. Should the Primates of the Anglican Communion be expected to make authoritative judgements on doctrinal, moral, and pastoral matters for the member churches of the Anglican Communion?

5. How are the Four Instruments of Anglican Unity and communion interrelated?

Interpretation of Scripture

—The Reverend Dr. John S. Pobee, province of West Africa

Tradition and Identity

A group or society's identity congeals around tradition. That tradition is expressed or couched in stories, myths, proverbs, music, symbols, and art. The social organisation, their authority patterns, and so forth are buttressed in those myths, traditions, and so forth. The scriptures of the Christian tradition represent such a development. Similarly, the well-known story of the Asante people of Ghana is articulated in such stories, e.g., the story of Okomfo Anokye and the golden stool, which is a powerful symbol and buttress of the coherence of the Asante nation.

Tradition and Language

Of course, tradition has to be translated and interpreted from one age and generation to another if it is to continue to have a binding force and authority. Herein lies the importance of language. Tradition, stories, myths, symbols, art, and music are the substance of language.

The English have a phrase, "taking coals to Newcastle." The phrase illustrates that language is more than syntax and morphology, or even words. Language carries a worldview and experience. The phrase, "taking coals to Newcastle," has its meaning in the historical fact that the city of Newcastle (in northeast England) was the centre of coal mining. So the language points to the superfluity of taking a commodity where it is already in abundance. Behind the terse English expression is a whole experience and understanding of reality.

Similarly, the Akan of Ghana never say baldly or bluntly that a chief is dead; they say "the chief has gone to the village." That language articulates a view that death is not *finis;* there is life of sorts after death; it is to be gathered with one's ancestors and to travel to a far-off land.

The contents of Scripture are couched in the language and idiom of contemporary contexts—some Aramaic or Hebrew and some Greek. The language of heaven presupposes a worldview of a three-decker universe—earth on which mortals live; heaven, or the firmament above, where God lives; and Sheol, the place of the dead, or the place below the earth. That was a Semitic worldview. We shall return to this when we discuss culture as a hermeneutic for interpretation. The first Russian astronaut returned from space proclaiming that he walked up in the space above and never saw God. Of course, this was a communist ideologue pulling punches at the Christian and Jewish cosmology. But in so doing, he failed to realise the symbolic nature of language, biblical language included.

Be that as it may, enough has been said to suggest that there is a work of translation and interpretation to be undertaken if the traditions of one age are to become meaningful, relevant, and gripping for another age. And this principle is true of biblical tradition, whatever we may claim about its sacredness.

Crucial Centrality of Scripture for Being Christian

In some circles the attempt to translate and interpret is threatening, if not taboo. Let me state unequivocally that while arguing for the necessity of translation and interpretation of tradition, the scriptures are a central part of the Church's tradition and identity, and they are crucial for the life of Christians.

The three cornerstones of religion are (religious) experience, ritual, and belief. At each of these points the scriptures of the Christian religion are crucial. The ritual as belief[1] must be translations and interpretations of the scriptures. The religious experience in one sense is the basis of our belief and ritual. The eighth-century prophet Isaiah-ben-Amoz "saw" and "heard" the Lord—i.e., he had a religious experience that made him proclaim God as holy (Isaiah 6) (belief). The apostle Paul had a religious experience of encountering the Lord Jesus on the Damascus Road: "Last of all, as to one untimely born, he (Jesus Christ) appeared to me. For I am the least of the apostles, unfit to be called an apostle, because I persecuted the Church of God. But by the grace of God I am what I am" (1 Corinthians 15:8-10). His religious experience gave him his identity as a Christian; it undergirded and authenticated his apostleship as that of the apostleship of the other apostles (1 Corinthians 15:7-8). The experience of encounter with the Risen Lord was undergirded and articulated in terms of the grace or unmerited favour of God, which was central to Paul's theology.

On the other hand, religious experience needs to be tested in the light of scriptures to ascertain how far the respective experiences are consistent with the received stories of Christian identity and style. Are they articulated in the tradition of Scripture?

The scriptures then are central to the life and work of Christians in their individual and personal life, as well as in communities and fellowship of faith. For that reason, the scriptures are more than just a document or piece of literature, even if they contain some of the most elegant and flowery language and excellent poetry (e.g., Psalm 23, Psalm 8, and 1 Corinthians 13). The scriptures are an instrument at the core of the identity of Christians and Church;

---

[1] I. M. Lewis. *Ecstatic Religion*. Harmondsworth: Penguin, 1971.

more critically, they are a tool for motivating the people of God—individually, severally, and corporately—to be Christian and to do mission.

For the foregoing reason, it is no surprise that the Reformers had the slogan *sola scriptura* (i.e., scripture alone). In this tradition we find the hallmarks of Anglicanism—Scripture, tradition, sacraments, the historic episcopate, and reason. Thus, Article vi, "Of the Sufficiency of the Holy Scriptures for Salvation" and Article vii "Of the Old Testament" of Anglicanism's *Articles of Religion* emphasize the importance and crucial centrality of the scriptures in the practice of Christian religion. We hardly need to recall the use of Scripture for Morning and Evening Prayer throughout the year.

The Lambeth Conference of 1998 reiterated this position when the Lambeth parents stated: "The congregation's life is to be wrapped up in and flow out of prayer and the worship of God. . . . This life is especially nourished by our study of Scripture, which is the source of our strength and our impulse to mission."

In taking the aforementioned stance, we discern fidelity to Scripture itself. 2 Timothy 3:14-17 states: "Stick with what you have learned and believed, sure of the integrity of your teachers—why, you took in the sacred scriptures with your mother's milk! There is nothing like the written Word of God for showing you the way of salvation through faith in Christ Jesus. Every part of Scripture is God-breathed one way or another—showing us the truth, correcting our mistakes, training to live God's way. Through the Word we are put together and shaped up for the tasks God has for us."[2]

When earlier we asserted the crucial centrality of scriptures for the Christian life, work, and mission, we were suggesting that our identity and motivation as God's people are determined not only by baptismal rite and repeated eucharistic renewal of baptism, but also—and perhaps more importantly—through the constant and continual renewal brought about by the study of and engagement with Scripture, which instructs in God's ways and message, offering challenge, reproof, and correction, all of which are indispensable to the process of forming, building up, and living as followers of God through Jesus Christ. Each time we encounter and engage Scripture, we embark on a process of engaging the vehicle for the transmission of the traditions of the earliest Christian community.[3] Let us simply put what I have been trying to say: every engagement with Scripture, especially interpretation, must have as its polestar the question "Scripture for what?" How does it contribute to defining our identity as ones "in Christ," and how does it give motivation for living, doing, and dying as Christ bearers in the contemporary world?

---

[2] Eugene H. Peterson. *The New Testament in Contemporary Language*. Colorado Springs, Colo.: NAVPress, 1993.
[3] C. F. D. Moule. *The Birth of the New Testament*. London: A. B. Black, 1962.

Translation and Interpretation

The *Articles of Religion* also have an article xxiv, "Of Speaking in the Congregation in Such a Tongue as the People Understandeth," which, in not many words, makes a pitch for what is called a *vernacular paradigm*[4] in missiological circles. Vernacular paradigm has been characteristic of the Church and the Christian faith as it has expanded around the globe. Thus, the scriptures and the Christian faith have been translated and interpreted into Greek, Latin, Celtic, Gothic, Armenian, Syriac, Coptic, Ethiopean, and so forth. Each translation was an attempt to let peoples of every tribe, tongue, and race understand the Word of God in the "tongue as the people understandeth." As such, every translation is necessarily interpretation.

The language of translation being interpretation points to some of the agenda. First, translation must be communication, which is more than stringing together words and sentences. Communication is about social relationships and creating situations of interacting meaning. The Christian scriptures emanated from particular contents, with a particular language, a particular worldview, and particular thought forms. In interpreting the Pentateuch or Pauline letters to our age, we are not just translating Hebrew and Greek words into our contemporary languages; we are also attempting to create social relationships between that world and ours through interacting meanings.

Second, such communication is most effective if it proceeds by symbolic rather than literal statements. Jesus' style of teaching through parables, stories, and so forth is the secret of its effective communication. Symbolism is not opposed to literal truth, rather symbolism makes the real more real.

For an African context, where many of the addressees of interpretation are non-literate, it hardly needs arguing that symbolism will be the most appropriate and effective means of communication. Needless to say, the very rational, propositional style, which has been an inheritance from the enlightenment culture, needs nuancing and revision.

Interpretation as Communication

Interpretation of Scripture is not only or even just erudition; it is communicating with particular people so that they are brought to accept and be confirmed in their faith in God through Jesus, Christ and Lord. We shall return to this point in a little while.

Today we live in an age characterized by a communications revolution, which can be pressed in the service of interpreting the scriptures. But we also hardly need reminding of how the same communications revolution

---

[4] Lamin Sanneh. *Translating the Message: The Missionary Impact of Culture.* Maryknoll, New York: Orbis, 1995.

leads to unbecoming consequences that can be especially divisive of society and community. So permit me to cite the Christian principles for communication as explicated by the World Association for Christian Communication.

(i) Communication creates community, revitalizing communities and communitarian spirit and overthrowing barriers that create exclusion.

(ii) Communication is participatory, with each person as subject of communication—each must enjoy freedom of expression and interchange of information on equal terms. The implications for the method of interpretation hardly need to be drawn out.

(iii) Communication liberates. In practice this means interpretation of Scripture should help people to articulate their own needs and to work together to find solutions to their needs. In this regard the interpretation of Scripture would help people encounter the biblical message as good news of hope and solidarity with the poor, the marginalized and the excluded.

(iv) Communication supports and develops cultures, enhancing values and symbols found in the people's cultures that contribute to their life and strengthen their community.

(v) Communication is prophetic in the sense that it stimulates critical awareness and helps people to distinguish between what is true and what is fake, between what is trivial and short-term on the one hand, and what is valuable and eternal.[5]

Today's interpretation of Scripture is done in a culture of communications revolution, the manifestations of which include periodicals, TV, radio broadcasting, videos, satellite transmissions, data banks, desktop publishing, software technology, CD ROM, Internet, and electronic networking. This vast array of possibilities does not automatically make for sound communication. The best use of the communication possibilities should mean discarding the formats that undermine the personal communication that is foundational in the study of Scripture and should also mean embracing the communication possibilities that foster more equality, more vitality, more relevance, and more inclusion into the life and thinking of the people of God. It is to this end that the five principles outlined above become important and helpful guideposts.

Let me put this another way: living in an age of communications revolution, we cannot but use it, at least some of it. But in so doing, we may never lose sight of the *telos* of the communication, which should give orientation to

---

[5] See Dafne Sabanes Plou, "The Impact and Media, Communications and Information Technology on Ministerial Formation and Theological Education," *Ministerial Formation* 75 (October 1996):28–29.

healthy and wholesome communication. And because we are from the Church and tradition which has the description *communion* in its self-understanding, that theological, religious, and spiritual word should be hermeneutic for the interpretation of Scripture. In other words, the study of Scripture should model and foster what is entailed in our self-understanding as communion, i.e., participation in divinity, fellowship, community, solidarity, inclusivity, and inclusiveness.[6] At the practical level, such a hermeneutic excludes the inherent atheistic-agnostic orientation of the Enlightenment culture; it also excludes the inherent individualistic orientation of the Enlightenment culture.

Vernacular Paradigm

What has been said above about translation, interpretation, and article xxiv of the *Articles of Religion* is in effect a pitch for vernacular paradigm for interpretation of Scripture. Let me delineate three elements of it.

First, commitment to the vernacular paradigm, whatever else it is, is also a political statement. It is political in the sense that it is a reaction to the medieval Roman Catholic Church, in which Latin was the language of discourse and was used, whether consciously or unconsciously, to domesticate and squeeze out all other interpretations and translations. It is political also in the sense that all nations, all tribes, and all tongues have a right to encounter God in their particular mother tongue. Literate persons, like non-literate persons, have a right to encounter God in Scripture in their own right and identity.

In holding out unashamedly for the political implications of the vernacular paradigm, one is in a sense making a return to what was said earlier about communication being prophetic. In today's world the gods of possessions, power, and pleasure are mightily working for death. The god of sectionalism has caused havoc and destruction. Surely genocide like tribalism is demonic, and biblical interpretation must be prophetic in confronting such evils. Needless to say, I am pleading for a reappraisal of the often-heard phrase of "keep religion out of politics."

Second, the vernacular paradigm also embraces what St. Augustine of Hippo called the "two books of life." On the one hand, as a Christian I have to engage the book of scriptures; on the other hand, I also have to take the book of life, i.e., the experiences, questionings, fears, hopes, and so forth of a particular people. In other words, the interpretation of Scripture is more than simply the transfer of knowledge or information; rather, it should be critical engagement and dialogue between the people's questionings, hopes, fears, and so forth. And the Word of God should endeavour to show the rel-

---

[6] J. Y. Campbell. "Koinonia and its Cognates." In *Three New Testament Studies*. Leiden: E. J. Brill, 1965:3–28; A. Bemile, et al. (eds.). Communio/Koinonia Strasbourg: Institute for Ecumenical Research, 1990.

evance of the biblical message to the story and circumstances of a particular people. This has epistemological implications for the educational process. For the present, let me signal that this means, among other things, that the process of education and translation or interpretation should not be from top to bottom; it is better from below, i.e., where the people are. Jesus' style of teaching confirms this approach. From the common and familiar experiences of people—the sowing of seeds, fishing, harvesting, the growth of seeds, and hazards of travel—Jesus led them to the deeper truth about the kingdom of God. The familiar missionary practice and method of *tabula rasa* (clean slate) needs a reappraisal.

Third, the commitment to the vernacular paradigm is also an option for culture as the hermeneutic and vehicle of interpretation. Culture is a world-taken-for-granted by a particular people, coming down the centuries from the ancestors. As E. B. Tylor defined it, it is a complex whole that exerts a directive, constraining, and dynamic influence over a particular people.[7]

Permit me to make four assertions about culture. First, culture is a system of symbols that operate at the imaginative level. As such, interpretation will necessarily be an intercultural communication and must necessarily take place at the imaginative level. Second, worldview stands at the core of culture and is, therefore, crucial for ultimate cultural decoding. Third, culture is the solvent of religion.[8] As Paul Tillich puts it, religion is the substance of culture and culture is the bearer of religion. There is no way an African, for example, can come to engage Scripture without his or her cultural identification with its heavy religious component. There is then a sense in which interpretation of Scripture amounts to inter-religious dialogue. It is precisely because this has not been done in Africa that there is this seepage of membership from the historic churches to the African initiatives in Christianity.[9]

For the foregoing reasons, the vernacular paradigm via the cultural hermeneutical route is the critical avenue of effective communication and interpretation.

Enlightenment Cultural Paradigm and the Pentecost Paradigm

So far, I have suggested that culture is the soul of a people. That is the classical anthropological view. But there is another type of culture that Europe and America and, through them, Africans and others, have imbibed. I refer to the Enlightenment culture, which among other things worships at the altar of rationality and individualism. This has been the

---

[7] E.B. Tylor. *The Origins of Culture Part I.* New York: Harper and Row, 1958. To Tylor's definition, let us add that there is empirical plurality of cultures. Therefore, no one culture may be exalted as normative.

[8] Paul Tillich. *Theology and Culture.* New York: Galaxy, 1959.

[9] John S. Pobee and Gabriel Ositelu II. *African Initiatives in Christianity.* Geneva: WCC, 1998.

motor of the scientific-technological developments of our time, of progress, of modernity. This culture deals in words like *fact, theory,* and *objectivity.* When these marks have been applied to the gospel story, there has been a temptation to exclude the credibility of miracle stories, ascension-resurrection stories, and so forth. As Walter Wink has crisply put it, "it pretends to be unbiased when in fact the methodology carries with it a heavy rationalistic weight which by inner necessity tends towards the reduction of irrational, subjective or emotional data to insignificance or invisibility. It pretends to search for 'assured results' and 'objective knowledge' when in fact the method presumes radical epistemological doubt which by definition devours each new spawn of 'assured results' as a guppy swallows her children."[10]

Permit me then to make some points on this heritage of the Enlightenment culture. First, there is no going back on the Enlightenment legacy of rationality. For it has shaped Western cultures to such an extent that today we cannot successfully divest ourselves of that legacy. In any case, the use of Logos in the incarnation story (John 1:1–14) and the description of humanity as bearing the image and likeness of God make room for rationality in the articulation of the biblical faith. So biblical interpretation must be rational. This is in no way to make a pitch for convoluted rationality.

But second, the Enlightenment model has also brought us face to face with what Winquist has called the "epiphanies of darkness."[11] The so-called rationality has not stopped the developed nations from exploiting and taking advantage of the weaker ones of the world. The rape of natural resources by the Developed World, their willingness to spend billions to pommel Kosovo and then to have a round table to raise funds for reconstruction, their willingness to sell armaments to Sierra Leone and Liberia to destroy their infrastructures and themselves and reluctantly try to raise funds for their reconstruction, the savagery in Bosnia, the genocide in Rwanda and Burundi—all are symptoms of the epiphanies of darkness. So the Enlightenment culture has not been an unalloyed blessing—it must be seen in perspective and reappraised.

Third, reality is not all rationality; it is also feeling, emotion, and passion. We have something to learn from the biblical word for "to know"—the Hebrew word *yada'*. The word signals knowing by the heart rather than by the mind; it signals engagement in lived experience. "Knowledge of God, therefore, is not measured by the information one possesses but how one lives in response to God."[12] Biblical interpretation should not only touch the mind

---

[10] Walter Wink. *The Bible in Human Transformation Towards a Paradigm for Biblical Study.* Philadelphia: Fortrers, 1973:6.
[11] Charles WinquiSt. *Epiphanies of Darkness: Deconstruction in Theology.* Philadelphia: Fortress, 1986.
[12] Cheryl Bridges-Johns. "From Babel to Pentecost: The Renewal of Theological Education." In John S. Pobee (ed.). *Towards Viable Theological Education.* Geneva: WCC, 1997:138.

but also the heart, feeling, emotion, and passion; for it is only when they are touched that there can be renewal and transformation.

In my recently concluded life as coordinator of the World Council of Churches' programme on theological education and ministerial formation, I initiated and prosecuted a three-year process on the viability of theological education. At the Latin American meeting of the process I proposed and utilized the paradigm of Pentecost as providing the ability to renew and give life to theology, ministry, and formation programmes. I do still believe that Pentecost does serve as an overall hermeneutic for interpreting our theological task, biblical interpretation included.[13] At the global consultation at which the regions of the world encountered each other around the same theme, Cheryl Bridges-Johns[14] built on it by pursuing the implications of the Pentecost paradigm for epistemology and ontology in the hope that it would help delineate the marks of quality, authenticity, and creativity in theological education. She argued that the Pentecost paradigm involves the inversion of the fund of knowledge and the inversion of subject and object.

Biblical Interpretation with Ecumenical Perspective

The Pentecost paradigm represents the unified voice *per contra* the divisions of the tower of Babel. It represents diversity and differentiation, which find a unity in the triune God, in Scripture, and in Church. The call for local interpretations can easily slide into some rabid nationalism, exclusivism, and chaos. The ecumenical perspective in the reading of scriptures has the capacity to guard against such things. Here what was said about communion above comes into its own. A number of things come to mind. (1) Each region, each congregation, and so forth must have the freedom and space to struggle with the one and same Word of God and to contribute it to the general pool of churches' readings of the same Word of God. (2) Each attempt at reading must be open to learn from and engage also the reading of the one and same word by other regions, other churches, and the other gender—how they have addressed the yearnings of their context—and also to learn from the errors of interpretation of the word of God. Learning is for mutual challenge, correction, and affirmation.

This is a tall order. We may not be able to apply each of the hermeneutical points in each and every case. But it should be possible to apply them in varying combinations for the illumination of people.

Silence as a Hermeneutic

Usually interpretation is understood in terms of somebody or some persons leading in the exposition of the text of Scripture. But I had a

---

[13] John S. Pobee. "Moving Towards a Pentecostal Experience." In *Ministerial Formation* 68. January 1995:17-22.
[14] op.cit.

different experience in Ethiopia during the dark days of *Mengistu Haile Mariam* and the Dirge. Churches were put under disabilities; some leadership had either disappeared or been made to disappear. Everything was being done to cripple the Church. It was not safe to be a Christian. Spies were inside the Church. It was in this context that we assembled for Bible study.

The text was Psalm 22. Four different persons read the text in sections slowly. The first piece, verses 1–5; the second, verses 6–13; the third, verses 14–18; and the last, verses 19–31. After each portion there was a pause of about eight to ten minutes, during which no one spoke; each person meditated on the word. At the end there was prayer, the Lord's Prayer, and then we parted.

Later, I interviewed some of the group and it was amazing to hear how similar their interpretations were: a sense of seeming abandonment by God. The evidence for this was their situation: feelings of embattlement by hostile forces and the seeming helplessness and hopelessness. Yet through all this there emerges a sense of hope in the Sovereign Lord of all history, leading to a sense of gratitude, courage, endurance, and praise.

With such an experience, I dare to suggest that interpretation may not always be verbal articulation; silently meditating on one's circumstances in the light of Scripture can also be illuminating and instructive. I believe that the Spirit of God does directly use the reading of Scripture to illuminate people.

I believe there is no one way of Bible interpretation, and no one style may be offered as normative. On the one hand, silent meditation on their circumstances in the light of God's word can be illuminating. Verbal exposition is also a possibility. Ritual, music, art, and symbols can be avenues of interpretation. In either case, there should be dialogue between the experiences and hopes of a particular people and the word of God. The idiom of a particular people is the wavelength at which a people can be engaged.

Presentation on Interpretation of Scripture

—The Reverend Dr. John S. Pobee, Province of West Africa

First, let me express my gratitude to the Archbishop of Canterbury and the ACC for inviting me to come. I hope they know what they have done, letting me loose in this company. Lord have mercy.

I asked for my text to be distributed yesterday. In my life, once I commit my thoughts to paper, the text loses its dynamism. I didn't want to come here to read it to you. Besides, we have had an experience here this week, whereby papers were read and we didn't have enough time to reflect. I thought you could read it in advance. I wanted to make sure that we would have enough time for dialogue. When we get to the dialogue time, don't be afraid to be sharp. I have lived all my academic life in the university. So I am not afraid of disagreement and argument. So try to be as sharp as you can. In the process, we shall have some clarity. So don't be sorry for this African. If you can give me a few knocks, by all means do so. But an African is like an Indian rubber ball; he can bounce back in style. Further, I wanted you to read my paper in advance because many of the participants here are not native English speakers; therefore, it can be difficult to hear. I think that in the Communion we have to be sensitive to that because we speak English with different accents and because it is not always easy to communicate.

But there is another reason. I am an African. I come from an oral culture. I bring this aspect of my culture to this meeting, and that is why I don't want to read my text. I want to be myself, to live my oral culture.

And finally, I want to communicate. We do not communicate by reading a paper when we are talking to people; therefore, I want to see your faces. I may look shy by wearing glasses, but I am not the least bit afraid to look you in the face, and I hope this is how we will continue. In the Communion we must learn to look each other in the face, face to face, and face the consequences.

I want to begin with something from 1 Corinthians 2:10–11 "These things God has revealed to us through the Spirit, for the Spirit searches everything, even the depths of God. For what human being knows what is truly human except the human spirit that is within? So also no one comprehends what is truly God's except the Spirit of God." So, unashamedly, I would like to invite us to pray.

> Holy Spirit, come; Spirit of God, we seek your wisdom;
> come and touch every heart, every mind, each soul, each
> body in this gathering, that through our proceedings here
> we may catch something of your mind in creating us for
> yourself. Spirit of God, come. Come, come. Amen.

The theme of this gathering is "The Communion We Share." I am giving this lecture in that context. I am not concerned about doing a Bible study. I am not concerned about giving a general lecture on interpreting Scripture. I am concerned, though, with how the interpretation of Scripture becomes a vibrant part of our search for Communion. And I do believe that slant is very critical for what we do. As we reflect theologically on this Communion, we are seeking to understand how Scripture underpins it. How does Scripture contribute to or help us to define this Communion?

The moment you use the word Communion, you are committed to a community concept. It is not a question of how *I* see it; it is how *we* see it—*we*, in spite of our differences. How do we read Scripture *together* so that we can be shaped into seeking communion with God and with one another. We do so not only as Anglicans. That is why I am glad that Sven Oppegaard, who spoke before me, is Lutheran. I am glad to see that Tim Galligan, a Roman Catholic, is here. We are in it together; not only Anglicans seek communion. And the ecumenical movement has rediscovered the basic ecclesiology to be a communion. We seek communion with others. The presence of the Lutheran and the Roman Catholic is a reminder that we have to seek this communion, not like a holy club, but in the company of others. And Scripture is the common inheritance of all who are in Christ. The issue is: How do we get a vibrant and viable interpretation of Scripture? I use viable in the sense that it is able to give life, to renew and to transform. We cannot seek communion and continue in the old ways. Something must give. We cannot be at the same place. We are being called to move. And therefore, for me the search for communion is to be linked with transformation. I am emphasizing that the interpretation of Scripture is not just intellectual gymnastics; it is about our life together, our transformation, and our renewal. Old-time and old-style polemics should be expunged from our common search for God through Scripture.

Let me make one more point before I get into the substance. When we use the word *interpretation,* people think of verbal articulation. Interpretation is not only or always by word of mouth. Our lives are supposed to be an interpretation of the gospel. So you can preach all the wonderful theology, but if your people know that you are a rotten person inside and they know all your secret views, you are an empty gong. Our lives are the interpretation *par excellence.* Please let us take that seriously. In Africa, the majority of our congregations are non-literate. We have to be adventurous enough to look for innovative ways of interpretation. Music and dance can be and have been means of interpretation. The hymns we sing, *Ancient and Modern,* or whatever we sing, are interpretations of Scripture. We seem to have exulted them to a point where even in Africa we keep on singing them—even the imagery of winter in a context where we have no sense of snow. Our music, our song, our dance can be vehicles of interpretation.

Why does the Church in Ghana continue to rigidly sing *Ancient and Modern* when its idiom is not the African's idiom? That it is another story. I think that by the time I die we will still be very much that.

Again, we do not interpret words. We interpret ideas, worldviews across cultures, generations, and genders.

So, to the text that I asked you to read yesterday. When we do interpretation, we are grappling with our identity. The scriptures as we have them are how various generations, various communities, grappled with God's challenge for them in their time and place. But since their challenges may not be identical with ours today, we dare not take them literally; we need to interpret them to our contexts. It is all part of our identity now; we cannot just get rid of it. But in the light of the response of the people to God's challenge for that time and age, what help do we get for looking at God's challenges today? Every time you come to interpretation, ask yourself: what is it that God is challenging us to today in the light of Scripture?

All too often we reduce that biblical thing to doctrines, theological formulae. This is inadequate. I want to say that it is something deeper than doctrine and theological formulae.

Let me suggest that the gospel is about the four Hs. It is about what it is to be *human;* this is what we mean by the incarnation—seeing the human face of God. It is about what it is to be *honest,* people of integrity. If you want chapter and verse, this can be found in Philippians 4:8. It is about what it is to be *humble.* Have this mind about you: he *humbled* himself obedient unto death (Philippians 2:5f). Let me say that it is also about having a sense of *humour.* When we get onto our biblical hobbyhorse, we are too serious for comfort. And God's way of dealing with us throughout history has been to show a heavy sense of humour. In that way, you have such strange statements as harlots going to the kingdom of God before you. You don't expect harlots to go, but in the strange humour of God, this is going to happen. This morning we were talking about the gay issue. In the humour of God, something will happen, but it is not for us to try to be self-righteous. Let us be humble and remember God's humour when we address difficult and troublesome issues.

Let me add one more thing to what this gospel is all about. I think the gospel tells us to live in eschatological expectation. Here we have no continuing city, here there is no abiding stay, and we look for the city, which is beyond. When my politicians are using all their power, I usually say to them: "Yes, you may run rings around us, but in the final analysis God will be God." To learn to look beyond the present to a future in God's hands. I think that is what my identity is all about. Not about doctrines, not about theological formulae, and please make sure that the four *H*s don't become theological formulae. They are very much existential things. And in order to carry that out, we use language. Language is only a tool. We have Semitic language, Greek language, English language, African languages, and so forth. Whatever the tradition is, it is for us to translate into new times.

What I try to say in the paper is that every translation is interpretation—the various texts that we have used (the Authorised Version, RSV, all of them).

If you compare them, they are all interpretations. That is how the Church has always behaved, and that is what I say to my African brothers and sisters: "Let's not continue to use the King James Version in our churches; it is not good for coherence. We have got to be part of that history of ours in which every age tries to interpret and translate."

I also said in my text that in the history of the Church we have always gone for the vernacular paradigm. I hope the word *paradigm* didn't give you any upset stomachs. I simply mean model or example. In the history of the Church, wherever the gospel went it took on the form of that place. So you have your Celtic texts, your Gothic texts, your Armenian texts, your Coptic texts, your English texts, and so forth. When are we going to be serious and have our own African text and paradigm? We should do it. Nobody should do it for us.

I also made a plea: that when we Anglicans made a commitment to the vernacular paradigm to use English in England, it was also a political statement. It didn't want to be dominated by the Latin of the Romans. It was meant to free them so that they could each hear the Word of God in their own language. Let's not get into this debate, stated as "keep religion out of politics." Remember that where two or three people are meeting, there is politics. But it is a question of doing the politics under what we know of the will of God. That is what our Bible study leader has been trying to tell us every morning. Please look around you and look at the issues God is asking you to tackle. It is in that dialogue that there will be vibrancy in biblical interpretation. Every time I have to preach when I get into the pulpit I am always looking and seeking who is sleeping. And the moment I see people sleeping I realize that I am not communicating. The sooner I get down from the pulpit the better. Something to watch. Interpretation is and should be communication. Are we in our interpretations touching the questions of people? Interpretation must touch the questionings of people. If you like another way of saying it, it must be contextual. What are the hopes and fears of the people as they encounter the one word of God?

In the text I talk about St. Augustine's "two books of life." There is Scripture and the Book of Life. Interpretation should be that encounter and dialogue between the Bible and Book of Life. What is my situation in Ghana asking me to face in the light of the word of God? We Anglicans love tradition in the early Church. Please, let's take that one seriously: two books, the encounter and dialogue between the two books. Again, that is what I see the Bible study doing—trying to say that we should hold a dialogue between the two books. You may disagree with the content and analysis, but that is what we should be doing.

My friends, at this stage of our lives we are captive to the Enlightenment culture. Even those of us from Africa by virtue of our education have been sucked into the Enlightenment culture. They think it is only the people in Europe who are victim of the Enlightenment. I think the Enlightenment culture puts an emphasis on rationality. And when we do Bible studies we want to see everything neatly done. Well, God's word is not like that. Our God is a God of surprises. And God is always making nonsense of our neat parcels. Further, reality is more than just rationality; it is also emotional and passionate. When we interpret Scripture, we must be able to reach the emotions of people. What we are doing is are trying to bring about transformation, and there can be no transformation without reaching the emotions. If you think it's only the brain that will do it, you lie; for I know that in my most intense moments my theology deserts me. The emotional element is critical. We have been brought up more or less to be suspicious of emotion. I hope you are not ashamed to say that you are in love with your wife. It is a reality; so let's not be just intellectual. And our membership in Africa rolled over to the African Independent churches; it is partly because they don't find emotional satisfaction in our pews. So if you want to be successful, let's take emotions seriously. Keep on appealing to the head, and you will preach to empty pews. Your life is in your own hands.

One of the things that I want us to remember out of that whole Enlightenment development is that we have been faced with, quoting Charles Winquist, the epiphanies of darkness. With so much pain around us, your interpretation must deal with the epiphanies of darkness. Otherwise, we shall not experience interpretation as the word of life; instead, it will be the word of death.

The last thing I want to say is that as I sit in Ghana and do my interpretation, Archbishop Carey is sitting in Lambeth doing his interpretation, and Archbishop Eames is sitting in Ireland doing his interpretation. Another person in the Caribbean is sitting there doing his interpretation in his context. We need a platform where together we will correct each other, affirm each other, and encourage each other. That is what I referred to in the text as the ecumenical forum—the platform where from our different interpretations we come to encounter each other and challenge and correct one another. In my vernacular we have a saying, "The one who is making a path cannot tell if it is going straight or crooked"; we need the other person to get it straight. It is only when I come to a meeting like this and engage with other people that I can begin to say, "Ah . . . I am on the right way." We need the Anglican Consultative Council, where together we can come with our differences. But let us not come to do things like the others are doing, because that is the mark of being developed. Come as you are. Encounter the other person in the process. We shall come to a clearer vision of God. I don't see the ecumenical thing first and foremost in terms of institutions. I see it as a perspective. In that forum it should be perspective. We shall see and perceive, hear, and understand.

I think we need a Pentecost paradigm—experiencing the Spirit to guide us into all truth, even in the region of Scripture, and not just some intellectual activity. That is why at the beginning of my presentation I invoked the Spirit. Because without the Spirit we cannot enter into the mysteries of God.

I had a note on silence. It was an experience I had in Ethiopia in those bad days. I believe God speaks to us in silence sometimes. When I look at the whole series of things, the frightening silence on the mountain where Elijah was hiding, God speaks out of that silence, and sometimes interpretation can become powerful in silence. Don't think it is always speaking. Call it meditation, call it anything. But sometimes it is good to cultivate silence in order to hear the Word of God speak to us today.

My friends, I thank you for this privilege of addressing you. You have the text already. What I want us to do is to go into our basic groups. You can chew me up, and then at some point we will come back here and I will be the lamb for the slaughter; you can punch me as hard as you like. But I hope in the process we shall move forward together. I did not intend to speak this long, but you see, if you don't read the text you run the risk of being unruly. So I have gone on much longer than I thought I would. Thank you very much.

Questions for Clarification

Question: Bishop Michael

When Nkrumah came to power, he used the Bible as a way of inviting his people to be his disciples. He said, "Seek you first the political kingdom and all will be added unto you." And now you said that in another language when two or three are gathered together there are politics. Church leaders in Africa are always in a dilemma, because whenever we say something about the Bible or about God, then politics comes in. How can you help us, as one of us, in terms of dividing politics and the word of the Lord?

Response

Yes, Nkrumah used Scripture. In a book I wrote, *Kwame Nkrumah and the Church in Ghana,* I tried to say that that approach was evidence of how strong the Church had been in the educational field. People knew the language of Scripture. But it was not as if he was committed to Scripture itself. That was my quarrel with him. He was using it in a political manner, a negative political use, without any commitment to it himself. He was doing a parody of a biblical saying.

But I think what I was trying to say in another way was this: If the whole earth is the Lord's, our mission is to bring everything under the purview of God's Spirit. When they tell me that "this is politics, we should not get into it," I don't allow that. You see, my problem is that every time I hear churches talking about doing projects, they are always treating the cases after the harm has been done, instead of going to the right source and getting the right orientation. If you have a development system that pauperises some people and then the Church comes to pick them up, we are not being fair to the

Church. We have got to go in early and say: "Look here, this kind of policy will lead to the destruction of our peoples." You don't wait for them to be destroyed before you go and pick them up. And that is why I don't allow this talk of "keep religion out of politics; keep religion out of economics." It doesn't help—all you end up with is broken bones, and then you pick them up and there is no way to secure the correction. One more thing to think about: Praying can be a political act. When I pray for Garang in Sudan, for Rawlings in Ghana, I am praying for God's help to influence political life and choices.

Question: Moderator of South India

Talking about intellect and emotion, you said that an intellectual sermon leads to an empty pew. So an emotional sermon leads to what?

Response

The emotion issue. I don't think you heard me right. What I was trying to say is that if you think developing a straight intellectual piece is what will change the world, you deceive yourself. But if you are able to touch the will and emotion of people to want to change, that will bring about enduring change. That is what I was trying to say. There is no way you can effect change without touching people's emotions. That is straightforward fact.

Hearing on Ethics and Technology

—The Reverend Eric B. Beresford

I want to start at the beginning. In one sense, the beginning of this session is the Lambeth resolution on technology and ethics, the resolution that provided the impetus for this session. But that is not the beginning I want to start at.

At the beginning of the book of Genesis, God addresses human beings with what is offered as both a task and a promise. God blesses humankind and says, "Be fruitful and increase, fill the earth and subdue it, have dominion over the fish in the sea, the birds of the air, and every living thing that moves on the earth."

From the earliest times we have been doing just that. We have shaped and adapted the natural world to serve our own ends, using and if need be transforming natural processes to provide ourselves with food, shelter, and clothing. Technology is not simply about the machines and interventions that have become so much a part of Western society and which are spreading into so many parts of the globe. It is about agriculture and arrows and all of the ways in which human beings have been able to adapt to their environment, or where possible, adapt their environment. For most of human history, our desire and capacity to dominate the created order seemed natural and proper, but then for most of human history it was also limited, not just in its effectiveness, but also in its capacity to undermine the very natural systems that it harnessed and redirected. In the West, this domination was often theologically justified, even in the Enlightenment, when the motivations were more rationalistic than theological. More recently, theologians have begun to insist that the notion of dominion does not give us freedom to do anything we choose with creation, but rather, it offers us the task and responsibility of stewardship. Our task, it is suggested, is the thoughtful and responsible management of creation. Other theologians have gone even further. From the observation that the primary divide in Scripture is not between human beings and the rest of creation, but rather between God, the Creator, and the creature, the created, they have developed more radical theologies of the organic wholeness of the created order of which we are a part. On these views the earth is viewed as an organic whole, or even as an organism; either as *Gaia*, the earth organism (Rosemary Radford Reuther drawing on James Lovelock) or as the *oikoumene* of God, the household of God (Larry Rasmussen, WCC).

The appeal of these more radical approaches is, I believe, linked to the fact that, increasingly, many of us experience technological development as profoundly ambiguous. Each new step, it seems, brings a new and often unadvertised cost, as our impact on one part of the earth's systems brings with it changes in other parts. What is more, the costs and benefits of technological development turn out to be rather unevenly distributed, both across different societies and, within individual societies, across different social groups.

I start with creation and with ecology because the question of technology, the question that motivates this hearing, is always at the same time a question about our relationship to the created order. It is about the nature and limits of responsible artifice if we are to live as citizens of the creation. I start with creation also because it is in the impact of our technological doing on the world around us, and on the world's capacity to sustain life, that the ambivalence of technology becomes clearest. In what I have to say today, therefore, it is important to remember that the Lambeth resolution on technology and ethics does not stand alone; it belongs with other resolutions and particularly with the resolutions on creation and ecology (1.8, 1.9). The themes of these motions are in fact the biblical themes of responsible belonging to the creation, of being responsive to the Creator.

But we have been asked today to think about technology and ethics, and that is probably a good idea, because it is always easier to think about particular problems caused by technology than it is to think about technology itself. Yet unless we think about technology and the nature of technology, I want to suggest that we shall always be in fire-fighting mode. We will always be responding to particular crises, but never really equipped to analyze the cultural assumptions that underpin technological development and that so often get us into trouble.

So what is technology? Our familiarity with the technological is so great that it is hard to remember what a new idea captured by the term *technology* is. It is actually a *neologism:* a word created by the combination of two others to form a new concept. The words *techne* and *logos* are, respectively, the Greek words for art, by which we don't mean art in the modern sense, but rather craft, the ability to make things, to create; and *Logos,* the word by which the Greeks pointed not just to the idea of a word but to reason and knowing. Technology thus involves what has been called, "a unique interpenetration of knowing and making" (Grant, *Technology and Justice*). Technology, I want to suggest, is not simply the practice of using tools, but rather a way of looking at the world, a way of framing questions and analyzing problems. In this latter sense, technology is something new in human history. It is the assumption that all knowledge can be measured in the effectiveness of its technique, its ability to predict and control. When Francis Bacon says knowledge is power, he is referring not to the power of authority—political, moral, or religious—but to the power of technique.

There are, broadly speaking, three ways of looking at technology that have been predominant in different phases of Western culture and that appear in different guises elsewhere. The notion of technology as unqualifiedly good predominates as one might expect at the birth of early modern science and technology. This is then displaced by a negative reaction, a demonization of technology that is associated, in part, with the experience of some of the negative effects of technological change, although it includes a rather romantic reaction against change and the sense of cultural loss, which tended to idealize earlier societies. Finally, there is the claim that technology is neither good nor bad in itself, but morally neutral. From this perspective, the questions that need to be asked are simply about the ends that technology serves.

Technology as Saviour: Unqualifiedly Good

The approach that characterized the early years of modern scientific and technological development is characterized as technology as saviour. Technology, it was hoped, would provide the cure for all of the ills of the human condition: physical, social, and intellectual. The English scientist Francis Bacon is characteristic of this view. For him, "knowledge is power," and he reasoned that if we had enough knowledge, we could use it to control nature and free ourselves from all the suffering caused by disease, want, and natural disaster. Such utopian points of view are by no means a thing of the past. In his recent book, *God and the Chip: Religion and the Culture of Technology,* William Stahl has traced a number of contemporary utopian scenarios that see promise of a transformed and renewed human culture, free from conflict or lack, just around the corner, all as a result of the benefits of technology, particularly computer technology. Implicit in this perspective is the assumption that technology equals progress and anyone who slows down the rate of technological development impedes progress. Also implicit in this perspective is the assumption that technology itself is infallible. When problems occur, it is due either to human error or to a foolish or malicious choice of the purposes for which a technology is used.

Let me simply point to two difficulties this point of view presents for us. The first is that this point of view assumes that the societies in which technologies are developed and used are rather monochrome. Utopians speak of the implications of new technologies for human societies as if the implications were going to be the same for all members of those societies, and I would suggest that this can be shown not to have been the case so far. Of course, the problem becomes even greater if you add the differential impacts on different societies. The problem is that our utopians are working with rather organic models of society, which tend to conceal the reality of social conflict: the reality that benefits for some members of society are bought at the expense of other members. It is all a matter of perspective. If you look from the top down, societies tend to look organic. Viewed from the bottom up, they look much more conflictual. To illustrate: nature always looks organic to the lion, but not to the lion's lunch. For Christians, the question is not simply a question about the nature of reality, but of the perspective from which we are called to look at reality. The second problem is that the utopians ignore our growing experience of what are sometimes called the "revenge effects" of technological development. DDT was supposed to save us from the damage that insects inflicted on our crops, but in the end it killed the birds that ate the bugs. The bugs, by contrast, simply became resistant to the poison. Cars were supposed to give us freedom and comfort; what they delivered though, in the places where I have lived at least, is gridlock and appalling air quality, with all the disease and early death that causes. Biotechnology is supposed to solve the problem of the world's food supply . . . Well, I guess the green revolution promised that one too!

Technology as Oppressor: Demonic

The second approach to technology I want to look at is the one that claims that technology is basically oppressive, even demonic. This is the point of view that sees technology as basically destructive of human persons and of human freedom. There are anti-utopias to match the utopias. The most famous include fictional works like Aldous Huxley's *Brave New World,* Charles Dickens' *Hard Times,* or, more recently, Margaret Attwood's *A Handmaid's Tale.* In all of these, it is the dark side of technology that is the focus of attention. The experience of technological societies is from this point of view, an experience of profound alienation. Mechanism takes control over human needs, relationships, and communities. Standardization, rather than individuality, becomes the norm. Don't you just hate it when your choice is a 32- or 34-inch waist and you're a 33? I am being flippant for a reason. Because it seems to me that this demonization of technology is a position that, from the very beginning, speaks of privilege and neglects the very real benefits that technology has brought to so many in the world, even where it has brought great cost. It has always seemed to me to be counterintuitive, if not simply self-contradictory, to fly around the world delivering indictments against the evils of technology from notes prepared on a word processor. However, the main reason why I don't wish to spend a long time discussing this rather negative assessment of technology is that, for the time being at least, it is the preserve of a few and has little if any impact on our wider culture. However, there are some points in this negative critique that are important and insightful, but I will return to them later.

Technology as Neutral: Tool

The last of the ways of looking at technology that I want to look at is one that looks at technology as neutral and value free, as simply tool using. Technology and technologies are, in and of themselves, neither good nor bad, it all depends on the purposes they are used for and the manner in which they are used. From this perspective, the problem is not technology, but rather how to encourage responsible use of technology. This is probably the most widespread approach to technology in Western society, and judging by the way in which technologies are appropriated in developing countries, there too. However, there are reasons to be skeptical of such a neat division between technology and its fruits.

Even in its beginnings, technological knowing was tied to social projects and social assumptions that, at the very least, we need to be aware of. For, while the aims of the projects were noble, there is reason to question the range of vision on which those aims were based. For Bacon, science was male, and nature, the object of science's gaze and of technology's action, was female. One does not need to be a feminist to feel some discomfort as Bacon proclaims that nature is the mind's bride and calls us to "make her your slave, conquer and subdue her." Even today, people speak of the destruction of the environment and depletion of the earth's resources as "the rape of nature." (Even John Passmore, usually very sensitive to the social implications of the sexualization of nature, tells us in his book, *Man's Responsibility for Nature,* that we are to see nature not as "a captive to be raped," but as a "partner to be cherished.")

There is ample evidence that this sexualization of technology continues into the present and functions to exclude, or at least place barriers to, the participation of women in certain areas of technological development. Try looking at any random sample of computer magazines from a news agent's shelf to see the images of women that are portrayed there. When they are present at all, the women represent only between one-third and one-tenth of the persons depicted in the magazines, and even then they are overwhelmingly depicted in stereotypical roles, e.g., as secretaries, as dependent on men, or as sex objects. When Christians affirm that in Christ there is neither male nor female, our claim is surely not that women are invisible, but that they are equal in grace and giftedness and, in their capacity, able to participate in the life of the Church and of society.

There are more concrete ways in which the particular perspectives driving technological development can be seen. I want to look at two examples, one related to the development of computer technologies and the other related to developments in the field of biotechnology, to show that technological development is actually linked with particular social arrangements. Computer technologies are extremely expensive and capital-intensive technologies to develop. Because of the need to attract large amounts of capital, one of the realities about computers is that their development has taken place in urban rather than rural contexts, because the capital is easier to come by there. Even with the move away from the larger centers, development is still occurring in urban contexts, usually near universities. As a result of this, computers come to embody certain urban values and assumptions, which make their appropriation in rural contexts less straightforward, at least in the first instance. While computers are very much a part of the rural scene now, linked with computers everywhere by means of the Internet, and while computers are now assisting in the breakdown of this simple dichotomy, we need to remember that we are twenty years into the home computer revolution in the west. Even now, Internet access and use is almost always easier and cheaper from cities.

Further, the need to communicate in this way is bringing to the fore another typical component of technological development, namely, the drive toward increased standardization of the goods available to us. This can cause some practical problems, but my main point is again that it points to a particular way of organizing social relationships. Finally, a factor that is not changing, the ability to attract large amounts of capital, is premised on the promise of economic growth. In times of economic stagnation or even deflation, it is extremely difficult to attract capital for investment in new technological developments. Once again, technological development is put in a very particular social context. Such development becomes dependent upon particular financial institutions and arrangements that those involved in technological development might be expected to support and protect. Added to this, the ability to continue to attract capital into the indefinite future assumes that economic growth can continue indefinitely. It assumes that it is, in principal, unlimited. Economic expansion and technological expansion are closely linked. Yet the difficulties involved in the pursuit of unlimited growth are now becoming obvious and acute.

In one sense, my second technological example might seem to be a response to the constraints imposed by limited resources. The promise of the biotechnology industry is, put simply, that genetically modified crops and farm animals will be more resistant to disease, more productive of the food we grow them for, and therefore more enabled to produce the food we need to feed the growing human population. There are two obvious responses to this promise. We can agree that the benefits are likely to be substantial. In principal, it looks as if we should be able to engineer plants that are more disease resistant and engineer cattle that produce more milk or sheep that produce pharmaceutical products that are difficult to produce by more conventional means. In principal, we should be able to manufacture human tissues in the bodies of animals, and this could contribute enormously to human health and life expectancy. We could go on. The other, obvious response is one of skepticism. We can point out that there are safety concerns that are far from being adequately addressed at this time. We can point to the dangers of the genes we have engineered into our pest-resistant plants being transferred to other plants, which will become extremely noxious weeds because they are resistant to the pests we were trying to get rid of, thus increasing rather than decreasing the amount of chemicals we need to use. Again, we could go on.

What both of these responses miss, it seems to me, are some of the prior questions. In a sense, they are both technological responses to a problem posed by technology. They frame their response in terms of success or failure of a particular technological project, but they don't question the project as such. Let me briefly go back over what it claims to offer. We are promised adequate food for the human population. However, the problem at present is not food production but food distribution, and there is considerable evidence that the biotechnology revolution (which by the way will make the industrial revolution look like a Sunday school picnic) will in fact worsen food distribution problems. Already, biotechnology companies are amassing patents on the biological resources of developing nations in a way that could make it extremely difficult for such nations to marshal those resources to meet their own needs in the future. Companies like Monsanto have been working on terminator genes—genes that would prevent farmers from being able to re-seed their fields from the crops they have grown, effectively ending the principle of farmer's privilege. Although Monsanto has backed off for the time being, it seems unlikely that they or other players in the biotech field are going to want to hold off indefinitely.

Returning to the promises. Perhaps we could use animals to grow human organs and tissues for transplant, but who will get the transplant? When we talk about improving "human health," it seems to me that we need to be a little more careful about asking whose health will be improved and what resources will be consumed in order to gain that improvement. Our past experience suggests that the health of a few may be bought at the cost of dwindling resources for many, and this is before we raise any questions about what might be appropriate limits to our use of animals.

Let me summarize with two characteristics that seem to me to be common to technological societies, and that will lay the basis for my comments about why a proper understanding of the nature of technological change is an issue for us, both as Christians and as representatives of the Anglican Church globally through the work of the ACC.

In the first place, a technological society will be one that will look at problems in terms of technology. It sounds like a truism, but what I am saying is that the interpenetration of knowing and doing that I referred to earlier means that a technological consciousness will proceed by asking what technique I must employ to deal with this or that problem. No problem will appear in principle insoluble to technique. Now this in turn means that such a society will be unable to see a decision to do nothing as anything other than a disguised action. We can see this clearly in a number of contexts. This becomes very clear when we look at debates about environmental development. Although the Rio conference embraced the "precautionary principal," which would put the burden of proof on those who wish to say that a novel development is safe, environmental regulation, in those countries with which I am familiar, has repeatedly put the onus on environmentalists to show that certain activities would be seriously damaging to sensitive habitat. Perhaps another area where we see this is in the area of reproductive technologies. Oliver O'Donovan has famously drawn a distinction between making and begetting. His concern is that a great deal of the rhetoric associated with the development in this field fails to be adequately aware of the difference between our offspring and the products of our inventiveness. While both making and begetting are at one level acts of the will, what we make has quite a different character from that which we beget. Until the advent of the new reproductive technologies, we would not have thought of "making" children. We bear or beget children. (O'Donovan uses only the language of begetting, which is rather masculinist, but his point about the intrusion of the language of technique remains.) Even now, the image of making sits rather awkwardly on our relationships to those who are the products of these technological interventions. They are not like the things that we make, things that we can do with as we please. Rather, they are like ourselves, or at least they become like ourselves. They not only share our nature, but they also share our history. Like us, they don't just exist, they live. They share hopes and fears, aspirations by virtue of which their lives can be measured as fulfilling and rewarding or tragic. The things we make may be valuable, but they never become part of the community as children are.

Technological society forces us to think in terms of making and doing. The response to a problem created by technology is a technological fix. The question is what to do now. Yet it seems to me that the Christian tradition has always wanted to talk about being as well as doing. Christians have generally insisted that consequences alone are not enough to justify an action. We do not generally quote with approval the maxim that "It is better for you that one man should die for the people, than that the whole nation should not perish" (Caiaphas according to John 11:50). This is one of the reasons for the importance of virtue in Christian ethics, an importance that is being recovered at the present time. Put simply, the relationship between acts and intentions is not like the relationship between cause and effect, because it is mediated through character. And without an understanding of the character of the individuals and communities involved, our ethical analysis will lack depth.

A second characteristic of technological society relates to our understanding of freedom. The goal of the technological revolution is in many ways freedom. Freedom from the necessities that nature imposes on us. We can now go further and faster, live longer and more healthily, than we could without technology. Technology frees us from a whole range of constraints. I have already pointed out that one problem with this analysis is that it tends to use the "we" in ways that are not helpful. We are not all equally beneficiaries of these new freedoms. A second problem is that the freedom described turns out to be a freedom of consumers rather than of participants. It is a freedom that is defined, in the first place, in terms of freedom from constraint. We are given freedom from, but it is not clear whether this can also be freedom *for*, or for *what*. Yet when St. Paul talks about freedom, it is surely the latter which is his primary concern. We are to be set free to become what God created and calls us to be. This is what Augustine had in mind when he spoke of the God in whose service we find perfect freedom. In fact, if we focus only on freedom as freedom from constraint, and ignore freedom as freedom *for*, then we risk a sort of moral abandonment: a situation in which we do not care what somebody decides, provided it is their decision.

What I have been doing in the last few minutes is sketching some indications of the types of motivations that might lead Christians to see technology issues as issues that they would wish to engage for theological reasons. I have tried to show that they are issues both for the community of the Church and for the wider communities of which we are a part, and indeed the whole created order. My account is necessarily sketchy—more a series of gestures than a sustained argument—both because of reasons of space and because what I want to do is to stimulate discussion rather than to lay out any definitive response. But even if we agree that these issues are important to Christians, we still need to ask why we should deal with them at the level of the Communion. To begin to suggest an answer to this question, I want to draw out for you some points from *The Virginia Report*. I do this not because I attribute any intrinsic authority to the *Report*, but simply for the pragmatic reason that it is one of the central preoccupations of this gathering. In any case, I will draw on principles that I might have easily found elsewhere in our Anglican heritage.

You might well ask, "How can *The Virginia Report* help us to understand technology and ethics?" At the most superficial level, the obvious answer is that it does not help us very much at all. Clearly, the primary concerns of *The Virginia Report* are far removed from the questions of ethics and technology or ethics and the environment. However, if we think less in terms of substance and more in terms of method, I think *The Virginia Report* has a great deal to say about why it would be helpful to address these issues at the level of the Communion.

For example, with regard to the principle of subsidiarity, the *Report* says that

> Decisions about the life and mission of the Church should be made [at the local level] and need only be referred to wider councils if the matter threatens the unity and the faithfulness of teaching and practice of the Church Catholic, *or where the local church encounters genuinely new circumstances and wishes advice about how to respond.* (p. 39, emphasis mine)

Also, when discussing the role of the Anglican Consultative Council, the *Report* says that it was formed because the 1968 Lambeth Conference

> recognized that there was a need for more contact between the Churches of the Anglican Communion than that provided by the Lambeth Conference every ten years by bringing together bishops, presbyters and laity, under the presidency of the Archbishop of Canterbury to work on common concerns. (p. 23)

Now it seems to me that both resolutions 1.9 and 1.12 from the last Lambeth Conference address themselves to developments that are giving rise to genuinely new circumstances. This is true of certain technological developments that are likely to fundamentally transform some key aspects of human life. (For example, developments in biotechnology are changing the way we manufacture medicines and are shifting the control of the food supply from the hands of farmers even further into the hands of a small number of multinational biotech companies.) It is also true of the substantial threats to the environment, locally and globally, that have given rise to a great deal of international concern, if very little concrete action to date. What I am suggesting is that the questions raised by technological change at this time, both as cultural phenomenon and in terms of particular technologies, are prime candidates for attention at the Communion level in terms of the priorities and approaches of *The Virginia Report*. Further, the urgency of these issues means that the more frequent gatherings of the ACC make this body a more flexible vehicle for reflection and source of initiatives than Lambeth can be. In terms of technological change, ten years might as well be a century. It is fascinating to note that the last conference did not address biotechnology issues. Why? I suspect because by the time the scope of the issues attracted sufficient attention, the planning was too far advanced.

In addition to this, I think there is a further motive for looking at these issues at the Communion level that, while consistent with *The Virginia Report*, draws on motivations only hinted at there. Both problems related to the implications of emergent technologies, such as the biotechnologies and information technologies, and ecological problems cross borders in such a way that they cannot be dealt with adequately without cooperation across the provinces. The pollutants that affect one province, the climatic changes in one area of the world, have their roots in another region of the world. Patents taken out on the genetic resources of one part of the world are owned by companies whose offices are in another part of the world, and the rules governing the restrictions that may be placed on intellectual property rights are set as part of international trade agreements. Once again, even though policies need to be set at the level of provinces, the only place they can be set constitutionally, there need to be adequate mechanisms for efficient consultation and sharing of information if those policies are to be effective. There needs to be some facilitation so that provinces can coordinate their efforts. In my reading of it, *The Virginia Report* supports the view that the ACC is one of the places where that consultation can take place. Given the nature of these questions and the sorts of expertise that would have to be drawn into a network working in this area, I would suggest that the ACC could be the most effective place.

The primary insights I take from *The Virginia Report* thus relate to the appropriateness of ACC involvement on these issues and to the most appropriate shape of that involvement (e.g., consultation, facilitation, information sharing, and so forth). However, there are a few theological hints that gesture toward the more substantial questions that need to be addressed in a way that may be fruitful. In discussing the context in which the Communion works at the present time the *Report* says,

> 1.3 What makes unity and interdependence particularly difficult today?
> In the last 200 years the world has seen extraordinary development in

the political, scientific, economic and psychological spheres. These developments have brought many blessings to the peoples of the world. At the same time there has been the disintegration of traditional cultures, values and social structures and unprecedented threats to the environment. The tension between blessing and disintegration creates a challenge to the unity and interdependence that the peoples of the world face.

Further,

> 1.4 . . . the omnipotence of scientific method and technology, and competitive individualism are no longer accepted without question. In many places there is a search for cultural, personal and social identity, which honors the integrity and value of cultural roots.

It seems to me that at these points we pass beyond questions of method to indications of substance. Matters related to emergent technologies and to ecological disintegration are not mere adjuncts to the questions of unity and communion. In a world divided around the impacts of these changes on particular populations, a point I have stressed repeatedly in this presentation, they are likely to become crucial points of tension. At the same time, they are therefore practical opportunities to show what it means to live in local communities as part of a global communion. Further, what we learn about how to live as a community comprised of many particular local communities will help us to bring a unique and important perspective to the debates in the wider political arena. In my view, there can be no way of looking at environmental issues or issues of technology and ethics that is abstracted from the particular social and political contexts where these realities have their impact. Given the reality of our life as "communion," an important concern of all of us, not just *The Virginia Report,* we are in a strong position to bring together particular local experience and reflective global analysis in a way that will meet the needs of the church and provide a creative and productive addition to the wider discussions that are beginning to take place about these problems all around the world.

The need to tackle these issues at the Communion level is further illustrated by what I take to be the most obvious weakness in my own presentation to you today. My sources and illustrations have been entirely Western and mostly European and North American. This is at one level inevitable because one can only see from where one stands. In fairness, I also think that the sorts of methodological moves I have made open me to hearing, indeed demand that I hear, a range of other perspectives. In part I have simply decided to speak with my own voice rather than appropriate the voices of others, but it shows clearly why we need to engage many voices across the Communion.

At this point the question is, How? And given the limitations of resources, this is an area where the original motion suggested that we make use of the technological capacities of the Internet and the World Wide Web.

Honduras External Debt

—The Right Reverend Leo Frade, bishop of Honduras

Before Mitch, we thought that we were poor. After Mitch, we wished that we could be as poor as before. Hurricane Mitch caused the worst natural disaster of the past two hundred years in the Western hemisphere, creating a catastrophe so vast that it destroyed human lives, livestock, crops, buildings, roads, and all kinds of infrastructure, consequently creating financial chaos of such magnitude that it will take years to solve.

Mitch was as devastating to Honduras as the issue of the world debt. Honduras owes at present $4.3 billion U.S. Dollars. The latest breakdown available of the debt is as follows in millions of U.S. Dollars:

Multilateral	$2,485.1
Bilateral	$1,475.9
Private	$339.0
Total	$4,330.0

About two-thirds of our debt is multilateral, and it is mainly owed to organisations of the Western Hemisphere. The largest creditor for Honduras is the so-called Banco Interamericano de Desarrollo, or in English the Inter-American Development Bank. This is a multilateral lending agency that is mainly financed by the United States. We owe them close to fifty percent of our debt. We also owe the World Bank, International Monetary Fund (IMF), the Central American Bank of Economic Integration, the Commonwealth Development Corporation, and other such multilateral creditors.

The bilateral debt is one-third of the total amount. Japan is our largest creditor, with $1.3 billion U.S. We also owe many European countries like Spain, the United Kingdom, France, Germany, The Netherlands, and Switzerland. We owe very little to the Scandinavian countries.

Some of the European countries like France, the United Kingdom, and Spain have forgiven or delayed the collection of their debts until the year 2001.

We also owe Canada and the United States. I must mention that President Clinton just forgave $65 million U.S. as a way to alleviate the debt. Of course, the U.S. Congress has managed to delay the approval of the bill that will make it official, so nothing has happened up to now.

Among the bilateral debts, we have some South-to-South debts with other larger South American nations and a very small amount of debt with other Central American nations and Mexico.

According to the Central Bank of Honduras and statistics of the World Bank, the foreign debt of Honduras is over $4.3 billion U.S. Dollars. We spend more than $600 million U.S. annually to service the debt.

Now, the bottom line of those numbers is that the country of Honduras has to pay $5.81 U.S. for each $1.00 U.S. we receive in loans in order to service the debt. You can imagine the negative social and economic impact of this very unjust treatment of what is considered the poorest of all the Spanish-speaking countries of the world.

The internal consequences we face are that for every dollar that the country is able to collect, we have to pay thirty-three cents of those dollars to service the debt. Thirty-three cents that could be used for education, medicine, social development, and so forth, but instead is paid to service the debt, leaving us with only sixty-seven cents.

The consequences of Mitch have worsened the economic conditions. Massive losses of lives (15,000 people died: 5,250 recovered bodies, 8,912 disappeared), more than two million people were displaced, and many towns and villages were destroyed. More than half of all the bridges of the country were lost, and most roads were made impassable. Most schools and hospitals were damaged, and many administrative centres were closed, as well as public services that were devastated. Authorities indicate losses of inventories and fixed assets—including infrastructure—amounting to about forty-nine percent of the GDP. Real GDP fell three percent in 1998 and was negative in 1999, compared with pre-hurricane projections of real gross domestic product (GDP) growth of more than six percent a year. The only way to face these deficits is to finance them through foreign grants, concessional loans, and debt relief.

Current revenue also declined to about 16 percent in 1998 and 14.5 percent in 1999. These figures are much less of what was projected for these years and are due to the reduction in receipts from income and sales taxes, as well as lower customs duties on imports of raw material and equipment associated with reconstruction efforts.

The private sector has indeed been extremely affected. The loan portfolios of several banks have been affected because of losses experienced by major borrowers.

In a nutshell, that is the situation of Honduras, the situation of almost six million people. A situation that is affecting our stability and our ability to develop the country. No development is possible if we are unable to develop the most important of all the capitals, which is the human capital. Our education, medical, and other social services are of bad quality, if they exist at all.

It is obvious that the situation of the foreign debt associated with the destruction of Hurricane Mitch accounts for much of our present predicament. But we see in the foreign debt an element of injustice that is self-evident. I'll give you an example.

About the same time of my consecration, almost sixteen years ago, the Honduran government got a loan from the Inter-American Development Bank, which is financed by the United States, in order to build a hydroelectric dam in a placed called El Cajon.

We borrowed $90 million and the money was used to build this massive project aimed to provide electricity to the country. Well, to make a long story short, more than ten years have passed and we have paid $196 million, just to service that particular debt. And hear this, we still owe the original $90 million.

The international outcry of protest given to that example of raw usury and exploitation of the multilateral lending institution forced them to modify the loan terms into more concessional terms. Just by modifying the terms and making them less inhuman, the nation is saving $14 million a year.

There are many examples of these kinds of loans that we have had to sign that make self-evident what Honduras and other poor nations of the world have been saying: "It is not that we do not want to pay our debts. *No*, the debts have been paid more than once already. What we want are humane terms devoid of usury and exploitation."

But we must be careful how we are being helped. What is going to be the price of being alleviated? What is the cost of exiting our recurrent debt problems?

Take the Heavily Indebted Poor Countries (HIPC) initiative, for example. In Cologne, Germany, the G7 or G8 continued to deal with an initiative aimed to reduce the overhang of the debt to the very poor countries of the world. Cologne supported faster, deeper, and broader debt relief for the poorest countries that demonstrate a commitment to reform and bring poverty alleviation.

The G8 nations, a group of industrialised countries, hoped that this initiative when implemented would release resources for health and education, thus helping to make the situation of the poor developing countries less acute and miserable.

Well, we hope that this time things will go better. The original HIPC plan was not only slow but also ineffectual. Only Uganda, Bolivia, and Guyana have benefited so far and only very stingily; thus, it has not made a real difference.

The problem with these faster, deeper, and broader cuts proposed by Cologne is that they will be accompanied by faster, deeper, and broader cuts of services to the poor, which are presently supported by social relief programs from the government. This heavy price that the poor will have to pay is because the HIPC initiative is bound to the execution of programs and conditions that, in practice, increase the social and economic inequalities within the Honduran society. Sadly for us, the HIPC initiative for Honduras does not contain any qualitative change that takes into account the destruction caused by Hurricane Mitch. Nor does it consider the challenge of reconstruction and transformation that Honduras must implement in the near future.

Honduras is among the twenty-six countries that have qualified to participate in the HIPC initiative, among countries like Benin, Ghana, Laos, and Senegal.

Please be aware that even after benefiting from any alleviation of our debt burden, we are going to be paying more to service our debt than we pay for education and health. This is in a country with a high infant mortality and close to fifty percent illiteracy. How many children's lives we could save and how many schools we could open if we really were able to be free from the world debt?

I must add for your information that none of the debt that Honduras presently has is due to the military. That type of help we got free from the Americans during President Reagan's days. Sadly there is always money for bombs and guns but very little for schools and hospitals. The first you can get for free but the others you have to get through loans.

Another thing that I should share with you about the Honduran case is how we always manage to end up where we first began. There is no question that the international community has been willing to help us due to the vast destruction of the hurricane. A large amount of money has flowed our way in order to help us. But please, also be aware that the help is just a small amount of what we really need. In many cases, the help consists in the form of a moratorium that is good for three years. There is no forgiveness of interest or capital. The help is not given without Honduras promising to pay it back.

In other words, at present we owe $4.3 billion. We are being "forgiven" $1.3 million to help us reconstruct, but at the same time we are taking a new debt of $1.3 million. The end result is that in the end, we end up in the same boat as we were in before. No real forgiveness happens for the most part.

A couple of months ago I was in Cheltenham, England, where I was invited to speak at the Greenbelt Festival on the issue of the world debt. While I was giving my address, I mentioned that we were praying in Honduras for the HIPC initiative to include Honduras. At the end of my speech I entertained questions. One of the persons in the audience was indignant that I could say that we were praying for Honduras to be part of the HIPC initiative. He tried to call my attention to my ignorance for saying such a thing. It was an anathema to his liberal ears. I answered him that I was perfectly aware of the accompanying results of the HIPC initiative and how they affected the people. But I also reminded him that we were not happy out of ignorance but out of hunger. Many times poor countries like Honduras have to commit to unjust, abusive terms in order just to continue living and developing. We have very few choices. Sadly, most of the choices are harmful to our people. The poorer you are, the worse you are going to suffer.

I must end by saying to you that the issue of debt cancellation must be seen not in financial or economic terms but in the terms of human lives. Most discussions on debt relief are happening in rich areas, and that indeed tones the discussion. If your surroundings don't bring about the urgency, as in Honduras or many of the developing countries of the world, if the surroundings don't show the urgency of the cancellation, then the discussion is toned in slowness and lack of urgency.

The discussions discount human lives and not capital. The net present value (NPV), which is the economic idea of discounting the money you are going to be lending and its real cost after it is paid back, looks only at the value of the capital and not at the lives that are permanently lost due to the lack of measures that could save them. We just look at the lack of opportunity for investment and not at the lack of humane conditions to survive.

We must strive to make sure that the debt relief issue is not a financial or a development problem. We are working with the wrong screen of qualification, we are developing the wrong plan, and we have the wrong institutions and people sitting down around the table where decisions are made. IMF people were sitting with government officials with no representatives of a people's forum present. I do agree with Lambeth's resolution 1.15, which states "that poverty reduction is more important than debt cancellation."

It also calls upon political leaders and finance ministers in both creditor and debtor nations to develop a new, independent, open, and transparent forum for the negotiation and agreement of debt relief for highly indebted nations and, in particular, to establish a mediation council to respond to appeals from debtor nations, identify odious debts, and determine debt repayments that prioritise basic human development needs over the demands of creditors.

We indeed must continue in our struggle as a church to make wiping the slate clean a reality. Not by degrees, with little nibbles. If a country qualifies, give it one hundred percent relief. This is not a giving away of money, remember, because the debt has already been paid several times.

Also note that Jubilee is not an everyday event. Fifty years is two generations; something that happens every two generations is an extraordinary event. We must remember that moral culpability is not only on the debtors for owing money, but also on the creditors that imposed impossible terms, making the debt unpayable.

We must also realise that the church relief organisations, even rock stars, have been rallying the people. This outcry has resulted in some relief. We must continue our struggle to end the slavery and misery of the debt and never cease to call for its cancellation.

We must continue bringing good news to the poor, proclaiming the release to the captives, recovering the sight of the blind, letting the oppressed go free, and proclaiming the Jubilee year of the Lord's favour (Luke 4:18–19).

The MISSIO Executive Summary

MISSIO, the Anglican Communion's Standing Commission on Mission, was established by ACC-9 in Cape Town in 1993 as the successor to MISAG II, with its members appointed for their first five-year term. MISSIO has met four times between 1993 and 1999. This report is respectfully submitted to ACC-11, meeting in Edinburgh in September 1999.

The main substance of this report is contained in chapters 4 through 7. Chapter 4 contains the report's major theological reflections on mission. Chapter 5 is a preliminary review of the Decade of Evangelism, with suggestions for the way forward. Chapter 6 contains a discussion of leadership training as this pertains to the mission work of the Church, and chapter 7 is a major review of international mission structures throughout our Communion. Chapter 8 is a case study of one church's struggle to deal with its historical legacy of cross-cultural mission, with pertinent reflections from three partner churches. Toward the end of most chapters, questions for discussion and reflection have been included, in the hopes that the report will be widely circulated and prove useful and informative to Anglicans throughout the breadth of our Communion.

The specific recommendations, on which ACC-11 is requested to act, are as follows.

Recommendations

- **A New Way of Meeting.** MISSIO chose, as a matter of policy, to hold each of its meetings in a different part of the Communion and took time to experience the life and witness of the local church in its own context. This was a good decision, enabling the commission to increase its understanding of the mission challenges and tasks around the Communion. The context in which one does mission contributes in no small measure to the theology of mission and the agenda for mission. MISSIO therefore recommends this way of working to those who will serve on the commission in the future and draws this model of working to the attention of ACC-11 and other committees, commissions, and networks of the Communion.

- **An Anglican Congress.** MISSIO warmly welcomed the 1995 proposal of the Joint Standing Committee of ACC and the Primates to hold an Anglican Congress. At its final meeting in Harare in April 1999, MISSIO continued to envisage such a congress, now contemplated for the year 2003. MISSIO's specific suggestions for a Fourth Anglican Congress are contained in a memorandum to the Secretary General of the Anglican

Consultative Council (appendix A).

- **A Meeting of Mission Agencies.** MISSIO is proposing a meeting of synodical, provincial, and voluntary mission agencies in the year 2001 (appendix A). This meeting will reflect on the roles and responsibilities of the mission agencies, as well as promote networking and mutual understanding among the older agencies and newer expressions of mission structures. MISSIO hopes the planners of the Anglican Congress will see the outcome of the mission agencies' conference as informing and enriching the Fourth Anglican Congress.

- **A Review of Leadership Training.** MISSIO, recognising that its surveys of the progress of the Decade of Evangelism within dioceses and provinces have highlighted the importance and problems of leadership training and clergy formation, therefore requests ACC-11 to initiate a review within the Communion of leadership training and clergy formation to identify trends, needs, and problems, as well as how they might be addressed.

- **The Decade of Evangelism.** At the time of MISSIO's final meeting, the Decade of Evangelism was still in progress. Many voices from around the Communion say that the decade has added great momentum to the ongoing witness of Anglicans worldwide, which will continue beyond the official end of the decade. In most provinces, much effort has been expended on empowering the laity. There was a new drive to include evangelism and mission into the curricula of many seminaries and theological colleges and an increase in persons participating in mission and evangelism training. Many provinces have expressed the need for deeper and wider training in mission and evangelism for both the laity and clergy. MISSIO therefore recommends:

  - That the provinces and dioceses of the Communion evaluate the lessons learned during the decade in their situation in order to continue and build on the momentum the decade has achieved and to keep evangelism as a high profile in the Church's mission.

  - That in particular the provinces, dioceses, and parishes develop and expand appropriate training to equip individuals and congregations for effective work in mission and evangelism

- **Inter-Anglican Standing Commission on Mission and Senior-Level Mission and Evangelism Staff Officer.** In response to the Lambeth Conference resolution 2.2e on "Mission and the Structures of the Anglican Communion," and having heard of the proposed recommendations of the ACC Joint Standing Committees' Priorities Working Group, MISSIO:

  - Endorses the proposal of the Priorities Working Group to continue a Standing Commission on mission;

  - Recommends that it be called the Inter-Anglican Standing Commission on Mission;

- Recommends that the Inter-Anglican Standing Commission on Mission have functions and membership as detailed on pages 58 and 59;

- Recommends that a senior-level mission and evangelism staff officer be appointed to the Anglican Communion Office;

- Recommends that the mission and evangelism officer be responsible for the functions listed on page 60.

- **Proposal for a Network of Anglicans in Mission and Evangelism (NAME).** In response to a referral from the Primates' meeting, MISSIO met with the organisers of a group known as the Network of Anglicans in Mission and Evangelism (NAME). Following the meeting, MISSIO discussed the group's proposal at length. Believing that a commitment to the mission of God should be recognised as an expression of our unity and wanting to encourage new expressions of mission, MISSIO recommends that the Anglican Consultative Council, on completion of the following steps, recognise NAME as a network of the Anglican Communion:

  - A positive review of the proposal by the provinces and major mission agencies, to be facilitated by the Anglican Communion Office (ACO).

  - Formation of a secretariat, or staff, and program committee by NAME that inspires confidence in the network's intentions.

  - Clarification of the membership of NAME, particularly the question of whether the network is open to people or organisations other than individual bishops and institutions or agencies.

  - The working out of a mutually acceptable reporting accountability to the Anglican Consultative Council. (MISSIO recommends that NAME liaise with the ACO staff officer for mission and evangelism.)

  - The establishment of a mutually acceptable working relationship with MISSIO, which takes account of MISSIO's mandate while enabling NAME to operate effectively and efficiently.

Foreword

—The Right Reverend Datuk Yong Ping Chung, bishop of Sabah, chairman, MISSIO

I am a convert to Christianity from a traditional Chinese family, all the members of which were also converted to Christianity. I always praise and thank God for the power of the gospel of our Lord Jesus Christ and for those who know Jesus personally and took great care in sharing Jesus with my family and me.

My journey from non-believer to believer, on to disciple, ordinand, deacon, priest, and bishop, continues to imprint upon my heart and mind the prime importance of mission and evangelism in the life of the Church. Thus, while I have tried not to lose sight of the "service and deeds" of the gospel, mission and evangelism have always been a prominent part of my ministry. Paul's passionate cry, "Woe is me if I do not preach the Gospel" (1 Corinthians 9:16), and "It has always been my ambition to preach the Gospel where Christ is not known" (Romans 15:20) have been a constant encouragement for me in my ministry.

The promise of "My grace is sufficient for you" (2 Corinthians 12:9) continues to call me to be faithful to mission and evangelism, while at the same time I know that God, in his own time, will give the increase. Thus I happily and humbly accepted the appointment as chairman of MISSIO in 1994, seeing it as an opportunity to pay the gospel debt to all those who respond to the call of God to mission and evangelism in the Anglican Communion. I was acutely aware of my own shortcomings in this task, but I was also confident and trusted that God would provide for our needs. Thus the eighteen members of MISSIO from different parts of the Communion met for the first time in Singapore (now part of my own home province of Southeast Asia). At that very first meeting I praised and thanked God for his abundant grace and provision. Here was a group of people chosen from our own Anglican family—they came with their own credentials and gifts, recognised by their own home church, totally committed to the mission and evangelism process of their own church, eager to be used by God to contribute to the effort of helping the Anglican Communion to turn from maintenance to mission mode.

We met four times in the course of the past five years. We prayed together, broke bread together, and studied the word together. We listened to each other's stories. We debated, argued, drafted, and redrafted together. We struggled together to make sense out of overwhelming experiences and diverse contexts. We offered our gifts and insights to be used by the Holy Spirit. This has been an experience of growth. Our report is but a partial reflection of our journey together.

We are also aware that there are many unsung heroes of faith of our Communion who engage in mission and evangelism in contexts of ongoing suffering and pain, caused by poverty, injustice, disaster, war . . . in short, human sinfulness. We want to acknowledge with deep gratitude and thanksgiving their faithfulness and commitment.

We, the members of MISSIO, present this report of our work. We pray that this record of our journey will be like a Chinese lantern put into the hands of our Communion to light our way to becoming a mission church. Indeed, the journey from maintenance to mission is a long one. I hope and pray our successor, the next mission commission, will in due time be another lantern in the hands of the Communion so that we can continue our journey of being a living Church of God in his world.

MISSIO Presentation

—Maureen Sithole

President, members of ACC, I am presenting to you a report from MISSIO. MISSIO was created through ACC five years ago, and the term of office ends this year. There are eighteen members in MISSIO, coming from fifteen different nations, who have worked hard and well together under the chairmanship of Bishop Yong Ping Chung.

We are presenting a report called "Anglicans in Mission: A Transforming Journey" which contains a theological reflection on the theme of mission as transformation. This picks up and develops some of the themes emerging from section 2 of the Lambeth Conference and includes comments on church growth, that is the five marks of mission: companionship in mission, reached people, the gospel, church, and culture. Those are some of the issues that this report looks into. It also includes an extended chapter on the Decade of Evangelism and highlights a number of principles and themes that have become apparent through a survey of provinces and dioceses. The overwhelming impression is how seriously the call for a decade of evangelism has been taken within the Communion and the variety of ways in which it has been carried forward. One of the main emphases has been on training and clergy formation, but patterns of training and clergy formation vary in different parts of the Communion.

The section, which looks at this formally, recommends that ACC initiates a review of leadership training and clergy formation to first identify trends, needs, and problems and how these might be addressed as a Communion. There is also a long chapter on patterns of international mission structures in the Anglican Communion.

This considers how the principles and practices of partnership have developed since the 1960s. New expressions of mission and mission connections are emerging, particularly multidirectional mission. The relationship of voluntary initiatives and more formal structures in forms of coordination, both within provinces and for the Anglican Communion, including a clear recommendation, that we need to take today for mission and evangelism are in response to a resolution from the Lambeth Conference.

The report concludes with a case study from Canada on the struggle for transformation within Canada as the terrible effects of Church and mission residential schools on the nation's first people become apparent, with apology, repentance, and restitution as the only possible responses. You will remember that in the report we gave you, we also gave you some other examples of how other countries have dealt with this kind of issue, and we would like you to actually look into that as well.

The commission also made specific proposals regarding a Communion-wide conference, which we dealt with the other day. I would not like to dwell on this, as we are still going to go back to the Anglican Congress. It also includes a recommendation that states that we should have another conference for mission agencies. This will be done in order to find out whether we can continue as partners or we can go into a companion basis with the mission agencies.

The other thing that the MISSIO dealt with was a group of bishops who came to visit MISSIO while in Harare. They wanted to start a network, and at the time they met with MISSIO, their name was AMEN. When they had the initial discussion with MISSIO, they did not have a constitution, they could not spell out in detail where the funding would come from, and they could not detail what their membership would be.

At the time they came to meet with MISSIO, their membership consisted of selected bishops and selected institutions, and MISSIO pointed out that we are a Communion that consists not only of bishops, but also of laity and clergy. MISSIO questioned the group about why, if it is going to be a network that supports the Communion, there are only bishops in the group. We do not have an answer to that.

We have a recommendation relating to that, that you will deal with when you break into groups. When you deal with the issue of that network, it is important that you're aware of the Anglican Communion's guidelines, which guide any grouping within the Communion who wants to start a network, and that the group does not comply with those guidelines at this time.

Now the other important thing is that, within their own structures, when the bishops left Lambeth, they had their own meeting, and after that meeting they went to their respective places and said that the Primates had agreed that they could form this network. In reality, the primates did not make a decision concerning the Network, but passed it on to MISSIO to make a recommendation to ACC-11.

At MISSIO we asked them not to do that, because it creates a lot of confusion within the family. If they want to become a network, we believe that they must enhance the work of the Communion and not start parallel structures. Otherwise, we are becoming a group that does not trust each other, a group that does not work with each other, a group that wants to do things with undercurrents. We want you—because you know the basic facts—to actually look at those things in order to see if we all agree that they should become a network.

Now the other thing we are going to do is divide the sections into different groups. Before we look at the different questions the groups are going to deal with, we thought it would be important for us to have some guidelines regarding what we expect you to do when you break into these groups—what our objectives are—so that you will have a focus for discussion and so that when you report to the group you will have the expected outcomes.

We are not using a talk-down kind of approach. We are asking you from the bottom to meet us halfway and meet those objectives.

The first expected outcome is that the ACC will have clear decisions about MISSIO's resolutions, which we will deal with later when we come back from our discussion groups. The second thing is on the future of mission.

The other thing is on the resolutions about theological education. Is it important that we have some kind of standard requiring that our theological education include lay training as well? You need to tell us that.

In addition to these items, you also need to make sure that you indulge yourselves in other aspects of the report, such as transformation, the Decade of Evangelism, change in structures for international world nations, and the Canadian case study. Use the case study as a basis, but relate it to your own context when you report back. And lastly, we request that you receive the MISSIO report and recommend it to the Communion.

We have also allocated questions to groups. Group 1 will deal with the question of transformation. Group 2 will deal with the Decade of Evangelism. Groups 3 and 4, within your own groups, will deal with the findings on the Decade of Evangelism, and you will be using your report to look at section 4 of the report. Groups 5 and 6 will deal with the patterns of international structures. Groups 7 and 8 will deal with training and leadership. Then all eight groups will deal with the issue of the struggle for transformation. We will also look at training for leadership, a mission Standing Commission. These are the expected outcomes. We will try to reflect them again in what you will be doing, so that you will have a focus.

Thank you.

ARCIC Presentation

—THE RIGHT REVEREND MARK SANTER, BIRMINGHAM, ENGLAND

I will begin by saying a few words about why we're dealing at all with an ecumenical text today, as well as something about who the Anglican-Roman Catholic International Commission (ARCIC) is, a word about how it works, and then what we hope to accomplish in this morning's session.

It's quite common for Christians to become impatient sometimes with the ecumenical movement, particularly when churches are facing such profound evangelical and prophetic mission challenges. Indeed, this meeting itself has been considering some of these challenges: the complexities of rapidly evolving technology and the questions of the injustice of the economic system globally. But it's useful to remember that theological dialogue on matters of faith and order cannot easily be dismissed as irrelevant. I would remind you of a very good quote from the 1958 Lambeth Conference that expresses this well, "A divided church cannot heal the wounds of a divided world." So we're engaged in ecumenical dialogue because such dialogue is an essential part of the healing of divisions, which obscure the gospel message of reconciliation and hope.

Now the ARCIC was established three decades ago by Pope Paul VI and Archbishop Michael Ramsey and was a pioneer really in terms of ecumenical dialogue between Christian churches. From the start it sought to tackle what many thought were insurmountable obstacles. It is a body to which members are officially appointed to represent the Anglican Communion and the Catholic Church worldwide. It has eight to nine members aside, plus the co-secretaries and, very importantly, an observer (a very active participant really) from the Faith and Order of the World Council of Churches.

Now how does the dialogue work? The purpose of the theological dialogue is to enable the two churches to recognise Christ in one another and to discover how, together, the faith can be expressed and lived. Because churches that live in separation inevitably become divided in the way they express the one faith.

So the method of ecumenical dialogue that has been followed by ARCIC since the start tries to draw us back to the scriptures and to the common tradition, and it seeks to avoid the later language, which has become polemical; these help us to express the common faith in fresh ways.

So we are at the stage in the dialogue when we have a new text before us. On the eve of Ascension Day in the Jerusalem Chamber of Westminster Abbey, this agreed statement, a copy of which has been circulated to us all, was released. It was a newsworthy event and even caused some surprise for members of both communions. But the work does not stop when the theologians and commission publishes the text. In fact, an important phase of the work begins, a phase that must involve the whole Church: laity, clergy, and those who have oversight, the bishops, in a process of receiving the text. Now we've heard from some places that when the text was published last May, some mistakenly read the document as if it were already a joint declaration of the two church authorities. It is not. It's a statement of theologians officially appointed by the churches, with an official mandate, but their work is now handed over to the Church at large for consideration. So we have the result then of the theological dialogue before us and now we begin a process of reception. A process that I hope will involve us all in studying and evaluating the text.

So the next stage, reception, is a process that cannot be rushed. For the next stage, which will develop over a period of several years, I hope that we will begin today a process that will set in place what needs to be done in the churches of our Communion to pay attention to and study effectively this document. In a real sense, the Anglican Communion begins the process today.

The purpose of this morning's sessions is really fourfold: First, to introduce to you this important text, to put it in context and to highlight some of its content. It is the first time that the publication has been before any instrument of our Communion. Secondly, it is to provide an opportunity for the members of the ACC to ask questions of clarification. There may be language and terminology and even concepts in here that are not familiar to us all. So we have an opportunity today, particularly in the presence of Bishop Mark, to ask some questions of clarification. I repeat: it's not for us to debate the theological content of the document today, but it's certainly a good opportunity to be able to go away with some initial questions of clarification answered, so that we're ready to begin to study it in-depth. Thirdly, I hope we will together be able to identify the questions and the resources, which the Communion will hopefully use over the next few years, that will help us study the text. It will be useful if, by the end of this morning's session, we have gathered some of your ideas and questions, so that the provinces, dioceses, and parishes can use them as they study the text. It would also be useful if you have an idea of any particular resources or study guides or whatever that the Communion might prepare in order to help this be received and studied across the Church. And lastly, to agree upon the timing and the process by which the group responsible for carrying this forward at the level of the Communion should do so. The Inter-Anglican Standing Commission on Ecumenical Relations will take a lead role in managing the study and reception of the statement, as is noted, if you've read my report in the convening circular.

What is good for us to establish is some kind of time frame, so we know how the churches can pace themselves in this study and when we might hope to hear back in the preliminary way about how this text is being received.

So today then, we actually begin the study by setting the questions, and the time frame, by clarifying any immediate issues of language and terminology, and in general by having an introduction to this report. I repeat, it is not for us today to say yes or no to the issues and the theological content contained herein, but it certainly is for us to give some guidance as to the future process and how we as a Communion will respond.

Perhaps I will just begin by thanking you and the organisers for asking me to participate in this. Obviously when I came here my primary role was to be the observer, but I am very glad to have this opportunity as a member of the commission to also talk a little bit about *The Gift of Authority*.

Now that David has explained something about our session, what I want to do before Bishop Mark speaks is to sketch in a little bit of the context for the statement.

Some people asked back in May, "Why is our ARCIC suddenly producing a statement on authority?" I hope that that isn't a question in the minds of members of the ACC, because I'm sure that you have been kept informed about the progress of the dialogues in previous meetings. The introduction to *The Gift of Authority*, paragraphs 1 to 6, already gives a little bit of context to what it wants to say, but I would like to take you into that a little to show where the statement is coming from.

First of all, it's very important to notice that the commission gave its document a subtitle, "Authority in the Church 3," to show that this new ARCIC statement isn't displacing its earlier work. Indeed not, because that earlier work from ARCIC in the final report has been officially evaluated by both churches. No, the earlier statements are the basis for this one, and you will have noticed that in the new statement, paragraph 1 lists some points of convergence that have come out of the previous work of ARCIC. But I think it would be quite unjust to the commission's intentions to imagine that that work can be reduced to just a list of points. Rather, I think the opening paragraphs of *The Gift of Authority* are an invitation to go back and reread that earlier work, which, let's remember, has been officially reflected on and evaluated by both our churches.

So ARCIC chose quite deliberately to build upon it, not to repeat it and not to try and give an exhaustive summary of it. So a question that may be worth considering this morning is whether this whole corpus of work on authority might need to be made available in some way for reflection by our churches.

Pope Paul VI and Archbishop Ramsey set up this dialogue between us when they met in 1966. Out of that visit came a joint commission: a proprietary commission to work out what this dialogue was going to involve and how it was going to go forward. That commission specifically highlighted the issue of authority in the Church, its nature, exercise, and implications. I quote from paragraph 20 of the Malta report, as it's known, the report that sketched out the form and direction that the dialogue ought to take. It says,

"A serious theological examination should be jointly undertaken on the nature of Authority. Real or apparent differences between us come to the surface in such matters as unity and indefectibility of the church and its teaching Authority, the Petrine primacy, infallibility and Marialogical definitions." So you'll notice that many of the themes, even in the new statement, were given to ARCIC by its authorities at that point.

When ARCIC had produced statements on the doctrine of the Eucharist and on ministry and ordination, it was to devote most of the succeeding years in that first phase to looking at this question. In 1976, the first statement looked at how the Holy Spirit keeps the Church under the Lordship of Christ. The commission claimed in that first statement to have reached a consensus, both on authority in the Church and on the basic principles of primacy. It did not say that all the problems associated with primacy, in particular papal primacy, had been resolved, but it did state (in paragraph number 24) that it believed that there was a solid basis for confronting them. So that's what the commission then went on in this first phase, before the publication of the final report. Five years later, in 1981, the commission did three things for our purposes. First of all, it published an elucidation, a document answering questions raised about the first statement on authority that it had produced. Secondly, it published a new, second statement on authority in the Church. And thirdly, it gathered together all that work, along with the statements on Eucharist and ministry and elucidations, as the final report and submitted it to the two churches to be officially evaluated. So that was a very important moment in this dialogue on authority.

ARCIC's second statement on authority looked particularly at universal primacy. In the elucidation they produced at that time the commission already stated that it had reached doctrinal agreement that "the Unity in truth of the Christian Community demands visible expression that such visible expression is the will of God and that the maintenance of unity at a universal level includes the episcopate, the oversight or leadership, of a universal primate" (from elucidation number 8). The new statement they produced at the time said that "a universal primacy will be needed in a reunited church and should appropriately be the primacy of the Bishop of Rome" (from elucidation number 9 of their second statement on authority). That statement registered further progress concerning primacy, although the commission did not claim that all disagreement had been resolved.

So that was the point that ARCIC had reached in its dialogue on authority by the time it concluded that first phase and published the final report.

The second phase of ARCIC's work, as this work on authority was beginning to be examined, was reflected on, received, and evaluated by our two communions.

I'm sure there is no need to remind you that both the 1988 Lambeth Conference, in resolution 8.3, and the 1991 Catholic Church response, after wide consultation in their respective churches, recognised that this early work of ARCIC on authority provided a basis for further dialogue and for progress.

Once there had been those official responses, ARCIC had a clearer idea of how its authorities wanted to continue this dialogue. The principal pointers that it took from those responses are those mentioned in paragraph 3 of *The Gift of Authority*. It's worth recalling, perhaps, that ARCIC does not set its own agenda. It takes its cue from what our churches ask it to do. It doesn't sit there thinking up what it ought to do. So by 1994 the commission was ready to continue dialogue on authority and it spent five years producing the statement that was published this May, which you have in front of you.

Bishop Mark is going to say something about its content in a moment. I just want to conclude by adding a few more important comments, which I think help to put it in its context. The first of these is that as the ARCIC commission was engaging in this further dialogue, which led to this statement, both our churches in different ways were also raising the question of authority in new ways for themselves and for ecumenical dialogue. I'm thinking first of all of the fact that in 1995 Pope John Paul wrote the first-ever encyclical letter on ecumenism. In it he reflected on a number of issues, but for our purposes we might recall in particular that he reflected at some length on the ministry of unity as he described the bishop of Rome. We might also recall the fact that it constitutes a difficulty for most other Christians; the Pope appealed for dialogue on that very subject, possibly enabling him to exercise this ministry in a way that is open to the new ecumenical situation (paragraphs 95 and 96 of the encyclical letter). There have been various responses to that invitation already. The Church of England's House of Bishops produced an extensive reflection called "May They All Be One." Other forms of response have been taking place. Perhaps I can say that ARCIC is also providing a contribution to such a response and one that certainly presents a challenge, I think, to my Church; for example, in the expectation expressed there that the exercise of this primacy by the bishop of Rome should be more transparent within the context of collegiality of the bishops.

The other way in which this issue was being raised up was of course in *The Virginia Report*. You've heard plenty about that already, so I don't think I need to say any more, except suffice to say that it is raising questions for Anglicans about teaching authority and how authority might work at the Communion-wide level, and even beyond, at the universal level. So I think ARCIC was working within that, if you like, new context. The second and final thing that I want to say about the recent situation is what has happened to this statement so far. Well, in one sense, it's very early; as David has emphasised, it's coming to an Anglican instrument for the first time today. It's only four months since it was launched, but quite a lot has happened and I just want to mention that very briefly. First of all, the only official version of this document is the English language one, which was produced by the commission, who works in English. However, this time we made an effort, which I think has not been made in the past, to make it as widely available in other languages as possible. So at the moment of its publication in English, it was also made available in translation in French, Italian, Portuguese, and in Spanish versions. They are not the official text; they are translations. But they are as good translations as we could get. Also, they were made immediately available on the World Wide Web, both on the Vatican pages and on the Anglican Communion pages. That's the first time that any ARCIC document has been issued in that way. They were also accompanied by some comments.

The commission offered some initial reflections that might help in reading the document. On our side, the Roman Catholic Church, this document was sent to every episcopal and bishop's conference in the world—not just those where Anglicans are a significant partner of the community, but to everyone, including the papal *nuncios*. One of my colleagues said that he thinks it's the first time we've ever sent a document to everybody at that moment of publication. We always publish these documents in a sort of house bulletin, which we send to everybody, but it's not quite the same thing. It was accompanied by a letter commending it for study and reflection, and a similar process was carried out by the Anglican Communion office, where the document was sent to every Primate. So it's now for our churches separately and together to begin a process of reflecting on its contents, discussing it, and eventually, in time, evaluating whether the Commission has indeed helped our two communities to come together on this question.

It's good to be with you this morning and to see some familiar faces. I think I'd like to start with an observation that I haven't written down. It's this: All of us engaged in ecumenism need to realise that we're talking not merely about the reconciliation of institutions or doctrines, but much more about the reconciliation of people in the one family of God. The infinite nurturing of friendship is an indispensable element of it[SLA25]. Tim Gallagher has been a friend of mine for twenty years, ever since when I was principal of a theological college and had a sabbatical term in Rome and he was the senior student of the English college in Rome. He was one of the people who made me feel very welcome indeed. I was present at his priestly ordination, and he was present at my episcopal ordination. That is part of ecumenism.

I'm very glad that he's set the context out so clearly. I speak, as you've been reminded, as the bishop who was co-chairman of the Anglican-Roman Catholic International Commission from 1983 until earlier this year.

What I want to start by saying is that, to remind you, in looking at this text on authority we are, so to speak, standing in the middle of a stream. A stream which, in the immediate view as we've been reminded, starts with Pope Paul VI's meeting with Archbishop Michael Ramsey in 1966. From that meeting in 1966, a third of a century ago, there has followed all the work of ARCIC. Our ARCIC agreed-on statements, evaluated by the churches that we've already heard about in this volume, on ministry and ordination and the first two statements on authority. Part of this ongoing stream of responses, which came from our two churches, has lead in turn to this new statement on authority. The background of this new statement includes not only this former work but also other work that the commission did—work on Church as Communion and *The Virginia Report*—important work that I think has been too little commented on and absorbed. Father Galligan reminded us of the Pope's invitation to the other churches to engage in dialogue with him on the question of the papal office as a ministry of unity for the whole Christian people.

But that only takes us back to 1966. There's a much wider context both of space and time. The dialogue between Anglicans and Roman Catholics is only one stream, so to speak, in the wider river of ecumenical dialogue; for example, the multilateral dialogue focus in the Faith and Order Commission of the World Council of Churches, lots of local or national dialogues, and the bilateral dialogues between particular traditions, such as ours with Lutherans or ARCIC.

The issue of authority comes up sooner or later in one form or another in every dialogue which addresses itself seriously to questions of community or unity. Sooner or later, if you're talking about working more closely together, you have to talk about who decides what in a way that is credible. That is the issue of authority.

In local or national dialogues, the issue of authority comes up on a local or national level. In global discussions, as we've discovered in our own Anglican Communion, the issue of authority comes up at a global level. How do we make decisions in such a way that we recognise we've made them? This issue of authority is simply inescapable. That is, so to speak, the dimension of space. The dimension of what it means to be in communion with our brothers and sisters throughout the world.

Also in this discussion of authority there is the dimension of time. Authority has been an issue in the Church ever since the days of the apostles. It is not a new issue. The apostles had to struggle to maintain unity in the Church, and their own apostolic authority was at stake in that struggle. The issue of authority was likewise central to the story of the split in the first millennium between the eastern and western parts of Christianity. The issue of authority was central to the tensions in the Church of the west in the fifteenth and sixteenth centuries, which lead to the schism of the Reformation. Questions about authority and obedience will be at issue in the Church until the end of time. A Lutheran said to me a few days ago that we (churches of the Reformation) think that authority is the issue; he thought that as far as we were concerned obedience is the issue. Worth thinking about.

Now, we Anglicans tend to focus on the question of the authority of the Pope as if that was the only difficult issue. Well, that is a cop-out. The authority of popes is only one of the questions. Another is the authority of bishops.

Equally problematic are the authority of kings and other civil authorities over and in relation to the Church. So the question is, Who speaks for the people as a whole and by what authority? So the question is of the local vis-à-vis the universal. What about the authority of scholars and theologians in the Church? And perhaps the deepest question of all is this: Do we really believe that Christ has given living organs of authority to his people, such that when it is necessary, the Church as a whole can recognise that it is being spoken to and spoken for in the name of the Lord?

Now if we are conscious of the dimension of ecumenism not only in space but also in time, it helps us to distinguish those elements of the Church's life rounded in Scripture itself that are integral to or constituent of the nature of the Church itself, and ARCIC talks a lot about that in the Church's communion. We distinguish between those essential elements and the particular forms which the life of the Church has taken from time to time. The Church always has been and still is changing, and so is the way in which authority is exercised in the Church.

Most of us have rather short memories, and so as far as the question of authority is concerned, we have to be very careful not to be so wedded to contemporary forms as in effect to excommunicate most of our Christian ancestors. For example, as Anglicans, we have become accustomed to synodical and representative forms of government. But if we were to insist on representation by democratic election as the only legitimate route which can properly hear the voice of laypeople in the Church, we wouldn't leave much space for the views or practice of St. Paul. In other words, we must always try to see our own particular situation in the context of the life of the whole Christian community, by which I mean the community both of space and of time. We are right to attend to what the contemporary world feels are legitimate and proper political structures, but we're also right not to absolutize them.

Now what I've been saying so far helps us, I hope, to understand the nature of this text before us.

Please remember that it took five years to prepare, so don't dismiss it in five minutes. Five years that presupposed both a prehistory and a story, which is still to follow. There's an important sense in which this is not a finished text. It's a contribution to a dialogue, which must continue, not only between Anglicans and Catholics, but also between and within every Christian community that is committed to unity in Christ.

So, please, this is a text that should be read with delicacy, attention, and respect. Each sentence, each paragraph should be read in the context of the argument as a whole, and it is a longer and larger argument than that which is contained between the pages of this little pamphlet.

This text should be read in the context of the wider dialogue between Christians of all communions about the nature of communion and authority in the Church. We already had some hasty comments from people who ought to have known better.

Your task as a council, I believe, is to help the people of the Anglican Communion to come to a measured, reflective, and responsible response that will contribute to a realisation of true unity among the whole Christian people. It's a process, which is bound to take time, patience, and hard work, as well as a willingness to listen to our Christian brothers and sisters. We should bear in mind as we try to evaluate this text that the question to ask is not so much "Is this recognisably Anglican or is it Roman Catholic?" but rather "Is it Christian and is it true?" There's nothing at all in the New Testament about Anglicanism, but there is a great deal in the New Testament about the unity that is required of all who belong to Christ.

Now the commission does not claim so much to have extended the areas of agreement of consensus already set out in its first two statements of authority as to have deepened their agreement.

May I simply draw your attention, quite briefly, to three particular areas where I believe we have gone deeper. First, and this is of great importance, some people have rushed to the end of the document and haven't reflected sufficiently so far on the first part. We have deepened our understanding of our biblical roots of the Christian doctrine of authority in the Church. The foundation of our work, based on St. Paul's teaching in 2 Corinthians 2, is our exposition of God's *yes* to humanity and humanity's *yes* or *amen* to God, both given once and for all in the person and work of *Jesus Christ*. We do not collude with the modern Western notion that all exercise of authority is necessarily corrupt. We insist that the authority that Christ lodged in his Church is a gift like all of God's gifts: it is subject in use to human corruption, but it remains a gift given for our good. Secondly, we have deepened our understanding of the relationship between the decisions of authority on the one hand and their acceptance or reception by the Church as a whole on the other. Here I'd make one point in particular, namely this: the importance of not playing off the exercise of authority and its reception against one another. They are inseparable elements in one process or operation. Thirdly, at the end of our statement we invite our two churches to consider ways in which we may exercise together the authority for proclaiming the gospel that Christ has entrusted to his people.

This is a proposal that is lessened and not all that it sounds. In fact, it's a matter of building on what we are already doing in many parts of the world. Think for instance of the significance of the joint decision-making that has contributed to our liturgical convergence. We talk in particular about the place of the Pope as the chief pastor of the Christian family, even before the whole family is holy reconciled.

You may want to ask for some clarification on that later on.

Parts of what the commission have said will sound unfamiliar to many of our people. That's because we've all been brought up to speak the language and to think the thoughts of a particular tradition. But in ecumenical dialogue we stop talking about only talking to ourselves and the members of our own family, and we start listening to our neighbours and to the ways in which they too have heard the message of the scriptures. The members of the commission do not claim to have spoken the last word on the issue of authority in the Church—far from it. But they do claim to be asking our two churches to address their minds to an issue that is inseparable from the question of unity. If we refuse to talk about authority, we are not serious about unity. Together with our brothers and sisters, and not apart from them, we are to ask ourselves, What is the nature of the authority that Christ has given to his people for the sake of their communion and unity, and in what ways is it to be exercised?

As we consider this statement, as with *The Virginia Report,* looking simply toward the issue of communion among Anglicans, we're not looking only toward the issue of communion between Anglicans and Roman Catholics. We're looking toward the horizon of visible communion of the one body of Christ between all whom he has claimed for his own. Our perspective is the visible, sacramental, ecclesial realisation of the faith that we proclaim every time we say that we believe in one holy, catholic, and apostolic church.

Just one final point. What you as a council now decide to do with this statement will itself be an exercise of authority. The way in which you invite the Communion to respond will itself exemplify an understanding or doctrine of authority. So part of the question before us is, What's the practice and what's the theory?

Study Questions for Small-Group Discussion on *The Gift of Authority*

The questions below were circulated to the Primates when *The Gift of Authority* was published in May to stimulate initial discussion. Are these the questions we need to ask the provinces at this stage of study? Are there any others? What resources will be helpful in the study and reception of the text? Are there any suggestions that should be passed on to the Inter-Anglican Standing Committee on Ecumenical Relations?

1. How does *The Gift of Authority* reflect the understanding and practice of authority, which the Anglican Communion has received?

2. What fresh insights into that understanding are suggested in *The Gift of Authority*, and how do these relate to the suggestions made in *The Virginia Report*?

3. How might these be accepted into the life of the Anglican Communion?

4. What consequences does the text have for deepening future Anglican-Roman Catholic relations at the local and provincial level?

Statement from the Co-Chairmen of the Anglican-Roman Catholic International Commission

FOR THE LAUNCH OF *THE GIFT OF AUTHORITY*

Westminster Abbey
May 12, 1999

1. **The Background: Official Anglican-Catholic Dialogue at an International Level**

In March 1966, the then Archbishop of Canterbury, Dr. Michael Ramsey, paid an official visit to Pope Paul VI in Rome. This inaugurated a new era in relations between the Anglican Communion and the Catholic Church, with the emphasis on Christian charity and sincere efforts to remove the causes of conflict and reestablish unity.

They decided to set up an official international dialogue whose work might lead to the unity in truth for which Christ prayed. The Anglican-Roman Catholic International Commission (ARCIC) took up this task in 1970. It is an international dialogue whose specialist members have been officially appointed to represent the Anglican Communion and the Catholic Church worldwide.

Three main dialogue topics were initially given to ARCIC: the doctrine of the Eucharist; ministry and ordination; and authority in the Church. Various agreed statements, issued as the commission carried out this work, were published together in 1981 as *The Final Report* and presented to the two churches for evaluation and reception. The Anglican Communion gave its official response in a resolution at the 1988 Lambeth Conference. The Catholic Church responded in 1991.

Since the publication of *The Final Report,* ARCIC has produced agreed statements on other important matters, on which it was asked to enter into dialogue by Pope John Paul II and Archbishop Robert Runcie when they met at Canterbury in 1982. *The Gift of Authority,* which is published today, is the fourth statement from this second phase of ARCIC's work.

We are happy to be launching this document in a location that dates from the time before our divisions. We hope this new statement will contribute to their healing. It is a document for Anglican and Catholic Christians in the many countries throughout the world where they live together. So it has already been sent to Anglican Primates and the presidents of Catholic episcopal conferences, and several translations are being made available on the World Wide Web.

2. **Why Has ARCIC Produced Another Statement about Authority?**

Even before the dialogue began, it was obvious that authority in the Church would require considerable attention. Authority, particularly the authority of the bishop of Rome, had been a key element in the division that occurred at the time of the English Reformation. For four centuries the Anglican Communion and the Catholic Church developed their structures of authority in separation from each other, and Anglicans lived without the ministry of the bishop of Rome.

The Final Report of 1981 devoted two agreed statements and an elucidation to the subject of authority in the Church. They already document considerable agreement, as follows, which has been acknowledged by both churches:

– About how authority operates in the Church;
– About the particular role of bishops;
– And, very importantly, even about the significance of the bishop of Rome in a reunited Church and the place his ministry has in God's providential plan for his Church.

Why then has ARCIC now returned to this issue?

- Firstly, because *The Final Report* itself recognised that, despite the considerable progress achieved, some serious issues still had to be resolved.
- Secondly, because the official Anglican and Catholic responses to *The Final Report* both requested ARCIC to do so. They indicated that the statement in *The Final Report* provided a good foundation for further dialogue. The principal points they put to the commission are mentioned in paragraph 3 of *The Gift of Authority*.
- Thirdly, it is hoped that this further statement will contribute to the discussion of authority that is taking place in both churches. Anglicans have been asked by the 1998 Lambeth Conference to reflect and study important questions about authority in the Anglican Communion raised in *The Virginia Report*, which was prepared for the conference. Among these questions is the issue of universal authority in the Church. Pope John Paul in his 1995 encyclical, *Ut unum sint*, has also called for a patient and fraternal dialogue about the ministry of unity of the bishop of Rome so that all can accept it.
- Finally, unless we can reach sufficient agreement about authority, which touches so many aspects of the Church's life, "we shall not reach the full visible unity to which we are both committed," as Archbishop Carey and Pope John Paul II said plainly when they met in 1996.

3. What Sort of Statement Is *The Gift of Authority*?

It is the product of five years of dialogue, patient listening, study, and prayer.

The commission has responded to the requests of our respective authorities. With their authorisation, it is now published as a statement agreed on by the commission and put before our churches for reflection and discussion.

The statement builds on all the previous ARCIC work on authority—hence its subtitle, *Authority in the Church III*. It therefore needs to be read alongside those earlier agreed statements. It is a closely argued, rich text, with every sentence important and leading toward its conclusions. It therefore will need careful study and reflection in our two Communions.

It is important to understand what the commission members have attempted to do: they have tried to express what they *believe* flows from our common shared faith; in other words, the members have engaged in dialogue as best they can as representatives of their two churches, not engaging in a kind of negotiation but attempting to express together what they believe faith demands.

The title of the new document gives a very important orientation. Rightly understood, authority in the Church is God's *gift*, to be received gratefully.

A scriptural image, taken from St. Paul's Second Letter to the Corinthians, is repeatedly used to keep before our minds the ultimate purpose of authority. Authority serves the Church's remembering of the *yes* God has given to humanity in Jesus Christ and enables its members to respond with a faithful Amen, as they walk Christ's way.

Then, agreement about how authority is exercised at various levels in the Church's life is outlined, including how the whole people of God bear the tradition across space and time, and the particular role bishops have in discerning and articulating this faith of the Church and ensuring that all the churches are in communion.

The document expresses agreement that the college of bishops can come to a judgement that, faithful to Scripture and consistent with apostolic tradition, is free from error (cf. number 42). This duty of maintaining the Church in the truth is one of the essential functions of the episcopal college (number 44).

The statement builds on the agreement about the bishop of Rome in ARCIC's previous work and offers agreement about his specific ministry within the college of bishops concerning the discernment of truth, which has been such a source of difficulty and misunderstanding. It seeks to make clear how in certain circumstances the bishop of Rome has a duty to discern and make explicit, in fidelity to Scripture and tradition, the authentic faith of the whole Church that is the faith of all the baptised in communion. The commission believes that this is a gift to be received by all the churches and is entailed in the recognition of the primacy of the bishop of Rome.

4. What Happens Next?

The detailed study of this statement will evidently offer challenges to both our churches regarding how authority is exercised in them. Some of these challenges are mentioned in the latter part of the document. The commission's task has been to enter into dialogue on an important and difficult issue. It believes it has arrived at further agreement, which it offers to our churches. It is for our authorities to decide in time if they do recognise our faith in this new agreed statement and how to address its consequences.

A Commentary on *The Gift of Authority*

THE LATEST REPORT

—Mary Tanner

May 1999

Introduction

(i) What Is the Background to the Report?

For Anglicans and Roman Catholics, agreement in matters of faith—sufficient agreement to bring us together and hold us together—is fundamental for full visible unity. Archbishop Michael Ramsey and Pope Paul VI initiated a theological dialogue in 1968 that has continued for more than thirty years. In 1981 a milestone was reached with the publication of *The Final Report* of the Anglican-Roman Catholic International Commission. It brought together agreed statements on the Eucharist, ministry, and authority. The *Report* was widely studied. Clergy and laity in both churches, in many parts of the world, were genuinely excited by the fact that in areas where our churches were once bitterly divided, we could now confidently claim substantial agreement.

The Lambeth Conference in 1988 affirmed what was said about Eucharist and ministry as "consonant in substance with the faith of the Anglicans." However, while both Communions recognised in the two texts on authority much with which they could agree, they also identified areas where further agreement needed to be reached: the relationship between Scripture, tradition, and the exercise of teaching authority; collegiality, conciliarity, and the role of the laity in decision making; and the Petrine ministry of universal primacy. Both churches were confident that the work that had already been done gave grounds for believing that further agreement was possible. Now, eleven years later, the commission offers more work on authority in *The Gift of Authority* (Authority III).

(ii) Why is This Report Important?

Both churches agree that we share a profound degree of communion based in our common baptism. Both churches are committed to making the gift of unity, which God has promised the Church, fully visible. Full visible communion entails the acceptance of a common authority. This in turn requires a shared understanding of authority. So, this further work on authority, with its deeper agreement, is vitally important if Anglicans and Roman Catholics are to live together in visible unity.

I. The Controlling Theme: God's Yes and Our Amen

The *Report* is not easy to summarise. Every sentence counts toward the building up of the whole. It repays slow and careful study. There is one controlling theme, imaginative and suggestive, which must be grasped in order to appreciate the advances in the understanding of authority being made in this report. The controlling theme is God's *yes* to our *amen* and us to God. God's will is to bring all people into communion with himself within transformed creation. In Jesus Christ, God not only affirms that purpose but also secures the outcome, demonstrating God's everlasting *yes* to us. In the faithful obedience of Jesus to the Father, Christians can recognise the perfect response of humanity, the perfect Amen to God and to God's purpose. In, with, and through Christ, by the power of the Holy Spirit, we speak our Amen to God and God's purpose for us. The life of the Christian and the life of the community of the Church are lived within the orbit of God's continuous *yes* to us and our attempt, through the grace of the Holy Spirit, to say Amen to God. The ministry of authority in the Church is to help the Church and the world to hear God's yes and to enable a response to be made to it. Within the framework of this controlling theme the exploration unfolds: first the nature of authority and then the way authority is exercised in the Church, including a ministry of primacy.

II. Authority in the Church (paragraphs 7 to 31)

The description of how authority functions in the Church moves step by step:

- Authority in the Church is gift, God's gift to his people, to enable the Church to live in the memory of God's *yes* made in Christ and to guide the Church to make its faithful response.

- The *yes* of the individual Christian to the purposes of God is said within the faith of the Christian community—the local community of believers and the community of the faithful of all times and all places. This community of faith through time and space passes on the revealed faith through a rich life of word and sacrament and through common life.

- Tradition is a gift received from the past, and the treasure to be handed on in varied circumstances and in continually changing times. What the apostles received and proclaimed is now found in the tradition of the Church, where the word of God is preached and the sacraments of Christ are celebrated. The scriptures occupy "a unique and normative place" by which the Church measures its teaching and action when faced with new insights and challenges. "Tradition," the *Report* says, is a "channel of love" making the gospel open to all people.

- The handing on of the tradition is the responsibility and work of the whole people of God. The Report describes this dynamic receiving and passing on of the tradition as being like a symphony in which different parts are played. The theologian has a role. Those entrusted with oversight have their special role in keeping alive the memory of what God did in Christ and the hope of what God will bring to fulfilment.

- Those with oversight have to be attentive to the mind of all the faithful (the *sensus fidelium*). In the life of the Church the mind of the faithful and the "ministry of memory" are always to be in reciprocal relationship.

Anglicans and Roman Catholics can agree on these things about authority in the Church; however, because the two Communions have lived separate lives, they need now to learn from each other's insights. They need to grasp the opportunity to share the mind of the faithful and the ministry of memory within a larger community of believers. In this way, Anglicans and Roman Catholics would share in receiving God's *yes* together and learn to respond together in a single Amen.

III. The Exercise of Authority in the Church (paragraphs 32 to 50)

The *Report* offers a key concept with which to understand the functioning of authority in the Church. All the faithful are called to travel together, to walk together on the way. The Greek word *syn-hodos* lies behind the English word synodality. Synodality refers to the life of all those who walk together within the tradition, those in the local church and those in the fellowship of all local churches across space and time.

(i) Synodality: Walking Together on the Way (paragraphs 34 to 40)

- The exercise of authority has a missionary orientation in keeping the Church faithfully to the purposes of God and to invite all people to respond to God with Amen.

- The bishop has oversight of the local church to lead churches in making their authentic Amen to God. The faithful have a duty to receive the guidance and decisions of those with oversight as they recognise God at work in the bishop's exercise of authority. The bishop's authority is not arbitrary. It works within the sense of faith of the community.

- No local church with its bishop is sufficient of itself. The local church lives in the tradition as part of, and together with, the whole Church. The local bishop, through membership in the college of bishops, plays a part in enabling the local church to walk together on the way with the whole Church. Together the bishops seek to discern and articulate the mind of the faithful.

Once again Anglicans and Roman Catholics can agree on these things about the exercise of authority within the walking together on the way of the whole Church, even if the way the two Communions structure their lives today is not identical. In the Anglican Communion bishops, clergy, and laity consult and legislate together in synods, where bishops play a distinct ministry in relation to matters of doctrine, worship, and moral life. Forms of synodality exist at the local, provincial, and world levels. The Primates' Meeting, the Anglican Consultative Council, the Lambeth Conference, and the Archbishop of Canterbury are instruments of synodality at the world level. In the Roman Catholic Church synodality exists in the meetings of bishops in episcopal conferences, in regional groups of bishops, when they visit Rome together. There has been a move to encourage the active participation of laypersons in the life and mission of local churches. Here the *Report* moves to a very important section.

(ii) Perseverance in the Truth: Discerning Together on the Way (paragraphs 41 to 44)

Both churches are faced with the question of how truth is discerned in situations of challenge. The participation of the whole body, together with those charged with the ministry of memory, is indispensable.

- In discerning, the Church can be confident in Christ's promise to lead into all truth. In special circumstances those with the ministry of oversight come to a judgement faithful to Scripture and consistent with tradition, which is preserved from error. "This is what is meant when it is affirmed that the Church may teach infallibly" (paragraph 42).

- The whole body of believers participates in discernment, not only those entrusted with the ministry of memory. Reception of teaching is an integral part of the process. And here comes a crucial sentence: "Doctrinal definitions are received as authoritative in virtue of the divine truth they proclaim as well as because of the specific office of the persons who proclaim them within the *sensus fidei* of the whole people of God. When the people of God respond by faith and say 'Amen' to authoritative teaching it is because they recognise that this teaching expresses the apostolic faith and operates within the authority and truth of Christ" (paragraph 43).

- There will be times when the *sensus fidelium* perceives a need for the Church to speak on a matter of faith and when it calls those with a ministry of oversight to speak. The episcopal college "has power to exercise this ministry because it is bound in succession to the apostles, who were the body authorised and sent by Christ to preach the Gospel to all the nations" (paragraph 44). The exercise of the teaching authority requires that what is taught be faithful to Scripture and consonant with apostolic tradition.

In this section, a step has been taken beyond the agreements reached in *Authority I* and *II*. The delicate balance maintained in the treatment of the infallibility of authoritative teaching, which belongs to the Church, and takes place under the guidance of the Spirit within the life of the whole community under certain circumstances, is important for both churches.

The *Report* has held together both the special services of a ministry of oversight and the role of all the faithful in the Church's ministry to teach infallibly. This has important consequences for both churches as they contemplate reform of their own lives today and as they consider the possibility for the joint exercise of authority in the future. Now the *Report* has reached the subject that many will be waiting for.

(ii)   Primacy (paragraphs 45 to 49)

It is a fact that forms of primacy exist in both churches. Anglican provinces have their Primate (the Primates' Meeting serves the whole Anglican Communion) and the Archbishop of Canterbury, who exercises a primatial role in the Anglican Communion. The *Report* reflects that:

- Primatial and conciliar aspects of the ministry of oversight belong together at every level of the Church's life.

- From the New Testament times Peter's role among the apostles strengthened the others. The bishop of Rome has exercised a ministry of primacy sometimes for the benefit of the whole Church and sometimes as a benefit to a local church, as when Gregory the Great supported Augustine's mission.

- Within his wider ministry the bishop of Rome offers a special ministry of discernment, which is often misunderstood. " 'Every solemn definition' is pronounced within the college of those who exercise *episcopé* and not outside that college" (paragraph 47). Because the bishop of Rome pronounces within the college of bishops, he proclaims not his own individual faith, but the faith of all the local churches.

- In order to teach, the bishop of Rome must discern under the guidance of the Holy Spirit and in fidelity to Scripture and tradition. The *Report* sums it up thus: "It is . . . the faith of all the baptised in communion, and this only, that each bishop utters with the body of bishops in council. It is this faith which the Bishop of Rome in certain circumstances has a duty to discern and make explicit" (paragraph 47).

The *Report* makes clear that the reception of the primacy of the bishop of Rome entails the recognition of this specific ministry of universal primacy. It is equally clear, and this is important for Anglicans, that authority is exercised by fragile Christians for the sake of fragile Christians. This is no less true of the successors of Peter. Indeed, Pope John Paul II in the papal encyclical, *Ut unum sint,* admits his own human frailty. The *Report* has gone a long way in examining those issues that were asked for by both Communions. It confidently claims that this understanding of authority and of its exercise is one that Anglicans and Roman Catholics can share. We have been helped to see that in the end, the aim of the exercise of authority and its reception is to enable the Church to say Amen to God's *yes*.

IV. Steps Toward Visible Unity: What Are the Challenges of the Report? (paragraphs 51 to 62)

The *Report* offers more than a theological statement. It recognises that both churches are churches in change as far as the exercise of authority goes. The Anglican Communion is reaching toward universal structures, which promote *koinonia*. The Roman Catholic Church is looking to strengthen local and intermediary structures. These changes are in fact complementary. The theological agreement offered in this report entails challenges to both Communions:

(i) Challenges to Anglicans (paragraph 56)

Is the Anglican Communion open to the acceptance of instruments of oversight whose decisions would in certain circumstances bind all?

Will the emerging new structures assist Anglicans to participate in the *sensus fidelium*, the mind of the Church, with all Christians?

To what extent does unilateral action by provinces, even after consultation, weaken communion?

The Anglican willingness to tolerate anomaly (for example in the different practices relating to the ordination of women) has led to impairment of communion in sharing Eucharist and in exercising *episcopé*. What consequences flow from that?

How will Anglicans respond to the question of universal primacy as it is emerging both in their own internal life and in ecumenical dialogue?

Very similar issues are treated in *The Virginia Report*, which the bishops at the Lambeth Conference invited the provinces to study for the sake of strengthening the unity and communion of the Anglican Communion.

(ii) Challenges to Roman Catholics (paragraph 57)

How far do clergy and laypeople in fact actively participate in the emerging synodal bodies of the Church?

Has the teaching of Vatican II on the collegiality of bishops been implemented sufficiently?

Has enough provision been made to ensure that consultation takes place between the bishop of Rome and the local church prior to important decisions being made?

How is the variety of theological opinion taken into account when decisions are made?

Do the structures of the Roman Catholic Church adequately respect the exercise of *episcopé* at all levels of the Church's life?

How will the Roman Catholic Church address the question of universal primacy as it emerges in the dialogue called for by the Pope in *Ut unum sint*?

These are sharp questions put to each church. Much hangs on the way each church answers them, not only in words but in the re-formation of its own life. The questions call for a systematic, radical self-examination leading to a renewal of our own exercise of authority and a commitment to exercise authority together within a visibly united Church.

(iii) Challenges to Both Churches (paragraph 58)

Both our churches are challenged not only to do together whatever they can, but also to be together as much as they can. Bishops are encouraged to work together at regional and local levels, to participate in international meetings, with Anglicans accompanying Roman Catholic bishops on visits to Rome, teaching and acting together, and sharing oversight of local ecumenical initiatives. It is unfortunate that the emphasis here is only upon episcopal sharing, especially in a report so keen to point to the inextricable relation between the ministry of oversight and the mind of the whole people of God. There is much that the bishops of both communions have to gain from listening to the laity of both communions, who today share together regularly in many areas of life and witness.

(iv) The Challenge of Universal Primacy: A Gift to Be Shared
    (paragraphs 60 to 63)

The final section of the *Report* offers an attractive portrait of the ministry of universal primacy exercised in collegiality and conciliarity, a ministry of the servant of the servants of God, who uphold legitimate diversity and enhance unity; a ministry exercising leadership in the world and in the lives of both communions, gathering for consultation and discussion. This portrait will surely rejoice the heart of many Anglicans and Roman Catholics who long to be in visible unity and in communion together with the bishop of Rome. They will find attractive the commission's suggestions:

- That Anglicans be open to and desire a recovery and re-reception under certain conditions of the exercise of the universal primacy of the bishop of Rome;

- That Roman Catholics be open to and desire a re-reception of the universal primacy of the bishop of Rome and the offering of such ministry to the whole Church of God.

It is striking here that the *Report* talks of a re-reception of the universal primacy of the bishop of Rome by both churches. It is not a matter of

Anglicans re-receiving from the Roman Catholic Church, but of both churches re-receiving together a renewed ministry of universal primacy.

V. What Are We to Do with the Report?

This report deserves to be widely and critically studied, preferably in groups that include both Anglicans and Roman Catholics who can interpret to each other their different experiences of authority and their hopes for a common exercise of authority in the future. The members of the official Anglican-Roman Catholic dialogue need to hear the reactions to their work from around the world. Those who exercise authority must guide the process of discernment and reflection on this report and urge that agreements issue forward in those "concrete steps" that were looked for in 1981. For without some changes being made in our lives and relationships, there will be little confidence in the effectiveness of the search for agreement in faith as one task on the way toward visible unity. *The Gift of Authority* is itself a gift, an instrument, to lead Anglicans and Roman Catholics to respond together to God's *yes* with a single Amen.

A Session on Urbanisation

—The Right Reverend Roger Sainsbury, bishop of Barking, Church of England

I hope you got the paper that we prepared for today's session toward an international program for the Anglican Communion. I would also like to say thank you for inviting us to share in this session. We are very aware of the friendliness of the people here and the sense of fellowship, and we want you to know that we have been praying for you as we know you have been meeting over the last fortnight. It seems that our prayers have been answered, so it's a joy to be with you here on the final day.

The origins of our presentation today go back to 1996, at an urban ministry consultation in Nairobi that was mainly sponsored by World Vision but had people from all denominations: the Roman Catholic Church, the Orthodox, and a small group of Anglicans. But the Anglicans were very representative of the whole Anglican Communion. There were people from Asia, South and North Americas, Australia, Europe, and Africa. And as some of you might know, it was one of the group from Africa, Halan Grace, that suggested at the end of the conference that the Anglicans meet together. So we did, there in Nairobi. The first question that we looked at was, Does the Church of England report "Faith in the City" have anything to say to the wider Anglican Communion?

The second question we looked at was a question that was posed at the 1998 Lambeth Conference, Is God planting churches in some of the most hurting parts of our cities? I think that we felt that very strongly in the African context. The third question that we were asked to look at was, Is urban mission and ministry going to have a place on the Lambeth Conference 1998 Agenda? The Reverend Andrew Davies and I, who attended that conference, took those questions back to the Church of England Urban Bishops Panel, which I chair. We shared these questions with some of the multiracial congregations in East London, for which I have responsibility, and on a visit to Chicago I also shared these concerns with an African American congregation in that city. We also tried to network widely through correspondence, and Andrew gathered stories of urban mission from throughout the Anglican Communion. And so we came to the Lambeth Conference itself, encouraged by those who were asking us to encourage the other missions to have a high place on the agenda at the Lambeth Conference. Early on in the Lambeth Conference there was a marketplace of events in the first week, and we looked at the opening verses in Mathew 11. Do you remember when John's disciples came to Jesus and said, Are you the one who is to come or should we look for another? In many ways this can be connected to the Bible studies you have had this week on the prophets. Are you the one who is to come, or should we be looking for another? Jesus' response about the excluded and the hurt—the excluded being welcomed, the hurt being healed, and the poor hearing the good news—made us ask at the marketplace event a very important question: Is the Anglican Communion good news to the poor in our cities? We wrestled with that and discussed that at that marketplace event. We also looked together at how can we learn from each other in our different cities' situations across the Anglican Communion, and one of the common themes that came out, which I understand has been coming out in this gathering as well, has been the effects of globalisation on all our cities—in different ways, but the impact is there. So we had that marketplace event, and then halfway through the conference twenty-five bishops and some ACC members, which are actually represented here, went to East London, and we looked at what was happening there on the grounds.

There is a copy of the report available today, because we wanted to earth the discussions in reality, in the real situation, that many Christians are facing in some of our poorer communities in the East End of London. As I mentioned in moving the amendments at the Lambeth Conference on urbanisation, it seemed to all of us that the whole question of urbanisation and urban ministry and evangelism was coming up in a whole variety of ways, in the Bible studies, section debates, discussions in plenary sessions, and in casual conversations we were having with each other. I wrote in a paper afterwards that it seemed to be the Holy Spirit saying to us that as we move into the next millennium urban mission and ministry is a very high priority. And after the passing of the resolutions at the Lambeth Conference, we had during that busy final week, when many people's minds were on other things, a large gathering of bishops and ACC members to discuss how are we going to take forward the resolutions on urbanisation that were passed.

At the conclusion of that gathering, the wide group representing the whole of the Anglican Communion said to us on the Church of England Urban Bishops Panel that they would like us to move forward to the next step, to talk to the Archbishop of Canterbury and the Secretary General of the ACC and to write and seek support from across the Anglican Communion for the resolutions that were passed at Lambeth. We did that and you will see at the back of the paper that there are people from across the Anglican Communion who said they wish to support this.

In South and North Americas these concerns were again shared. Dr. Andrew Davies went to the Peace and Justice Conference in Korea and shared these concerns there too. There seemed to be a growing reality that the resolutions on urbanisation passed at Lambeth were very important for the whole Anglican Communion. We were encouraged by that; in fact, Andrew commented that the e-mail lines grew hot with people saying that urban mission should be a priority for the Anglican Communion as we move into the next millennium. So that is the story of how we have arrived today and why it's so good to be with you. The different people represented here are going to share in this presentation.

The Right Reverend Laurie Green, bishop of Bradwell, Church of England

The Lambeth Conference participants acknowledged the extraordinary momentous nature of the challenge to us of both urbanisation and globalisation and the way in which these two work together. We are becoming more urban, clearly, and we are becoming more global. These two factors have recently grown and developed out of the recognition of the extent at which they are now threatening to overwhelm us. They are staggering in their magnitude and their influence, and we are finding that many of the old answers are being eclipsed, eclipsed by the sheer scale of these processes. So during this presentation this morning, we will hear how others are ahead of us in this field: economists, sociologists, politicians, big finance houses, and business corporations—they are all researching globalisation and urbanisation, and on the back of that research they are making strategic decisions accordingly. They know that if they don't find ways of working with these powerful processes, they will be swept aside by them. We are all learning that the new technology on one hand, and the powerful economy on the other hand, are now combining to make the world a much smaller place—globalisation. Globalisation is not value-free; it brings with it certain values: specifically values of the marketplace—competition and profit. Everything and everyone can become a commodity with the powerful processes of globalisation taking over. It works largely through cities; that's the interconnectedness. It works through the cities, urbanisation, and on out into the rural areas. We will pick up on that sometime later, but the dynamics of this are so subtle that globalisation also surges into local feeling, local localisation. So there is the global and the local interacted, or what some sociologists have called *globalisation*. The two working together makes it very difficult to unpick. These processes are leading to the exclusion of many sections of our societies: women, children, and ethnic groups, even whole nations marginalised from the powerful forces. Change affects the North and the South. The depopulation and the urban decay we encounter in the inner cities of post-industrial North America and Europe, that inner city decay, are just as much a part of the scene as the exploding cities of the South. Our question is, Is the Church up to speed on all this? We know that many of you are deeply concerned and very active in urban ministry, urban evangelisation, urban mission, and urban theological reflection, and our Archbishop of Canterbury has certainly sponsored many initiatives in this direction, but this morning we are hoping to present to you some glimpses of these new challenges, the new dimension of these challenges, and to look at how they are impacting the Church, particularly the Anglican Communion. Impacting our theology, impacting our understanding and practice of evangelism, impacting how we operate alongside those in strength and alongside those in need in our wider mission. The work that Bishop Roger described revealed how engaged many are in the Communion, and that engagement has raised questions of how we might be better connected. There are bits going on here and bits going on there, but with globalisation we need to have an overview if we are to really understand the processes that are forcing all this change. We need to be better connected, better informed about the resources, experience, and expertise that we have and that is building up.

This morning we have a number of stories, reflections, and facts to share with you from Japan and Brazil. Dr. Andrew Davies will take up the stories of the Americas and Asia. In these reflections and stories we hope to capture, in snapshot form, something of the range and the challenges facing the Church—the churches of the Anglican Communion in particular—in an urban world on the verge of the twenty-first century. The six stories will give us just a glimpse of the Church's mission on these new frontiers; everything is so new. We will share just a handful of reflections and stories, but there could be so many more. They would all be different, and yet they would all reveal the scope, need, and experience that we have to share in the worldwide Anglican Communion. This short tour may be something like the Sarmise had in mind when he encountered his audience to consider the city before them and encountered God within it. Walk about Zion, go all around her, count her towers, consider well her walls, examine her palaces that you may tell the next generation that such is God, our God for ever and ever (Psalm 48:12-14). We will present these snapshots and our reflections and proposals, and then later on in the morning we hope that you will share your experiences with globalisation and urbanisation. So let's begin now with a short video clip about Mexico City, from a recent educational program produced by our own open university. This clip poses this question, To whom does the city belong? It encourages us to encounter the many-layered life of the city and those who have a stake in its future.

Some Remarks on Issues of Urbanisation in Japan

—The Reverend Samuel I. Koshiishi

At the end of August, the Japanese government announced the results of a 1998 population census. According to that report, nearly fifty percent of the total population of Japan was concentrated in the three metropolitan areas of Tokyo, Nagoya, and Osaka. This unbalance of the population has caused some serious difficulties in our society in the political sphere; the unbalance between representatives to the diet and the size of the electoral body has been an issue of hot debate. In the economic sphere, the dichotomy between privileged urban and impoverished rural residents is getting to be serious.

Some analysts say that the dropping of the price of land in those big city areas after the bursting of the bubble-economy is the main reason for the increase of the city dwellers, though, I am not quite confident of that analysis. For from the very beginning of modernisation, the population policy of the Japanese government was to create a surplus population and to shift the industrial structure from the pattern of primary industry dominance to secondary or tertiary industry dominance by using this surplus population, while at the same time extending the military forces. Thus, the concentration of the population in the urban area should be understood as the continuation of the basic thrust of modernisation.

While preparing this presentation, I was amazed to see the figures of the distribution of labour force, even though I had studied Japanese economic policy, especially population policy, at my undergraduate school. When I wrote an essay about the population policy of our nation, the available statistical data was the census of 1960, and I can't realise how far the change of our industrial structure has gone. It was in 1960s that our industrial structure was drastically transformed, along with the energy policy change from coal to oil. It was also the time when our nation joined the OECD and began to get into a wider international market, when the Tokyo Olympics were held, and when many domestic seasonal migrant construction workers emerged. The drastic mobilisation of the population as a result of all of this had gradually ruined the traditional way of life during this period of time. It was also the time that the so-called nonsect radical student movement was quite active. And it was a time when industrial pollution, some of which had started nearly a century ago, was found to cause illness like Minamata Disease.

Enlarged Gap between City Centres and Rural Areas

In the following two decades, however, these tendencies have been enormously extended. This drastic change in Japan is a result of its deeper involvement in the global market, in which the principle of minimum cost with maximum profit is consistent. International market competition reflected domestically in the decay of agriculture and primary industry. For in the international market raw materials are much cheaper and more abundant than domestic production. Thus, the gap between central city and local areas was widened. In June, I had a chance to visit the northernmost island of Holikaido and was able to visit some towns which have been in decline, both in number of people and economy. These towns are mainly located on the east seacoast. Except for small-scale fishing and agriculture, there is no major industry, and because of the rapid development of motorization, these places become inconvenient and the people tend to move out. For example, in one of these towns more than half of the population was engaged in public service. Most of the inhabitants were simply left there because of their incompetence either by age or physical or mental condition. The local governments that lose massive numbers of people are in such financial difficulty to provide jobs to their taxpayers that they tend to initiate building projects for public facilities, like roads or piers, that are scarcely used. This kind of public investment often causes unwanted damage to the natural environment. Even though not so many people are aware, this unbalance between central cities and rural areas is one of the most serious issues and needs dealt with immediately.

Harsh Competition and the Principle of Economic Efficiency

The involvement of a nation in the international competitive market has domestically produced a very harsh competition among the people, mainly for getting prestigious jobs concentrated in central cities. It is said that after the bursting of the bubble economy, unemployment was increased. However; it may signify the new dimension of international competition rather than provisional phenomena. Among the unemployed, the middle managers and skilled workers are eminent. To survive in the global market competition, firms tend to reduce general administration, and the system so-called McDonaldism tends to be adopted in food services and constructions. There is a quite interesting story in our food industry. Because of cost efficiency, the Tokyo Central Fish Market now provides pre-sliced fish for sushi bars; thus, well-trained sushi cooks are fired. Restructuring is now one of the most popular words in Japan. It is true that unemployment has increased, but it doesn't necessarily mean that job opportunities are decreasing. The job that a skilled worker used to do now becomes the one that almost anyone can do. Then the form of employment has changed from the stable permanent type to the provisional unstable one. The downsizing of enterprises has an effect on the real estate market, and office buildings have a difficult time finding tenants. Thus, there is almost no demand for new buildings. The construction business relies very heavily on daily labourers, and those who used to engage in this kind of daily work are easily becoming the homeless through this lack of demand of new buildings. This is particularly the case in Osaka. However, the other side of the coin is in the area of tiny food service enterprises, like restaurants, bars, and so forth. It can be said that a big portion of expatriates engage in this area of work.

Post-tradition, Pluralism, Uncertainty, and Confusion

This unprecedented situation signifies that the traditional way of life and traditional values have been abandoned. The traditional way of life has been destroyed by losing the population in rural areas and by the massive number of newcomers in the cities. Throughout the period of modernisation parents have encouraged their kids to get into a well-qualified school to win the life-long race. It already contradicts the traditional way of life. Still the parents may tell their kids the same thing as their own parents told them, even though to graduate from a well qualified university is not a guarantee for success anymore. Thus, a survey that was carried by some mass media on the occupation preference of high school students shows that their most preferred one was public servant. On this outcome someone commented that it shows the low self-esteem of young people. But I would think that this occupation preference of our young people shows their quest for stability, not only stable employment and stable income in the future, but also some stable social life or place of security right now. Modernisation has produced in Japan the dissolution of the traditional way of life and values and fragmentation of the people. Although not so many people are aware of it, the situation, which has made our young people yearn for a secure place, has also brought social anxiety to our people as a whole. This anxiety might be reflected in strange new legislation measures, such as the guidelines for a U.S.–Japan Defence Cooperation, a wiretap, and a national anthem and flag. On the one hand, the Japanese government would promote a huge profit for military industries, which may go along with the global economy, and on the other hand, it would still stick to the traditional nationalism. Against this background, it is quite understandable that the people with mental disorders have enormously increased in recent years.

Some New Seeds for the Mission of NSKK

As you can easily figure out from the NSKK statistics attached in the reference, our church is a tiny and dispersed entity in our society. Except for the dioceses of Tokyo, Yokohama, and Osaka, each diocese has tiny local parish churches, most of which hardly seem able to survive. Although many people are aware of the critical situations of our church in general, like aging of the membership, the decrease or complete disappearance of young people, and so on, there is not any organised work to find out the mission task of NSKK as a province.

However, at diocesan, parish church, and individual levels there seem to be some programs in various scales to provide affirmation and security to the people in need. In a depopulated area in the northern islands, a priest has become deeply involved in the community development activities through the area YMCA. In Osaka, an institution that was originally dedicated for Korean residents in Japan has developed its service into the area of people with mental disorders. In Nagoya, the Diocesan Anglican Youth Centre provides services to protect the homeless, as well as operates a school for children whose parents are mostly overstayed expatriates. In Tokyo, one parish church has provided a facility with clean and secure space at a reasonable cost for children who are patients with intractable diseases and their families who come from distant places for hospitalisation. These services would be new seeds of the ministry of NSKK and should be encouraged and coordinated. I do hope they will be an impetus to each diocese to look at its ministry freshly against the unpredictable and ever-changing world.

NETWORKS

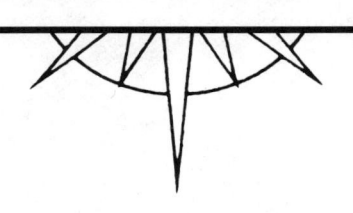

Presentation by NIFCON

NIFCON is the Network for Inter-Faith Concerns in the Anglican Communion.

Part 1. How the Network Could Operate

Part 1 is to help ACC members to see the information that NIFCON receives and to consider in groups how to respond. Canon John Sargant, convenor, and The Reverend Dr. Israel Selvanayagam are members of the NIFCON Support Group.

Part 2. Report on the International Consultation at Jos, Nigeria, July 1999

An example of the regional conferences which NIFCON recommends are held between Lambeth Conferences. They are arranged by the Theological Resources Network of the Evangelical Fellowship in the Anglican Communion (EFAC) and are designed to focus on the political aspects of Islam, which affect several Anglican provinces. Dr. Ida Glaser, director of Faith-to-Faith, helped to design the consultation.

Part 3. What is Involved in Monitoring Christian-Muslim Relations?

The NIFCON Support Group has begun to plan a pilot project or case study, which will show what is involved.

Part 4. Planning Ahead, Resources and Resolution

NIFCON's work is mandated but not resourced. Mr. Ghazi Musharbash, member of the finance committee and of the Joint Standing Committee.

Draft Resolution on Inter-Faith Concerns, September 23, 1999

This council:

(a) Affirms resolution vii of Lambeth Conference 1998, "On Relations with People of Other Faiths";

(b) Charges the Network for Inter-Faith Concerns (NIFCON) to study and evaluate Muslim-Christian relations and report regularly to the Primates' Meeting and the ACC;

(c) Will continue to consider how to resource NIFCON adequately both in personnel and finance;

(d) Supports NIFCON's interim plan of seeking ways to continue its work and to undertake this new charge as and when resources become available.

(This is based on the words of resolution VI.1 of Lambeth Conference 1998.)

Part 1. How the Network Could Operate

(The quotations that follow are from replies written at the Lambeth Conference.)

NIFCON asked, What is your interfaith situation?

a. "I chair the Leaders of Faith Communities Forum—Christian, Hebrew, Buddhist, Muslim, Hindu." Melbourne, Australia

b. "Muslims constitute a real danger for us." Boga, Congo

c. "Religions here coexisted for years. A six-religious conference organises activities, such as seminars, social activities, and information." Hong Kong

d. "There are always tensions and clashes between Hindu Fundamentalists with Muslims and Christians." Bombay, Church of North India

e. "Our interfaith relationship is fairly cordial, (but) varies from one part of the country to another. The adherents of African traditional religions live and let live. But not the Muslims, especially in the far north, the middle belt, and a few isolated cities and towns in the south." Akure, Nigeria

f. "In the forum Nigeria Prays, Christians and Muslims pray together." Niger Delta, Nigeria

g. "Christianity and Islam are wrestling." Yirol, South Sudan

h. "The main challenge is to strengthen a frail interfaith organisation." United States

In the next fifteen minutes, in groups, please look at the quotations below. In your situation, which of the four perspectives is more important than the others? Are there any other interfaith concerns, issues, or challenges for further exploration? Please be ready to report these in one or two sentences.

NIFCON asked, What are your interfaith concerns, issues, and challenges?

1. Social or political perspective

i. "Christians have given support to religious minorities at times when tensions arise, e.g., before the Gulf War. Heads of faiths have taken joint stands on a number of social and moral issues." Australia

j. "To engage in sustained dialogue with Islam as a promising and urgent matter." England

k. "Initiating relationship, reconciliation, and goodwill between Hindus and Muslims." Bombay, North India

l. "To have knowledge of one another's beliefs and practices, to respect each other, to honestly accept areas where they should agree to disagree, and to cooperate in serving the common needs of our country gladly." Nigeria

2. *Cultural perspective*

m. "I like to see more interfaith sharing and cooperations in education and social services." Hong Kong

n. "It is important to work sometimes together, e.g., in the funeral service and other big occasions in which Muslims and others are allowed to join in." Sudan

o. "The main challenge is to strengthen a frail interfaith organisation." United States

3. *Theological perspective*

p. "Fear of 'selling out' the gospel of Jesus Christ and his uniqueness. Understanding God in other religions." England

q. "There is a division between those who see it as their priority to evangelise those of different faiths, and those who are interested in theological cooperation." A young steward at the Lambeth Conference

4. *Mission perspective*

r. "Educating Christians in the notions of dialogue, particularity, and (shared) witness." Australia

s. "When a Muslim becomes Christian, the Muslims hate him and look for ways to kill him." Congo

t. "The main issue among Christians is how to live together bearing witness in unity to the One Name we all bear—Lord Jesus Christ." Nigeria

u. "The Church has to catch up with interfaith awareness and strategy for mission." South Africa

Part 4. NIFCON Is Planning Ahead: A One-Page Summary

A. The NIFCON Support Group presented a six-page paper, "Inter-Faith Concerns in the Anglican Communion and the Strengthening of NIFCON," to the Secretary General of ACC dated October 30, 1998. We are grateful to The Reverend Colin Chapman, who initiated this plan after attending the Lambeth Conference as a consultant.

B. Since networks are the preferred way of addressing specialist concerns within the Anglican Communion and since the role of NIFCON has been affirmed by Lambeth 1998, the support group would like to work as closely as possible with the ACC and Lambeth to find ways of consolidating and extending the work of NIFCON. It needs to be clear about its role, to have a higher profile, and to be properly resourced.

C. The Lambeth Conference Resolution vi.1 does five significant things:

- It spells out the marks of what we believe to be a genuinely Christian approach to people of other faiths.
- It recognises the special possibilities for Anglicans in interfaith work because of the nature of the Communion.
- It recognises the status of NIFCON and affirms its role in the Communion.
- It recommends that NIFCON be charged to monitor Christian-Muslim relations and reports regularly to the Primates' Meeting and the ACC.
- It recommends that the ACC consider how to resource NIFCON adequately both in personnel and finance.

D. Our immediate priorities are as follows:

- To invite three bishops in different parts of the Communion to be presidents.
- To form a network of properly authorised, active, and committed correspondents, and to have a lead bishop for interfaith concerns for every province or country within the Communion.
- To clarify what is involved in monitoring Christian-Muslim relations.
- To contact other bodies who are already active in Christian-Muslim relations.
- To begin study and evaluation on a small-scale pilot project, recognising that new funds need to be found for the real work to be done.

E. Resources: NIFCON's work is mandated but not resourced.

We have identified three options open to the ACC:

- **Option A:** Continue NIFCON as at present, with a convenor one day a week at the expense of the diocese and a budget of £3,000 a year.

This has been adequate until now, but will not enable any response to the Lambeth resolution.

- **Option B:** A half-time convenor and a half-time person for monitoring.

This would cost about £31,000 a year, the absolute minimum for achieving any of the plan.

- **Option C:** A full-time convenor and a half-time person for monitoring.

We foresee this kind of budget, which will be required within two years or so, to resource both the network and the monitoring project.

Resolution vi.1 of the Lambeth Conference 1998

On Relations with People of Other Faiths

This conference:

(a) having heard about situations in different parts of the world where relations between people of different faiths vary from cooperation to conflict, believes that the approach of Christians to people of other faiths needs to be marked by:

   (i) commitment to working toward genuinely open and loving human relationships, even in situations where coexistence seems impossible;

   (ii) cooperation in addressing human concerns and working for justice, peace, and reconciliation for the whole human community;

   (iii) frank and honest exploration of both the common ground and the differences between the faiths;

   (iv) prayerful and urgent action with all involved in tension and conflict, to understand their situation, so that everything possible may be done to tackle the causes of conflict;

   (v) a desire both to listen to people of all faiths and to express our own deepest Christian beliefs, leaving the final outcome of our life and witness in the hands of God;

   (vi) sharing and witnessing to all we know of the good news of Christ as our debt of love to all people, whatever their religious affiliation.

(b) recognises that by virtue of their engagement with people of other faiths in situations all over the world, Anglican Christians are in a special position to explore and develop genuinely Christian responses to these faiths;

(c) also recognises that the Network for Inter-Faith Concerns (NIFCON) has been established by the ACC at the request of the last Lambeth Conference as a way for sharing news, information, ideas, and resources relating to these concerns between provinces of the Anglican Communion;

(d) recommends:

   (i) that NIFCON be charged to monitor Muslim-Christian relations and report regularly to the Primates' Meeting and the ACC;

   (ii) that the ACC consider how to resource NIFCON adequately both in personnel and finance;

   (iii) that all the other official Anglican networks should be encouraged to recognise the interfaith dimensions to their work.

International Family Network

—Dr. Sally Thompson, network coordinator

May 1999

1. Introduction

The year 1999 is the twelfth anniversary of the International Family Network (IAFN). Regular IAFN newsletters are published in *Anglican World*. In addition, five hundred copies are printed separately and sent to people who request them—free to those in the Two-Thirds World. One of the aims of the network is to reach and reflect "grass roots" projects. Publishing information about such projects affirms their work—which is often unknown to the wider Church—and provides an international canvass for problems and issues affecting families throughout the Anglican Communion. It is a practical way of utilising the variety and riches of the Anglican family to produce a unique educational resource for the different provinces and cultures to learn more about each other. The newsletters, through their project examples, also provide a stimulus to further action.

2. Newsletters Published Since IAFN's Report to ACC-10

- *Strengthening Marriage* (Michaelmas 1996)
- *HIV and AIDS and Young People* (Advent 1996)
- *Moving Families: Migration: Immigration and Asylum* (Easter 1997)
- *The Challenge of Parenthood* (Michaelmas 1997)
- *Young People: Risk, Exploitation and Abuse* (Advent 1997)
- *Families and Disability* (Easter 1998)
- *Families: The Challenge to the Church* (July 1998). A separately produced briefing for the Lambeth Conference that was distributed to all bishops and their spouses.
- *Women's Voices: Lambeth 1998* (*Anglican World;* Easter 1999). Reported some of the issues raised during the Spouses' Programme; separate printed copies were sent to all spouses.

3. Lambeth Conference

In addition to the newsletters produced (see above), the network coordinator helped to plan the social issues portion of the Spouses' Programme and, with Maureen Sithole, an ACC member, led workshops on issues of women and violence. These were oversubscribed, and additional sessions were requested. The coordinator also took workshops on the family network. The conference provided many new contacts, which will benefit IAFN's future work.

4. Assessment of IAFN'S Work

Articles are being received from an increasing range of countries, with more people asking to become members. Comments received on the newsletters have been favourable, e.g., "excellent, punchy and serious" and "looks great, is well presented and so human." *Families: The Challenge to the Church* was affirmed by Lambeth Resolution iii.10. Extra copies of *Women's Voices* have been requested by many—organisations as well as individuals, e.g., the National Council of Churches in the United States, the provincial office in Canada, and the Diocese of Melbourne.

The coordinator is regularly asked to speak on international family issues, e.g., at the Centre for Anglican Communion Studies, Selly Oak College, Birmingham, and at the 1998 Mothers' Union Worldwide Conference.

5. Current Work

Two more newsletters are being produced for 1999:

- *Prostitution* (to be published in *Anglican World;* Trinity 1999)
- *Single-Parent Families* (*Anglican World;* Michaelmas 1999)

6. Future Work

Members' suggestions for themes for future newsletters include:

- Men and families
- Family concern for the environment
- Prison and the family
- Faith and the family
- Divorce
- The role of grandparents

7. Plans for Development

Active consideration is being given by the management committee to the suggestion made during the Lambeth Conference at a consultation hosted by Canon John Peterson that an important way to carry forward the work of the network would be to hold conferences for practitioners on family issues. These could be either regional or linked with the proposed Anglican Congress. Such meetings would widen contacts for the network and facilitate "grass roots" involvement. They would be written up either as newsletters or reports for members.

The seven-year-old computer, provided by the Children's Society in 1992, ceased functioning in the year 2000 due to the millennium bug. We hope to obtain new equipment, which will give us access to the Internet and e-mail.

8. Funding

For the past twelve years funding has been obtained from United Kingdom sources (the Children's Society, the Church of England Board for Social Responsibility, the United Kingdom Diocesan Bishops, the Scottish Episcopal Church, and the Mothers' Union). The publication of *Women's Voices* was made possible by a special grant from the United Thank Offering, United States. Several of these United Kingdom grants are now coming to an end as they are time-limited. To enable IAFN's work to continue, further financial help must be found, and the possibility of funding from the United States is currently being explored. The minimum budget required to continue the newsletters is £20,000 per annum. This covers the salary of the coordinator (part-time), office expenses (telephone, postage, stationery, and so forth), design, and some printing costs. The publication of the newsletters in *Anglican World* greatly reduces IAFN's expenses for printing and postage. The network office accommodation is provided free, and the Children's Society, a major voluntary organisation linked with the Church of England and the Church in Wales, gives professional support (e.g., for the management committee and the control and auditing of IAFN's accounts). Additional funding would be required to enable the development work outlined in section 7 of this report.

The Anglican Indigenous Network

Ka'a`awa, Hawaii
June 1999

The Anglican Indigenous Network (AIN) is comprised of English-speaking indigenous Anglicans: the Maori of New Zealand (Aotearoa), Australian aborigines and Torres Strait islanders, Native Hawaiians, Native Americans from the United States, and the indigenous peoples of Canada. An organizational meeting of the key leaders from the U.S., Canada, New Zealand, and Hawaii was held in Hawaii in December 1991. One year later, at our first full-scale meeting in Hawaii, AIN adopted its mission statement:

> We are indigenous minority people living in our own lands. We are committed to the Anglican tradition while affirming our own traditional spirituality. We have discovered that we have many things in common: a common spirituality, common concerns, common gifts, and common hopes. We believe that God is leading the Church to a turning point in its history and that the full partnership of indigenous peoples is essential. Therefore we pledge to work together to exercise our leadership in contributing our vision and gifts to transform the life of the Christian community.

Subsequent meetings were held in New Zealand in March 1994, when Australia and the Torres Strait Islands joined the network, in Alaska in September 1995, and in Canada in July 1997. Because of the expense of the Canadian Synod and Lambeth in 1998, the next gathering was scheduled for September 1999 in Hawaii.

In between the international gatherings, delegations from member countries have attended events of local significance to our network partners. Examples include the summer training programs in New Zealand and the consecrations of four indigenous bishops in that country; the celebration of five hundred years of survival of Native Americans following Columbus' arrival; the signing of the new Jamestown Covenant between leaders of ECUSA, Native Americans, and Alaskans and Native Hawaiians; consultations on the Indigenous Theological Training Institute (ITTI), United States; and meetings of the Anglican Council of Indigenous People, Canada.

The mutual support provided by AIN at its biannual meetings and by participation at national events contributed in large part to the creation of the Canadians' New Covenant to work toward self-determination in 1994, the adoption of a statement of self-determination by the indigenous peoples of the American Episcopal Church in 1995, the development of the Native Hawaiian Ministry and Leadership Training Program, and the establishment of ITTI. These are all areas of concern identified by AIN during its meetings over the last seven years.

Following the July 1997 meeting, AIN members implemented a recommendation that a permanent working group of the heads of theological programs be formed to address common concerns. The first working group meetings were held in California in November 1997, and a follow-up meeting was convened in August 1998 in New Zealand.

In addition, another working group to produce theological material addressing such topics as native spirituality and native perspectives on the gospel held its initial meeting in Hawaii in May 1998. An expanded group, including the bishop of Alaska, met in Portland in October 1998 and again in Minneapolis in June 1999. Tangible results of this interaction will be available in the *First Peoples Journal of Theology*, an annual publication that is scheduled to make its debut in January 2000.

The July 1997 meeting in Canada also urged indigenous bishops to meet at Lambeth to discuss common concerns. That meeting resulted in a letter sent to the conference addressing some of these issues.

It is AIN's intention that these working groups will continue to engage in substantive ongoing discussions and will report back to the larger biannual gatherings, making appropriate recommendations for action.

A Supplementary Note to the AIN Report

—WHATARANGI WINIATA, AOTEAROA, NEW ZEALAND, AND POLYNESIA, ON BEHALF OF THE ANGLICAN INDIGENOUS NETWORK

September 20, 1999

1.0 Included in the papers for ACC-11 is a report, dated June 1999, on this network. This was written and distributed before the latest meeting of the network, which took place in Hawaii earlier this month.

2.0 The Anglican Indigenous Network (AIN) met from September 8 to 12, 1999, in Hawaii, and this note covers some of the emergent thinking within this network. Recommendations from the network for consideration by ACC-11 are included.

3.0 The June 1999 report that is contained in the ACC-11 papers contains some historical commentary on the AIN. Attached to this note is an appendix with a little more on the history of this group.

4.0 Approximately thirty people attended the meeting in September. All five parts of the current membership of the network were fully represented (five each); in addition, some observers were present. Lively debate marked the occasion and there were many signs that the networking throughout the 1990s has encouraged members to build new relationships among themselves and with their non-indigenous partners. The five meetings of the network, funded by the members themselves, and the sharing that has occurred have been confidence-enhancing and initiative-producing.

5.0 New covenants between some of the members and their non-indigenous partners have been confirmed at major national events.

6.0 There have been initiatives in education. One is the founding of the Indigenous Theological Training Institute (ITTI) in the United States, which will launch a journal early nest year to facilitate its work. Another is the establishment by Te Pihopatanga o Aotearoa of a centre of higher learning in ministry, *atuatanga*, and social services, which has just had its first undergraduate degree approved by the New Zealand Qualifications Authority.

7.0 The network has reaffirmed the 1992 mission statement (see the opening paragraph of the June 1999 report) and formulated a process by which to encourage more indigenous minority peoples living in their own lands to participate. This process, which will draw on the practice of inviting observers, will be followed for the sixth gathering of the AIN, which is scheduled to be held late in 2001 in Cairns, Australia.

8.0 The last few paragraphs of the appendix to this note comprise a summary of the proceedings of the meeting in September. The paper by Bishop Mark MacDonald, to which reference is made, received a lot of attention and is relevant to the current ACC discussion on structures within the Anglican Communion. *The Virginia Report* offers insights into the implications of cultural and contextual variations that are helpful to the work being done by the AIN.

9.0 This network is of the view that the Anglican Church must review its own constitutional arrangements. The AIN believes that the Communion must consider how we might audit and, as appropriate, alter the structures of the Church to reflect the promises and expectations of the many treaties between colonisers and indigenous (and now minority) peoples. The AIN has in mind, in particular, those treaties to which the Anglican Church, and the wider Christian Church, were parties in one way or another. The network reflected on the reasonably new constitutional rearrangements in the Church in Aotearoa, New Zealand, and Polynesia and on recent community-wide constitutional developments in Canada.

10.0 This subject will be on the agenda in Cairns in 2001. Matters of authority, jurisdiction, and self-determination in the Church's own house will be addressed. The AIN is of the view that the Church can be more effective in its advocacy of justice and equity for all, including the indigenous peoples who are minorities in their own land and are ineffectual in persuading their governments to fulfil treaty and related obligations. However, the Church must get things right in its own house, including the ACC.

11.0 The AIN would welcome a review by the ACC of the nature of the relationship between the ACC and those indigenous peoples who are minorities in their own lands. The AIN would be happy to work with the Secretary General in this respect.

12.0 Coordination of the affairs of the Anglican Indigenous Network until the meeting in 2001 will be a responsibility of Bishop Whakahuihui Vercoe of Te Pihopatanga o Aotearoa within the Anglican Church of Aotearoa, New Zealand, and Polynesia.

13.0 This network would welcome consideration by the ACC of ways and means by which the network might be assisted, financially and otherwise, in its promotion of the Church's mission.

14.0 Recommendations:

(a) That the report of the Anglican Indigenous Network be received.

(b) That the ACC note that the Anglican Indigenous Network is looking at ways by which to encourage greater participation in the network's activities by indigenous minority peoples living in their own lands.

(c) That the ACC note that the Anglican Indigenous Network has an important role to play to assist the Church to find its way forward to ensure that the potential contribution of indigenous people to all aspects of the life of the Church is enhanced, constantly.

(d) That the Secretary General of the ACC consult with the AIN on the suitability and appropriateness of the current arrangements for the participation of the indigenous peoples in the affairs of the ACC and report, as appropriate, to the Joint Standing Committees.

(e) That the Standing Committee of the ACC be asked to consider how the ACC might provide assistance, including, but not exclusively, financial, to advance the activities of the AIN.

Anglican Peace and Justice Network Meeting

—Eskith Fernando, Sri Lanka

Seoul, Korea
April 14 to 21, 1999

Thirty-two participants from twenty-four provinces of the Anglican Communion met in Seoul, Korea, where the Anglican Peace and Justice Network (APJN) held its ninth meeting from April 14 to 21, 1999, at the Sangan Institute of Management at Yonsei University. The meeting was hosted by the Anglican province of Korea.

The network took time to understand and respond to the situation in Korea. It visited the DMZ, saw the pain and violence of being in a divided nation, and applauded the leadership given by the churches, including the Anglican Church, in relation to reconciliation and unification of Korea. It is recommending that the Anglican Consultative Council send a delegation to North Korea. It also visited inner city sites where the Anglican Church is serving the community, responding to the needs of the victims of recent economic upheaval in Korea, the homeless, and the unemployed.

Among the concerns that received the attention of the network was globalization, a phenomenon from which no country appears to be able to escape. As the world advocates this trend as the way forward economically, the network seriously questions whether market forces can deliver justice to the poor and the oppressed.

For years now the network has focused on the international debt burden. The APJN affirmed the statements made at Lambeth 1998 and heard about actions for debt relief and cancellation of debts for the highest indebted poor countries. Most of the group of seven (G7) countries are finally addressing this crisis through various forms of legislation, and it was heartening to note that the voice of the Church is being heard in the halls of power.

In light of the increased power and influence of Trans National Corporations, APJN continues to support the development of an International Corporate Responsibility Code developed by church bodies in the United States, United Kingdom, and Canada.

The network met at a time of immense suffering for the people of Yugoslavia in general and Kosovo in particular. War sadly seems to be the final answer to evil. In recent human history Iraq and Kosovo stand out as examples where the just war theory has been evoked. Indeed, to many Christians the just war theory is attractive given the intransigence of the leaders of these states, but many more are uncomfortable with modern warfare as a means to conflict resolution. The network called for examining what sources of spiritual power utilizing nonviolence could be drawn upon in the face of grave injustices. What price are people willing to pay for a nonviolent paradigm to resolve conflict and evil in the name of peace? And how can the Church help to empower the United Nations to be a nonviolent instrument of peace?

The network also reaffirmed the APJN statement of 1996, "Landmines, Transfer of Weapons and Violence" and commended the Lambeth Resolution i.11 on nuclear weapons and called for their total abolition.

Meeting in Seoul was an appropriate venue to examine the urbanization process. Migration to the cities will pose new challenges to churches in the new millennium. Poverty among many countries has created a huge population of migrant workers, resulting in a range of issues both in the receiving and sending countries, requiring the churches to take a leading role in seeking justice for these workers. The problem of oppression of women in Africa and Asia was discussed and made an ongoing item of concern for the network.

The Great Lakes region of Africa, which has experienced prolonged instability and suffering in recent years, was high on the agenda. The network agreed to send a delegation to the region and encourage the churches and governments in their work for peace and reconciliation in that part of the world. The network heard from other areas of conflict, including Sri Lanka and Israel and Palestine. Last year the network made a pastoral visit to Sri Lanka.

In response to the Lambeth resolution on homosexuality, to engage in dialogue with the gay and lesbian community, the APJN heard a presentation from two such groups from Seoul, Korea. The emphasis of the presentation focused on the human rights aspect of gay and lesbian people. The network agreed to continue to consider the justice dimensions of the debate as a contribution to the dialogue called for in the Lambeth resolution.

As in the past, the APJN will communicate its views on the many matters discussed via a report to the provinces, the ACC, the Primates, and other relevant authorities for action.

Coming to Seoul

At the invitation of the Anglican province of Korea, over thirty members of the Anglican Peace and Justice Network (APJN), representing twenty-four provinces of the Anglican Communion, met on the grounds of Yonsei University in Seoul, Korea, from April 14 to 21, 1999. It was very much a family meeting, where concerns of individual provinces and dioceses of the Communion were on the table, as well as shared issues, of which APJN has long been aware, that were presented to the full meeting by committees charged with investigating and discussing them in-depth.

In this summary of the meeting, the committee reports are presented first, followed by in-depth reports from the provinces and some dioceses of the Communion. The overall tone of the reports—both those from committees and those from provinces and dioceses—is frank. If readers had not understood before, they will certainly learn here that the concerns of the Anglican Communion have become the concerns of a cohesive global family.

The committee reports, of course, reflect the collective opinion of APJN members on a number of world and regional issues. But they also reflect concerns that reach into the lives of people around the world from every country and faith community. Concerns, for instance, about the realities of globilization, the international debt burden, the worldwide trend toward urbanization, and the ways in which the problems and issues of nations and regions tend to come together in cities. And all of these issues are reflected in the report "Migrant Workers," which, in turn, informs some of the key issues raised in "Asian and African Women," whose lives are frequently impacted by the effects of migrant work on family structure in many communities.

Issues surface, reflected in these reports, that are obviously going to grow in significance in the very near future. For instance, an extensive and quite eye-opening report on "The Dimensions of Age" begins to make us aware of the worldwide implications of a population that is living longer.

There are also the immediate, active concerns of the APJN as a collective sounding board for the Communion. There are two papers on "Alternatives to War," in light of international involvement in Kosovo and potential involvement elsewhere. And there is attention paid to problems in Korea, the host country. The group considered the problem of "Korean Re-Unification" and lifted up the ways in which Christian churches are attempting to become partners in a healing process. Members of APJN made a visit to the DMZ, the dividing line between the estranged nations of the peninsula. And they considered ways to continue the dialogue launched at Lambeth in 1998 regarding the Church with its gay and lesbian members in a panel on homosexuality.

The provincial and diocesan reports are evidence of the trust level within the Communion and the degrees of difference of opinion that are possible within this amazing worldwide body. For instance, the area-wide problems reflected in the committee presentation on Africa's Great Lakes countries are pinned down in great detail in reports from Rwanda, Burundi, Tanzania, and so forth. And world economic problems, especially as they are reflected in the lives of people in developing countries, are explored strikingly in the article from Brazil. The report from Sri Lanka allows us a window into the political and ethnic complexities of the island nation we may not have had before. The comments from the Church of the province of Southern Africa give us a glimpse of a mountain that has been moved there and the problems yet to be overcome.

It is impossible to look at this collection of documents and not find a positive message. It is all about the willingness of people in a family to share their problems and concerns with each other for mutual understanding and support, and to move together to accomplish agreed-upon goals. It is also a statement about the realities of the complex world we all share.

Somehow, no matter how challenging and even daunting some of the problems raised here may seem, the fact that a group like the APJN is the instrument for addressing them head on—you will see very little dodging of issues here—is encouraging. Perhaps more than encouraging, it is something to make us proud of the spirit of the Anglican Communion in mission.

Welcome Address from Archbishop Chung

Dear brothers and sisters in our Lord Christ!

We are gathered here in Seoul, Korea, to join the Anglican Peace and Justice Network from all around the world. I welcome you all. As you know, this is the last year of the twentieth century. The next year opens the new millennium. It is timely and very meaningful to have the APJN conference at this particular moment anticipating the twenty-first century. Even after more than fifty years, the Korean peninsula is still divided into north and south. In this land where the fear and anxiety of war remains, having the APJN conference bears a quite symbolic meaning.

According to the scriptures, God has created the world in which humankind shares a common humanity; therefore, each person has equal dignity and value. That God-given dignity and value must not be hurt. Unfortunately, however, sin has penetrated into humanity, and human dignity has been wounded. The power of evil has created divisions between humans, and the strong oppress the weak. The harmony among human societies has been ruined. Up to now, the history of humankind has been stained by endless conflicts and violence between tribes and nations. God has sent Christ Jesus to bring an end to all these divisions in this world. Through his passion, death, and resurrection, Jesus has established reconciliation and peace between God and humanity and between peoples. "Peace be with you." This was the first word that Jesus spoke to the group of his disciples after his resurrection (John 20:19). He has also called his followers to be peacemakers among peoples.

"Blessed are the peacemakers, for they shall be called sons of God!" (Matthew 5:9). We are here in response to that call to be Christ-followers, in other words, peacemakers. I urge you to take this APJN as a wonderful opportunity to respond to our Lord with grateful hearts and joy.

You will surely discuss these issues deeply and profoundly, but let me remind you of the Lambeth resolutions around some issues. First, the issue of international debt and economic justice. Those poor nations in the Third World borrowed a lot of money from the First World nations for economic development and poverty reduction. On the contrary, they have become poorer countries than before. Poverty has rather been accelerated, and these nations are unable to pay the debt. They lose autonomy to international creditors, and their societies are restless under the burden. In order for the hundreds of millions of people in these unfortunate nations to protect their equal human dignity, debt cancellation is a necessary step, concluded the Lambeth Conference. Now, how to make this happen is our task.

Second, the issue of social justice and peace. It is not unusual to hear almost everyday about violence, international refugees, starvation, the extermination of indigenous peoples, and civil war between tribes. Particularly what is happening in Kosovo is very tragic. A number of Kosovo people have been killed by the extreme means of racial cleansing. NATO's air attacks are also increasing the number of deaths in the former Yugoslavia. No one can exclude the possible danger of turning this situation into a worldwide tragedy. It is surely time for prayer while urging a peace process to stop the war.

Third is the issue of Korean unification. Lambeth Resolution v.26 tells that the conference supports the efforts of the Korean National Council of Churches (KNCC), including the Anglican Church of Korea. Korea's division was not a Korean choice. The ideological confrontation between superpowers victimized this nation to pay such an unbearable price for a long time. Now Korea is the only divided nation. To end this, the reunification of Korea is necessary and urgent. The Anglican Church of Korea has actively participated in KNCC's efforts to achieve reunification. Father John Lee recently visited North Korea as chair of the unification committee in KNCC. As president of KNCC, I also try to be an active part of Korean Christian churches' efforts for reunification. President Kim Daejung's so-called Sunshine Policy is to seek reunification by helping North Korea in many ways. North Korea is suffering from economic difficulty and severe food shortage. Noting that to help North Korea in need will be a road for reunification, the Christian churches in the south, with KNCC as the centre, try to help the north continually with food, fertilizer, and medical products.

James 3:18 tells that the fruit of righteousness is sown in peace by those who make peace. You are all peacemakers. And your efforts will certainly bear the fruit of righteousness. God's blessing will be upon you all. It is a blessing and joy itself to work for peace because Christ himself is our peace (Ephesians 2:14). I hope this meeting held in Korea will be a chance for you all to gain a better understanding of the Korean situation. May this Seoul conference be a stepping stone for the Anglican Peace and Justice Network to make a great contribution to our dear Communion and world peace.

Thank you and God bless you all!

Sermon at a Liturgy for Peace in Seoul Cathedral
—Bishop Prado
April 16, 1999

Christ has died; Christ is risen; Christ will come again.

Easter is a great time to work on peace and justice. In fact, the Easter season calls us to rejoice in a God who refuses to leave the dead forever dead. Jesus did suffer a violent death. But God had no intention of letting Jesus rest in peace. He gives death no permission to hold Jesus as a permanent victim of other people's injustice and violence. Resurrection is God's answer to those who think death and violence have the last word.

During Easter we praise God's great act in raising Jesus from the dead. We believe that God's grace will be shared with us and that our own deaths will not be the final word.

Our faith teaches that we will share in Jesus' resurrection on the last day. But our faith is not restricted to remembering Jesus' resurrection. The question is: what happens to our faith in resurrection between Jesus' resurrection and our own lives? How do we live without faith in resurrection until our own last day?

Looking to our world today, we cannot deny the suffering and violence that is killing so many people everywhere. Of course, we have here today people who have suffered very bitter things.

What does our faith in resurrection say to all this and to all of us right now? We are an Easter people. Our challenge is to understand the history of human suffering in the light of Jesus' resurrection. It means that we have to take God's part in protesting and denouncing injustice, oppression, and violence. As Christians, we have to resist the forces of death in the midst of life.

Death is not only our own personal death. Death is part of our human social reality. Death is something deeply rooted in the social structures of our community. Death is around us in the midst of life. The death of those killed by the market's priorities; the political death of those oppressed; the death of the hopeless and alone; the death of thousands killed by militarism; death by torture; death everywhere; painful death.

To accept death as a "regular" part of our life in society or to accept it as inevitable, is to empty Christ's resurrection of its power for us today. Resurrection is not about reform. Jesus' resurrection was God's radical revolution—a real transformation from death to abundant life.

A resurrection faith faces the cross and fights against the oppressive powers of our society. Our calling is to live as God's chosen people. They refuse to kneel to the powers of death; they fight against violence and oppression that is used as a means to maintain economic and political power.

The resurrection of Jesus is the witness that the Suffering Servant is God, who cannot be held in death. And God works for liberation and abundant life. We know the reality of resurrection when we see new life and transformation in the life struggles of the poor and oppressed.

Powerful witnesses of God's life are visible in people who risk their lives struggling against the oppression inflicted on their sisters and brothers. We see similar hope and power in the disciples, who see in the dark what no one else sees. For all this we rejoice. It is always Easter. And the Lord is with us—right here and right now.

Living that same Easter faith, we will be stronger for the struggle. No one should be left for dead. Resurrection takes place when we defy reality. Even if, from a human point of view, Jesus' life was a dead failure. Nevertheless, the disciples began to discover that Christ was still alive. And he had rejected life based on power and wealth. He had gone through pain, death, and resurrection—and this was also to be our way, the way of his followers.

Our networking together during these last fourteen years has produced lots of good fruit, seeds of resurrection, growing awareness, deeper commitment and solidarity, and newer and more demanding challenges to the Anglican Communion. Despite our mistakes and few resources, God keeps calling us, as all other Christians, and other faiths, to witness to God's original intention of love, liberation, and healing. May God keep us walking together, sharing the same bread, recognizing the Lord with us in our lives and vocations.

On behalf of all our provincial representatives, my fellows and companions, let me say how thankful we are, to God and to you, for your kind hospitality and support.

Let us all offer to God's glory and for the transformation of our human family our prayers and work for more concrete signs of resurrection in our society. I'll conclude with a poem and prayer:

> He is Risen! That through him, we may rediscover faith: in ourselves, in our world, in our God.
>
> He is Risen! That through him we may rekindle hope for the abandoned,
>
> for the despairing, for the dreamless.
>
> He is Risen! That through him we may restore love to those from whom we have kept it, to those who are most near us, to those we will never meet, to all and everything.
>
> He is Risen. Alleluia!

Minutes of APJN Business Meeting

April 20, 1999

Communications

A web site for APJN will be established shortly after the meeting through the auspices of Episcopal Church in the United States (ECUSA). A page will be available to each province to post written reports and to update the Communion on local issues.

Most of the membership now has e-mail addresses, which will greatly facilitate communications between meetings. Emerging technology is now more accessible and is changing the landscape of communication across the Communion in dramatic ways.

UN Observer

Much time was spent discussing the future of the office of the Anglican observer to the UN. A letter to the Secretary General of the ACC and the Archbishop of Canterbury will be written to convey the following points:

- There should be transparency in the search process.
- A clear job description with accountabilities should be shared widely, inviting applicants from throughout the Communion. The relationships of the office to Canterbury, to the ACO, to the Primates, to the ACC, and to networks and other constituent groups should be spelled out. APJN desires a close working relationship with the office, as both have overlapping concerns and can undergird one another.

   The incumbent should be experienced in international relations and theology. The successful candidate would be expected to work ecumenically with other church nongovernmental organizations (NGOs) at the UN. The person could be lay or ordained and come from any province of the Communion. The search committee should operate under an equal opportunity policy.

- The search committee should be made up of persons widely representative of the Communion. APJN has members who could serve well on such a committee.
- Looking to the future, the committee now advising the office might be better broken into two committees: one to be responsible for fund-raising only and the other to be more representative of the whole Communion, offering direction and advice to the office as well as the ACC.

Site of next meeting: Aotearoa (New Zealand). South Africa and Sri Lanka offered to host the meeting to follow Aotearoa, probably in 2002. The Steering Committee will make the final determination.

Steering Committee

The committee elected Jenny Te Paa, Vivian Sau Lin, Themba Vundla, Brian Grieves, and Luiz Prado to serve on the Steering Committee.

The following task forces were created:

    Globalization: Mark Bennett, Joy Kennedy, and Frank Rwakabwohe

    Alternatives to War: Valerie Martin, Pie Ntukamazina, Mark Bennett, and Robert Okine (Naim Ateek will also be asked to serve)

    Human Sexuality: Jenny Te Paa, Brian Grieves, and Themba Vundla

Members will seek ways to connect with existing coalitions on world debt and urbanization. The Steering Committee will be responsible for continuing the progress made in inclusivity in the network.

The members approved letters to the Sudan churches, the NCCC-Brazil, and made several recommendations to the Anglican Consultative Council (which can be found in the full report of the meeting).

An invitation for an APJN delegation from the representatives of Burundi, Rwanda, and Uganda was received and referred to the Steering Committee for implementation.

APJN Participants

Name	Province
Joy Kennedy	Canada
Miguel Palacious	IARCA (Central America)
Reverend Dr. Jae Joung Lee	Korea
Sara Afshari	Jerusalem and Middle East (Iran)
Reverend Themba J. Vundla	Southern Africa
Lin Sau Lin	Hong Kong
Reverend Harold M. Mwang'ombe	Kenya
Delene M. Mark	Southern Africa
Mark Bennett	Jerusalem and Middle East (Egypt)
Reverend Mkunga H. P. Mtingele	Tanzania
Suhail Dawani	Jerusalem and Middle East (Jerusalem)
Most Reverend Andrew Mya Han	Myanmar
Reverend Naim Ateek	Consultant
Geoffrey Kayigi	Rwanda
Eksith Fernando	Sri Lanka
Reverend Andrew Davey	England
Jenny Te Paa	Aotearoa
Right Reverend Pie Ntukamazina	Burundi
Right Reverend Luiz Prado	Brazil
Reverend Samuel I. Koshushi	NSKK (Japan)
Frank Rwakabwohe	Uganda

Name	Province
Reverend Brian J. Grieves	ECUSA
Tom Hart	ECUSA
Reverend Jeremiah Guen Seok Yang	Korea
Reverend Francis Joo-yup Lee	Korea
Most Reverend Robert G. A. Okine	West Africa
Andrew A. Tauli	Philippines
Jossette Randrianarison	Indian Ocean
Valerie Martin	Wales
Right Reverend Michael H. G. Mayes	Ireland
Priscilla Ju-young Lee	Korea

Section 1: Areas of concern

Korea Reunification

During the conference in Seoul, Korea, the APJN had an opportunity to visit the DMZ at Panmunjom and to hear a number of reports on the great variety of reconciling work, initiated by the Korean National Council of Churches as long ago as the 1970s, and subsequently taken up at a political level.

The Anglican Church of Korea, as one of the main instigators in the establishment of the KNCC, has been involved in this process of reconciliation since the very beginning.

The first open discussion on the subject of reconciliation was held outside Korea. Subsequent developments led to a public declaration in 1988, which consisted of a penitential recognition of the problems and injustices caused by continuing division and of detailed proposals for the political structuring of a reconciliation process that might lead to eventual reunification.

Although the political process has so far made faltering progress, the steps that have been taken have been based largely on the programme outlined by the KNCC in 1988.

The APJN believes that the work of the KNCC has much to offer to other areas of the world, particularly to East Asia as a whole, where continuing division perpetuates mutual injustice, hatred, and fear. It commends the record of that work to the wider Anglican Communion for careful and detailed study.

The APJN further submits the following resolution to ACC-11:

In order to facilitate the process of reconciliation and reunification in the Korean Peninsula, the APJN requests ACC-11 to:

(a) Offer the active support of he Anglican Communion to the Korean National Council of Churches in its admirable work in the realm of reconciliation and reunification; specifically, APJN recommends to

ACC that it send a delegation to the Korean Federation in North Korea under the auspices of the ACC and the Anglican Church in Korea.

(b) Encourage the government of North Korea to avail of such opportunities as are presented to it to hold part of the programme of World Cup 2002 within its jurisdiction.

(c) Support the government of South Korea in its Sunshine Policy, based on mutual respect and mutual recognition, aimed at transcending the paralyzing consequences of the Cold War in order to create new political structures that will enable North and South Korea to move forward together in harmony and peace.

Urbanization: Peace, sustainability, and justice toward a holistic mission

Our encounter with the city of Seoul has given us critical perspectives on a city that is rapidly expanding, accompanied by rapid social change and economic upheaval. In Seoul's Bong-chan House of Sharing, the House of Freedom's work with the homeless, and in the parishes we visited on Sunday morning, we witnessed the Anglican community striving to be faithful to Christ and to the vision of his kingdom in this challenging context.

In the House of Sharing we found an inspiring model of the Christian community in solidarity with the urban poor, with those who find themselves most powerless as the city government remodels their areas and the economic recession bites deeper.

Building new community is a primary task for Christians in urban areas where traditional patterns of community life have not flourished, where planning and design militate against good social relationships, and where minority groups find themselves marginalized. Christians must also ask vital questions concerning the sustainability of the urban environment, the impact of their communities, and the work in which they are engaged. Sustainability concerns not just ecological issues but also questions the structures of participation and the creation of dependency.

In our encounter with urban Korea, we have discovered many common challenges that face those who work in urban contexts. Cities often act as microcosms reflecting the tensions, divisions, and power structures of national and global society. In 1996, the UN Center for Human Settlements-HABITAT reported to its second summit in Istanbul on the state of an urban planet, which has now reached the symbolic point where over half the planet's population lives in towns and cities. The report, *An Urbanizing World* (Oxford 1996), outlines the varying patterns of urban growth and the impact of urban areas on other parts of nations. It also highlights how urban poverty is often greatly underestimated because of the juxtaposition of great wealth and crushing poverty within cities. The report poses this question: What will make cities places where people want to live, rather than places into which they are forced to move to eke out an existence that is merely about survival?

To these ideas we would add the concerns of the APJN, which we find concentrated in cities, often in destructive patterns of life. There is the proliferation of micro-arms, drugs, and increasing urban violence. There are also issues of difference and diversity, and the need to plan cities in ways that promote peaceful coexistence and exchange. And there is indebtedness and the need for new, community-oriented financial structures. We are also concerned about the plight of children and young people, for whom exploitation and lack of hope are barriers to growth and wholeness. We recognize that there is often a connection between political corruption and urban decay.

Cities are the nodes of the globalisation process, as the urban revolution is matched by technological transformation in ways we often find difficult to monitor or change. We encounter new forms of poverty and social exclusion as the spatial dimensions of the city change. We also encounter the exciting phenomenon of marginalized groups and social movements discovering their capacity to use global networks to enhance their cultural, religious, and community life. At the same time, we are aware of sophisticated, clandestine global networks dealing in drugs and small arms, which exploit both urban and rural poor.

Cities will be the vital arena of the Church's mission and ministry in the new millennium.

We need structures that will keep us aware and informed about resources (human and written), ongoing programmes, new responses to the urban context, and patterns of Church engagement, as well as theological and sociological work. We must make connections between international peace and justice issues and the experience of urban communities. We must also raise these issues in existing forums, diocesan partnerships, other ACC networks, and regional groupings.

We welcome the Lambeth Conference's resolution calling for the churches of the Communion to participate in renewing, redeeming, and regenerating our urban communities through holistic mission and ministry; and we look forward to dialogue between this network and the proposed project on urbanization.

Migrant Workers

Searching the sheep and seeking them out . . . (Ezekiel 34:11)

Asians and an increasing number of Africans and Hispanic Americans coming from highly indebted poor countries compose the majority of about 125 million migrant workers worldwide. They are those who have left their homes and countries in search of better opportunities in foreign lands because of

- abject poverty, joblessness, and landless-ness;
- inequitable distribution of wealth, the widening gap between rich and poor, and the burden of the international debt;
- trade globalization and economic injustice;
- armed conflict, political oppression, and abuse of political power;
- cultural, social, and religious intolerance.

Although stories of success have been encouraging, they are outweighed by tragic stories about the destruction of the lives of people. All of the people leaving home are in search of a more compassionate environment and a dream of a better tomorrow. Instead, many have found themselves facing oppressive conditions that lessen their dignity as human beings. Worse, more and more of these migrants are forced to accept

- the pain of separation from families;
- the oppression of being forced to leave home to find work;
- the harsh consequences for migrant workers who overstay and work as illegal undocumented labourers in inhospitable receiving countries;
- the adversities of some migrants who are forced to give up their Christian faith and embrace a new religion in order to stay on in host countries and suffer, nevertheless, environments of ethnic hostility.

Often overworked, sometimes underpaid, the human rights of migrant workers are generally unprotected by the laws of host countries. And their welfare is often ignored by the embassies of their own countries. The physical and mental health of migrants is often endangered by neglect and withheld treatment. Many migrant workers return home indebted, disabled, and ill, both physically and mentally.

In the harsh environments in which they live, some migrants escape responsibility through the abuse of alcohol and prohibited drugs. Others have been sexually abused, flogged, or even imprisoned and held hostage until their families have raised enough money to ransom them. In some cases, migrants have been killed or have, in despair, committed suicide. Sometimes the families of migrants receive only their bodies, with little or no explanation of how they died.

The facts reviewed up to this point attempt to show the human face of the migrant workers issue. However, there are also broader consequences. Many of the migrant workers come from traditional societies and their issues tear at the fabric and even threaten the continuing existence of these societies. Traditional societies have become increasingly subject to the tremendous social and psychological pressures brought on by the absence of breadwinners, many of them women and mothers. These pressures sometimes result in broken homes and broken bodies.

In the face of these problems, how have our churches—specially in the receiving countries—responded? How should they respond? How should they search the sheep and seek them out? How should they ease the burdens of the oppressed, the poor, the suffering? And how many migrants must lose their faith in a just God before the churches give them sanctuary?

Many questions have been asked. Much has been said. Much more needs to be done. Let no more tomorrows come before our churches seriously recognize the plight of migrant workers as an issue of justice requiring urgent action.

APJN, as part of its Christian responsibility and mandate, takes the side of vulnerable, exploited, and marginalized migrant workers. APJN commits itself to their empowerment and offers them its services and support as expressions of our obedience to God's commandment to love our neighbours.

APJN appeals to the churches of the Anglican Communion in sending and receiving countries, and to countries that were once created by immigrants and developed by migrant labour, to take a leading role in the search for justice for the least of these, our brothers and sisters.

APJN urges the governments and state policy makers to

- repeal all unjust and anti-migrant laws and policies.

- enact legislation to protect the rights and promote the well-being of migrant workers and their families.

APJN calls upon the provinces of the Anglican Communion to call on the twenty signatory countries needed for the 1990 United Nations Convention on the protection of the rights of all migrant workers and their families to become an international law and to immediately

- sign and ratify the UN Migrant Convention (if they have not previously done so).

- begin to abide by and implement the provisions of the convention.

As members of APJN, we

- urge our brothers and sisters of all faiths, in ecumenical coalitions, in partner NGOs, and in government offices and agencies to work for the liberation of migrant workers.

- commend this report to the Anglican Consultative Council (ACC) and to the provinces of the Anglican Communion and their constituent dioceses for their proactive endorsement and support.

- express and reaffirm our commitment to Christ, to one another and to the people we profess to serve in faithful response to God's purpose for us all.

Asian and African Women

More than half of the population of the world consists of women. It is estimated that two-thirds of them are living in the undeveloped countries and developing countries, mainly in Asia and Africa.

Women and children have been the most affected by wars, international debt, and even natural disasters.

Women in many African and Asian societies do not enjoy the status of equal citizen. Instead, they are frequently treated on the same level as servants. As we know, history has shown us that women are true pillars of society and struggle for justice in all of life's situations. Women provide loving emotional stability to both family and societal life.

The majority of migrant workers in today's world are Asian and African women who are subject to violence, abuse, and exploitation. These women are not protected by any regulations. Due to lack of education and skills development, most of these women are limited finding employment as domestic workers, industrial workers, or farm labourers. Many societies discriminate against women with regard to education and equal opportunities, even though, in the context of Asian and African women, they are the breadwinners.

It is important for the Church in Asia and Africa to acknowledge that women are the majority and, therefore, provide the bulk of the income available to fund our basic needs. In both the Church and family context, women are not the decision makers, even though they are the income generators.

This meeting has also listened to stories from specific Asian countries, where female fetuses are sometimes aborted and girl children are killed due to their sex.

In Hong Kong, the status and condition of women is totally different. Hong Kong is a very prosperous and rich city. Women's rights and needs have been recognized. The government of Hong Kong has just established an Equal Opportunity Commission to deal with the problem of sexual and gender discrimination.

As the Church, we acknowledge that it is our duty to address the injustices that women in African and Asian countries live with every day. We know that their needs are for capacity-building, particularly in the area of literacy and skills training. Much would be gained if the Church community could fund educational programmes for women or support overseas study opportunities for them—or even just help them to get started by helping to establish equal opportunities for women's education. As the Church, we encourage the inclusion of women in church leadership roles as a crucial way of involving women in the total life of the Church. And last but not least, we propose that the issue of injustice to women around the globe be a specific focus of the next APJN meeting.

Globalisation

Globalisation is an issue that cannot be escaped and is a fact of the shrinking world that we live in. We are told that there will be many benefits to peoples from many countries. We are told that economically this is the way forward—that countries must bring down barriers and enter the world market. This is preached as the way of the future, but there are many discrepancies. Economies are to be open, but in most cases borders are being closed. Money and funds should flow freely, but in most cases they flow in one direction, not two. Resources and opportunities are open to some but become more closed and inaccessible to others.

- What is the controlling factor in such a process?
- For whom are the benefits?
- What contribution and direction does the Church have in this case?
- What party will ensure justice for the weak, the oppressed, the alien, and the outcast?
- Can the market forces deliver such justice?
- Can the market forces bring prosperity to nations that lack resources to build an economy? Who will wait for them to catch up?
- Is the good of the shareholder the only common good that should be considered?

> Woe to those who make unjust laws, to those who issue oppressive decrees, to deprive the poor of their rights and withhold justice from the oppressed of my people, making widows their prey and robbing the fatherless. What will you do on the day of reckoning, when disaster comes from afar? To whom will you run for help? Where will you leave your riches? (Isaiah 10:1–3)

In the light of the increased power of TNCs in matters of trade, investment, technology, development, and even national, social, and political policies, we reaffirm the APJN 1996 support for the work on Benchmarks for Global Corporate Responsibility and gladly receive the final document brought to us at APJN 1999. We add our support to the developing International Corporate Responsibility Network and recommend the Benchmarks for commendation by the ACC.

Globalisation in some cases threatens the national sovereignty of countries that find themselves in difficult circumstances in the world marketplace. This is an important area for consideration.

Suggestions:

- That a working group be formed to consider the theological perspective and also to explore other economic models that may be viable.

- Consult with the work already carried out by the WCC.
- Consider what kind of body needs to be in place to recommend and implement safety restrictions on the progress of globalisation and the nature of its impact.
- We recommend that the ACC discuss the theological understanding and the role of the nation-state in our present global system.

International Debt Burden and Jubilee 2000

We affirm the resolutions made at Lambeth 1998; in particular, we are aware of the urgent need for the cancellation of international debt to alleviate suffering in many countries. The churches to date have been able to make a difference. Most of the group of seven (G7) countries have come up with good resolutions in the last six months, and we have heard at this conference that Japan may also be ready to make a commitment.

As an illustration, we consider the case of Brazil. In 1989, Brazil owed $115.5 billion; between 1989 and 1998 it paid $225 billion in interest. However, in 1998 it still owes $235 billion (Central Bank of Brazil). In other the words, the country is getting deeper into economic trouble, although a huge amount of its international debt has been paid. This pattern we feel, must come to an end.

We wish to affirm the work of the Jubilee 2000 campaign globally—what it has already achieved and what it is continuing to do with churches and government bodies—in raising awareness. There is still much work for the Church to do. We call on the Church to be involved in the independent, fair, and transparent process (Lambeth 1.15b) of ensuring that the cancellation of debt of the most indebted countries takes place immediately, and that a new system of credit is put in place.

There are a number of issues that we feel are important and must be kept in consideration:

1. The problem is at least twofold. First, that creditor countries maintain power over debtor countries through crippling debt. And secondly, that some debtor countries are irresponsible in their use of funds, plunging their countries into worse crises. Some control over both of these instances needs to be in place.
2. Whatever new model or solution comes into being, there is the problem of paternalism. Jubilee means to release the captive, not to maintain control. This requires some level of trust and responsibility and must be achieved through agreed instruments.
3. The decision-making process must include both debtor and creditor countries so that concerns of each may be considered and there may be agreement on the action taken.

The democratic process is important. The involvement of civil society is key to ensuring that accountability and transparency are achieved. The involvement of civil society implies providing concrete education for citizens around the issues of the debt burden and Jubilee 2000.

Recommendations for action:

1. The ACC should take up the Lambeth plan to commit 0.7% of its income to international development programmes; we affirm this.
2. There is a need for IMF and other agencies that are involved in providing financial resources to be also mindful of the social impact of structural adjustment programmes.
3. There should be a focus on involving women in the decision-making process that involves how resources are spent.
4. Churches and other NGOs should allocate resources to provide for grassroots education on this kind of economic issue.
5. New economic and relational structures should be established between debtors and creditors based on mutual partnership in service to people, rather than on economic gain.
6. Consider stopping debt repayment and channelling those payments into a fund directed at improving living standards of people in debtor nations. Debtor countries could agree on the terms of such an agreement and set up structures for its implementation.
7. Work together with other agencies and women's groups so that a balanced approach is achieved.

The efforts of ECUSA in support of a debt relief bill before the U.S. Congress is affirmed.

The Church needs to be the prophetic voice, taking the lead in searching for alternative patterns of reducing poverty, empowering nations to achieve development, and protecting those who are lacking resources. It may be that there is a price to be paid by those of us who live in creditor nations. As Christ's ambassadors in the world, we should be willing to acknowledge that our lifestyles need to change in order to achieve the goals of justice and a fair use of resources. The cancellation of debt and the consequences affect us all, not only those in debtor countries. Globalisation and international markets are controlled by market forces and the need to return dividends to shareholders. The Church needs to challenge this pattern to ensure that justice is done.

Regional Conflicts: The Great Lakes Region

The Great Lakes region of Africa is comprised of the countries of Burundi, Kenya, Rwanda, Sudan, Tanzania, Central African Republic, Uganda, and the Democratic Republic of Congo.

The region has experienced prolonged instability; thus, it has had a lack of peace and justice for quite some time. It is now engulfed in a war that has drawn in other countries for differing reasons. It was hoped that after the fall of the late Mobutu Sese Seko in Congo that there was going to be peace and stability in the region. These hopes were quickly dashed when President Laurent Kabila, who took over from Mobutu, decided to side with Rwandese refugees (former defeated army and Interahamwe militia) who had not abandoned their genocidal mentality and were planning to invade Rwanda; he also started supporting rebels opposed to the Ugandan government.

Kabila also expelled the Banyarnulenge, who actually brought him to power, denying them their right to Congolese citizenship; in this move, he actually committed genocide against Rwandophone (Kinyarwanda-speaking) Congolese.

This policy sparked a rebellion that has been backed by Rwanda, Burundi, and Uganda for reasons of security and, ultimately, survival.

Following this rebellion, President Kabila appealed to the heads of state of some countries who, motivated by (personal) economic interests rather than political or humanitarian interests, unilaterally decided to give him military support in equipment and men. The countries in this category include Zimbabwe, Angola, Namibia, Chad, and Sudan.

The conflict has become multinational and requires a multidimensional approach to resolve it.

Associated Problems

As a result of the war in the Great Lakes region, many thousands of people have been killed; others have been displaced or uprooted. Property has been lost, and Tanzania hosts a very large number of refugees. Burundi counts a large number of internally displaced people (refugees in their own homeland!). Those displaced are obviously traumatized by what they have gone through. Disease is on the increase. There is also concern about food supplies. A lot of resources that would otherwise be invested in the countries involved in the conflict are being wasted in the sense that they have been diverted to the war effort.

In Rwanda, although genocide took place almost five years ago, few of those who committed it have been brought to justice. The UN approved an International Criminal Tribunal (ICTR) for Rwanda in Arusha. And yet Tanzania has proved extremely slow in letting it perform its task. As the saying goes: delayed justice is justice denied! The genocide survivors feel let down by the UN, both before and after the genocide. The picture of UN troops being pulled out right at the time they were most badly needed is still fresh in the survivors' memories. It is more especially so when the testimony of General Romeo Dallaire, who was the commander of the UN troops, clearly states that the UN kept quiet despite alarming reports he sent before the genocide; namely, asking for authority to intervene and stop the slaughter.

In Burundi, the democratization process was set back by the killing of the first elected president in October 1993, after only three months in office.

The many refugees who sought asylum in neighbouring countries launched repeated attacks from the border. This has been another source of insecurity in the region.

Conflict Resolution Attempts

President Chiluba of Zambia has been trying to mediate in the Congo conflict. The Organization of African Unity (OAL) and the UN have called on the parties involved to put down their arms and enter into negotiation. President Kabila does not accept negotiation because he stubbornly persists in speaking of outside aggression, instead of admitting to the existence of a Congolese rebellion.

The churches have tried to intervene, but the situation is complex. The parties involved stick to their respective positions as a consequence of Kabila's unwillingness to face reality. In the meantime, people continue to be killed!

What Can the Network Do?

The churches of the region need support to respond to the many challenges raised in this conflict. Peace building involves change of attitudes and practices. This is a long-term process. However, in the shorter term:

- The churches in the region need network solidarity and understanding.
- The uprooted people (both internal and external) need increased assistance.
- The churches need facilitation to continue the process of pursuing peaceful means of conflict resolution.

The sister churches of the North should lobby their respective governments to control the flow of arms to the region. Efforts should also be made to stay in close communication with the churches in the region in order to maintain an accurate picture of the situation and be able to relay unbiased information to the respective governments, local media, and human rights organizations.

Specifically for Burundi. The APJN is pleased to hear of the changes taking place in Burundi, especially that the sanctions which were imposed on Burundi have been suspended and political talks are going on in Arusha and Tazania, as well as in Burundi. An urgent appeal is made to those fighting to end the war, since innocent people are the most affected by this crisis. Both internal and external dialogues between the government, the parliament, and political parties (Burundians who are both inside the country and those outside) should be encouraged. It is the mission of the local church in Burundi to continue the role of mediator and to hold seminars on peace, power sharing, and reconciliation.

Specifically for Rwanda. The APJN supports the Church in Rwanda in its initiatives toward reconciliation. Ways and means should be sought to enable the Church to take a step further and pursue the action on a larger scale. The Church should be assisted financially to take the lead in showing compassion to the needy, especially helpless genocide survivors and other war victims (for instance, victims of landmines). The necessity to assist the Church in responding to the need, for instance, for popular education is recognized; this might, in the future, protect the innocent population from manipulation by selfish politicians.

The Anglican UN office should lobby in order to effect some improvement in the ICTR process in Arusha; true justice is a prerequisite to reconciliation.

Israeli-Palestinian Peace Process

The APJN expressed its deep concern about the Middle East peace process and about the freezing of that process by the present policy of the Israeli government, formulated because of forthcoming national elections in May.

The APJN expresses its solidarity with the Palestinian people in their search for self-determination and an independent state that can coexist in peace with the state of Israel. It also urges that Jerusalem be a shared city for the three faiths and their peoples, and open to everyone.

We call upon the ACC to write both parties, urging them to continue their efforts to strengthen the peace process so that both parties may enjoy equal rights and live together in dignity and harmony as children of God, embracing the position of the Lambeth resolution.

On an Alternative to War (Paper 1)

For thousands of years, our world has been using war as the final answer to conflict resolution. Similarly, in today's world, when everything else fails—diplomacy, negotiations, economic sanctions, moral pressure, and so forth—military power is used against the aggressor under the pretence that it will restore justice. Some cases in point from recent history would be Iraq and Kosovo. The just war theory has been evoked in both these conflicts and seemed attractive to many Christians.

At the same time, more and more Christians are uncomfortable with war as an instrument for conflict resolution, even in the face of a Milosovic or a Saddam. Where are other effective sources of power that Christians can draw upon in the face of grave injustice? What alternative strategies and methods can Christians lift up before a world that is tired of the destructive nature of war, even when it is perceived by some as just? What is our theology of the cross; and how can it be of help to us in arriving at those alternatives?

From one theological perspective, the cross reflects the vulnerability of God and God's experience of helplessness in the face of evil powers that are able to crucify the innocent. In the scheme of redemption, the reality of the resurrection had to be preceded by the reality of the cross, of total vulnerability and helplessness. We, therefore, see a need to accept this principle of loving vulnerability as a legitimate way of addressing evil.

How can we translate this theological foundation practically?

1. One way, which must be more seriously explored, is to impress on governments the need to begin training huge numbers of people as armies for peace. Instead of military training, they would be trained in nonviolent resistance. In areas of conflict, these "armies" would be dispatched with no military arms except their moral presence, acting as human shields in the face of the aggressors, even at the risk of losing their own lives. Such actions have been practiced on a small scale at different times and in different places and have had considerable success. They need to be tried on a larger scale. Obviously, they demand the total conversion of our world's political and other leaders for a new approach to conflict resolution. It will take time and this new strategy will require continuous refinement, but it is worth considering. Some of us believe that its rate of success will be greater than its rate of failure.

(An important follow-up is to request churches and governments to invest in more serious research in peace studies, with a focus on alternatives to war.)

2. Empower the UN so that it can be, as much as possible, nonpartisan and impartial in its decision making and more effective in implementing its resolutions.

3. Demand that the United States and Britain see their role within the UN and not above it.

On an Alternative to War (Paper 2) : Kosovo Situation

The heart of many recent conflicts in Kosovo has been tied up with memories of pain and aggression in the paSt. Past suffering becomes the fuel for tomorrow's conflicts. It is not difficult to remind people of how they have been treated unjustly in the past and should fight to prevent it from happening again.

Such a mind-set cannot produce lasting peace. Peace can come only through forgiveness and reconciliation. First there must be a shared desire for peace, a willingness to pay a price to achieve it. This is the model that Jesus presents to us. Reconciliation with our Father came at a great price, but through sacrifice, not through law and punishment.

There are a number of concerns that we have in relation to the means that are presently being employed to bring peace:

1. How do we deal with a leader such as Milosevic? His people are the ones who suffer the consequences of his actions, and in many cases, the retribution that is aimed at such a leader becomes that leader's tool to rally support.

2. What alternative role can the Church present in the light of the cross and its vulnerability?
3. How can the role of the UN be enhanced by the Church offering just and peaceful alternatives to what is presently being done?
4. What price are we willing to pay, as God's ambassadors, when we commit ourselves to peace?
5. We recommend that a task force be set up to investigate the options open to our Communion, and how these options for peace could be implemented. One suggestion has been that an army of peace volunteers be set up by the churches; volunteers who are willing to go to a country at war, meet with its people, and stand with them in the conflict but peacefully protesting the action of the warring parties, forcing them to consider other alternatives. Such a suggestion has a cost! Training, transport, logistics, and possibly lives. What price will we pay for peace?

Implementation:
- A web site should be set up.
- A forum for discussion should be established.
- A task force should be formed to make suggestions and lobby for their acceptance.

On Landmines, Weapons, and Violence

We reaffirm the APJN 1996 statement on landmines, transfers of weapons, and violence and uphold Lambeth resolution i.11 on nuclear weapons.

As we have reflected on these matters in the current context, we wish to add our voice to the demands for the total abolition of nuclear weapons and weapons of mass destruction. We urge all provinces and the ACC to demonstrate their commitment to this by joining with other civil society campaigns, such as Abolition 2000, and to actively oppose NATO's first-strike policy.

We further urge that these issues be examined for their impact on the sustainability of the planet and all species and peoples.

The New Dimensions of Age

—SUBMITTED BY RIGHT REVEREND MICHAEL HARE DUKE

In Britain we are waking up to the implications of the demographic changes that are taking place in the world as a result of the increasing number of people surviving into old age. In Britain, over the next thirty years, the number of pensioners (retired persons) will double and the number of people over eighty-five will increase proportionately. As a result, by 2040 A.D. there will be only two working people per pensioner, compared to 1961 when the proportion was four to one. These figures could make economists blench.

Who will provide the wealth to sustain the costs of pensions and care? They also provide a warning for politicians, since they mean that Grey Power has come of age and a high proportion of the electorate will be demanding support for either themselves or their parents. The media have sometimes called this situation the "Age Time Bomb."

It is not acceptable for a Christian community to use such a problem-centred approach. Old age is not a threat but an opportunity for service. We need to rethink the stereotypes that lie behind these assumptions.

The Royal Commission on Long Term Care has set the scene for a new attitude toward aging with a quotation in a report published in March 1999: "The moral test of Government is how that Government treats those who are in the dawn of life, the children; those who are in the twilight of life, the elderly; and those who are in the shadows of life, the sick, the needy, and the handicapped."

Practical thinking may be dominated by the statistics, which show the staggering increase in the proportion of old to young across the world. The situation, however, requires a moral response that shifts the argument from the mathematics of the cost of care to an appreciation of the gifts that older people bring to society.

The Report sets out its basic assumptions:

> Older people are a valuable part of society and should be valued as such. Old age will come to increasing numbers of the population and this should be seen as a natural part of life and not as a burden. Old age represents an opportunity for intellectual fulfilment and for the achievement of ambitions put on hold during working lives. To compartmentalize old age and to describe old people as a problem is intolerable morally and practically.

At the moment, it is the affluent countries of the North that are beginning to confront the new situation. Nevertheless, the statistics apply almost worldwide, and in some cases the change is almost more dramatic. In India in 1920, the age of life expectancy was twenty-five. In 1980 it had risen to fifty-three, and in 2020 it is projected that it will reach sixty-eight. This dramatic change will pose the same questions to the Indians about infrastructure, health care, family life, and the understanding of death that have arisen in northern countries.

The facts of demographic change have implications:

- Economically: Who will bear the cost of maintenance of the older generation?
- Politically: How will the older generation make its influence felt? Through the voting power they can mobilize? What will this do to the allocation of resources?
- Socially: How will society structure itself to provide adequate care for the increased number of elderly?
- Theologically: How do we understand old age and death?

Some of these questions require an answer at a social level in terms of policy, and some are a matter of pastoral care at an individual level. In respect to the latter, the churches need to think out their view of old age. This is not a time of increasing uselessness but a time for growing in new ways spiritually, discovering God in an ability to look back with gratitude, and also to enjoy the apparent diminishment of the present. It is a time for contemplation and not activity; but this is also a dimension that contributes to the wholeness of society. The older members can witness to priorities other than creation of wealth and career advancement.

We have become obsessed with the appearance of youthfulness and devalue the gifts of age. By contrast, the Psalms offer an alternative picture: "I am become like a bottle in the smoke" (Psalm 119:83). Here the image of the person is as the old gnarled wineskin hanging in the corner by the fire. The leather of the wineskin has become hard and cracked in the smoke, assuming all of the characteristics of age—against which Oil of Olay and other cosmetic products promise protection. But the outer appearance does not matter; within is the wine that has matured with the years.

Theologically, old people need to discover their value, the ability to see life from a mature point of view—perhaps because they have grown beyond the fear of what others think. Such a position sets a person free to make unlikely friendships, support unpopular causes, and to be a resource to those who are on the margins of society. It has been discovered in Scotland how much older people can contribute to society as volunteers. Most of those who care for others are pensioners (retired people). They look after older relatives; they are baby sitters for their grandchildren, enabling the parents to go out to work; and they listen to problems when nobody else has the time. Above all, they can provide an element of stillness in an increasingly frenetic world.

The Old Testament carries something of this vision. Micah and Zechariah dreamed that:

> Each man will sit under his vine and fig tree with no man to trouble him. (Micah 4:4)
>
> Aged men and women once again will sit in the squares of Jerusalem. (Zechariah 8:4)

Part of the quality of Messianic times will be a fulfilled old age:

> No more shall there be an infant that lives but a few days, or an old person that who does not live out a lifetime, for one who dies at a hundred years shall be considered a youth, and one who falls short of a hundred will be considered accursed. . . . Like the days of a tree shall the days of my people be, and my chosen ones shall long enjoy the work of their hands. (Isaiah 65:20–22)

To work with such an understanding is part of the pastoral care of the individual. This is especially relevant in an aging community where so many church congregations are made up of the elderly. It is part of the justice structures of the kingdom in which nobody is disregarded, to combat the ageism in society that sets arbitrary dates for retirement, sees older people as unemployable, and pushes them to the margins of society.

Longevity produces its special problems among those who fear that they have outstayed their welcome in this life and almost imagine that God has forgotten to "call them home." This, too, needs a special kind of spirituality, something more than passive waiting. Modern medicine has taken control of both birth and death and given the opportunity of choice. This opportunity produces a variety of ethical and theological responses. In addition, in a society that has little experience of living with age, the onset of Alzheimer's disease, for instance, can pose cultural problems. All the expectations are that age brings wisdom, not dementia. The consequent disruption of stereotypes can be distressing.

At the Commonwealth Heads of Government meeting in 1998 in Edinburgh, I listened with distress to a consultant psychiatrist from India. First he described how his culture revered age and made a celebration for a person reaching their sixtieth birthday. Then he went on to the case study of an old lady admitted to an old people's home. The warden of the home was particularly concerned about the safety of personal property and so was most careful to collect any jewellery her patients had in their possession. One particular old lady failed to understand the intention of the warden and imagined that her jewels, which had been taken into safekeeping, had been stolen. She was brought to see the staff psychiatrist because of her delusion. She continued with her story and then began to search in her sari for her lost jewels. The nurse who accompanied her began to slap her to control her inappropriate search. In spite of the culture's traditional respect for old age, this elderly Indian woman was treated like a naughty child because the caregiver lacked any cultural norms to guide her in the newly developing situation.

There are various voices giving a lead to ways of finding a new ethic. Hans Kung has done work on a "Global Ethic," which won acceptance at the World Parliament of Religions in Chicago in 1993. Within Britain, Age Concern has mounted a Debate of the Age, supported by a number of working papers on "Values and Attitudes." They identify an acceptable view of old age, but suggest that it depends on "epigrammatic validity," a phrase attributed to Frank Cioffi (who remains unidentified). Is this sufficient authority for a basic principle like "an individual's entitlement to the respect and protection of the community and to equal access to its opportunities does not vary with age or life expectancy"?

Similarly, the International Year of the Older Person, established by the UN, sets out five principles for the treatment of older persons: independence, participation, care, self-fulfilment, and dignity. These can be deduced from the premises set out in the UN charter, but if they are to carry weight in practical policy making, do they require some stronger underpinning?

There are ethical questions for older persons themselves. How far do they use their political muscle to gain advantage for themselves—better pensions and social provisions, a disproportionate share in health care, housing rights, and transport? What should their attitude be to their children and grandchildren in the matter of inheritance of wealth? How do they balance the advantage of their family against the good of the community?

It may be that such problems exceed the concerns of APJN, yet they are all part of the pattern of a just, participatory, and sustainable society, which was the original formulation of the WCC that led to Justice, Peace and the Integrity of Creation (JPIC).

These are issues with which we are wrestling in Scotland—particularly as we engage in the Debate of the Age in preparation for the millennium. These issues cannot be avoided by any society as it comes to take seriously the demographic shifts in our world.

Panel on Homosexuality

The Anglican Peace and Justice Network (APJN), in response to the Lambeth resolution to engage in dialogue with the gay and lesbian community, heard a presentation from both lesbian and gay men's organizations from Seoul, Korea. Much of the emphasis of the presentations focused on the human rights aspect of gay and lesbian issues. The speakers noted that the Church is a major source of repression of homosexuals and asked that the power of love given in Jesus Christ be used as a basis for understanding and accepting gay and lesbian people.

The APJN recognized deep divisions on the subject of homosexuality that surfaced after the Lambeth resolution, especially the section on how Scripture is used to discuss homosexuality and on the blessing of same-sex unions and ordaining those involved in same-gender unions. These concerns exist largely in the Anglican Communion's northern provinces, but also emerge elsewhere in the Communion and should not be seen exclusively as a Western subject. The network agreed to continue to consider the justice dimensions of the debate over homosexuality, in the hope of contributing to the dialogue called for in the Lambeth resolution.

Network Recommendation to the ACC September Meeting

The Network asks the ACC to affirm that human rights exist for all people and that there can be no exceptions to the universal principles of those rights in the UN declaration, including the rights of gays and lesbians. Further, the ACC is encouraged to recognize that homosexual persons are children of God and to affirm that section of the Lambeth resolution that assures the Church's gay and lesbian members "that they are loved by God . . . and are full members of the body of Christ." This affirmation is crucial to the well-being of our church communities where gay and lesbian members are present. Finally, the network asks the ACC to consider ways in which dialogue on Anglican approaches to interpretation of Scripture may be implemented so that the Communion may better engage the general subject of human sexuality.

The Anglican Communion International Refugee and Migrant Network

—The Most Reverend Ian George, Archbishop of Adelaide, Chairman

May 1999

1. The network last met in May 1992 in Jordan. Twenty-five people, representing the Communion at large, met in Amman for eight days. A number of resolutions were passed and an executive appointed. It does not appear that the executive has ever met and no papers are available from the ACC office.

2. In late 1997, the Archbishop of Canterbury asked Archbishop Ian George, Archbishop of Adelaide, South Australia, to revive the network. Of the twenty-five people present in Amman, only three are known to be still active in the work of the Communion.

3. The Archbishop of Canterbury invited the chairman to the meeting of the Joint Standing Committees of the Primates and the ACC in Canterbury, England, from March 12 to 16, 1998. At that meeting, the chairman presented a general report on what might be done, and there was extensive discussion.

4. The following key points emerged.

    a. We are witnessing the greatest movement of peoples around the globe since the collapse of the Roman Empire. The causes are political, racial, religious, economic, and ecological.

    b. There are between twenty and thirty million persons who come within the UN HCR definition of a refugee at this time (i.e., a person outside his or her own country of origin who is unable to return owing to a reasonable fear of persecution on political, religious, racial, or other grounds).

    c. There are probably up to forty million persons at this time displaced but remaining within the borders of their own country of origin.

    d. At least one hundred thousand of these people (according to the UN HCR) are in dire straits and without resettlement in the near future will perish. That number may now have been significantly increased due to the escalating crises in Sudan and the Balkans.

e. A significant percentage of the world's refugees and displaced persons are Anglicans.

f. Only a few countries in the world have remained recipients of refugees and asylum seekers. This number has increased recently due to the needs of the Kosovars. Nevertheless, Great Britain, the United States, Canada, Australia, and New Zealand are the main long-term receiving countries. All these countries have significant Anglican communities.

g. While the WCC has a particular concern for this area, not a great deal seems to be being done. However, at the recent WCC assembly in Zimbabwe there were over forty workshops devoted to issues relating to refugees and forcibly displaced persons. An amazing number of countries, especially in Africa, are receiving refugees from neighbouring countries or coping with internally displaced persons. It is evident from that assembly that Anglicans are actively involved in assisting refugees and displaced persons in many areas, usually on a temporary basis.

5. There was considerable agreement that the Anglican Communion with its widespread membership and influence could do a number of things very effectively; among them are the following:

   a. **Advocacy.** Obviously the Anglican observer to the United Nations has a crucial role to play here. The loss of humanitarian concern and the rise of economic rationalism make it particularly important for the churches to be heard in this area.

   b. **Response to immediate need.** There are many agencies already in the field and there is no need for us to create another. However, the Anglican network could be a major supplier of invaluable, accurate information, which is so lacking at this stage. This could greatly assist the Archbishop of Canterbury's Anglican Communion Fund, the Presiding Bishop's Fund for World Relief, and similar bodies in various countries.

   c. **Preparation for the future.** There are many funds and agencies that respond to immediate need, but few are considering the needs of refugees and asylum seekers for the future. Those already in camps have a desperate need for vocational training to enable them to find effective repatriation or resettlement.

   d. **Resettlement.** The Anglican Communion is already active in this area, but there is a great need for what is being done to be communicated and for more networking among those involved.

   e. **Education.** Most dioceses in First World countries appear to have more pressing problems than responding to overseas refugee and aid problems. The person in the pew is usually blissfully ignorant of what is going on.

f. **Political questions.** It appears that few of our churches or agencies are involved in tackling governments on policy, challenging priorities, and seeking to change conditions in many countries that cause refugee problems.

6. Oxford meeting, July 1998

As a result of the meeting of the Joint Standing Committees in New York with Mr. Richard Parkins, who runs Episcopal Migration Ministries, and then in Toronto with Mrs. Elsa Musa, who runs the refugee section of the Canadian Primate's World Relief and Development Fund, we were able to plan a small conference at Oriel College, Oxford, immediately before the Lambeth Conference. A range of Primates was invited to send representatives, but it was very difficult to get replies. We were expecting Bishop James Ottley (Anglican Observer to the UN), who suddenly had to go into the hospital for surgery. Bishop Ghais Malik from Egypt was unable to come at the last moment because of his wife's illness. Archbishop David Gitari appointed Bishop Stephen Kewasis Nyorsok, bishop of Kitale (province of Kenya). There was no answer from Archbishop Moses Tay of Singapore, and no bishop was appointed from the Church of England. Mrs. Elsa Musa was to represent the Canadian province but was forced suddenly to go to Eritrea to check on her family after the resumption of war with Ethiopia. Mr. Richard Parkins from ECUSA attended and Bishop Richard Harries of Oxford attended for one day.

The conference discussed:

a. The purpose of the network

b. The theological basis

c. The development of a mission statement

d. What is being done?

e. What resources are available to us?

f. What could we attempt?

g. How can we arouse interest in the Anglican Communion?

h. Advocacy

During the three days a useful visit was made to the Refugee Research Centre at Ruskin College.

A document containing the mission statement and agreed objectives was prepared and is appended to this report as appendix A.

7. Lambeth Conference 1998

a. Spouses' Conference

As a result of discussion with the Archbishop of Canterbury and Mrs. Carey in March, the chairman was invited to conduct two workshops at the Spouses' Conference; they were reasonably attended and spirited, and discussion took place. Part of the value of the exercise was to give an opportunity to some bishops' wives who had either been refugees or experienced the situation to express their feelings and recount their experiences.

b. Section 1. Human rights and human dignity

There were many stories from those who had direct experience of the problems of refugees and displaced persons throughout the Communion in this section and subsection. An appropriate resolution was passed and is attached to this report as appendix B. It is to be noted that the Communion has committed itself:

1. To promote a greater awareness of the problems.
2. To pray for those who are affected by them.
3. To encourage effective advocacy.
4. To promote greater cooperation within the Anglican Communion.
5. To designate contact persons in every province to develop and guide this work.
6. To encourage the revitalisation of the network.

It is important to note that the Primates were requested to designate contact persons to work for greater cooperation and to enable a greater commitment of personal material resources for the work in the meeting of ACC-6 (see Proceedings of ACC-6, page 126, resolution 391984).

c. Informal discussions during Lambeth

It was possible for informal discussions to take place between Mr. John Rea (Scotland) who is a member of the ACC Standing Committee and has been appointed the liaison person for the network, Bishop James Ottley, Bishop Stephen Kewasis Nyorsok, Bishop Richard Harries, and Bishop John Perry of Chelmsford, who has indicated an interest in this work, together with the chairman. As a result, the chairman was invited to attend the advisory council to the Anglican Observer at the United Nations when it met in New York, December 1–2, 1998. It was useful to be at that meeting, but unfortunately it coincided with Bishop Ottley's announcement of his resignation and most of the interest and energy of the group was taken up with that.

8. What is the present situation?

a. A submission was made in April 1999 to Trinity Church, Wall Street, New York, for funding for one year ($15,000 Australian) for a half-day per week assistant to the chairman and the setting up of certain office equipment to begin to network with every province and diocese in the Anglican Communion. This is intended to develop an information-sharing exercise on the Internet and is the basis for effective advocacy. No reply from Trinity Church has been received as yet.

b. It is likely that a small meeting will need to be held to discuss the best way of proceeding to increase the effectiveness of advocacy within the Communion. It has been suggested that that would appropriately take place in an area where the needs are currently great, probably in some area of Central Africa.

9. Conclusion

The network needs the earnest prayers of the ACC and the Primates' Meeting and the increasing focus of every part of the Communion if anything is to be done effectively in the area. The problem is immense, as we all know, and can only be addressed by tackling some very specific targets and acquiring some administrative assistance to get the network moving again.

Appendix A
The Anglican Communion International Migrant and Refugee Network

Preamble

The gospel of Jesus Christ calls us to recognise our oneness with all human beings as part of God's creation and as recipients of God's unconditional love. Our Lord calls us through our baptismal covenant to love and care for the stranger, the dispossessed, the uprooted, and the marginalised as our neighbour. We, therefore, affirm the need for the Anglican Communion to commit itself to the alleviation of the suffering of millions who are uprooted and forcibly displaced from their communities, families, and friends.

Mission

The mission of the Anglican Communion International Migrant and Refugee Network is to serve as a catalyst for encouraging prayer, concern, and action on behalf of uprooted and forcibly displaced persons.

Objectives

A. Promote within the Anglican Communion greater awareness of the plight of uprooted and forcibly displaced persons. To accomplish this, the network will:

- Promote programs of theological education of clergy and lay leaders, which underscore the scriptural and doctrinal basis for welcoming and caring for uprooted and forcibly displaced persons.

- Promote programs of spiritual formation, which guide Anglicans to have greater concern for uprooted and forcibly displaced persons.

- Encourage the development of skills in pastoral ministry to serve uprooted and forcibly displaced persons.

- Encourage leadership initiatives within the Anglican Communion, such as the development of pastoral letters by bishops, participation in public forums, and the cultivation of the media to promote understanding of the plight of uprooted and forcibly displaced persons; participation in conferences; and training that emphasises the responsibilities of Anglicans to serve uprooted and forcibly displaced persons.

B. Recognise the plight of our Anglican brothers and sisters who are victims of forcible displacement and who need our prayers and support and commend the exceptional courage and leadership exercised on behalf of these victims by certain members of the Anglican Communion.

C. Encourage the development of effective advocacy on behalf of uprooted and forcibly displaced persons within the Anglican Communion, as well as within its individual provinces. Such advocacy should focus on the policies and practices of appropriate international bodies, especially the United Nations, the World Council of Churches, and those of individual governments as these affect the well-being and safety of uprooted and forcibly displaced persons.

D. Promote recognition of the needs and contributions of refugees, asylum seekers, and immigrants within our parishes and communities and develop policies to combat forces that inhibit hospitality to these new members of our societies.

E. Encourage prayer, worship, and study experiences that express the solidarity of the Anglican Communion with uprooted and forcibly displaced persons.

F. Promote greater cooperation within the Anglican Communion on behalf of uprooted and forcibly displaced persons by:

- Designating contact persons in every province whose responsibility would be to develop and guide this work. (All Primates were requested to this as expressed at the sixth Anglican Consultative Council, in 1984. See Proceedings of ACC-6, page 126, resolution 39.)

- Increase the commitment of personal and material resources on behalf of uprooted and forcibly displaced persons.

G. Seek opportunities to link the work of the network with other ecumenical bodies, locally, nationally, and internationally.

Appendix B
Lambeth Conference 1998

Resolution 1.5: Uprooted and Displaced Persons

This conference commits its members to:

(a) Promote within the Anglican Communion and beyond a greater awareness of the plight of uprooted and forcibly displaced persons, including indigenous peoples, and the causes of such disruption, including Third World debt, religious conflict, economic deprivation, political oppression, and environmental degradation;

(b) Recognise the plight of our brothers and sisters who are victims of forcible displacement and encourage prayer, worship, and study experiences which express the solidarity of the Anglican Communion with uprooted and forcibly displaced persons, commending the exceptional courage and leadership exercised on behalf of these victims by certain members of the Anglican Communion;

(c) Encourage effective advocacy on behalf of uprooted and forcibly displaced persons within the Anglican Communion, as well as within its individual provinces;

(d) Promote greater cooperation within the Anglican Communion on behalf of uprooted and displaced persons by designating contact persons in every province whose responsibility would be to develop and guide this work, and by increasing the commitment of personal and material resources for this work (all Primates were requested to this as expressed at the sixth Anglican Consultative Council in 1984; see Proceedings of ACC-6, page 126, resolution 39);

(e) Encourage the revitalisation of the Anglican Communion International Migrant and Refugee Network to assist the Anglican Communion in this work.

International Anglican Women's Network 1999

—LIZ BARNES, COORDINATOR

It gives me great pleasure to deliver a report on the activities of the International Women's Network for the past year. The year has been an exceptionally exciting one, and the response to the formation of this network from the provinces has been so encouraging. We now have representation in thirty-five of the provinces and contact with numerous women's organisations within the Anglican Communion. Our database has in excess of 150 names and addresses.

The results of the questionnaire, which was sent to the various names received from the Primates, were well received and far exceeded our expectations. This proves the necessity of this network and the important role it will play in the future. (A schedule of these results will be tabled at the meeting.) It is most encouraging and enlightening to learn of the various needs, what the women of the Church require, and what they will be expecting from the network.

I was most privileged to attend the Mothers Union World Wide Council meeting in July 1998, which enabled me to obtain further contacts. However, the exposure that the network received at the ACC networks booth in the Marketplace at Lambeth was tremendous, encouraging, and of the utmost importance. Not only were we able to promote the vision, but also we were able to listen to views, ideas, and requirements. It was so gratifying to realise that this network is perceived with such postiveness and commitment by all who visited the booth. I was also privileged to address the Spouses' Meeting on the network and received a great deal of encouragement from those present. My visit to Lambeth was such a wonderful experience, both personally and spiritually. My grateful thanks to all those who were responsible in making the trip possible.

The time has now come to put into action the results of the questionnaire and begin, in earnest, the work expected by the women within the Communion from this network. The contacts we have made to date may be divided into three categories—the provinces that can be contacted by e-mail, those that can be contacted via fax, and those where the only means of communication is the unreliable postal services. The latter, fortunately, is the smallest of the three groups. It has been decided that communication will take the form of a "Gazette" (a copy will be presented at the meeting), the format of which will be based on the issues itemised in the platform for action from Beijing.

We have been most fortunate to have had our own web site donated and beautifully designed, on the lines of the "Gazette," and it will be up and running by the end of July 1999. (Full details and visual material will be tabled at the meeting.) This, too, will play a vital role in the success of this network and certainly will give the necessary and required exposure. To maintain a web site has a cost as does postage and faxing, and I sincerely hope that the generosity experienced so far continues.

Finally, this report would not be complete without thanks to certain people: the Reverend Canon John L. Peterson, the Reverend Canon Alice Medcof, and Dr. Sally Thompson for all the love, support, and encouragement, and especially to Almighty God for affording me the opportunity to be involved in this most exciting and important venture.

International Anglican Youth Network

—Peter Ball, for the Inter-Anglican Youth Network

July 1999

The partnership with the Church Mission Society (CMS) proved extremely successful in bringing together young Anglicans for the Gathering in August 1997. A varied programme was arranged, including a residential conference at Lampeter in Wales, as well as visits to dioceses in England, Scotland, and Wales. In addition, the participants in the Gathering attended Greenbelt, which is an annual Christian Arts Festival; they contributed to the worship and led a workshop at this event.

Maintaining contact with participants since the Gathering has been through a regular prayer diary circulated to everyone, and there has been regular communication with most provinces. This prayer diary is to be maintained but will be distributed on an annual basis in the future. We have also been able to circulate resource material for Youth Sunday to friends and colleagues in the provinces; this is produced in England by an ecumenical group and made available to the Youth Network.

The Gathering conference presented an opportunity to reflect upon and consider the themes of the Lambeth Conference. A report was prepared and submitted to the Lambeth Conference, which proved to be a way in which the voice of young adults could be heard by the bishops. There was a plenary session at the Lambeth Conference on youth work, which was introduced by the bishop of Horsham and Pete Ward, the Archbishop's adviser in youth ministry. This plenary featured a video presentation of interviews with Gathering participants from different provinces and a live interview with some participants who were able to be at the Lambeth Conference.

One of our constant concerns has been to increase the profile of the network. At the Lambeth Conference we were able to do this by participating in the Marketplace with a display stand. Several young adults were available during the conference to talk with bishops and visitors. We were delighted to be supported by the Church of England Children's Society and the Anglican Family Network in putting this display together.

A significant way in which young adults were also involved in the Lambeth Conference was as stewards. Several participants from the Gathering were successful in applying to act as stewards and found this to be a challenging, sometimes tiring, but very worthwhile experience.

The last few years have been busy for the Youth Network. We have rejoiced in being able to come together for the Gathering in 1997 and in being able to make a contribution in different ways at the Lambeth Conference. We look forward to building on these experiences and developing our work further as we move into the new millennium

It had been hoped that a meeting of the network might have been arranged in 1999, but this has not been possible. Discussion will be taking place around the time of the meeting of ACC-11 to plan for the next network meeting.

ANGLICAN CONGRESS

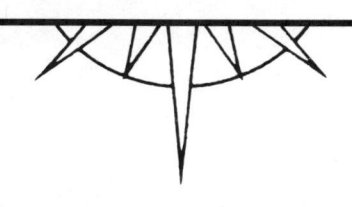

An Anglican Congress in the New Millennium: A Background Paper for ACC-11

As early as the Anglican Consultative Council meeting in Singapore in 1987 an outline for a "possible model for the future" Anglican Communion work was suggested, allowing "periodically there could be an Anglican Congress with wider representation from the dioceses of the Anglican Communion." There have been two Anglican Congresses, one in 1954 and the second in 1963. The only other similar type of gathering took place in 1908 in London, called the Pan-Anglican Congress.

The Lambeth Conference of 1948 called "that a Congress representative of the Anglican Communion be held." The General Convention of the Episcopal Church of the United States extended an invitation in 1949 for a congress to be held in the Diocese of Minnesota. Invitations went to the bishop of each diocese and missionary district and included inviting one priest and one lay delegate from each diocese. The 1954 topics included vocation, worship, message, and work.

Following a resolution of the Lambeth Conference of 1958, another Anglican Congress, and this time by invitation of the Anglican Church of Canada, was convened in August 1963 in Toronto. The two continuation bodies of the Lambeth Conference following 1958, the executive officer for the advisory council for mission strategy and the Lambeth consultative body, were responsible for the preparations for this congress. Bishop Stephen Bayne led these efforts.

Out of the second congress came the acceptance of the document entitled "Mutual Responsibility and Interdependence in the Body of Christ," which was described by Dr. Donald Coggan, then Archbishop of York, as "of absolutely first importance." This document was the basis for cooperative mission work within the Communion.

Much has happened in the life of the Anglican Communion since the 1963 congress, including the formation of the Anglican Consultative Council authorised by the 1968 Lambeth Conference and the establishment of the office of the Secretary General of the Anglican Communion. The Secretariat in London serves all the instruments of unity of the Anglican Communion: namely, the Lambeth Conference, the Primates' Meeting, the Anglican Consultative Council, and the Archbishop of Canterbury in his international role.

In considering the possibility of holding a third Anglican Congress, attention would need to be paid to:

- The purpose of the event
- Its relation, if any, to the instruments of unity
- The serious issues raised in appendix II of the Inter-Anglican Theological and Doctrinal Commission's 1996 *Virginia Report*
- The appropriate representation for each diocese and the mechanism for selecting representatives

- How the congress would be funded, including pre- and post-congress expenses
- Which church would initiate an invitation to provide hospitality
- How the officers of the Communion would engage in pre-congress preparation and post-Congress follow-up

The Joint Standing Committee of the Primates and the Anglican Consultative Council meeting in March 1995 came to a general agreement that a large gathering of Anglicans should be held. It would be in the form of a celebration, meeting in small groups for business and the whole number gathering for festival events. The year 2003 was suggested as being a midpoint between two Lambeth Conferences. It was felt that the congress should be held in a place where the Anglican Church was experiencing growth, with Africa being the most appropriate place. Considerations include: accessibility, moderately priced accommodation, and a country where visa regulations would allow for a representation of the Communion easily to attend.

The Inter-Anglican Theological and Doctrinal Commission in an appendix to *The Virginia Report* gave a cautious opinion on the place of an Anglican Congress in the life of the Communion. While the commission did not see a congress becoming a fifth instrument of unity, it did acknowledge that a congress might from time to time offer the Communion an opportunity for renewal of its life witness and mission. The ACC meeting in Panama in 1996 called for a feasibility study and a committee to examine a process for a congress. Meetings have been held in this regard. The Joint Standing Committees of the Primates and ACC in their March 1998 meeting stressed the importance of the role of laity in the Church and how this proposed congress could help strengthen that. They gave approval to "the proposal to hold and plan an Anglican Congress early in the twenty-first century."

The feasibility group, in consultation with ACO staff, prepared a report to ACC-11. MISSIO, the Mission consultation of the Anglican Communion, in April 1999 was interested in the idea of a congress and in a note to the Secretary General made some suggestions of how to proceed.

Support for the idea of an Anglican Congress has come from some provinces, including the Anglican Church of Australia, the Church of England, and the Church of the Province of Southern Africa. The latter made specific suggestions about topics and issues that it felt were of global significance. The Anglican Communion Office has begun receiving names of possible clerical and lay representatives who might assist in consultation about planning our congress. The feasibility group meeting in London drafted a possible mission statement:

> Christian witness in today's world requires listening, speaking, and sharing in the joys and pains, as well as the mutual concerns, of our global family. An Anglican Congress can strengthen that witness as well as challenge the Communion, laity and clergy alike, to move into the future affirming God's people and committing itself to God's world, God's creation. By speaking the truth in love, walking together by faith, and being open to the Holy Spirit, we can then, through our baptism in Christ, celebrate with "a new heart and a new spirit" being confident that "the truth shall make us free" (John 8:32).

New Heart, New Spirit: Fourth Anglican Congress, 2003

This paper represents the work of the Anglican Congress feasibility group meeting in London from May 13 to 15, 1999. The committee included Presiding Bishop John Paterson, Ms. Judith Conley, Mr. John Rea, Ms. Maureen Sithole, and Bishop Fernando Soares, along with the Secretary General and staff members.

Purpose

Christian witness in today's world requires listening, speaking, and sharing in the joys and pains, as well as the mutual concerns, of our global family. An Anglican Congress can strengthen that witness as well as challenge the Communion, laity and clergy alike, to move into the future affirming God's people and committing itself to God's world, God's creation. By speaking the truth in love, walking together by faith, and being open to the Holy Spirit, we can then, through our baptism in Christ, celebrate with "a new heart and a new spirit" being confident that "the truth shall make us free" (John 8:32).

The congress will be grounded in and nourished by:

- Our scriptural faith
- Our common baptism
- The complementary ministries of lay and ordained
- The richness of experience of our global Church
- Our witness to Christ
- The goodness of God's creation

Within this broad purpose, the congress will provide opportunity for:

- Celebration
- Sharing
- Affirmation
- Consultation
- Mutual appreciation and understanding

Through the following specific objectives:

1. To celebrate the richness and diversity of lay ministry worldwide
2. To identify examples of mission and ministry, as well as the structures and processes that enable mission and ministry, at every level in the Church's life.

Venue

It is important that there is strong local support. The organisation of the congress should be a joint venture between the host church and the Anglican Communion Office. There will have to be clarity about the financial commitment of the host church.

Venues, which are to be investigated, are Hong Kong, Cape Town, Accra, Nairobi, Gaborone, and Amman.

Membership

It is suggested that each diocese in the Communion should be asked to send a group of five, of whom three should be lay and at least one person should be a woman and one person should be under the age of twenty-eight. The recommendation in appendix II of *The Virginia Report* is:

> Membership of the Congress should include laity, deacons, priests, and bishops. The Archbishop of Canterbury would preside and be accompanied by a number of Primates, as well as by other bishops. Efforts should be made to symbolize the personal, collegial, and communal aspects of the ministry of the Archbishop. At the same time as the unity of the Church is made visible, the recognition of the diversity of God's gifts should also be expressed. There should be opportunity to show how plurality and unity are held together within the one fellowship.

Funding

The treasurer will be seeking financial information from the suggested venues in order to put together a cost appraisal for ACC-11.

Programme

There will be celebration of Anglican diversity and unity through worship, Bible studies, and the telling of stories.

Appendix II of *The Virginia Report* states: As an international congress, it would not be appropriate for decisions or resolutions to be taken. A message to the Communion might be an appropriate form of communication (May 1999).

Anglican Congress Feasibility Data: Preliminary Financial Appraisal

—MICHAEL NUNN, DIRECTOR OF FINANCE AND ADMINISTRATION

August 11, 1999

This paper summarises the financial implications of a decision to hold a congress in the year 2003.

Cost Considerations

At this stage, accurate cost estimates are not available. Some costs, i.e., travel and accommodation, can be estimated with reasonable confidence. Other costs, e.g., preparatory meetings, additional staff requirements, communications needs, and so forth, can only be guessed at until more detailed planning is done.

It is anticipated that the organisation of a congress would be a joint venture between the Anglican Communion Secretariat and the host church.

The experience of the 1998 Lambeth Conference indicates that, as plans are formulated and requirements specified, costs will increase. This was particularly true in the area of technical support—public address, video link systems, translation equipment, and so forth. Such costs can only be determined accurately in negotiation with suppliers, preferably in the host country. In the meantime, generous assumptions have to be made about the potential cost.

It is assumed for cost purposes that the representation will be five delegates per diocese as suggested by the ACC-11 design group. There are 621 dioceses, giving a total of 3,105 delegates. Allowing for consultants, communicators, stewards, a chaplaincy team, translators, staff, and guests, the estimated numbers are 3,515, of which it is assumed 3,155 would be fee-paying (all the delegates and half of the communicators).

Possible Venues

The ACC-11 design group suggested a number of alternative venues for consideration. Three of these, i.e., South Africa, Hong Kong, and Jordan, have confirmed that suitable facilities are available. Costing information has been provided from each of these venues. Travel costs used have been provided by MTS and adjusted to allow for inflation.

Travel Costs

It is anticipated that, in principle, delegates and some communicators will be responsible for their own travel costs. The total costs of flights, in round figures, are calculated as follows:

South Africa	£3,067,000
Hong Kong	£3,358,000
Jordan	£3,260,000

Costs of visas and travel to and from airports in the home countries will be additional to this.

Congress Costs

The congress budget would need to be financed by fees charged to the delegates (plus some communicators).

Combining figures from the host churches with estimates of other expected costs, the budget totals currently appear, in round figures, as follows:

South Africa	£2,808,000
Hong Kong	£7,979,000 (net of local subsidy)
Jordan	£3,548,000

As there is a tremendous difference between these figures, it should be explained that in South Africa university facilities are envisaged, whereas in Hong Kong it would be necessary to use a convention centre and hotel accommodation. The figures for Jordan are more tentative, but hotel accommodation is envisaged. It is not clear if university accommodation can be used in Jordan. If so, the cost would be significantly less.

It must be emphasised that these cost estimates are preliminary and approximate. If it is decided to hold a congress, a lot more work will need to be done in looking at the detailed requirements and the consequent costs. Furthermore, currency fluctuations can make a significant difference to the sterling figures before 2003.

The cost estimates, as they stand at present, are attached as appendix B, expressed in sterling. An additional note giving the Hong Kong data in Hong Kong dollars forms appendix D.

Based on the present figures, there would be a need to charge a fee of about £890 ($1,425) per person to meet the budget for South Africa, £2,529 ($4,050) for Hong Kong, and £1,125 (or $1,800) for Jordan.

A schedule of the fee implications for the member churches is attached as appendix C. Appendix D combines fees and airfares.

An Assistance Fund

Because of the considerable inequities in the world economy, it is clear that many delegates would need assistance with the costs of attendance. The extent of the help needed could be arrived at only in consultation with the member churches. It is likely to be considerable.

Using the Lambeth Conference as a point of reference and assuming the average travel cost for the participants was £750, the total fees plus fares (bishops and spouses together) were about £2,700,000 ($4,300,000). Of this, some £760,000 ($1,200,000) was met from the assistance fund. Most of the assisted churches provided some part of the cost from their own resources.

In understanding the figures, two significant factors need to be kept in mind. (i) The Lambeth Conference was partially financed by the Inter-Anglican budget and other donations. (ii) The Lambeth Conference assistance fund finished in surplus. Total contributions were £1,200,000.

For the congress, using the lowest set of figures (South Africa) and allowing for some cost escalation overall, the total fees and fares (for five delegates as opposed to two at the Lambeth Conference) could be in the region of £6,000,000. Thus, unassisted dioceses would need to produce over twice as much to cover their own fees and fares as was the case for the Lambeth Conference. Assisted dioceses, arguably, might require the equivalent of the help they received for the Lambeth Conference, plus the full cost of the additional three people who would be attending the congress. A rough calculation based on this assumption indicates a possible need of £2,470,000 ($3,950,000). Hopefully, other factors will come into play to reduce this need. It is possible, for example, that the individuals chosen to attend may be able to find resources to support themselves, rather than be dependent on their dioceses. However, it must be assumed that a substantial fund may be needed.

Fifteen churches contributed to the Lambeth Conference assistance fund in the following bands:

1				£555,000
1				£340,000
2	Between £80,000	and		£100,000
1				£35,000
2	Between £10,000	and		£20,000
8	Up to			£5,000

To accumulate a fund of £2,470,000, the contributions would need to be about double the amounts contributed for the Lambeth Conference assistance fund.

The contributing churches would therefore need to meet their own costs at more than double the Lambeth Conference level and possibly contribute twice as much to the congress assistance fund as they did to the Lambeth Conference assistance fund.

Cash Flow Requirements

Substantial costs will be incurred ahead of the congress in administration and preparatory meetings. It will therefore be necessary to request early payment of a proportion of the congress fees and early contributions to the assistance fund, possibly twenty percent in each case.

Quality of Data

It should be understood that, at the time of preparing this paper, the amount of hard data available about congress costs is limited. The data on airfares and accommodation costs is largely based on reality, but some of the other figures are guesswork.

Between now and the council meeting in September, it may be possible to improve the quality of the data. If necessary, I will provide an update of this information at that point.

Meanwhile, again in the light of the South Africa figures, a minimum target cost estimate of £6,000,000 (including travel) is probably not unrealistic. The Hong Kong figures are much higher and indicate a total net cost in the region of £11,300,000. The Jordan figures, which are less certain at this stage, indicate £6,800,000.

A Smaller Congress

The ACC-11 design group has suggested five representatives per diocese. This supersedes an earlier suggestion of four per diocese. Clearly, a smaller congress would reduce the cost. Reduction to four representatives would reduce airfares by twenty percent. The congress budget, however, would not decrease to the same extent. The accommodation costs would reduce pro rata, but other costs (administration, preparatory process, and so forth) may not be very different.

It is estimated that on the South Africa figures, the congress budget would decrease by 5.5 percent. The fees per person would be higher, as the fixed costs would be shared among fewer people. The overall reduction in cost to the member churches (fares and congress costs combined) as a result of a reduction to four representatives per diocese is estimated at thirteen percent. Estimated total costs (reducing from the £6,000,000 "minimum target cost"' estimate) become £5,200,000.

It is estimated that on the Hong Kong figures, where the accommodation costs are a greater proportion of the total, the reductions would be 9 percent on the congress budget and 12.5 percent overall. Estimated net costs become £9,900,000.

It is estimated that on the Jordan figures, which are more tentative than the others, the reductions would be eight percent on the congress and fourteen percent overall. Estimated costs become £5,900,000.

Anglican Congress: Presentation

—Mrs. Judy Conley, United States

I'd like to begin this presentation with a reference to something that I heard earlier. Professor John Pobee opened his remarks by stating that he did not want to read his paper, because in order for him to be himself he wanted to speak to us face to face. He wanted to be related to the community, and this has been a thread throughout the presentations that have been made—the thread of face-to-face dialogue and the need for being in community or, if you will, the Communion. So, I would like to suggest that the presentation that Maureen Sithole and I will make today illustrates the premise for the Anglican Congress. What I will do is ask you to refer to the first sheet in your notes, which is dated September 18, Saturday, 10:00 A.M. What I will do—rather than to rehearse verbatim all that you have before you—is to attempt to offer a brief history of how we got to this point and highlight certain areas in the report that I think would be helpful for you to know before you entertain a resolution that will be presented on behalf of the Standing Committee.

At ACC-10 in Panama it was decided by way of resolution that the Standing Committee would be asked to entertain a feasibility study, to be done by several members of the Standing Committee, to determine whether or not this would be something that we could consider as a body. The feasibility study began with the Secretary General and me gathering some data—just preliminary data—from our travel agent, to find out where the most feasible place would be for such an event to be held. We did that, and we did some further work on what we thought might be helpful, and it was presented to the Standing Committee. The Standing Committee then approved what we had done, and we met this past May with the design committee. You will see the results from the meeting with the design committee in the resolution. On the pink sheet on the first page, I would like to call your attention to the fact that there have been two previous Anglican Congresses, the first in 1954 and the last in 1963, which was approximately thirty-six years ago. The second congress came to the acceptance of the doctrine entitled *Mutual Responsibility and Interdependence in the Body of Christ*. This document was the basis for cooperative mission work within the Communion. In 1995, the general agreement was that a large gathering of the Anglican Communion should be held, and that was then highlighted once again in *The Virginia Report*, devoting a whole section—appendix II—to the reference of an Anglican Congress. The Priorities Working Group report, which you have, also emphasises the need for such a gathering. You will hear again, when the MISSIO report is offered, an affirmation of the need for such an event. In addition to the groups that I have mentioned, several of our provinces have suggested and offered their support for an Anglican Congress, those being the Anglican Church of Australia, the Church of England, and the Church of the Province of Southern Africa.

I would like to now read on the blue sheet the purpose of the Anglican Congress.

The Christian witness in today's world requires listening, speaking, and sharing in the joys and pains, as well as the mutual concerns of our global family. An Anglican Congress can strengthen that witness, as well as challenge the Communion, laity and clergy alike, to move into the future, affirming God's people and committing itself to God's world, God's creation, by speaking the truth in love, walking together in faith, and being open to the Holy Spirit. We can then, through our baptism in Christ, celebrate with a new heart and a new spirit, being confident that the truth shall make us free. And we have agreed that if this is accepted, we would like to use the theme that has been highlighted—a new heart and a new spirit. On the back of that page, what we have done is provided a way for you to see that this will not be just a body, but an inclusive body:

> "The Archbishop of Canterbury would preside and be accompanied by a number of Primates, as well as by other bishops. Efforts should be made to symbolise the personal, collegial, communal aspects of the ministry of the Archbishop. At the same time, as the unity of the Church is made visible, the recognition of the diversity of God's gifts should also be expressed. There should be opportunity to show how plurality and unity are held together within one fellowship."

You have on the yellow sheets a fairly in-depth feasibility study on our finances and what the financial implications are for such an event. We have looked at several different areas of the world and have offered you three in terms of where we think it would be most feasible to hold such an event—South Africa, Hong Kong, and Jordan. I had the privilege of being in South Africa this past summer, so I have a very good sense of what the cost will be there, and I would suggest that there is a strong possibility that they might be even a little less than what has been offered. I will end my portion of the presentation and ask Maureen to present the resolution to you, but I would like to leave you with three questions to respond to when you deliberate on the resolution.

The first is, Is mutual responsibility and interdependence not a two-way street? The second is, If the laity can provide most of the funding for the Primates and bishops to meet, can they not in turn exercise their leadership under pressure and assist this primarily lay-led event? And finally, I go back to something that our Secretary General mentioned in his presentation, although he did not use the initials, and it's WWJD: What would Jesus do?

UNITED NATIONS

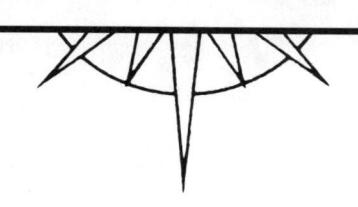

Anglican Communion Office at the United Nations: Overview Report of the Anglican Observer at the United Nations, 1994-1999

—THE RIGHT REVEREND JAMES HAMILTON OTTLEY, ANGLICAN OBSERVER

Acknowledgements

May I first begin with a word of thanks to God for his abundant blessing and the strength that he has given me during my tenure as the second Anglican Observer at the United Nations. I would especially like to acknowledge with gratitude the strong support that Trinity Church has given to the Anglican Communion Office at the United Nations through the Trinity Grants Program. Trinity Church has been instrumental in its support for the office since its inception in 1991 and continues to be a strong advocate for this ministry, which serves the worldwide Anglican Communion. The Most Reverend Edmond Browning, recent Presiding Bishop, and the present Presiding Bishop, the Most Reverend Frank L. Griswold III, and the Episcopal Church in the United States have played a tremendous role in supporting this ministry by providing office space and many other resources that facilitate the office's daily activities. Archbishop Carey has been most gracious and very supportive of this ministry, as has the Anglican Consultative Council under the able leadership of the Reverend Canon John Peterson. The advisory council of the Anglican UN office has been a continuing source of financial and advisory support and counsel at various stages of this ministry.

Thanks must be given to the bishop of the Diocese of Long Island, the Right Reverend Orris Walker; the bishop of New York, the Right Reverend Richard Grin; the bishop of Connecticut, the Right Reverend Coleridge; and the bishop of Southern Ohio, the Right Reverend Herbert Thompson. Thanks also to the persons who have served as staff members and volunteers during the time that I have been in the office: the Reverend Don Cichelli, Mrs. Magdaly Zayas, Ms. Barbara Hernandez, Ms. Ruby Norfolk, the Right Reverend Theophilus Annobil, the Reverend Johncy Itty, Ms. Nancy Courtner, the Reverend Jeffery Golliher, Miss Yasmeen Granville, Mr. Richard Mugenzi, Ms. Megan VanHart, Ms. Carolyn Gayle, Mr. Richard Kim, and Ms. Attiba Pertilla.

Introduction

The Anglican United Nations Office is a unique ministry where the Anglican family demonstrates its care and concern for those who are suffering social, political, and economic injustice. This office plays a key role in actively working to affirm the dignity and well-being of all seventy million members of the Anglican family in 165 countries around the world.

The Anglican United Nations Office facilitates the delivery of the vast resources of the United Nations to improve the quality of life for the people of the Anglican Communion. The Anglican UN Office also focuses on human needs by bringing biblical and theological perspectives into dialogues involving spiritual leaders, heads of governments, and leaders of major international and nongovernmental organizations (NGOs).

The Anglican UN Office not only is a high-level diplomatic forum for advocating the concerns of member churches of the Anglican Communion, but also is deeply involved at the forefront of a number of social issues. The office is the Anglican Communion's direct link with the United Nation's 184 member states, 12 social service agencies, and 2,500 nongovernmental organizations from around the world that interact at various levels to implement the goal of the UN charter "to promote social progress and better standards of life in larger freedom."

As the second Anglican Observer, I began my ministry in this office in October 1994. In my brief four-year tenure, I strongly believe that we have made tremendous progress in expanding both the dimensions and scope of the activities of the Anglican United Nations Office. Much of my time has involved traveling, attending various meetings, giving speeches and sermons, and attending a variety of diplomatic, religious, and social functions related to the ministry of the Anglican UN Office. We have also been involved in arranging meetings at the UN for bishops and others of the provinces of the Communion. Forums have been part of our *modus operandi*.

1995

The list of activities involving this office during my four-year tenure began with attending the social summit in Copenhagen, which is the United Nations World Summit Conference for Social Development. I then travelled to the Great Lakes region of Africa in 1995, stopping in Burundi and then in Rwanda, to serve as a mediator between the government and other forces in Burundi. There my visit coincided with the visit of Archbishop Desmond Tutu, who served as president of the All-African Conference of Churches. In Rwanda, at the invitation of Archbishop Carey, I explored the opportunities for promoting reconciliation and a peaceful transition toward a stable government and to help prepare the way for Archbishop Carey's visit to Rwanda in May of the following year. The Anglican Church in Korea then invited me to Korea to discuss concerns about the just settlement of the comfort women case, where a number of Korean and other Asian women were brutalized in areas under Japanese occupation during World War II. I attended a meeting on the ethical and spiritual dimensions of social progress organized by the UN Secretariat; this meeting took place in Bled, Slovenia, and focused on ethical and spiritual issues as they shape the direction of social progress in countries throughout the world.

During the beginning of my tenure I also had the pleasure of visiting a number of churches and diocesan conventions, including the dioceses of Philadelphia, Ohio, and Long Island. Speaking at these forums afforded me an opportunity to relate the global ministry of the Anglican Communion Office at the United Nations in local terms and to develop a fuller awareness of major political, economic, social, and religious issues confronting our global community.

The problem and issue of land mines was of concern to our office and ministry and a major issue with which a number of countries throughout the world continue to struggle. In responding to this problem, I wrote to President Clinton and members of his cabinet regarding the situation. In response to our efforts, President Clinton personally wrote to us to acknowledge the gravity of the matter and steps his administration would be taking in trying to resolve this issue.

In September of 1995, I had the opportunity to represent the Communion and also speak on behalf of the World Council of Churches at the Fourth World Conference on Women at the United Nations.

I informed both the religious and secular communities in our world that there were indeed alternative perspectives on issues of gender and social development than those advanced by other members of the household of faith.

As this office is also a ministry for the promotion of human rights, we were involved in advocating the successful release of the nephew of Ms. Rigoberta Menchu, the Nobel Peace Prize Laureate, from Guatemala. This office then coordinated with other NGOs, UNHCR, and the State Department to advocate for refugees' safety in Guatemala. Efforts are being made to minimize the tensions surrounding refugees' return. In the latter months of 1995, my office was also involved in several other ministries, such as promotion of the advancement of women, protection of the rights of the child, special refugee cases, French nuclear testing in the Pacific, and educational resources programs.

1996

In 1996 this office was involved in several activities as well. As the Anglican Observer I had an opportunity to engage in a variety of multifaceted tasks that raised the profile of the office and the Communion. Among the many diverse activities assumed by this office was meeting with a number of ambassadors, including British ambassador Sir John Weston, Ambassador Victor Marrero of the United States, Ambassador Rex Horoi of the Solomon Islands, Ambassador Dejammet of France, Ambassador Reyn of Belgium, Ambassador Terence of Burundi, Ambassador Castaneda-Cornejo of El Salvador, Ambassador Petrella of Argentina, and representatives from many other countries around the world. I also spoke to many government leaders from Latin America, Africa, Asia, Europe, and North America, both at United Nations functions and in other forums. This office also played an important role that year in helping the indigenous people of Salta, Argentina, to have their voices and grievances heard by government officials. Without our intervention in this matter this may not have been possible. This office continued its effort in sharing information about the consequences of land mines on civilian populations of the world. Our office was invited to share our thoughts and ideas at various permanent missions to the UN, and our support was actively sought by the then UN Secretary General, Boutrous-Boutrous Ghali, in his effort to both continue and strengthen his leadership at the UN.

That same year our office entered talks with UNICEF about opportunities for partnership in promoting development in war-torn areas such as Liberia and other places. This dialogue with UNICEF also focused on how young people conscripted as child soldiers during the conflict in Liberia could be reintegrated into civil society. The Communion office also served as a liaison between UNICEF and the Anglican Church in Uganda, and as a result of our involvement, the Church in Uganda received support for its AIDS ministry. In the area of human rights, the office was active on a number of different issues that year.

1. We wrote and urged the General Assembly to actively work to strengthen the resources made available to the International Criminal Tribunal, which oversees the prosecution of individuals convicted of crimes of genocide in Rwanda.

2. We contacted the U.S. Congress and wrote to one of its members regarding the increasing reports of conditions of slavery and servitude in Mauritania.

3. We were in contact with the Secretary General over the issue of Tibet and through the UN have sought to urge the government of the People's Republic of China to guarantee the protection of fundamental human rights in Tibet.

4. We participated in a multi-religious service that launched the UN study on the impact of armed conflict on children. Archbishop Desmond Tutu gave the keynote address at this event.

5. We met with Ambassador Victor Marrero, one of the U.S. ambassadors to the UN, in order to express our deep concerns about Zaire and to determine what steps the United States and the UN will undertake to expedite humanitarian relief efforts. (This meeting took place two days prior to the U.S. commitment to send troops.)

That same year the Anglican Communion Office played an active role in the fifty-second session of the United Nations Human Rights Commission in Geneva, Switzerland. It had the opportunity to interact with a number of governmental and nongovernmental representatives on a wide range of different issues related to human rights and the preservation of peace and security. The commission's mandate was to examine the broad spectrum of human rights in their civil, political, economic, social, and cultural contexts.

The human rights concerns centred around situations in Cuba, southern Lebanon and western Bekaa, Iran, Zaire, Equatorial Guinea, Myanmar, Afghanistan, Iraq, Sudan, the territory of the former Yugoslavia, Rwanda, and East Timor. The Anglican Office also spoke out on the behalf of those who were still being victimized as a consequence of the political situation in Sudan at the UN Human Rights Commission meeting.

The Anglican Office was also deeply concerned about the harsh impact of the international debt crisis and effects of structural adjustment programs. Adding to that our office was also concerned and committed to finding ways in which provinces and dioceses of the Anglican Communion could strengthen their work in caring for the environment. Our office participated at the United Nations conference on cities (Habitat II), which was held in Istanbul, Turkey. We are especially concerned about environmental issues, as they relate to the broader question of sustainable human development.

The final issue the office focused on that year was disarmament. Our office conducted research into how church structures at the local level can get involved in promoting the cause of peace. Part of this involves lobbying governments and international organizations to support measures that eliminate illegal land mines and the sale and transfer of arms, munitions, and other weapons of mass destruction.

1997

This year began with the Anglican Communion Office establishing links between our office and various churches throughout the Anglican Communion, and also with facilitating dialogue and cooperation within ecumenical circles. In June of that year I was invited to the House of Bishops of the Church of the Province of the West Indies to share information about the Anglican United Nations office as it relates to the UN. I was also invited and had the opportunity to attend an important meeting in Johannesburg, South Africa, which was chaired by the Archbishop of Central Africa, the Most Reverend Khotso Makhulu, who discussed issues affecting the ministry of the Church on the continent of Africa. That same year I was invited to attend the Universal Congress of the Panama Canal, which took place on September 7 to 10, 1997. This meeting allowed us to continue to develop our relationship with the Church of Panama. This meeting also enabled the local church, its leadership, and its people to have their views shared in a global forum that will affect the Church and people there after the year 2000, when the canal will be handed over to Panama. This of course, is a human rights issue for the people of Panama.

Our office also sought to strengthen the cordial ties it already enjoys with the UN Centre for Human Rights. The office was especially asked to consider the possibility of inviting the special rapporteurs of the Secretary General and the Human Rights Commission to provide briefings to church organizations and other nongovernmental organizations.

In May of that year the office hosted a major conference on the international debt crisis. The participants of this conference offered informed, unique, and plausible insights into some of the problems associated with overburdening debt and underdevelopment.

In July of that year the Reverend Johncy Itty and I participated in a meeting regarding the fifty-third session of the UN Human Rights Commission in Geneva. In speaking before the commission, the Reverend Itty called upon member governments of the commission to "work to preserve the territorial integrity of countries that are parties to a cease-fire agreement."

The Anglican Communion Office that year also worked on many other issues with the consultation and cooperation of various governments through their permanent missions at the United Nations. To cite one example, the office was actively involved in responding to a request from the Archbishop of Canterbury's office to look into the human rights situation in Myanmar. The Reverend Itty represented the office and met with the United Kingdom mission to United Nations to discuss that situation and to share our concerns about the political climate within that nation.

This office was also involved that year in the Ministry of the Environment. The Reverend Cannon Jeff Golliher (staff member for the environment) represented the office of the Anglican Observer and was a very significant presence at the meeting of the Commission on Sustainable Development. Dr. Golliher also participated as a member of the World Council of Churches team.

This office on the issue of global economics was very concerned that the current debt crisis was and still is one of the most pressing international problems that faces the world today. The Round Table Conference on the International Debt Crisis provided an opportunity for theological ethicists, investment bankers, economists, social scientists, clergy, experts in the areas of business and finance, and representatives from domestic and international organizations to meet together over a two-day period to evaluate and develop policy proposals and recommendations. The final policy paper, with recommendations, which resulted from this meeting, was circulated throughout the wider Anglican Communion.

For the Ministry in Peace and Security issues, Bishop Theophilus Annobil represented the Anglican UN Office and was active in the meetings of the disarmament commission of the UN. This commission did not limit itself to nuclear disarmament, but also discussed the campaign to eliminate the use of antipersonnel mines as weapons of war.

The latter months of 1997 found the office making efforts toward development and funding issues. Ms. Nancy Courtner, then the office's development coordinator, coordinated a forum discussion with distinguished speakers on the topic entitled "Religion . . . Cause or Cure of Global Conflict?" The office then hosted a luncheon reception honouring twelve archbishops from various parts of Africa, ambassadors, and other key donor prospects.

1998

This year began with several issues and activities, among them a meeting attended by myself, Bishop James Ottley, and Bishop Paul Moore, retired bishop of New York, along with Ms. Gillian Martin Sorensen, assistant Secretary General, Office of External Relations at the UN, to discuss concerns and issues about human rights on a global scale.

In March of that year I met with Mrs. Joanne Fox-Przeworski, director of the United Nations Environment Programme, of the New York regional office, to discuss environmental and ecological issues as they relate to sustainable human development.

In April, the Anglican Communion Office met with a senior official of the IMF and sought to continue its ongoing dialogue with that body on matters related to poverty and sustainable development. The Reverend Dr. Johncy Itty, associate for human rights, and I represented this office during discussions with Mr. Justin B. Zulu, director and special representative of the IMF to the United Nations.

In that same month, the Anglican UN office also participated in a meeting at the Lawyers Committee for Human Rights, which dealt with issues related to human rights in the occupied territories in Palestine. The Reverend Dr. Johncy Itty represented the office at this program, which included representatives from Human Rights Watch and other international human rights organizations.

In May of that year, this office hosted an informational discussion forum dealing with United Nations reform. The program was held at Trinity Church, Wall Street, and attended by a number of distinguished clergy, laypersons, and executives from the Wall Street area.

On the issue of human rights in Africa, the Anglican UN office in response to a request by the Archbishop of Canterbury to look into the political situation in northern Uganda, met with UN Department of Special Political Affairs representatives to discuss the human rights situation, particularly relating to the abduction of children from Uganda to Sudan to be used as soldiers or as wives—a situation that continues to take place within that region.

In July of 1998, the Anglican UN office hosted an informational meeting on the international debt crisis at the Episcopal Church Center in New York. The Reverend Dr. Johncy Itty, who spoke on my behalf as I was recuperating from surgery, moderated the meeting. The principal speakers that afternoon were Dr. Richard Jolly, economist for the United Nations Development Programme; Ms. Carole Collins of Jubilee 2000; and Dr. Justin B. Zulu of the International Monetary Fund.

In the following month the Reverend Dr. Johncy Itty represented the Anglican UN office at a meeting on peace and security issues at the U.S. mission to the UN, participating in discussions with representatives of other religious and nongovernmental organizations and with Ambassador Soderberg on security issues that were before the UN Security Council.

In September The Reverend Dr. Johncy Itty and I represented the office at a meeting with the World Bank. There we engaged in discussions with Mr. Alfredo Sfeir-Younis, the representative of the World Bank. Three points were touched upon:

1. The bank is committed to the eradication of poverty.
2. The bank values the input of NGOs.
3. Key issues of environmental sustainability and financial development.

The conclusion to this year had our office involved in a series of meetings including a conflict resolution forum on Rwanda, a meeting at the UN on the loss of the U.S. vote in the General Assembly due to debt, meetings on the ongoing conflicts in Congo, Sudan, Angola, Liberia, and Sierra Leone, and a conference on the global humanitarian emergencies of 1998 and 1999. Our office was also invited to attend the fiftieth anniversary of the Universal Declaration of Human Rights in New York, which I attended.

1999

Although we are merely in the third month of the year (at the time of this report), this office has been involved in activities, forums, and discussions on a variety of subjects. On January 8, we were invited by the Lawyers' Committee on Human Rights to attend a briefing discussion on human rights violations in southeastern Turkey. A Turkish lawyer briefed us on some of the human rights violations that occurred to her and those continuing to occur to the citizens of that region. Mr. Richard Sabune, a representative of the Anglican Communion office, attended. On the fourteenth of that month our office was invited to attend a briefing at the UN Plaza for U.S. NGOs. On the thirtieth of that month Mr. Sabune also attended a meeting on the global reconciliation service project in Rwanda hosted by Ms. Virginia M. Swain of the Center For Strategic Change in Boston and the Reverend Erisa Mutaabazi, an Anglican priest from Rwanda who is studying in the United States. Other distinguished guests were also in attendance, including human rights lawyers based in Rwanda and in the United States, professors of political science and African Studies, artists and sculptors, and representatives of other NGOs. This was the second meeting between this office and that of Ms. Swain.

In February the UN Mission to the UN and Security Council representatives invited the Anglican Communion Office and other NGOs to a briefing on current global conflicts. Mr. Richard Sabune-Mugenzi and I attended this meeting.

Further Comments and Recommendations

Allow me to say how much I have enjoyed the exercising of the ministry as the Anglican Observer at the UN. I can also say that my colleagues have worked with the same dedication and commitment. They have worked timelessly and unselfishly for this ministry on behalf of the Communion. There have been many hardships endured; however, I am grateful for the strength that comes from God, and thus allowed for a ministry of this nature to move forward even in the face of adversity. As I leave this office I thought it relevant to leave some impressions that might be helpful as you move toward the selection of the next Observer.

1. The Archbishop of Canterbury, the Anglican Consultative Council, the Primates of the Anglican Communion, the advisory council to the Observer and the Office should engage in a dialogue as to the need, philosophy, and accountability of and for the office. It is crucial that the Primates of the Communion have a greater voice in the direction and ministry of the office. There is a need as well for a greater ownership and responsibility for the office by the Primates.

2. There seem to be two ideas at present about the direction of the office. One approach views the office as an advocate on the issues of poverty, justice, and inequality; it views the office as assuming a prophetic and pro-active role in these areas. The second demands that the office not assume a prophetic role in these areas.

    You are aware that this office raised the issues of the international debt crisis, land mines, ecology, globalisation, the need for interfaith dialogue, and women and children as they relate to the issue of poverty in this world.

    We live today in what is described by many as a global village; however, the overwhelming proportion of jobs, and thus of people, are not global. In fact, they are local and regional. Their fate and standards of living depend on the global economy that is controlled by interconnected multinational corporations. "In a world with a population of 5.9 billion (October 26, 1998) the corporations directly employ 70 million workers, but these workers produced 11% of the world's total private output, and the global value of their sales in 1992 was US $5,500 billion, which is 25% more than the total value of world trade in that year" (UNRIED News, no. 19, page 4).

    These are issues that constantly face the United Nations. What is to be the role of the Anglican Observer?

3. The non-prophetic model might view the office as a door knocker and assume a most ceremonial function. In terms of purpose, the question is then to what end?

    Sometime ago I highlighted the ambassadorial function of the Anglican Observer and was rebuked publicly. Since then, however, it is curious to note that the term has been used to refer to the function of the Observer as one who listens, gathers information, and interacts with people. As you can see, this model does not lift up the prophetic ministry model, which is demanded by various churches of the Anglican Communion in the Developing World. It does emphasize listening and the gathering of information, but never pro-active advocacy. Irrespective of the decision on the model taken, the prophetic ministry of the Church should not be guided by the foreign policy of any country where our churches are located; nor should it ever serve the particular interests of any foreign service. Prophetic ministry should not be confused with programs on the social issues of the United Nations. I never saw this office as a program office, but as one that lifted up issues that affected our lives in the world in which we live in. We never had the staff or the money to do programs.

4. Where should the office be? New York seems to be the logical place. If possible, proper residence should be sought within the city, with adequate space to receive guests.

5. The Observer should be from a developing country and his or her term in office should be for three years and renewable. It should be clear what renewable means. In any event, the term of office should be clear from day one.

   How the office is to be funded needs to be made clear before the next Observer is contracted.

6. Sometime after the second year, an evaluation of the office should be made. The Observer's point of view should be read and shared with others, if the evaluation is shared.

7. The advisory council needs to be regularized as I stated at its last meeting. The terms need to be stated clearly, i.e., years of service and what is to be expected as a member of the advisory council.

8. I would like to close by saying that the issue of human rights is in the forefront of many considerations at the United Nations and should always be a part of the concerns of this office.

In conclusion, there is much to learn and much to give as a church. We have a very special model to share as a multiethnic, multilinguistic, and multicultural community of faith, which celebrates unity in the midst of diversity.

I strongly believe that this is a very unique, special, and worthwhile ministry of the Anglican Communion. During my tenure, we have been affirmed by others at the United Nations and the wider community for our prophetic and educational ministry and witness on behalf of the churches of the Communion.

As I move back and forth on the city blocks that separate my office and the United Nations, I come to a small park that looms large in my mind. To get to the United Nations, one must descend a stairway that leads to the park. The stairway hugs a wall on which words from the prophet Isaiah are inscribed: "They shall beat their swords into ploughshares, and their spears into pruning hooks; nation shall not lift up sword against nation, neither shall they learn war any more."

These words form a beautiful, lofty vision of humanity at peace—planting, cultivating, nurturing; this vision of humanity busy bearing life, not destroying it.

It is this vision that has sustained our ministry here. A vision that sends us marching on with hope for peace and justice and a vision that celebrates life and not death.

May the Lord continue to bless us all.

The Anglican Observer's Office at the United Nations

Summary of discussions of the Joint Standing Committee of the ACC and Primates prepared for the meeting of ACC-11, Dundee, Scotland, September 1999.

The Joint Standing Committee has given careful and lengthy consideration to matters relating to the UN Anglican Observer's office at each of its meetings in the three years since ACC-10 in Panama.

In particular, the following issues have been addressed:

- the strategic importance of the Office budgetary provision (24,000 pounds sterling per annum)
- job description (see "Ministry Mission Statement")
- lines of accountability
- role of the New York Advisory Council
- membership of the New York Advisory Council
- relationship to the Office of the Archbishop of Canterbury
- relationship to the Anglican Communion Office
- relationship to the Primates
- relationship to Anglican Communion networks
- the possibility of ecumenical co-operation/communication with the member churches of the Communion

We have received reports both in person and in writing from the Observer and have had the opportunity to consult with the then chairperson of the advisory council, Mr. Tom Chappell.

It is clear that there are still some differences in perception of the role and function of the office. The advisory council has worked very hard to raise a large amount of money on an annual basis to support an expanded office. The Joint Standing Committee has been consistent in its view that a more modest operation is all that is needed.

Bishop James Ottley's contracted period of employment has now been completed, and we have an opportunity during this interregnum to achieve a common understanding of all the matters in the above list, prior to any new appointment being made.

The Joint Standing Committee is grateful to the Episcopal Church in the United States (ECUSA) for the provision of office space and support for the office of the UN Observer. During the present interim period, the staff of ECUSA are offering oversight and support, and this is gratefully acknowledged. It is important that this interim period should not exceed six months, if at all possible.

The Joint Standing Committee has been asked for representatives to meet with members of the advisory council in January 2000 in order to work through all these matters and move to making the next appointment, in order that the work and presence of the office at the UN continue in the best possible manner. It will be important that such a meeting take place, with good preparation having been undertaken beforehand.

This will provide an important opportunity for the ACC to make clear that the office of the Anglican observer at the UN is an ACC post, to which we are all committed. The advisory council has an important part to play, but it should be made up of official representatives of the Communion as and where possible, of the Archbishop of Canterbury, and of supporters of the office from around the United States and the Communion.

Accordingly, the Joint Standing Committee recommends the following to this meeting of ACC-11:

1. That the gratitude of the ACC be expressed to the members of the advisory council for their work in support of the office of the Anglican Observer at the UN.

2. That the office of the Anglican Observer at the UN be continued, subject to the following:

    2.1 That the Joint Standing Committee ensures representation at the proposed January 2000 meeting with members of the advisory council and satisfies itself on the following matters:

    2.1.1 The role of the Observer and the number of staff in the office;

    2.1.2 An agreed job description for the appointment of the next Observer;

    2.1.3 Line management arrangements through the Secretary General of the Communion;

    2.1.4 Clear lines of accountability;

    2.1.5 Location of the Observer's office;

    2.1.6 Possible ecumenical cooperation;

    2.1.7 The role of the advisory council and appointment by the Standing Committee of the chairperson of that Council;

    2.1.8 A working budget for the next five years; and

    2.1.9 Contributions to that budget.

2.2 Subject to the Standing Committee being satisfied on these matters, an appointment committee comprising representatives of the Archbishop of Canterbury, the chair and vice chair of the ACC, the Secretary General, and a representative of the advisory council be authorised to select and appoint a new Observer for a term not to exceed five years.

2.3 That budgetary provision be continued as recommended by the Inter-Anglican Finance Committee.[1]

Office of the Anglican Observer at the United Nations

The finance committee has noted that consideration is being given to the appointment of a new Observer with a suggestion that it be for a five-year period. It notes also that projections from the treasurer of the advisory council in New York envisage a staged increase in the Inter-Anglican budget contribution to the budget of the office from its present level of $40,000 to $60,000 in the year 2002.

In the light of this and the previous history of this post, the committee would like to make the following observations and suggestions:

- The committee recognises the great potential value of an appointment to this strategic ministry.

- The Inter-Anglican budget does not reflect the staged increase assumed by the advisory council treasurer. At this point, it is not practicable to increase the Inter-Anglican budget contribution to the office.

- The New York Advisory Council is a voluntary group, not a legal entity, and can have no legal obligation or liability in relation to the financing of the office.

- The committee advises very strongly that no contract of employment should be signed until sufficient financial support is guaranteed.

- Guaranteed support might conceivably be secured through the establishment of a substantial endowment.

- Subject to the securing of financial support, the finance committee suggests that the office should be limited to an Observer with secretarial help and should not expand beyond that.

---

[1] From the report of the Inter-Anglican Finance Committee to the Joint Standing Committees.

A Millennium Prayer

God,
We praise you,
We bless you,
We worship you,
We give thanks to you
For the great love shown to us
By the birth of your Son,
Jesus Christ, two thousand years ago.

Born in Bethlehem,
Child of Mary,
Loved by Joseph,
Friend of Magdalene and John,
Our Saviour:
Revealed in word and sacrament,
Christ, the way, the truth, and the life,
The same yesterday, today, and forever.
Our only hope.

May your Holy Spirit be our guide
As we celebrate our Christian faith
In this new millennium year of jubilee,
Reconciliation, and forgiveness
That we may proclaim with united voice,
Christ has died!
Christ is risen!
Christ will come again!
and bear witness to your love in this broken world.

Blessed be God.
Amen.

—from *Anglican World*

Prayers for the Anglican Communion

O Almighty God, our heavenly Father, who hast called us to be members of the Anglican Communion and to a partnership of churches in all parts of the world: grant, we beseech thee, that we may understand the mission which thou hast entrusted to us, and our duty to those who are separated from us; that penitently recognising our failings in the past, we may go forward in unity and love to the fulfilment of our common work, through Jesus Christ our Lord.

—based on a prayer of the Pan-Anglican Congress, 1908

Almighty God, our heavenly Father, who in thy providence hast made us members of a great family of churches: we pray thee to pour out thy blessing upon the Anglican Communion throughout the world. Grant that we and all its members be faithful to the trust which thou hast committed to us, and advance thy honour in the cause of Christian unity and mission, through Jesus Christ our Lord.

—parish prayer

Resolutions of the Eleventh Meeting of the Anglican Consultative Council

Resolution 1: Welcome to New Provinces—Anglican Church of the Central America Region

Resolved that the Primates having assented, this ACC-11 meeting in Dundee, Scotland, welcomes into membership of the Anglican Consultative Council the Anglican Church of the Central America Region.

Resolution 2: Welcome to New Provinces—Hong Kong Sheng Kung Hui

Resolved that the Primates having assented, this ACC-11 meeting in Dundee, Scotland, welcomes into membership of the Anglican Consultative Council the Hong Kong Sheng Kung Hui.

Resolution 3: Standing Committee Report

Resolved that the report of the Standing Committee of the ACC be received.

Resolution 4: Inter-Anglican Finance Committee

This ACC

(a) Receives the report of the Inter-Anglican Finance Committee; and

(b) Adopts the budget set out in the committee's report subject to the continuing monitoring by the Standing Committee as prescribed in the constitution;

(c) Recognises with gratitude the strong commitment of many of the member churches to the support of the Inter-Anglican budget and the generous support that has been given by the Compass Rose Society membership;

(d) Encourages the member churches to support the Inter-Anglican budget in the coming years;

(e) Acknowledges the generous support given by the Episcopal Church in the United States of America, the Church of England, the Anglican Church of Canada, Trinity Church, Wall Street, and others in assisting in areas not reflected in the core budget of the council.

Resolution 5: Assessments

This ACC asks the Joint Standing Committee to examine the present system for assessing the financial contribution from provinces and report to ACC-12 with recommendations on appropriate criteria on which to base assessments.

Resolution 6: Constitutional Amendments

(a) That the amendments to the constitution set out in the constitutional documents be adopted and referred to the provinces for ratification in accordance with article 10.

(b) That the amendments to the bylaws set out in the constitutional documents be adopted with immediate effect.

(c) Resolved that the *Guidelines for ACC Meetings* set out in the constitutional documents be adopted with immediate effect.

(d) That the Standing Committee consider, and if it thinks fit, adopt an appropriate legal structure for the ongoing work of the council within the framework of a limited company in accordance with legal advice and any directions of the charity commissioners for England and Wales, but so far as possible in all other respects in accordance with the existing constitutional arrangements.

Resolution 7: Anglican Communion Priorities, Strategies, and Budgets

ACC-11

(a) Thanks the Anglican Communion Priorities Working Group for their paper;

(b) Agrees that there are two priorities for the Anglican Communion, namely mission and ecumenism (as they are defined and elaborated in the Anglican Communion Priorities Working Group paper);

(c) Recognises that

   i)   Communications

   ii) Enabling the Communion to meet at various levels

   iii) A strong and effective secretariat

   are all essential for achieving the two Anglican Communion priorities;

(d) Affirms that priorities in the future may be proposed by

   i)   The Archbishop of Canterbury

   ii)   The Primates

   iii) The Anglican Consultative Council

   iv)   The Lambeth Conference

   v)   The ACC Standing Committee

   vi)   The Primates' Standing Committee

   vii) Commissions and networks

   viii) The Anglican Communion Secretariat

(e) Affirms further that the priorities must be decided by the ACC or the Joint Standing Committees.

Resolution 8: ACC Membership

(a) This ACC thanks the membership subcommittee for the work done in response to motions 6, 9, and 26 of ACC-10 and receives this report.

(b) This ACC, noting the additional funding that would be needed in relation to any expansion of the membership of the council or the Standing Committee, considers that no change to the present arrangements can be justified at the present time but requests the Standing Committee to keep the matter under review.

Resolution 9: ACC-12

This ACC

(a) Accepts with gratitude and pleasure the kind invitation of the Most Reverend Peter Kwong, the Archbishop of Hong Kong Sheng Kung Hui (HKSKH) to hold ACC-12 in the Hong Kong Special Administrative Region, People's Republic of China;

(b) Authorises the Standing Committee or such subcommittee as the Standing Committee may think fit to liaise with HKSKH regarding the timing, venue, and incidental arrangements for ACC-12; and

(c) Agrees to make financial provisions for ACC-12.

Resolution 10: Anglican Observer at the United Nations

(a) That the gratitude of the ACC be expressed to Bishop James Ottley for his services over the last four years as Anglican observer at the United Nations and to the members of the advisory council for their work in support of the office of the Anglican observer at the UN.

(b) That the office of the Anglican observer at the UN be continued, subject to the following:

   (i) That the Joint Standing Committee ensures representation at the proposed January 2000 meeting with members of the advisory council and satisfies itself on the following matters:

   1. The role of the observer and the number of staff in the office;
   2. An agreed job description for the appointment of the next observer;
   3. Line management arrangements through the Secretary General of the Communion;
   4. Clear lines of accountability;
   5. Location of the observer's office;

6. Possible ecumenical cooperation;
7. The role of the advisory council and appointment by the Standing Committee of the chairperson of that council;
8. A working budget for the next five years; and
9. Contributions to that budget.

(ii) Subject to the Standing Committee being satisfied on these matters, an appointment committee comprising representatives of the Archbishop of Canterbury, the chair and vice chair of the ACC, the Secretary General, and a representative of the advisory council be authorised to select and appoint a new observer for a term not to exceed five years.

(iii) That budgetary provision be continued as recommended by the Inter-Anglican Finance Committee.

Resolution 11: MISSIO

This ACC

(a) Receives the report of MISSIO to ACC-11, "Anglicans in Mission: A Transforming Journey";

(b) Notes the positive experience of MISSIO in holding each of its meetings in a different part of the Communion, thereby experiencing the life and witness of the local church in its own context, and encourages this way of working to the future commission and to other bodies of the Communion as appropriate;

(c) Endorses the MISSIO proposal to hold a meeting of synodical, provincial, and voluntary mission agencies in the year 2001 to reflect on the roles and responsibilities of the mission agencies, as well as to promote networking and mutual understanding among the older agencies and newer expressions of mission structures;

(d) Asks the Joint Standing Committee to consider the MISSIO suggestion to initiate a review within the Communion of leadership training and clergy formation to identify trends, needs, and problems and how they might be addressed;

(e) Encourages

(i) The provinces and dioceses of the Communion to evaluate the lessons learned during the Decade of Evangelism, with a view to continue and build on the momentum the decade achieved and to keep evangelism as a high profile in the Church's mission; and

(ii) Provinces, dioceses, and parishes to develop and expand appropriate training to equip individuals and congregations for effective work in mission and evangelism;

(f) Recommends the continuation of a Standing Commission on mission that would be called the Inter-Anglican Standing Commission on Mission and Evangelism and that would have functions and membership as detailed on pages 58 and 59 of the MISSIO report, "Anglicans in Mission: A Transforming Journey";

(g) Asks the Joint Standing Committee in consultation with the Inter-Anglican Finance Committee to consider the appointment of a senior-level mission and evangelism staff officer to the Anglican Communion Office when the funds are available, to be responsible for the functions listed on page 60 of the MISSIO report, "Anglicans in Mission: A Transforming Journey."

Resolution 12: Network of Anglicans in Mission and Evangelism (NAME)

This ACC-11

(a) Welcomes and appreciates the desire of groups within the Communion to assist the Communion in its mission and evangelism responsibilities.

(b) Hopes that, in time, it will be possible to welcome the Network of Anglicans in Mission and Evangelism (NAME) as a network working with the Inter-Anglican Standing Commission on Mission and Evangelism.

(c) Requests that NAME comply with the ACC-10 guidelines for networks.

(d) Resolves that for this to happen the following steps must be completed to the satisfaction of the ACC Standing Committee:

   (i) A positive review of the proposal by the provinces and major mission agencies, to be facilitated by the Anglican Communion Office (ACO).

   (ii) Formation of a Secretariat, or staff, and programme committee by NAME that inspires confidence in the network's intentions.

   (iii) Clarification of the membership of NAME, particularly the question of whether the network is open to people or organisations other than individual bishops and institutions/agencies.

   (iv) The working out of a mutually acceptable reporting and financial accountability to the Anglican Consultative Council, by NAME liaising with the Secretary General.

   (v) The establishment of a mutually acceptable working relationship with the mission commission that takes account of the mission commission's mandate while enabling NAME to operate effectively and efficiently.

   (vi) Compliance with other recommendations of MISSIO as set out in appendix B of its report to ACC-11.

(d) Asks the Standing Committee, once all requirements have been met regarding NAME as a network member, to bring a recommendation to ACC-12.

Resolution 13: *The Virginia Report*

This council, noting that *The Virginia Report* was introduced to ACC-10 (Panama 1996) and that Lambeth 1998 welcomed the report and requested the Primates "to monitor a decade of study in each province on the report,"

(a) Requests the Primates to ensure that opportunity is given at provincial and diocesan level for careful and critical study of the report.

(b) Asks that a summary of the report in simple language be made available by the Anglican Communion Office in order to assist further study.

(c) Recommends that *The Virginia Report* be studied by others, such as those working in theological seminaries.

(d) Suggests that seminars be organised as soon as possible to train leaders to facilitate the study of *The Virginia Report* at the local level.

Resolution 14: Anglican Congress

This ACC

(a) Receives the report on the proposed Anglican Congress;

(b) Welcomes the positive suggestion of the Archbishop of Canterbury during the ACC discussion that an Anglican Congress should be held in association with the next Lambeth Conference;

(c) Notes

   (i) The discussions, which date back to ACC-9;

   (ii) Various expressions of support for such a congress;

   (iii) The comment in *The Virginia Report* that acknowledges "the creative opportunity an Anglican Congress might, from time to time, offer the Communion for the renewal of its life, witness, and mission"; and

   (iv) The estimated cost structures and advice of the Inter-Anglican Finance Committee;

(d) Recommends

   (i) That there should be an Anglican Congress in association with the next Lambeth Conference;

   (ii) That such an event should be held in the first decade of the twenty-first century at a place to be determined by the Archbishop of Canterbury in consultation with the Joint Standing Committee;

(iii) That for the congress the Archbishop of Canterbury invites the diocesan bishop and on behalf of the Primates and the ACC invites four other persons, of whom three should be lay and at least one person a woman and one under the age of twenty-eight; and

(e) Requests the Archbishop of Canterbury, the Secretary General, and the Joint Standing Committee to put in hand such planning and financial provision as would make this congress a reality.

Resolution 15: *The Gift of Authority*

The Anglican Consultative Council, recalling that the 1988 Lambeth Conference encouraged ARCIC "to continue to explore the basis in Scripture and tradition of the concept of a universal primacy" and that areas for further work identified at that time included the relationship between Scripture, tradition, and the exercise of teaching authority; collegiality; conciliarity; and the role of the laity in decision making; and the Petrine ministry of universal primacy,

(a) Welcomes the publication of the report entitled *The Gift of Authority: Authority in the Church III* and all other reports of ARCIC II, which have yet to be considered;

(b) Expresses its appreciation to ARCIC for these agreed statements, in particular for *The Gift of Authority*, which seeks to address the issues identified at Lambeth 1988 and to deepen the agreement expressed in previous statements on authority;

(c) Commends these reports to the provinces for careful and critical study over the next five years, particularly with a view to considering any outstanding issues of ecclesiology and authority;

(d) Directs the Inter-Anglican Standing Commission on Ecumenical Relations

   (i) To facilitate and monitor the process of response to *The Gift of Authority* and the other reports that the member churches of the Communion will undertake;

   (ii) To ask helpful questions to the member churches of the Anglican Communion based on the suggested questions circulated to the Primates in May 1999 and those offered by ACC-11; and

   (iii) To report to ACC-13 in 2005.

Resolution 16: Report of the Anglican Peace and Justice Network

This ACC

(a) Receives the report of the Anglican Peace and Justice Network dated April 1999;

(b) Welcomes the breadth of issues with which it is engaged and commends the report to the provinces for reflection and action.

Resolution 17: International Debt—World Bank and IMF

The Anglican Consultative Council, meeting in Dundee between September 14 and 25, 1999, representing the thirty-eight provinces of the Anglican Communion;

- Noting with profound concern the continued burden of unpayable debt upon the poorest people of the world;
- Conscious of the great significance of the biblical and theological concept of Jubilee;
- Recognising the dramatic success of the campaign led by the Jubilee 2000 coalition to bring to the attention of the governments of the world, and to people in general, the moral scandal of unpayable debt;

Resolves,

(a) To call upon all member churches of the Anglican Communion to take action urgently with their governments on the basis of resolutions i.15 and v.2 of the 1998 Lambeth Conference;

(b) To communicate directly with the president of the World Bank, the president of the International Monetary Fund, and the heads of governments of the G8 nations on the occasion of the annual meeting of the World Bank and the IMF to request both urgent action on the basis of agreements reached at the G7 summit in Cologne in June 1999 and further radical action to alleviate the intense suffering in many countries of the world;

(c) To urge Anglicans, together with ecumenical partners, people of other faiths, and all people of goodwill to engage in dialogue with governments of the world in order to seek ways to ensure that the UN targets for halving abject world poverty by 2015 are met.

Resolution 18: International Debt Burden and Anglican Giving

ACC-11 endorses the Lambeth Conference resolution i.15 k and renews Lambeth's call to Primates to challenge their dioceses to fund international development programmes recognised by provinces at a level of at least 0.7 percent of annual total diocesan income.

Resolution 19: International Debt—Anglican Development Projects

This ACC

Noting that,

- The debt under which the countries of the Third World suffer is a shared responsibility, thus it is also necessary to share the solution;

- The transfer of technology has been a very costly process, since such technology has been the property of powerful nations; and
- The authorised loans to countries of the Third World has, in many cases, through abuse benefited only a few;

Now

(a) Resolves to strengthen our efforts and advocacy in favour of the cancellation of the international debt of poor countries;

(b) Asks each of the delegates to ACC-11 to send a letter to each of the presidents of the countries in the group of seven (G7) to the president of the World Bank and to the president of the International Monetary Fund urging the cancellation of the international debt of poor countries;

(d) Encourages the identification of development projects in poor countries or regions that have the potential to generate resources and provide local employment.

Resolution 20: East Timor

This ACC

(a) Expresses

   (i) Deep concern over the East Timor tragedy following the referendum on independence in the territory;

   (ii) Appreciation of the work of the UN in moving forward possibilities of peace and justice for the East Timorese and their progress toward independence;

   (iii) Support for the ministry and human rights work of the Indonesian Communion of Churches (PGI) and assures the PGI and its member churches of our continuing prayers; and

(b) Calls on

   (i) Anglicans to press their political leaders to urge the Indonesian government and army to assist in bringing an immediate end to human rights abuses against the people of East Timor;

   (ii) Anglicans throughout the world to pray for the restoration of peace and justice and a cessation of guerrilla activity in East Timor;

   (iii) The world community to give every possible assistance for the rehabilitation and development of East Timor and its people; and

   iv) Anglicans to pray for the safety of the members of the UN peacekeeping forces and all those ministering to the religious needs of the troops.

Resolution 21: Israel-Palestine Peace Process

In the light of recent positive developments toward reaching a just and lasting peace settlement in the Middle East, this ACC

(a) Heartily endorses Lambeth Conference Resolution v.20 on the Holy Land.

(b) Asks the Secretary General to write to the Israeli government and the Palestinian authority urging them to continue their efforts to strengthen the peace process so that all involved may enjoy equal rights and live together in dignity and harmony as children of God.

(c) Asks member churches to continue praying for and encouraging the peace process.

Resolution 22: Sudan

This council

- Noting with deep sadness the continuing war in Sudan, with all the attendant suffering and destruction;
- Welcoming the renewed commitment of all the churches of Sudan to work together to seek peace;
- Recognising and congratulating the Episcopal Church of Sudan (ECS) in its centenary year for its continued courageous and faithful ministry in the face of antagonism, poverty, and division;

Resolves,

(a) To express its indignation at the government of Sudan in the confiscation of the headquarters of the Diocese of Khartoum in Omdurman;

(b) To urge the Sudanese government to bring to a rapid conclusion the proceedings against two Roman Catholic priests and others currently in detention in Khartoum;

(c) To support and encourage the Christians of Sudan in their ministry for peace and justice and to appeal again to the government of Sudan and other parties to the conflict to resolve the war in a peaceful spirit;

(d) To request the Archbishop of Canterbury personally to make the Sudanese government aware of the strength of feeling of the council on these matters;

(e) To renew its commitment and the commitment of all the churches of the Anglican Communion to pray for peace in Sudan and to act together in support of the Sudanese people;

(f) To send its warmest greetings

    (i) To the centenary celebrations of the ECS due to take place in December; and

(ii) To the meeting of the Provincial Synod due to take place in February in Nairobi.

Resolution 23: Cuba

This ACC-11 reaffirms resolution v.9 of the 1998 Lambeth Conference (and its predecessor resolution from Lambeth Conference 1988) calling for the cessation of the U.S. embargo against Cuba.

Resolution 24: Korea Re-unification

This ACC, at the request of the Anglican Peace and Justice Network (APJN), in order to facilitate the process of reconciliation and reunification in the Korean Peninsula,

(a) Offers the active support of the Anglican Communion to the Korean National Council of Churches in its admirable work in the realm of reconciliation and reunification;

(b) Requests the Joint Standing Committee to investigate the possibility of sending a delegation to the Korean Christian Federation in North Korea under the auspices of the ACC and the Anglican Church in Korea and, if feasible, to implement the same;

(c) Supports the programmes based on mutual respect and mutual recognition of the government of South Korea that are aimed at transcending the paralysing consequences of the Cold War in order to create new political structures that will enable North and South Korea to move forward together in harmony and peace;

(d) Encourages the government of North Korea to avail itself of opportunities presented to it, such as to host part of the programme of World Cup 2002.

Resolution 25: Nuclear Weapons

This ACC-11, at the request of the Anglican Peace and Justice Network,

(a) Urges all provinces to demonstrate their commitment to Lambeth Resolution i.11 on nuclear weapons.

(b) Urges all provinces to study and critically assess NATO's first-strike policy.

Resolution 26: Land Mines and Arms

This ACC

(a) Endorses Lambeth Conference Resolution i.13 concerning land mines.

(b) Calls upon Anglicans throughout the Communion to work with other Christians in their provinces to establish more effective control on the production, sale, and distribution of arms and weapons.

(c) Commits itself to bringing, with its ecumenical partners, these concerns before the United Nations.

Resolution 27: Network for Inter-Faith Concerns (NIFCON)

This council:

(a) Affirms Resolution vi.1 of Lambeth Conference 1998, "On Relations with People of Other Faiths";

(b) Charges the Network for Inter-Faith Concerns (NIFCON) to study and evaluate Muslim-Christian relations and report regularly to the Primates' Meeting and the ACC;

(c) Asks the Joint Standing Committee to continue to consider how to resource NIFCON adequately both in personnel and finance;

(d) Supports NIFCON's interim plan of seeking ways, in consultation with the Joint Standing Committee, to continue its work and to undertake this new charge as and when resources become available.

Resolution 28: Women's Network

This ACC-11

(a) Receives the report from the women's network;

(b) Notes the support from the various provinces for the decade of the churches in solidarity with women;

(c) Appreciates the initiatives and decisions from some provinces to give a quota of representation of women in their decision-making structures; and

(d) Commends and requests all provinces to set a women's desk at the provincial level.

Resolution 29: Urban Network

ACC 11

(a) Thanks the groups and individuals who have worked together so far on these significant issues and encourages them to work together to bring these issues before the churches of the Anglican Communion;

(b) Encourages those who are creating an urban network to continue to work toward being recognised in due course as an official network of the Anglican Communion and recommends that they are in touch with the Secretary General to discover the guidelines by which networks are recognised;

(c) Welcomes the proposal of a project to identify and develop urban resources in the Anglican Communion;

(d) Asks the urban network to prepare a further report for ACC-12 regarding the scope and viability of a "Faith in an Urban World" Commission.

Resolution 30: Co-opted Member of ACC

This ACC requests the Spanish Reformed Episcopal Church to nominate a person who would be willing to serve as a co-opted member of the council in accordance with paragraph e of the schedule of membership. The Secretary General should be notified of the nomination before the next meeting of the Standing Committee for ratification by it, and in default of such a person being so nominated, a casual vacancy shall be deemed to have occurred for the purposes of bylaw 6.

Resolution 31: Resolutions of Thanks

Resolved that the eleventh meeting of the Anglican Consultative Council thanks God for the ministry of so many whose dedication and service have enabled the council to do the work of the Church:

For our President, Archbishop George Carey, whose personal commitment, clear proclamation, pastoral compassion, and involvement in the daily life of the council inspire us.

For our Chairman, Bishop Simon Chiwanga, whose wisdom and experience have been a grace and strength to us.

For our vice chairman, Presiding Bishop John Paterson, whose steady hand has guided the work of the council.

For the Secretary General, the Reverend Canon John Peterson, whose enthusiastic presence and immense energy encourages us.

For the design group, led by Presiding Bishop John Paterson, assisted by Bishop Bernard Ntahoturi, Mr. John Rea, Ms. Maureen Sithole, and Bishop Fernando Soares, who enabled us to diligently discharge our responsibility to the agenda.

For the Inter-Anglican Finance Committee, chaired by Archbishop Robin Eames, assisted by Ms. Judith Conley, Archbishop Alwyn Rice Jones, Mr. Ghazi Musharbash, and Bishop Fernando Soares, for their leadership on financial matters.

For the nominations committee, led by Mr. Samuel Arap Ng'eny, assisted by Archdeacon Barbara Clay and Archdeacon Bryan Williams, who helped us discern our future leaders.

For the resolutions committee, led by Canon Dr. Christina Baxter, assisted by Ms. Wong Fung Yi, Mr. Bernard Georges, the Reverend Robert Sessum, Mr. Robert Tong, and Mr. Bernard Turner, who helped us express our minds and will clearly.

For the Bible studies prepared by Bishop Leo Frade, which challenged us in our Christian walk.

For the worship team, led by the chaplains, the Reverend Paul Gibson and Father James Milne, and the organist, Mr. Matthew Edwards, who directed our hearts and minds in common prayer.

For the communications team, led by Canon Jim Rosenthal, assisted by Canon Margaret Rodgers, The Reverend Dr. Ian Douglas, Mr. Chris Took, Mrs. Veronica Elks, Mr. Ian Harvey, and Mr. Manasseh Zindo, who enabled us to speak to the world.

For the executive assistant to the Secretary General, Mrs. Deirdre Martin; the Secretariat, headed by Miss Marjorie Murphy and assisted by Mrs. Helen Bates, Miss Fiona Millican, and Mrs. Barbara Stanford Tuck; the treasurer, Mr. Michael Nunn, assisted by Ms. Rosemary Palmer and Mr. Graeme Smith; and for the travel officer, Ms. Ann Quirke—for their dedication and skills in serving the council.

For the legal advisor, The Reverend John Rees, for his counsel on legal and constitutional matters.

For the director of Ecumenical Affairs, The Reverend Canon David Hamid, for assisting the ACC with its ecumenical and doctrinal agenda.

For the Archbishop of Canterbury's staff, Dr. Herman Browne, The Reverend Canon Andrew Deuchar, and The Reverend Lesley Perry, for assisting the Archbishop.

For our partners in full Communion:

> the Right Reverend Joseph Mar Irenaeus—Mar Thoma Syrian Church of Malabar
>
> the Right Reverend Joachim Vobbe—the Old Catholic churches of the Union of Utrecht,
>
> for enriching the life of the council with insights from their churches.

For our ecumenical partners:

> The Reverend Dr. Alan Falconer—Faith and Order, WCC
>
> The Reverend Timothy Galligan—Roman Catholic Church
>
> The Right Reverend William Boyd Grove—World Methodist Council
>
> The Reverend Sven Oppegaard—Lutheran World Federation,

whose presence reminded us of the Church beyond the Anglican Communion.

For speakers and presenters:

> Bishop Mark Dyer on the instruments of unity and *The Virginia Report*
>
> The Reverend Dr. John Pobee on the interpretation of Scripture
>
> The Reverend Eric Beresford on technology and ethics

Bishop Leo Frade on international debt

Bishop Bruce Cameron, The Reverend Dean Fostekew, and The Reverend Clive Wylie on Mission 21

Bishop Mark Santer, The Reverend Timothy Galligan, and The Reverend Canon David Hamid on ARCIC

Dr. Ida Glaser, The Reverend John Sargant, and The Reverend Dr. Israel Selvanayagam on the Network for Inter-Faith Concerns (NIFCON)

Archbishop Glauco Soares de Lima and The Reverend Samuel Koshiishi on urbanisation

Bishop Roger Sainsbury, Bishop Laurence Green, and The Reverend Canon Andrew Davey on the Anglican urban network,

who, each in their turn, informed and challenged us in the great issues before the Church.

For our hosts:

The Most Reverend Richard Holloway, the Right Reverend Neville Chamberlain, the Right Reverend Bruce Cameron, and Ms. Pat McBryde, who opened their hearts and their arms to offer us unforgettable hospitality and witness.

The First Minister of Scotland, the Right Honorable Donald Dewar, for his presence with us in Edinburgh.

The Lord Provost of Aberdeen, the Lord Provost of Dundee, and the Lord Provost of Glasgow, for their warm welcome and kind hospitality.

For the interpreters, the Reverend Paula Mayer, Mrs. Dominique MacNeill, Ms. Ruth Lambert, Mrs. Dorothy Evans, and the Reverend Rogelio Prieto, who opened the meeting to Spanish and French speakers.

For the West Park Centre staff, Eve Anderson, Anne Bishop, and all who assisted in the dining room, the conference centre, and the villas.

For the volunteers from the Scottish Episcopal Church: Ms. Pat McBryde, the Reverend Clive Wylie, the Reverend Dean Fostekew, Mr. Rob Whiteman, Ms. Jean Forbes, the Reverend Joe Morrow, Mrs. Judy Robinson, Mrs. Judith Edmond, the Reverend Kathleen Dall, Mrs. Olive McAusland, Ms. Mary Affleck, and Mrs. Margaret Knox.

For the drivers: Bishop Neville Chamberlain, Bishop Michael Henley, Bishop Ted Luscombe, the Reverend Canon Bill McAusland, the Reverend Canon Richard Jones, the Reverend Edmund Marquis-Faulkes, the Reverend Canon Jim Wynn-Evans, the Reverend Canon Malcolm Richardson, the Very Reverend Robert Breaden, Mrs. Diana Chamberlain, Mr. Donald Chamberlain, Mr. Ed Creany, Mr. Colin Humphries, Mr. Alan

Nicoll, Mr. Ian Turnbull, Mr. John Dilks, Mrs. Dilks, the Reverend David Campbell, the Reverend David Elder, and the Reverend Darren McFarland.

For members whose last meeting was ACC-11: the Very Reverend David Richardson (Australia), Mr. Robert Tong (Australia), the Right Reverend Bernard Ntahoturi (Burundi), Venerable Barbara Clay (Canada), the Right Reverend Bernard Malango (Central Africa), the Right Reverend Fernando Soares (Portugal), the Right Reverend Phillip Newell (Australia), Mr. Michael Kututwa (Central Africa), the Right Reverend Sylvestre Tibafa Mugera (Congo), Canon Dr. Christina Baxter (England), Mrs. Brenda Sheil (Ireland), Mr. Samuel Arap Ng'eny (Kenya), Venerable Nelson Nyumbe (Sudan), the Reverend Canon Mkunga Mtingele (Tanzania), and the Right Reverend Mark Dyer (United States); for their dedication and commitment to the work of the wider Anglican Communion.

For the Reverend Kevin Franz and the participants in the sensitive and informative hearing on human sexuality in Edinburgh, which offered the members of the ACC an opportunity to listen and reflect.

Resolution 32: Prayers and Greetings

Resolved that this eleventh meeting of the Anglican Consultative Council sends its greetings and assurances of prayer to the following:

The Bishop of Rome, His Holiness Pope John Paul II, with prayers for his apostolic, evangelical, and ecumenical ministry as Christians approach the third millennium of the birth of our Saviour Jesus Christ;

The Ecumenical Patriarch, His All Holiness Bartholomeos I, with prayers for the patriarchate in Constantinople and with thanks for the relationships between the Orthodox churches and the churches of the Anglican Communion;

The moderator of the central committee of the World Council of Churches, His Holiness Aram I, with thanks for its work on behalf of all of us who pray for growth among Christians in faith and order, life, and work;

His Eminence Cardinal Edward Cassidy of the Pontifical Council for Promoting Christian Unity; Dr. Ishmael Noko, General Secretary of the Lutheran World Federation; Dr. Joe Hale, General Secretary of the Methodist World Council; and Dr. Konrad Raiser, General Secretary of the World Council of Churches; for enabling ecumenical partners to be with us who have enriched our fellowship;

The Most Reverend Antonius Jan Glazemaker, Archbishop of Utrecht, and the Old Catholic churches of the Union of Utrecht; and the Most Reverend Dr. Alexander Mar Thoma; for ensuring the presence of representatives from churches in Communion who make visible our unity in Christ.

The Last Word

—THE REVEREND CANON JOHN L. PETERSON, SECRETARY GENERAL OF THE ANGLICAN CONSULTATIVE COUNCIL

December 6, 1999, Feast of St. Nicholas

As we stand on the threshold of the third Christian millennium, it is important for us to look back as well as to look ahead. We look back to a particular moment in time knowing full well that the Scripture says that "to God a thousand years are like one day" (Psalm 90:4). Our pilgrimage takes us to Nazareth and Bethlehem. It was in Nazareth that a young woman said her *yes* to God. It was in Bethlehem that God chose to reveal to the human world the Word made flesh, Jesus Christ. It was Jesus who taught us that if we continued in his word we would truly be his disciples. John 8:32 puts it succinctly: "you will know the truth, and the truth will make you free" (NRSV).

The Compass Rose, the symbol of the Anglican Communion, has at its centre these words from St. John's Gospel. These words become for us Anglican Christians the centre of how we remember Jesus' coming among us. To realise Jesus' assurance that he is with us always, even to the end time. We recommit ourselves, our communities, our dioceses, our parishes to Christ's mission, Christ's service, Christ's call.

The Anglican Consultative Council, at an important point in its history, met in Scotland in a spirit of celebration. For more than thirty years the ACC has been a representative council of laity, clergy, and bishops in the Anglican Communion. It is at an ACC meeting that the Church truly gathers together as one body in Jesus' mission. When we come together as the ACC, we come with our memories, our hopes, our anxieties, our petitions, our thanksgivings, our supplications, and our intercessions. It is always our hope that at these gatherings God's word of forgiveness and promise will permeate all that we do. Our confidence in Jesus, even in the midst of the many struggles and failures that we face as a worldwide Church, is summed up well in the words of Mother Julian of Norwich in her *Showings,* written in the fourteenth century when she prayed: "Lord Jesus I have heard you say sin is necessary but all will be well. All will be well, and every kind of thing will be well."

ACC meetings are times of great joy. One of the great joys of this particular meeting was our exposure to the small but vibrant province of the Scottish Episcopal Church. To hear its dreams and aspirations for its Christian witness and testimony in the clamour of busy city streets, such as in Glasgow with its poverty and multiplicity of needs, and in the serenity of mountainous rural villages, where indeed the gospel message needs to be shared as well, was a testimony to the exciting Mission 21 programme that the Scottish Episcopal Church presented to ACC-11. That presentation demonstrated our interdependence upon each other as representatives from Australia, Canada, Ireland, Kenya, Japan, Nigeria, Sudan, New Zealand, Uganda, and Wales all asked if they could indigenise the Scottish Episcopal Church's Mission 21 programme "back home." The response was so great that the Scottish Episcopal Church is doing a pilot scheme with two provinces before venturing out to all ten provinces.

To me one of the most exciting realisations of our Communion during the latter part of 1999 was the one hundred years celebration of the Episcopal Church of the Sudan. This centenary celebration was one that was carried in the midst of civil war, degradation, poverty, separation, loss, and almost every other word that expresses the evil that can disrupt the lives of human beings today. However, out of all this comes the vibrancy of worship and the testimony of a people who truly walk in the light of the Lord. The Episcopal Church of the Sudan hopes that it now sees the light at the end of the tunnel, for it knows, as true disciples of Jesus Christ, that the "truth will make you free."

Sudan symbolises so much for us as an international family. It has been the focus of our prayer and attention for so long. Like Southern Africa, Jerusalem, Sri Lanka, Burundi, and Northern Ireland, we as a family long for peace and tranquillity among the people of God, our family. If we are going to celebrate any kind of true millennium in the years 2000 and 2001, we must receive inspiration from people like those from the Sudan, who know the difference in their lives because Jesus has come into our world. The people of Sudan also give us the opportunity to truly see what it means to share and witness in the world. But in our often complacent and selfish world in which we find ourselves, the Sudan also lays before us the need to resolve in our hearts and minds to work for the coming of Christ's kingdom on earth. As we stand on the threshold of the millennium, might we take seriously the Jubilee. All of us can benefit from a Jubilee.

Some of the true attributes of a Christian are the abilities to create, to overcome, to endure, to love, and to transform. These are the words of Ben Okwe in his book *Mental Fight:* "Every day is a New World, our future is greater than our past."

As an organisation I see the ACC's future being built directly upon its past. The eleventh meeting of ACC was a turning point, for there was a recommitment of its members to seek and respond to the challenges, the sufferings, and the dreams that await us as a Church in the new millennium.

As the ACC met daily for worship, I could not escape the power of the words of the Magnificat. Mary's song of liberation and praise has inspired Christians in the most difficult circumstances. What is true for Mary, the mother of our Lord Jesus Christ, is also true for us. Mary sings: "His mercy is for those who fear him from generation to generation, he has shown strength with his arm, he has scattered the proud in the thoughts of their hearts, he has brought down the powerful from their thrones and lifted up the lowly, he has filled the hungry with good things and sent the rich away empty."

The Magnificat is our song as well. I truly believe the action of the Anglican Consultative Council has put us on a road, as a global Church, to seek and promote peace, to heal the wounds that so many bear in conflict, war, and pain. We are called upon to make true sacrifices in order to serve the world in Jesus' name. The decisions made at ACC-11 talked about treasuring God's creation and God's people. Its resolutions, its work, its discussion, its deliberations all pointed to the ACC's desire to build a firm foundation for the children of the world and to show respect for those of later years. As we recall thirty years of the ACC, a hundred years of the Episcopal Church of the Sudan, and two thousand years of Christ's presence in the world, may we be drawn together in love and peace, not being afraid, but knowing that through God's grace we may find our future in Jesus' hands.

Directory of Provincial Secretaries of the Anglican Communion

The Anglican Church in Aotearoa, New Zealand, and Polynesia
    Mr. Robin A. I. Nairn
    General Secretary/Treasurer, The Anglican Church in Aotearoa, New Zealand, and Polynesia
    P.O. Box 885, Hastings, NEW ZEALAND
    Street address: 114E Queen Street, Hastings, New Zealand
    Office: 64 (0)6 878 7902
    Fax: 64 (0)6 878 7905
    E-mail   gensec@hb.ang.org.nz

The Anglican Church of Australia
    Reverend Dr. Bruce Norman Kaye
    General Secretary, The General Synod, Anglican Church of Australia
    P.O. Box Q190, Queen Victoria Post Office
    Sydney, New South Wales, 2000, AUSTRALIA
    Office: 61 (0)2 9265 1525
    Fax: 61 (0)2 9264 6552
    E-mail   anglican@ozE-mail:.com.au

Igreja Episcopal Anglicana do Brasil
    Reverend Canon Maurício José Araújo de Andrade
    General Secretary, Igreja Episcopal Anglicana do Brasil
    Caixa Postal 11 510
    Porto Alegre, RS, 91720-150, BRAZIL
    Office: 55 (0)51 339 7666
    Fax: 55 (0)51 339 7666
    E-mail   m_andrade@ieab.org.br

The Episcopal Church of Burundi
    Reverend Pascal Bigirimana
    Provincial Secretary, The Episcopal Church of Burundi
    BP 2098, Bujumbura, BURUNDI
    Office: 257 224 389
    Fax: 257 229 129

The Anglican Church of Canada
    Venerable James B. Boyles
    General Secretary of the General Synod,
    600 Jarvis Street
    Toronto, Ontario, M4Y 2J6, CANADA

Office: 1 416 924 9192
Fax: 1 416 924 0211
E-mail jboyles@national.anglican.ca

The Church of the Province of Central Africa
Reverend Richard Chance
Acting Provincial Secretary
P.O. Box 769
Gaborone, BOTSWANA
Office: 267 353 779
Home: 267 313 895
Fax: 267 352 075
E-mail acenter@info.bw or rjchance@info.bw

Iglesia Anglicana de la Region Central de America
Reverend Hector Monterroso
Provincial Secretary
Apartado 58a, Guatemala City, GUATEMALA
Office: 502 (0)2 369 0669
Fax: 502 (0)2 369 0669
E-mail iarcahfm@infovia.com.gt

Province de L'Eglise Anglicane Du Congo
Reverend Molanga Botola
Provincial Secretary, Province de L'Eglise Anglicane Du Congo
CAC-Bunia, P.O. Box 25586, Kampala, UGANDA
Street address: BP 798, Bunia, Republique Democratique Du Congo
CAC-Bunia, P.O. Box 21285, Nairobi, KENYA

The Church of England
Mr. Philip John Courtney Mawer
Secretary General, General Synod of the Church of England
Church House, Great Smith Street
London, SW1P 3NZ, ENGLAND
Office: 44 (0)171 898 1360 or 44 (0)171 898 1000 (central switchboard)
Fax: 44 (0)171 898 1369
E-mail: synod@church-of-england.org or philip.mawer@c-of-e.org.uk

Hong Kong Sheng Kung Hui
Reverend Andrew Chan
Provincial General Secretary
1 Lower Albert Road, Central, Hong Kong, PEOPLE'S REPUBLIC OF CHINA
Office: 852 2526 5355
Fax: 852 2521 2199
E-mail: office1@hkskh.org
Web site: www.hkskh.org

The Church of the Province of the Indian Ocean
    Reverend Emile Victor Rakotoarivelo
    Provincial Secretary
    Box 8445, Tsaralalana, 101-Antananarivo, MADAGASCAR

The Church of Ireland
    Mr. Robert H. Sherwood
    Chief Officer and Secretary
    Church of Ireland House, Church Avenue
    Rathmines, Dublin, 6, REPUBLIC OF IRELAND
    Office: 353 (0)1 497 8422, ext. 200
    Fax: 353 (0)1 497 8792
    E-mail: chief@rcbdub.org

The Nippon Sei Ko Kai (The Anglican Communion in Japan)
    Reverend Samuel Isamu Koshiishi
    General Secretary, The Nippon Sei Ko Kai
    65-3 Yarai Cho, Shinjuku-ku
    Tokyo, 162, JAPAN
    Office: 81 (0)3 5228 3171
    Home: 81 (0)3 5382 3220
    Fax: 81 (0)3 5228 3175 (provincial office)
    E-mail: general-sec.po@nskk.org

The Episcopal Church in Jerusalem and the Middle East
    Right Reverend Riah Hanna Abu El-Assal, Bishop in Jerusalem
    St. George's Close, Box 19122
    Jerusalem, ISRAEL
    Street address: P.O. Box 75, Nazareth, Israel
    Office: 972 (0)2 627 1670 or 972 (0)2 627 2932 or 972 (0)50 309 277
             or 972 (0)6 655 4017 (Church Nazareth)
    Home: 972 (0)6 656 2726
    Fax: 972 (0)2 627 3847 or 972 (0)6 656 3649 (Church Nazareth)
             or 972 (0)6 657 6507 (St. Marg. Host)
    E-mail: Riahasal@netvision.net.il or edioces@netvision.net.il (Dio of
             Jerusalem)

The Anglican Church of Kenya
    Mrs. Susan Nzisa Mumina
    Provincial Secretary, Church of the Province of Kenya
    P.O. Box 40502
    Nairobi, KENYA
    Street address: CPK, Language School Building, Off Bishop's Road,
        Nairobi, Kenya
    Office: 254 2 714 752 or 254 2 714 753
    Fax: 254 (0)2 714 750

The Anglican Church of Korea
    Reverend Chae-Yul Kim
    General Secretary, The Anglican Church of Korea
    3 Chong Dong Chung Ku,
    Seoul 100-120, REPUBLIC OF KOREA
    Office: 82 (0)2 738 8952
    Fax: 82 (0)2 737 4210

The Church of the Province of Melanesia
    Mr. Nicholas M. Ma'aramo
    Provincial Secretary
    P.O. Box 19
    Honiara, SOLOMON ISLANDS
    Home: 677 205 49
    Fax: 677 210 98

La Iglesia Anglicana de Mexico
    Right Reverend Benito Juarez-Martinez
    Bishop of Southeastern Mexico and Provincial Secretary
    Av Las Americas #73, Col. Aguacatal, 91130 Xalapa
    Vera Cruz, MEXICO
    Office: 52 (0)5 550 2863 or 52 (0)5 616 2490
    Fax: 52 (0)5 616 4063

The Church of the Province of Myanmar (Burma)
    Reverend Samuel Htang Oake B.A.
    Provincial Secretary
    P.O. Box 1412, 140 Pyidaungsu-Yeiktha Road, Dagon PO
    Yangon, MYANMAR
    Office: 95 (0)1 272 668

The Church of Nigeria (Anglican Communion)
    Venerable Samuel B. Akinola
    General Secretary, Church of Nigeria
    Provincial Secretariat, 29 Marina, P.O. Box 78
    Lagos, NIGERIA
    Office: 234 (0)1 263 3581 or 234 (0)1 263 5681
    Fax: 234 (0)1 263 1264

The Anglican Church of Papua New Guinea
    Mr. Howard Graham
    National Secretary, Anglican Church of Papua New Guinea
    Box 673
    Lae, Morobe Province, PAPUA NEW GUINEA
    Office: 675 472 4111
    Fax: 675 472 1852
    E-mail: acpng@global.net.pg

The Episcopal Church in the Philippines
   Reverend Rex R. B. Reyes
   Provincial Secretary, Episcopal Church in the Philippines
   Provincial Office, P.O. Box 10321, Broadway Centrum
   1112 Quezon City, PHILIPPINES
   Street address: Cathedral Heights, 275 E. Rodriguez Sr. Ave., Quezon City, Philippines
   Office;   63 (0)2 707 591/2/3 or 63 (0)2 721 5061
   Fax: 63 (0)2 721 1923
   E-mail: ecp@phil.gn.apc.org

L'Eglise Episcopal au Rwanda
   Reverend Josias Sendegeya
   Provincial Secretary
   BP 2487, Kigali, RWANDA
   Office: 250 73 213 or 250 76 338
   Fax: 250 73 213 or 250 6504

The Scottish Episcopal Church
   Mr. John Stuart
   Secretary General, Scottish Episcopal Church
   21 Grosvenor Crescent
   Edinburgh, EH12 5EE, SCOTLAND
   Office: 44 (0)131 225 6357
   Fax: 44 (0)131 346 7247
   E-mail: Scot_Episc_Church@ecunet.org

Church of the Province of Southeast Asia
   Datuk Robert Jacob Ridu
   Provincial Secretary, Church of the Province of Southeast Asia
   c/o P.O. Box 347
   Kuching, Sarawak, MALAYSIA
   Street address: McDougall Road, 9300 Kuching, Sarawak
   Office: 60 (0)82 472 177
   Fax: 60 (0)82 426 488

The Church of the Province of Southern Africa
   Mr. Rob S. Rogerson
   Provincial Secretary/Treasurer
   P.O. Box 1932
   Cape Town, 8000, SOUTH AFRICA
   Office: 27 (0)21 45 1557
   Fax: 27 (0)21 45 1571

Reverend Canon Luke Luscombe Lungile Pato
   Provincial Executive Officer, Church of the Province of Southern Africa
   16-20 Bishopscourt Drive, Bishopscourt

Claremont, 7700, SOUTH AFRICA
Office: 27 (0)21 761 4193
Fax: 27 (0)21 761 2531
E-mail: peocpsa@cpsa.org.za

Iglesia Anglicana del Cono Sur de America
Sr. Rolando Dalmas
Provincial Secretary, Iglesia Anglicana del Cono Sur de America
Casilla 6108
11000 Montevideo, URUGUAY
Fax: 598 (0)2 962 519
E-mail: rdalmas@chasque.apc.org

The Episcopal Church of the Sudan
Reverend Nelson Koboji Nyumbe
Provincial Secretary, Church of the Province of the Sudan
P.O. Box 110
Juba, SUDAN
Office: 249 Juba 20 065 or 249 Juba 20 040
Fax: 249 (0)851 20 065 (from 12:00 P.M. United Kingdom time is the best time to get faxes through)

The Anglican Church of Tanzania
Reverend Canon Mkunga Humphrey Percival Mtingele
Provincial General Secretary, Church of the Province of Tanzania
P.O. Box 899
Dodoma, TANZANIA
Office: 255 (0)61 21 437 or 255 (0)61 324 574
Home: 255 (0)61 324 270
Fax: 255 (0)61 324 565
E-mail: mmtingele@maf.org or cpt@maf.org

The Church of the Province of Uganda
Reverend Canon Dr. George K. Tibeesigwa
Provincial Secretary,
P.O. Box 14123
Kampala, UGANDA
Office: 256 (0)41 270 219 or 256 (0)41 271 218 or 256 (0)41 271 219
Home: 256 (0)41 271 081
Fax: 256 (0)41 251 925
E-mail: coups@uol.co.ug or COUnet-ps@Mukla.gn.apc.org
Telex: 61196 UNEMAS UG

The Episcopal Church in the United States of America
Reverend Patrick Mauney
Deputy for Anglican Relations and Provincial Secretary
The Episcopal Church Center, 815 Second Avenue

New York, NY, 10017, USA
Office: (212) 922 5413
Fax: (212) 983 6377

The Church in Wales
Mr. J. W. David McIntyre
Secretary General / Provincial Treasurer
39 Cathedral Road
Cardiff, South Glamorgan, CF1 9XF, WALES
Office: 44 (0)1222 231 638
Fax: 44 (0)1222 387 835
Web site : www.churchinWales.org.uk (provincial)

The Church of the Province of West Africa
Mr. Nat N. Stanley
Acting Provincial Secretary, The Church of the Province of West Africa
Bishopscourt, P.O. Box 8
Accra, GHANA
Office: 233 (0)21 663 595
Fax: 223 (0)21 669 125
Telex: 2075 SNAFR GH

The Church in the Province of the West Indies
Mr. Idris Reid
Acting Provincial Secretary, The Provincial Secretariat
c/o Church House, P.O. Box N-656
Nassau, BAHAMAS
Office: 1242 322 3015 /6 /7
Fax: 1242 322 7943
E-mail: cpwi@bahamas.net.bs

The Church of Ceylon
Right Reverend Kenneth Michael James Fernando
Bishop of Colombo
Bishop's House, 368/2 Bauddhaloka Mawatha
Colombo 7, SRI LANKA
Office: 94 (0)1 696 208 or 94 (0)1 684 811 (Direct)
Home: 94 (0)1 695 539
Fax: 94 (0)1 684 811
E-mail: bishop@eureka.lk
Cable address: EPISCOPUS COLOMBO

Iglesia Episcopal de Cuba
Right Reverend Jorge Perera Hurtado
Bishop of Cuba
Calle 6, No. 273 Vedado

Havana 4, 10400, CUBA
Office: 53 (0)7 32 11 20 or 53 (0)7 31 24 36
Home: 53 (0)7 3 56 55 /3 80 03
Fax: 53 (0)7 3332 93

The Church of North India
Dr. Vidya Sagar Lall
Provincial Secretary, Church of North India
CNI Bhawan, Post Box No 311, 16 Pandit Pant Marg
New Delhi 100001, INDIA
Office: 91 (0)11 373 1079 or 91 (0)11 371 6513
Home: 91 (0)11 373 1079
Fax: 91 (0)11 371 6901
E-mail: sagar@cnisynod.org
Cable address: "SYNOD" NEW DELHI
Web site: www.cnisynod.org

The Church of South India
Reverend G. Dyvasirvadam
General Secretary, CSI Synod Secretariat
P.O. Box 688
Royapettah, Chennai 600 014, INDIA
Street address: 5 Whites Road, Royapettah, Madras 600 014, India
Office: 91 (0)44 852 1566 or 91 (0)44 852 4166
Fax: 91 (0)44 852 3528
E-mail: csisnd@md3.vsnl.net.in
Cable address: SOUTHSYNOD MADRAS-600 014

The Church of Pakistan
General Secretary, The Synod, Church of Pakistan
Cathedral Close, The Mall
Lahore 54000, PAKISTAN
Office: 92 (0)42 374 190
Fax: 92 (0)42 225 536

The Church of Bangladesh
Mr. Samarendra Bayen
Provincial Secretary, Church of Bangladesh
St. Thomas' Church, 54 Johnson Road
Dhaka-1100, BANGLADESH
Office: 880 (0)2 238 218 or 880 (0)2 236 546
Fax: 880 (0)2 238 218
Cable address: St. Thomas Church, Dhaka - 1100